IT SPEAKS TO YOu

MAKING KIN OF PEOPLE, DUODJI AND STORIES IN SÁMI MUSEUMS

LIISA-RÁVNÁ FINBOG

ISBN 978-1-64504-296-9 (Paperback)

ISBN 978-1-64504-297-6 (Hardback)

ISBN 978-1-64504-298-3 (E-Book)

Library of Congress Control Number: 2023934239

Printed on acid-free paper

This book is part of *Community Wisdom*

Series Editor: Jennifer Markides

"Dego gođus, laktit duodji ja muitalusat."

To all my kin and the stories they carry, and to all the duojárs that have thaught me to weave.

Table of Contents

CHAPTER 1: GIISÁ

"IT SPEAKS TO YOU"

MAKING KIN THROUGH PEOPLE, DUODJI
AND STORIES IN SÁMI MUSEUMS

ÁVNNAS MUITALA MO GALGGAT BARGAT/ THE MATERIAL TELLS ME HOW TO WORK —A PROLOGUE

"It speaks to you", a practitioner of duodji once told me. Duodji is a customary practice of creation, involving aesthetics, knowledge[s] of materials, place and season, as well as a Sámi holistic worldview that touches upon spirituality, ethics and the interrelational qualities embedded in the multiple world[s] of creation. The duojár in question, Unni, was one of several that I had invited to an event that I curated in December of 2019. The event, which had been convened jointly by Office for Contemporary Art—Norway (OCA) and Norwegian Crafts (NF) in relation to the United Nations International Year of Indigenous languages, was titled "Båassjoeraejken Tjïrr—Returning (to) the Language of Our Ancestors". My intent was to facilitate for conversations and workshops in which several practitioners within the fields of Sámi and Indigenous aesthetics were to reflect on if and how their practice is intimately linked with their ancestral languages and the landscapes in which they evolved. Before we began, one of the invited participants who is a good friend, ᑕᖅᕋᓕᒃ [Taqralik] gifted me one half of a hairless seal skin that she had brought with her from her home community ᑰᔾᔪᐊᖅ [Kuujjuaq], in Nunavik, in what is today known as Quebec, Canada.

Together, a group of us was smelling it, touching it, and rubbing it between our hands, testing the thickness and elasticity of it. I was saying how I already had some ideas as to how the skin would be used, and others offered even more suggestions. "The skin", Unni said "it speaks to you". In North Sámi, the language of my áhčči, this is expressed as 'ávnnas muitala mo galggat bargat'[1], or 'the material shows you the way'. In the practice of duodji, the will of the material is important. Your work, your practice, and your birrasat, or surroundings, is a combination of different voices; the voice of the material, of your surroundings, and of your ancestors' teachings take part in shaping your own practice. All of this is conveyed in duodji, and duodji as such teaches us to listen and to seek consent. And this is what Unni meant when she said that the skin spoke to me.

INTRODUCTION

In duodji, even if it is individual hands that shape the work, you are never alone in your practice. Aside from the will and consent of the material you are working with, the experience of those before you are also voiced in the practice. To duddjot [to practice duodji] then, is to remember and listen to all of these voices, working collectively to produce something that is *vuogas*, beautiful as well as functional. "*We let the material lead the way, we talk about the meaning and the process, we create*", says Laara, a young South Sámi duojár from the Swedish side of the border (05.04.2018). The same holds true for this book. An exercise in the building of kinships across time, borders and sii-das [communities], the following work brings together both collec-tive and individual stories, memories, epitaphs, and reflections on the many processes that create, negotiate, and reinforce Sámi identities and mediate Indigenous sovereignty through the practice of duodji and within the boundaries of museums. A collaborative and reciprocal process, my words as such appear as if I was slowly doing duodji and creating a form out of multiple voices. In that sense, this is a work of and by duodji, reflecting the many dialogues that I have had with myself, my own practice, other duojárs and their practice, museum collections, museum staff, and objects, though I collectively refer to all of these as verdde, meaning friends in [North] Sámi.

Drawing on these multiple stories and voices, this book traces, firstly, how the process of killing knowledge, or the epistemicide fol-lowing the colonisation of Sápmi worked to disrupt the knowledge[s] contained in the practice of duodji. Secondly, it looks into the work

---

1 The exact translation is "material tells how to work".

16

that is being done in Sámi communities today to re-remember various practices within duodji and in the process re-establish or/and mediate Sámi identities and sovereignty, and how museums—with their vast collections of Sámi heritage objects—play into these processes. More to the point, in this book I do the following three; to start, I disregard the conventional translation of duodji as 'craft' (Nielsen 1979), and I consequently re-conceptualize the practice with the intent to re-establish it as a Sámi epistemology, a system of knowledge; Second, I examine how the practice of duodji may affect the identity of the duojár; and lastly, I investigate the role that Sámi museums have come to occupy in the relationship between identity, duodji, material culture and sovereignty. By engaging in discourses of material culture and duodji by way of these four topics, the study at hand **explores the emergence of identities and sovereignty at a material level, asking what objects and cultural belongings in museums may reveal of the mediations of being and becoming Sámi, of establishing Indigenous sovereignty** and furthermore, **in what ways duodji is involved in said process.**

MAKING KIN

To make kin is in many ways an abstract exercise, but throughout my work on this book, to me it has become clear that forging kinship comes from connecting with all your relations, be they human, non-human beings, entities, land and waters, or your surroundings, in deep respect and reciprocity. "*Everything connects*", we are all part of "*a system of interdependency*" where all "*are equally relevant*", a duojár once told me when we discussed the idea of a Sámi philosophy (Ovlla 24.04.2019). In this, he reflected the core of most Indigenous-based philosophies and worldviews, where this is a stated truth; everything is relational, and to live a good life, what we call *birgejupmi*[2] in North Sámi, is to honour all of our relations, making kin of them as it were. Sharp eyes might recognize the term, 'making kin', having spotted it in the writing of Donna Haraway. And indeed, I have found and borrowed the term in/from her writings as a way to conceptualise that in the interrelational character of our world/s, "*we require each*

---

2   Birgejupmi is difficult to translate into English. In Norwegian we would perhaps compare it to "livsfornødenhet", which means to have just enough of everything—not too much, but not too little—to get by. As I've heard it used in everyday contexts however, birgejupmi should be thought of as 'good life'.

other in unexpected collaborations and combinations [...]. We become-with each other" (Haraway 2016:4). By no means do I intend to make use of 'making kin' as a theoretical lens. Instead, I use it in the sense that it reflects the interrelatedness that is so present in Indigenous world/s, including one that is Sámi. Or, as the Dakota[3] scholar, Kim Tallbear (2016) articulates it; *"making kin is to make people into familiars in order to relate"*.

A CRITICAL INDIGENOUS METHODOLOGY AS STARTING POINT

Regardless, the following work is very much centred in the act of making kin, and thus Sámi and Indigenous concepts and perspectives. This expands far beyond a simple use of Sámi terminology. Ever since 'first contact' in the context of colonialism happened, the story of Indigenous peoples' has been one *"of 'no speak' and no voice. It has been a story of silence, of invisibility, of conquest, marginalization and power-lessness"* (Goduka 1999:26). As a consequence, Indigenous knowledge systems, as well as our worldviews, perspectives, and values, have been equally silenced, what in Sámi is *jávohisvuohta*[4], and disregarded—undoing kin, rather than making. The Sámi scholar, Rauna Kuokkanen (2008a:60) has conceptualized this silence as an *epistemic ignorance*. This refers, as she explains it, to the ways in which academic theories and practices ignore, marginalize, and exclude other than dominant western European epistemic and intellectual traditions; the latter distinguished, not as a particular location or social group, but rather as a collective philosophical, moral, and scientific doctrine that is widely accepted as being the dominant collective discourse as far as research goes.

For Indigenous scholars such as myself, the challenge is to overcome said ignorance. Not because we ourselves suffer from this ignorance, but because we feel it keenly in the academic fields we move within and between. When I began to consciously think of situating my research within a critical Indigenous methodology, I was warned to remember where I was. The person who gave me this warning meant it kindly. Their concern was that the institution where I was employed,

---

3   Dakota is the name of an Indigenous people whose homelands are found in what is today known as U.S.A.
4   In Sámi *jávohisvuohta* means 'being silenced', and *jávohuvvan*, is how we refer to the group or people being silenced (e.g., Somby 2016:19)

the University of Oslo, did not perceive Indigenous studies as a viable academic consideration, far less included it in their curriculum. For me however, such kindness is killing. Because it teaches us that to get by as academics, we must centre our projects in the established paradigms[5] of Western thought. It thus perpetuates the belief that as Indigenous people, we are worth less and so is our knowledge[s] and systems of learning. And, if there is one thing I have learned as an Indigenous scholar, it is that our systems of knowledge are not lesser. It is not a competition, not a question of better or worse. It is simply a matter of how you approach the world, and how you think through it.

In its broadest sense, Indigenous methodologies can be *"understood as a way of being in, thinking about and interacting with the world—the thinking behind the doing"* (Smith 2019:3). As I see it, methodology can never be reduced simply to a systematic analysis of the methods applied in the field of a study. On the contrary, methodology is very much the lifeblood of who we are and what we do, the knowing of our self, intersecting with the world. In short, Indigenous methodologies are rooted in Indigenous Peoples' ways of being and making sense of the world (Kovach 2009:25), but how do we go from acknowledging the validity of our Peoples' holistic perspectives to implementing them into our scholarly efforts?

I do not pretend I have a sure answer. Nor do I really think that any one of us will find one homogeneous truth. After all, the idea that reality can be comprised into an *"objective scientific/rationalistic thought that [...] the universe [is] from a purely mechanistic and materialistic standpoint"* is the prerogative of Western science (Goduka 1999:26). From the starting point of Indigenous perspectives, there is instead a multitude of ways in which Indigenous ideas and ways of being may be prioritized within research endeavours. In this book, the ways that I have implemented are presented in the form of storytelling and the practice of duodji.

INTRODUCING THE GIISÁ

Storytelling means stories, and the stories told in this book are mainly collected from duojárs. This choice rest on multiple reasons. Firstly,

---

5   I understand the use of paradigm in line with Thomas Kuhn ([1962]1996:10) definition of the term as a "universally recognized scientific achievements that [...] provide model problems and solutions for a community of practitioners".

as I am myself a practitioner of duodji, a duojár, I have an extensive network of people to talk to and with. Second, though duodji is an important part of Sámi society in general (Lehtola 2006), many of the complexities inherent in duodji escape those that are themselves not familiar with the practice. It has been considerably less demanding to speak on concepts and practices with those who already knew them even if they did not always have the words or Sámi terminology to articulate them. In this, I have not differed between professional duojárs or duojárs that simply practice duodji for their own—or their family's—purpose. I do recognize that there has been a tendency in recent years to associate the title of duojár with an institutional education or profession (Inga 15.01.2018). Still, in the words of Merete Kuhmunen, who is herself an exceptional duojár, "*if you duddjot then you are a duojár*" (12.09.2019).

Before I continue, I would like to add a note of clarification. There is a marked difference between the duodji practice of men and women (Eikjok and Gjørv 2007:110), the former relating more to *garraduodji*, wherein hard materials such as bone and wood is preferred. The latter, more often than not, engage in *dipmaduodji*—soft duodji that centres on materials such as fabrics, skin, leather, and yarn. Though dipmaduodji by all appearances was highly regarded in the past, in present day, there is a tendency to think of it as second to garraduodji, the latter of which has typically been defined as 'kunsthåndverk', or craft art. Additionally, the lines of transference have mainly been gendered in that women have taught other women, and men other men (Balto 1997).[6] For my own part, this means I mostly practice within the realm of dipmaduodji, and my social network with other practitioners reflects this by being largely focused on other women. As a consequence, this book is very much focused on practices as they relate to women, with 43 of 48 verdde being women.[7] However unintentional, this does aim attention at gender, and the differences in practices of duodji, colonial experiences, and processes of identity-formation and acts of sovereignty.

In addition to duojárs, I have also collected stories from objects, museums, and museum workers. These have all been gathered in what I think of as a *giisá*.

---

6   Though research on Sámi transference of knowledge have overlooked female contributions, focusing mainly on male practices (Kuokkanen 2007a:83).

7   See Appendix I.

FIGURE 1-1 THE GIISÁ IN MY ÁHČČI'S CHILDHOOD HOME HAS ALWAYS BEEN A SOURCE OF WONDER. CONTAINING IMAGES OF LIVED LIVES, AND OF PEOPLE BOTH PAST AND PRESENT, THE GIISÁ MOST CERTAINLY IS A TREASURE CHEST WHICH CONTAINS KNOWLEDGE. THE PICTURES SEEN HERE ARE SOME FROM THE GIISÁ IN QUESTION, INTERSPACED WITH PICTURES I HAVE COLLECTED FROM MY TJIDTJIE'S FAMILY AS WELL AS THOSE FROM MY OWN COLLECTION.

If I were to translate the word, images of a wooden chest meant to store one's belongings comes to mind. In the present day, however, the giisá usually store valuables, such as silver or *risskut*[8], which is the jewelry you use with your gákti, a piece of clothing that has been developed collectively for generations and that is deeply embedded in Sámi cultural values and meanings.[9] Other times, the giisá serves a different purpose.

In my áhčči's home for instance, there is a giisá that has been used to store pictures, and with them the stories of the people depicted. The giisá has as such functioned as an archive of memories and of life-stories that have persevered, sometimes against all odds. I imagine the stories collected in this book to be stored in a similar, if metaphorical giisá; an archive collecting and sharing many stories from many Sámi.

There are perhaps those that would disagree with the giisá as an allegory, citing that in the past the giisá was very personal and a place where you put your things to keep them out of the way and out of sight. While it is true that the giisá may be used to hide things, this is no obstruction to its use as a metaphor. On the contrary, what is contained in a giisá may certainly be that which you want to keep away, but the stories of Sámi struggles and resistance have for far too long been hidden and silenced because as a People, we have been bound by

8   Risskut is the plural of risku, a term for a brooch of silver or bone used with the gákti. Solju is another term for it.

9   See the section on gákti under chapter 4, on rematriation for more on the history of the gákti.

the chains of a 'colonial wall', "*a psychological barrier designed to control, confine and contain a [N]ation by internalized colonialist subjugation of colonizer domination*" (St. Germain 2014:iii).

This speaks quite persistently to why the giisá is my chosen metaphor. Despite our stories being silenced, I believe the time is ripe to share them with a broader audience. So too do those that with great generosity gift their stories for such a purpose. In that sense, we are offering the giisá, opening it up for others to see. In this, I also take some inspiration from the fact there is a precedent for the giisá being a treasure chest from which "*knowledge is brought out and used*" (Pettersen 2011:187).

The stories in the giisá are numerous. They are also of various distinctions. Some are happy and some are sad, while others are angry or even bitter. They all bring with them distinct flavours that certainly have the potential to colour the direction of each chapter. In this, my role has mainly been as the curator in that I have selected and interpreted the stories of the giisá. This is especially pertinent in my choice of implementing the 'prologue'. In Indigenous writing, a prologue is what "*structures space for introductions while serving a bridging function for non-Indigenous readers*".

At the same time, these prologues indicate that what will follow is "*woven throughout the varied forms of writing—analytical, reflective, expository—there will be story, for our story is who we are*" (Kovach 2009:3,4). In this sense, I do bring my own experiences and stories into the analysis. Whilst such is rarely encouraged within a Western academia, it is as I will explain in later chapters, the essence of any train of thought born from the Indigenous experience. As such, though I certainly write from my academic perspective as an archaeologist and museologist, so too am I writing as a Sámi Indigenous scholar and duojár.

Fitting the theme of the giisá, within the pages of this book is also found the pictures that go with some of the stories. They are, of course, never used without permission, but they are necessary. This is a conscious choice based, not simply on a desire to add aesthetics—though it certainly does help in that department—but because it has allowed me to present images, moments in time, when emotions, concepts, and descriptions of happenings have not been possible to convey with words alone; employing what Sámi scholar Harald Gaski refers to as 'lohkat govaid' or reading images.[10] The inclusion of pictures has thus allowed me to probe more deeply into my analysis, as well as provide context for readers.

WHY DUODJI?

As this book is museological in character, few would be surprised at its interest in museums. Duodji, on the other hand, might be more surprising. And yet, I make no excuse; the work ahead is truly a labour of love born from my long-time fascination with museums, as well as a great love for duodji. In that regard this book is an attempt at combining the two. The idea of making such a merger came when I was working on my masters in museology, which briefly touched upon the link between Sámi museums and the practice of duodji in processes of negotiating Sámi identities. My interest in the latter goes far beyond the mentioned timeframe however, beginning when I witnessed, as a child, the women in my communities coming together to converse, and gossip, if truth be told, whilst working on their projects.

FIGURE 1-2 EARLY PICTURE FROM MY CHILDHOOD. IN IT, TJIDTJIE IS TAKING A SMALL BREAK FROM HER DUODJI TO FEED MY YOUNGER BROTHER, ÁNDARAS.

---

10 I first heard Gaski speak on the concept of 'lohkat govaid' on April 27th, 2021 during a gathering convened by the curatorial group, of which I was a member, for the Sámi Pavilion at the International Art Exhibition of La Biennale de Venezia in 2022. The intent was to create a space to address the building of a Sámi-led publication to accompany the exhibition.

I was raised in Oslove, which is the South Sámi spelling of Oslo, the capitol of Norway. As such, I resided quite far from my parents' home communities, which by way of inheritance is also my own. *Tjidtjie*, my mother, is South Sámi, and her home community lies in the area of Vaapste [Vefsn] in Nordland, on the Norwegian side of the border. My áhčči is from Skánit [Skånland] in Troms, albeit now Troms-Finnmark, which is also on the Norwegian side of the border even if our homelands reach beyond and far into the Swedish side. As will no doubt be noticed, I thus use both South Sámi and North Sámi terms and concepts, which reflect my positioning in both cultures.

Quite early on, tjidtjie realized, I think, that the frequent gatherings with other Sámi women doing duodji, was one space that could immerse me in both languages and cultural practices. From early childhood then, duodji became one of the ways I was able to connect with my Sámi heritage. Later on, when I began to practice duodji more seriously, I naturally sought similar arenas. It was here I first noticed the connection between people rediscovering their Sámi heritage and duodji. It is from here that the themes and lines of inquiry in this book take their shape.

The relevance of duodji as the focus of my research, also lies in the fact that while duodji is how we name a cultural practice; it is also the term for the products of said practice, its objects and things. Largely due to the colonial past of museums (Lonetree 2012) and thus the colonial legacy of museum collections, many Indigenous people today make a connection between sovereignty and cultural heritage. Or rather, they connect the loss of one with loss of the other (Gabriel 2008:14). Repatriation, and by extension objects, has consequently become one of the ways in which Indigenous people seek to restore their *"spiritual independence"* and initiate *"language renewal, cultural revitalization, intellectual property rights, land rights and health and well-being"* (Simpson 2008:67), and thus their sovereignty as Peoples'. Nowhere is this more visible than in the wealth of literature that, in recent decades, has called attention to the importance of material culture in Indigenous strategies to materialize and negotiate identities as well as acts of sovereignty (Clifford 2004, Webb 2006, Krmpotich et al. 2013, Peers 2013).

SÁPMI, SÁMI AND SOVEREIGNTY.

Sovereignty, or more to the point, Indigenous sovereignty is thus a key concern in this book. While easily construed as a buzzword, forming jargon that is specific to Indigenous academic communities as an analytical lens or conceptual phrase, sovereignty is, in fact deeply embedded in the complex processes and strategies to achieve cultural integrity and self-determination on multiple levels. While it is true that sovereignty as a concept has been used in association with governance models wherein a community or nation has independent authority, or autonomy, this meaning has been contested. Rauna Kuokkanen (2019:19) for instance, has noted that the mainstream view on sovereignty is limited as it mostly pertains to legalistic and state-centered definitions. For Indigenous Peoples', whom by their very definition are stateless or *"homeless in one's own land"* (Jernsletten 2000:53), this understanding of sovereignty serves only to exclude because it undermines our holistic worldviews and the collective characters of our societies; reproducing the idea that *"'Indigenous' and 'nation' are two terms that seem incommensurable"* (Simpson 2012:7).

FIGURE 1-3 THIS PICTURE WAS TAKEN IN VENICE DURING THE 2019 BIENNALE AND DEPICTS ONE PART OF RICHARD BELL'S PROJECT TITLED ABORIGINAL EMBASSY WHICH AMONG OTHER, PROBLEMATISE SOVEREIGNTY.

In "Restructuring Relations: Indigenous Self-Determination, Governance and Gender" Kuokkanen (2019) instead suggests a relational approach to sovereignty, applied to mean self-determination of lives, territories, cultures, and languages despite the long-time struggle of Indigenous Peoples to gain their recognition as Nations from colonial powers. This sovereignty is a:

> [...] spiritual notion: the ancestral tie between the land, or 'mother nature', and [...] peoples who were born therefrom, remain attached thereto, and must one day return thither to be united with our ancestors. This link is the basis of the ownership of the soil, or better, of sovereignty. It has never been ceded or extinguished (First Nations Constitutional Convention 2017).

The above quote is admittedly taken from "the Uluru statement of the Heart" that was issued in 2017 when 250 Aboriginal and Torres Island Indigenous leaders gathered at the First Nations Constitutional Conventions. But it also holds in a general Indigenous context.

The interrelatedness between land and people is essential in understanding Indigenous sovereignty, and it materializes in many and various ways. This is a grounded normativity, a concept that privileges Indigenous contexts and relationships born from "*land-connected practices and longstanding experiential knowledge that inform and structure our ethical engagements with the world and our relationships with human and nonhuman others over time*" (Coulthard 2014:13). Indigenous sovereignty is informed by these relationships.

To show how sovereignty materialize in a Sámi context I shall use an example that focus on language, at least on the North Sámi language, with which I am most familiar—not that language in any way, shape or form is simple. Our language is, after all, the essence through which our lives are revealed, both by way of the spoken word, but also through the articulations in which our perspectives and realities are expressed (Gaski 2013:116-18).

Take Sápmi and Sámi for instance; the former, Sápmi, is how the homeland of the latter, the Sámi People, have been, and is, referred to amongst ourselves, and as Sámi, we were and are the People living on her.[11] In the [North] Sámi language, to be Sámi is the accusative of Sápmi, and conversely Sápmi is the nominative of Sámi. In languages

---

11 Research into Finno-Ugric languages seem to confirm that Sámi/Sápmi have its etymological root in the old word 'Šämä', which seems to exist back to the earliest variations of Sámi languages, and it is even then associated with the meaning of 'land' (Hansen and Olsen 2004:47)

of case grammar, accusative and nominative are forms of a noun used to signify the direct object of a verb, or the subject of a verb, respectively. Embedded in Sámi language, we thus find the land-based philosophy that is so typical of Indigenous, and indeed a Sámi worldview. This relationship is *"the foundation of Indigenous ideology and culture"* and it *"constitutes and is constituted by the interconnection of memory, life and culture, which are embedded in Country"* (Barrett 2015:112). In other words, our sovereignty as Indigenous is embodied, embedded in our relations and those that are made kin (Moreton-Robinson 2007).

As a colonial strategy, however, language is often used to bodily alienate the people from the land (Jernsletten 2011:4). Instead of Sámi, the people were as such designated as "Lapps", a term that is today regarded as a highly derogatory word for the Sámi people. No longer Sápmi, the Sámi homelands instead became Norway, Sweden, Finland, and Russia. During the Sámi movement of empowerment in the 1960s onwards, Sápmi was reconnected with the Sámi people to enhance that despite not being internationally recognized as such, the Sámi was still a Nation (Stordahl 1996:89). When I use Sápmi and Sámi, I am in reality using a precise vernacular to assert the Sámi as the people of an *unceded* Sápmi, as no treaties or other agreements exists of Sápmi being entered into another Nation state[12]. *"We have never been conquered in war and we have never signed agreements with any state"* (Magga 1996:76), yet Sápmi has been divided by four different Nations; borders drawn on paper, and also enforced unto the land on which we live.

Despite this focus on language, the question of sovereignty is one that I find to be deeply connected to most aspects to do with Sámi life; whether expressed in educational spaces, rights to land, to continue practicing Sámi livelihoods, or engagements within the field of cultural heritage. In this book, my focus is primarily on the latter. That is not to say that issues of sovereignty do not intersect. They do, but I think that looking into the sovereignty of the Sámi is greatly eased by doing so within a set space, or a boundary as it were. To me, that space is museums. More specifically I focus on Sámi museums on the Norwegian and Swedish side of the border. I also reflect on and discuss non-Sámi museums as a way of contrasting.

---

12 I use unceded in the context of an international language of Indigenous rights, when reflecting situations where land has never been ceded (Øyvind 2020).

TERMS OF USE

The concepts and terms used in this book will for the most part be discussed, described and/or defined in my chapters on theory and methodology. There are nevertheless some terms, such as sovereignty, that should be clarified at an even earlier stage. Besides sovereignty, another important term is Indigenous. Many of my peers at an international level have shared with me their opinion that Indigenous is a term created by colonizing powers and as such it should not be used in any way, shape, or form. Instead, the convention has become to refer to a Peoples sovereign naming, such as Sámi, Cree, Māori, etc. Still, there is a certain value in the term. The Sámi historian Henry Minde argues that Indigenous should be understood and used as an international identity that can unite people that are Native to different territories, but who nonetheless share an imposed colonial experience (Minde et al. 2008). As such, I will be using Indigenous in the following discussions.

As to my use of Indigenous, I always capitalize the term as it is a proper noun. I have noticed that many scholars and researchers do not do so, but for me it is a matter of respect and an acknowledgement that we, as sovereign Peoples', resist the colonial claims on our homelands and thus we do not recognize the borders separating our families, communities and homelands. In Sápmi for instance, the use of capitalized Sámi and Indigenous express how our communities are situated on different side of the borders and not in Countries. Additionally, though it is not my native tongue I am writing in English. As such, I am communicating in a language that always capitalizes Nations and Nationalities. As we define ourselves as Nations, the same courtesy should be applied to Indigenous, and also the sovereign terms of Indigenous Peoples'.

Here, I would also like to add a note on the use of English as my working language. Before I started writing this book, the majority of my academic writing was in Norwegian. On rare occasions I did write small essays or articles in English. As for using a Sámi academic language, I asked to do so when I began my education as an archaeologist at the University of Oslo in 2004. The reply I received back then was that it was within my right to have my final exams in Sámi, but they—the institute of archaeology—could not guarantee that it would be graded due to not having competency in Sámi languages.

In hindsight, their lack of competency was not my problem and had I pursued the matter perhaps things would stand very differently today. Nonetheless, with my decision to situate this book in an Indigenous methodology also came the choice of writing in English because it allows me the use of a well-developed academic vernacular of Indigenous make. It also allows me to add Sámi into said vernacular. This is one small way in which I am able to oppose the epistemic ignorance that currently has academia in its grasp.

Another small note is my use of Sámi terms. As explained, Sámi is a case grammar language, meaning that one word may have multiple spellings and endings depending on case. I have however, done a linguistic anglicisation. As a result, Sámi words are kept in their nominative form. When speaking of something in plural, I simply add an -s. Gákti is thus singular, and gáktis is the plural form.

Duddjot is another important term. In Sámi, to duddjot designate the practice of duodji, and there are those that distinguish between *duddjot* and duodji, citing the latter as the objects made from said practice (e.g., Guttorm 2017:163). I have chosen not to do so myself, as I find it moves dangerously close to creating a binary opposition between the two terms, which would only encourage the cartesian dualism so prominent in Western thought (e.g., Goduka 1999:27), yet foreign in a Sámi worldview (Oskal 2007). Though at times I refer to duddjot as a practice, I equally, if not more so, speak on the 'practice of duodji'.

When I speak of duodji as museum artefacts, I have chosen to use the term heritage object intermittently with objects and things or duodji. I borrow the term from the American interdisciplinary scholar James Clifford (2004:16), who suggest heritage object to be applied to objects of significant value in their communities of provenience, or source communities, thus materializing as sites of memories and communication. In this context, source community refers to both the groups of Indigenous people from which the artefacts were collected in the past, as well as their present-day descendants (Peers and Brown 2003:2).

STRUCTURE

As I initially stated, this book is not only on the subject of duodji, but also of duodji. To reflect such, I have chosen to structure my chapters by the principles of the practice. More to the point, various practices of duodji has been chosen to act as structural elements to help me focus my thought process and shape my writing.

In **bárket**, we begin our story with the early days of colonialism, preparing the context for understanding the coming discussions and analyses. Quite contrary to the exotic images of an Arctic people, the nature of whom is childlike and naïve, that so often has been disseminated by history (Schefferus 1673), this is a more mature tale. The colonial experience of Indigenous people is ugly. This is also true with regards to the Sámi. *"One might call colonization a way of war"* (Jernsletten 2011:45), and as such, bárket document the ways in which war has been waged on the Sámi; on our lands; our languages; our cultural integrity; our livelihoods; and our very sovereignty. Putting on the lens of epistemicide, or the colonial process of killing knowledge, as an analytical tool, this chapter follows the Sámi colonial experience from 'first contact' to the 20th century, emphasizing how deliberate acts of epistemicide was used to erase Sámi knowledge[s] and practices, and how so many of the Sámi people eventually emerged as *jávohuvvan*, a silenced People.

Ruvdet take its starting point from bárket, as it explores what the colonial implementation of epistemicide sought to unravel by revealing the Indigenous Sámi worldview that is at heart in our ontologies, our epistemologies and our axiologies. Depicting a specific Sámi epistemology that is deeply connected with the act of making kin, the chapter highlights how the Sámi way of being, doing, and knowing is born from the interrelatedness of the world [which is one of relations]. This brings to light the reciprocity in between spaces, which have been rooted in people, in land and waters, as well as spirituality, in other beings and entities. By doing so, ruvdet share the complexities that seeds our Sámi world/s and seek to understand how these intricacies materialize through stories and storytelling.

There is a continued emphasis on stories and storytelling in **riessat**, where the theoretical framework is conceived of. Here I develop an idea of duodji as literature; the documents and archives that is expressed in stories and through storytelling. Riessat thus works to change our perception of duodji, revealing it as a sophisticated system of knowledge deeply embedded in both the practice and the objects. Though not intended to provide an image of duodji as a standardized theory, the chapter nonetheless extrapolate certain aspects of the practice; transforming them into analytical tools or concepts by which I create a theoretical boundary for detecting, understanding, and interpreting processes of recentering Sámi identities.

In **čuoldit,** the work of duojárs is understood from the theoretical boundary designed in riessat. Here then, we are presented with the theory in practical terms as čuoldit search out and examine various processes of regaining Indigenous sovereignty through the recentering of identities. In this, the giisá provides the clues, offering up a particular entry point through one specific story that discuss the belief in ancestral knowledge as a component of Sámi knowledge systems. By way of such belief, this chapter ends up following several verddes' and their mediations of duodji as practice and focused through specific acts of revitalization, or what I prefer to term re-remembrance.

The focus on memory continues in **bearalduodji,** but more as it pertains to an interaction with museums as memory institutions. Opening the discussion, we are served with a problematisation of heritage objects remanded into the custody or ownership of museums outside of source communities. Again, the giisá offer a point of departure with a story that details accessibility, which reveals the multiple complexities that come into play when duodji is transitioned from objects of use to museum artefacts. Here, the consequences of such material movements are also discussed in light of both the loss and later restitution of Sámi identities and sovereignty.

The last chapter, *šiella,* summarize my discussions, and outline some pertinent thoughts and conclusions

CHAPTER 2: BÁRKET

"THIS LAND ON WHICH OUR ANCESTORS LIVED"

COLONIAL PROCESSES IN SÁPMI AND THE (ATTEMPTED) DESTRUCTION OF SÁMI KNOWLEDGE[S].

WHAT DO I KNOW OF SÁMI CULTURE? —A PROLOGUE

In the autumn of 2018, I travelled to the city Båddådjo, or Bodø as it is called in Norwegian, with the intent to participate, as an observer, in a weekend-course in the making of a Pitesámi gappte. I flew in from Oslo on a Friday morning and as my flight arrived early, I had some free time before the course, which was scheduled to begin that evening. I spent that time in the city centre, having arranged to catch up with an old friend over lunch. After, I ended up finding a charming little coffeehouse where I spent the remainder of my time before leaving for the course. By all accounts, the café was popular with the locals, and it soon filled up with people until there was no vacant tables left. I was interrupted from my reading by a woman asking if she could share my table, and we soon came to be talking. No doubt having registered that I spoke in a Southern dialect, she asked me what I was doing all the way up North. I answered her and explained about the course I was to attend later that day. At my reply, she asked me if my interest was due to me being Sámi myself. After I confirmed my ethnicity, she became quiet and she remained so for quite some time.

I returned to my book, not thinking much of it. Båddådjo is actually quite close to my tjidtjie's home-community, merely a three-hour drive away. As a child and young teen, I spent the majority of my summers there living with my aahka [grandmother]. I have fond memories of the place and good friends and family that still lives there. But I also have not so fond memories due to the blatant racism that Sámi may experience from some of the Norwegian locals. I simply assumed that this woman was precisely one such local and decided that the better part of valour was to simply ignore her. As it turned out, my assumption was false. After 10 or maybe 15 minutes she picked up our conversation.

"My grandmother hated the Sámi. She wanted no part in that culture. When I was little, sometimes I would hear her talking about those "filthy Lapps". I didn't understand why they were [filthy], but you know, I didn't really care. I wasn't one after all. Then, when she [grandmother] got old she started to forget things. She regressed, I guess. And suddenly she talked Sámi. That's how I discovered that my family was really Sámi. Today I know I am Sámi, not Norwegian. And I think of my grandmother with sadness. What drives a person like that? What had she experienced before meeting my grandfather that made her feel as if she had to hide who she was and to call her own people filthy Lapps to keep others from knowing that she was really herself a Lapp? That is what Norwegian heritage gives you. I want no part of that, [but] what do I know of Sámi culture?"

I was shocked, not so much by her story, because it is, I'm sad to say, not unique. Rather what disturbed me was the frank candidness she delivered her story with. Perhaps she recognized my feelings, because she continued speaking in a slightly explanatory tone of voice: "If I allow myself to think on it too much, I want to cry". We continued talking with one another for an hour or so before I had to leave. But I remember our meeting with great clarity. I think of her often, and I wonder if she still feels like crying (Ájsa 23.06.2018).

INTRODUCTION

The intricacies that reveal themselves in matters of identities as seen in the prologue, are always numerous and varied, not to mention complex. More so perhaps when the identities in question are Indigenous in origin. In large, the reason for such is, I think, that the Indigenous experience is characterized by a history of colonisation, oppression, assimilation and other trauma, which inevitably becomes a necessary point of reference, so deeply intertwined with the social formation of Indigenous self—both past and present—that it may be difficult to see a culturally based identity without also taking into account these social and political processes (e.g., Alfred 1995, Minde et al. 2008, Hernes 2017, Hansen 2015). That is not to say that what defines our

Indigeneity are negativities alone. On the contrary, within the Indigenous experience there are also dynamic engagements of resilience and
resistance.

It seems to me, however, that stories of colonial violence, of resistance,
and of resilience, no matter their geographical origin, in large have been
hidden or silenced (Minde 2005:16, Hirvonen 1999, Somby 2016); em-
braced by the quintessential saying, 'out of sight, out of mind'. As was articulated in a recent study on the untold stories of Sámi women, *"[l]ean gi-
erddahallan jávohisvuođas"*, I have had to bear the silence (Somby 2016:8,
my own translation). In the research tradition then, albeit one that is of a
Western thought, most of the sources in connection to Sámi cultures have
been written by 'outsiders'—the States, the Church, travellers and Western
scholars (Jernsletten 2011:24, Storm 2017:62).[1] Aside from the dynamics
of power implied herein, no doubt the scarcity of written sources of Sámi
origin owes much to the fact that Sámi cultures were, and very much still
are, oral cultures (Schanche 1995), and history, as we all know, is written.
This does not mean that the stories are not there; *"they exist"*, only they do
so "as *[...] oral literature"* (Jernsletten 2011:3).

Still, there is a low visibility of Sámi perspectives in the history
books, in research and within academia in general (Hirvonen 1999,
Berg 2001, Dunfjeld-Aagård 2005, Bergstøl 2008, Somby 2016). As
such, the context that I discuss, analyse, critique, and problematize
within, may not be immediately accessible to non-Sámi, and even
some Sámi, readers. Responding to the very real possibility of said
context being inaccessible to many, the following chapter aims to create a context—not in any attempt to rewrite history, no matter how
necessary I think that might be. Instead, I will simply lay out, in extremely broad lines, what in my opinion is some of the vital points of
the colonial history in Sápmi. Here, I would caution the reader that I
am most familiar with the colonial processes as they occurred on the
Swedish and Norwegian side of the border as this is where my home
communities lie. The exploration ahead is very much, I suspect, characterized by such a fact. But considering that my verdde for the most

---

1   In the rare event that sources may be traced back to Sámi authors, they have seldom been understood holistically, or at worst been misunderstood and/or twisted to fit an outsider perspective (Gaski 2011). Here I am
thinking of "Muitalus Sámiid Birra" published in 1910 that was written in Sámi by Johan Turi. In addition to
his written words, Turi added any pictures that he himself drew, implementing a methodology which would
facilitate the readers to also 'lohkat govaid'. Nevertheless, as his non-Sámi contemporaries lacked the knowledge to understand that Turi's art was sources equal to his written words, they only got fragments of the story
that Turi wanted to tell (Gaski 2011:12).

part have their homelands in the same locations, I think it reasonable to focus on said areas.

Another point of concern in the following is the switch between a Sámi and a more general Indigenous context. Although I discuss the relationship between Indigenous and Sámi experiences in more detail in the next chapter, ruvdet, I will for now state the following: it is not my intent to generalize or homogenize Indigenous experiences. Nonetheless, I do believe that regardless of our specific Nations, as Indigenous people we share many similarities—be it our present concerns of sovereignty, or our stories. As a result, in the following chapter I do discuss both Indigenous experiences at a more general level as well as Sámi experiences specifically. The main focus is on the latter, however, which is also why the starting point for this chapter comes from the content of the giisá, or more to the point, from the prologue above.

The story that was shared with me in Báddådjo, is one of heartbreak. It details the story of a grandmother whose self-hatred became the foundation on which she built her life, and it continues with a granddaughter whose grief upon discovery was only a prelude to the grief she felt upon realising what it was that she herself had lost. At first glance, this story might seem a tragedy, but one of personal discovery. The more you listen, however, the more you realize that it is in fact, only a fragment of a much larger narrative that concerns the entirety of the Sámi people. I chose this story as a starting point because it illustrates how colonial strategies work; the dynamics that over time forced upon a woman an ethnic stigma so great that rather than living as Sámi, she chose to pass as Norwegian—even to her husband and children. And these are the strategies that, according to Anders Larsen[2], a Sámi schoolteacher that worked actively to support Sámi languages in the early 20th century, has left "*no Sámi youth [...] that has not been damaged in soul*" (quoted in Hidle and Oterbech 1917:35, my own translation).

What both the granddaughter in the prologue and Larsen speak of is, in my opinion, a textbook example of *lateral violence*. Originating in the work of early theorists in Africa (Fanon [1963]2007, [1967]2008) and Latin America (Freire 1970) to explain some of the internal pro-

---

2   Larsen was also the founder and long-time editor of the Sámi newspaper 'Sagai Muittalægje', which was founded in 1904.

cesses induced on the colonized, the term describes what happens when people who find themselves in a position of powerlessness direct their dissatisfaction, either covertly or overtly, towards each other or inward toward themselves. Lateral violence is caused by the many strategies of colonialism, be it segregation, assimilation, or the systematic dehumanization of Indigenous people to justify the stealing of their lands, languages, and knowledges.

Although these strategies are no longer being actively pursued—at least not in ways we would recognize– many would perhaps choose to focus on the fact that they are a thing of the past (e.g., De L'Estoile 2008). After all, the Western concept of time as linear inevitably mean that *"settler narratives [...] distance themselves from the horrific crimes committed against Indigenous peoples and the land"* (Estes 2019:24). But the legacy of colonialism is ongoing, and the trauma that it implies still impact on the continued existence of Indigenous people. In relation to mainstream populations, for instance, Indigenous people often suffer poorer physical and mental health, lower income and education levels, elevated levels of prejudice and racism, and are far more likely to be the victims of sexual abuse, domestic violence and the aforementioned lateral violence (Chandler and Lalonde 1998, Duran 2006, Eliassen et al. 2013, Øverli et al. 2017). The British social anthropologist, Paul Connerton (2011:16), has defined all of these as the physical manifestation of a *historical trauma*. To briefly explain the concept, Connerton defines historical trauma as the *"routinized forms of suffering"* or structural damage and/or violence caused, in this case, by colonialism and its associated strategies. Typical of such trauma is that it affects a community, or Nation, as a whole rather than simply at an individual level alone. That is to say, even if someone has not directly experienced the cause of historical trauma on their body or person, like the granddaughter in the prologue, they are still afflicted by the history of it (Dankertsen 2014). In this chapter, though I will not pretend to offer a comprehensive exploration of all the possible strategies and consequences of colonialism, I will nonetheless discuss the approaches that I feel have been especially harmful to Indigenous Sámi identities and sovereignty. To help me do so, I concentrate my discussion around the term *epistemicide*.

Initially coined by the Portuguese sociologist Boaventura de Sousa Santos (2008) to describe the systematic destruction of knowledge[s], epistemicide describes the effect of globalization on countries perceived to be underdeveloped, and where local knowledges are slowly being overwritten by the imported knowledge systems of the West. Epistemicide, however, works in a number of ways and it is especially relevant in the context of colonisation and Indigeneity where it implies:

> [...] the deliberate destruction of other cultures. The destruction of knowledge (besides the genocide of [I]ndigenous people) is what I call epistemicide: the destruction of the knowledge and cultures of these populations, of their memories and ancestral links and their manner of relating to others and to nature (Santos 2014:18).

TO BÁRKET—MAPPING MY STRUCTURE

To organize the structure in the following, I take my inspiration from another concept. To be fair, more than concept, to **bárket** is in truth a practice within duodji. One of the many steps necessary when tanning and preparing animal hides, to bárket describes the process of storing the hides in large containers imbued in decoctions that have been made from dried bark. This process not only help colour the skin, but also work to make the hides waterproof. To treat the hides such, is an important step in preparing them for making duodji. Inspired by bárket, this chapter has a similar purpose in that it metaphorically gathers the themes, or bark, needed to prepare the hide, or this book for making duodji, or analysing the empirical material. With epistemicide as my focus, I thus collect my bark in the shape of two important events, starting with 'first contact'.

The reason I start with first contact, is that the colonial experience differs, both in spans of time and of place. That is also true of the Sámi colonial experience, where contact in certain areas preceded the colonial expansion by large stretches of time (Jernsletten 2011:42). Though first contact has various implications, my use of it as a term is strictly in the anthropological sense of a first meeting between people of two previously unknown cultures. Of course, arguments may be made that there is nothing about the term that restricts it to a benign use, as it far too often has been followed by asymmetrical relations embedded in contexts of imperialism and colonialism (Solbakk and Hansen 2006, Dunfjeld-Aagård 2005).

FIGURE 2-1 THIS SHOWS HIDES THAT HAVE BEEN HUNG TO DRY AFTER THEY HAVE BEEN BÁRKET. IT IS IMPORTANT THAT THEY DRY NATURALLY BECAUSE USING HEATERS WOULD MAKE THE SKIN THOUGH AND DRY, THUS DIFFICULT TO WORK WITH. THESE HIDES HAVE BEEN PREPARED BY DUOJÁR, PIA JANNOK, WHO HAS ALLOWED ME TO MAKE USE OF IT IN THIS BOOK.

Forewarned by the fact that first contact is a typical prelude to colonisation, the next section, discussing the colonial expansion into Sápmi, is a natural transition. Within the frame of said colonial process, I engage with two hugely different examples of epistemicide. One that is very visible, and undeniably loud, as it centres on the very public confiscation and attempted eradication of Sámi religious tools in the 17th century. The other example is stealthier, expressed as a covertly 500-year long period of assimilation, which eventually forced upon the Sámi a shame so great that many felt it necessary to shift their ethnicity.

I have chosen these two events because they had a massive impact, not only on identity, but also on the practice of duodji. Of course, interspaced in-between and around these two examples, I take small detours to establish some necessary bridging points to help the reader understand both the history of a People, but also why there is a need to shed light on the relation between Sámi sovereignty, identities, duodji and museums.

OF 'FIRST CONTACT'.

Every story, no matter how unpleasant, has a beginning. As beginnings go, the story of 'first contact' as it relates to the Sámi and the neighbouring Norse and Slavic communities is difficult to date. Archaeological material suggests that a gradual development of differing ethnicities happens within Fenno-Scandinavia sometime during the last millennium B.C.E.[3] (Olsen 1984:153, Hansen and Olsen 2004:4, 52-149).[4] As a source, this does little to foreshadow the events to come. Nor is any warning given if we look to the earliest sources of a literary nature. The earliest written record of contact between the Sámi and other cultures we find in Tacitus[5] account of Germania[6] from the first century C.E. (Tacitus [98]1997:94-5).[7] Some later sources, such as Fjordane and Porcius dating to the 6th century C.E., also make reference to the Sámi, but neither can be said to paint a picture of exploitation or subjugation (Hansen and Olsen 2004:47). On the contrary, if we shift the focus back to archaeology, the sources from this time indicate that there was a peaceful co-existence between the Sámi and their Norse/German/Slavic neighbours with both trading relations, as well as inter-cultural marriages, being quite commonplace (Storli 1991, 1994). What I find interesting about these interpretations is not so much what is being said, but rather what they indicate.

The Norwegian archaeologist, Inger Storli, has argued that trade and matrimony between the Sámi and Norse was connected. Looking at burials from the latter part of the Iron Age (500-1030), which in Scandinavia is termed the Viking Age (800-1030), from the Northern areas on both the Swedish and Norwegian sides of the border, Storli has found that some female burials of a Norse character would include Sámi grave goods, and that some female burials of a Sámi character include Norse grave goods.[8] From this, she concludes that

---

3   B.C.E. is an abbreviation for Before Common Era and is used as a secular option to replace the traditional B.C., or Before Christ. Similarly, C.E, or Common Era is used instead of A.D., or Anno Domini meaning "in the year of the Lord".

4   It is not the intention of this book to explain Sámi ethnicity. I would urge anyone interested in learning more to look to the collaborative work of historian Lars Ivar Hansen and archaeologist Bjørnar Olsen (2004) that give a good view of archaeological and historical sources pertaining to such.

5   Gaius Cornelius Tacitus was a senator of the Roman Empire and considered to be one of its greatest historians. His work "Germania" is thought to be the most complete account of Germania that still survives

6   Germania was the roman term for the Northern territories past the Alps.

7   It should be noted however, that there is some disagreement as to whether Tacitus is describing the Sámi, but an overall majority agrees that he does make mention of the Sámi, which is what I too am assuming.

8   The difference in burial customs is extensively discussed by archaeologist Audhild Schanche (2000), and I

cross-cultural marriage may very well have happened as an exchange between trading partners to affirm their mutual commitments (Storli 1991:115-19). Though the interpretation seems valid, I would still like to point out one major concern.

EARLY INDICATION OF COLONIALISM?

Similar to many other Indigenous communities, *"women in Sámi society historically had a form of equality with men, characterized by a complementarity of domains, roles and tasks"* (Kuokkanen 2007a:74). It is not my intent to support an idea of Sámi society prior to colonisation as matriarchal[9], but there is evidence to suggest that with an eventual colonisation also came a change in the structural relations between genders, and not to the better if looked at from a female perspective (Kuokkanen 2007a). As I read Storli, her interpretation completely disregards that there might be a difference in how the Sámi and the Norse structured their systems of gender. This leads me to conclude that either her interpretation takes shape within the assumption that Sámi gender roles mirrored the Norse relation between genders at this time, or colonial processes had already begun. Both possibilities are equally serious. If it is a case of the former, then assumptions about a Sámi past have been made, not on the basis of Sámi oral sources, but rather on colonial ideas and stereotypes.[10]

As to the latter argument, both Rauna Kuokkanen (2007a), and Bonita Lawrence (2003), who is a professor of Sociology of Mi'kmaq[11] decent, has argued that systems of gender discrimination and hetero-patriarchy[12] in general is a constituent process in the colonisation of Indigenous communities. If, as Storli suggests, Sámi women at this time had become tools of trade as it where, might not this be indicative that the customary equality of sexes had begun to become eroded, and replaced with a highly asymmetrical system of gender? If so, it is

---

would direct anyone interested to learn more to her work.

9   This was more a popular image created during the Sámi ethnopolitical movement to distinguish the Sámi from surrounding cultures (Kuokkanen 2007a:76).

10   One example is when Storli find support for her interpretation in *"several independent sources of the 18th century"* (Storli 1994:115, my own translation) that detail how Sámi men had a practice of wife swapping, which lead to them "lending" their wives out to non-Sámi officials, who of course documented these encounters (see Odner 1989-7).

11   The Mi'kmaq are a First Nation People Indigenous to the areas now known as Canada's Atlantic Provinces and the Gaspe Peninsula of Quebec as well as the north-eastern region of Maine, USA.

12   This is a socio-political system in which cisgender males and heterosexuals have authority over cisgender females and other sexual orientations and gender identities.

not too large of an inference I think, to suspect that colonial processes were already at play sometime in the Viking Age. Storli's findings correspond with some literary sources, but these are all of a much later date and none have come from the Sámi themselves (Nielssen [2012]2019:89). I would thus urge some caution in interpreting these sources.

To conclude, while it may seem as if the relationship between the Sámi, at least those of the male variety, and the neighbouring Norse tribes was one of equilibrium, there is also evidence to suggest that colonial changes had begun to appear. Still, attempting to determine for sure whether the relationship between the Sámi and the Norse was one of equality or characterized by imbalanced power structures is no easy task.

Historically there has been a tendency to view the relationship between the Sámi and the Norse during the Viking Age as asymmetrical, with the former being suppressed and exploited by the latter (e.g., Gjessing 1973). No doubt the literary account of Othere of Hålogaland is one of the reasons why (Storli 1994:105). In 890 C.E., Othere, who was a Viking seafarer and tradesman visited the court of Alfred, the then King in the Anglo-Saxon kingdom of Wessex. In his account, Othere speaks of his home to the far North in what is today Nordland and Troms on the Norwegian side of the border. He also tells Arthur of the Sámi people living on *his* land, who pay tribute to him in rich furs and animal skins, bird feathers, whale bones and ropes made of the skins from whales and seals. He concludes that a majority of his wealth is actually owed to his imposing taxes on the Sámi living in close proximity (Simonsen 1957:68). Though Othere makes no mention of this himself, the Norwegian historian Lars Ivar Hansen and Norwegian archaeologist Bjørnar Olsen (2004:66), figures that the taxation in all likelihood is an aspect of a reciprocating relationship where in return for their tax, the Sámi got both easy access to specific commodities and/or military protection. This interpretation is perhaps more easily understood if one looks to the relational experience of the world that was, and still is, typical of a Sámi worldview.

THE SÁMI GIFT AND THE NORSE TRIBUTE

As is the case with many Indigenous philosophies, the Sámi has long manifested their relations and/or connections through gift-giving.

This is not, by any means, to ensure the reception of a "counter-gift",[13] but more for the reason of acknowledging that the world is made up of relations and the gift is one way of ensuring a harmonious co-existence with all of these (Kuokkanen 2007b:65, e.g., Pettersson, Bäckman, and Kjellström 1979:134). This is a logic that is quite different from "*the logic of exchange that prevails in modern society and through which the gift giving practices and philosophies of [I]ndigenous societies are commonly interpreted (and thus, misunderstood)*" (Kuokkanen 2007b:66). In their interactions with the Norse, it is quite possible that the Sámi engaged in a culturally derived practice of acknowledging relations that the Norse had no concept of, and as such no way of truly understanding, and so they assumed a reciprocal relationship of tribute to exist.[14]

This perceived reciprocity was one of the major cornerstones in his findings when the Norwegian archaeologist, Knut Odner during the early 1980s' published his treatise on Norse/Sámi interactions during the Iron Age wherein he challenged the reigning interpretation of the latter being subjugated by the former. In "Finner og terfinner: etniske prosesser i det nordlige Fenno-Skandinavia," he instead postulated that the two cultures had a relationship characterized by reciprocity and collaboration; the Sámi, in their capacity as hunters and trappers, provided valuable commodities, and in return they got valuable metals, such as iron, and military protection (Odner 1983:80, 92-3, 116-7). Odner's suggestion had support in historical sources. Especially from the German ecclesiastical chronicler, Adam of Bremen, who in 1160 wrote that both iron tools and grains were beneficial gains in trade for the Sámi. Despite being 300 years apart, both Adam of Bremen and Othere, thus cite the Sámi as valued, if unequal, trading partners.

Odner found support for his hypothesis in archaeological material (Zachrisson 1984, Storli 1991, Henriksen 1996). The Swedish archaeologist Inger Zachrisson (1984:16-7, 22) for instance, has remarked that from the 11th century onwards there is a clear change of Sámi sacrificial material; whereas previously blood, bones, fur and skin of animals was the primary gift, now came the addition of silver. This

13 Though the gift does imply a response-ability whereby a gift is responded to by acknowledgement of the larger whole in which humans is but one small part.

14 This is not unique to a Sámi context. In 1840, when the Treaty of Waitangi was signed, from the British perspective the treaty was meant to secure sovereignty over New Zealand. For the 46 chiefs in Bay Island, each given two blankets and a small quantity of tobacco, the exchange was meant to ensure the retention of Māori authority alongside British governorship (Henare 2005:1)

sacrificial material is likely an expression of Sámi gift giving, where *sjiele*, the South Sámi term or *šiella*, the North Sámi term, are gifted to the land and spirits to maintain and ensure a good relationship with one's relations (Turi [1910]1987:159, Strompdal 1954:42, Dunfjeld 2006:201, Jernsletten 2009:119). Silver then, is most likely an added valuable gain from trade. The literary sources corroborated by archaeological material is as such in support of Odner. But, as we have already seen, archaeological material may, on occasion, suit several arguments depending on context. And as one may imagine, Odner's theory is not without objections.

There are two main criticisms against Odner. Firstly, his assumption that Sámi society was egalitarian (e.g., Odner 1983:117). To Odner, the trade between the Sámi and the Norse was a large inducement to the social stratification of the latter, but for some reason he did not consider that the exchange of valuable goods could have had a similar impact on the former. Archaeological materials from the Iron Age might indicate differently (Storli 1991, Schanche 1994). Looking to specific structural remains of settlements in the mountainous areas of what is today Norway and Sweden, as well as hoards of metal and burial goods, Storli (Storli 1994:99, 103, Schanche 1994:84-5) has argued that there is a Sámi process of social stratification happening as early as the 10th century C.E. It is likely, she continues, that this new elite did develop as a direct result of the trade with the Norse. In fact, the aforementioned appearance of sacrificial silver is just one material expression of said elite being created (Storli 1994:104). This elite would also be the same people that she argued had cemented their trade agreements by intermarriage.

Another objection to Odner's interpretation, is his dating of Sámi ethnicity. Though Odner (1983:116) see a marked difference between Norse and Sámi ethnicity somewhere during the late Roman period and early Migration period between 300–600 C.E., he believed that ethnicity of a pan-Sámi nature only happened sometime during the 16th century when colonisation intensified. The idea being that only in the face of a colonial expansion or intrusion did the Sámi see a need to unify their ethnic expressions. Today, however, the prevailing interpretation is that Sámi ethnicity developed sometime during the pre-Roman Iron Age, or within the last millennium B.C.E. (Olsen

1984:153, see Hansen and Olsen 2004: 4, 52-149 for more details).[15] Bjørnar Olsen (2004:23) has even entertained the idea that some cultural variations indicating a developing Sámi ethnicity may be traced even further back, but he hesitates to define them as Sámi, which is really not surprising.

According to Norwegian archaeologist Edel Berg (2001:82), it is quite commonplace for archaeological remains in the Nordic countries to be seen in light of political implications when one is arguing for a Sámi ethnic affiliation. The demand for legitimation is thus far greater then when one is arguing a Nordic and non-Sámi affiliation. As has been remarked by Ole Henrik Magga (1996:78), the first president of Sámidiggi, the Sámi Parliament on the Norwegian side of the border;

> We cannot say anything about ethnic relations in those old times [...]. But this does not prevent editors of atlases, magazine articles, newspaper articles and tourist brochures to write and speak about "Norwegians 10,000 years ago" in Northern Norway [...]. In this way a past that most probably is a Sámi past and certainly not a "Norwegian" past in the narrow sense is stolen from us daily. For ordinary people, the question naturally arises: when and from where have the Sámi come to Norway? In this way we are deprived of our past in a very clever way.

Despite the criticisms raised against Odner, his main narrative, in which the Sámi and the Norse were equals in status, rights and opportunities, is still considered credible by most. In fact, even some of his harshest critics give this interpretation their overall support (e.g., Storli 1994:106). I do feel the need, however, to mention that some sources and consequent interpretations indicate that the early trade between the Sámi and the Norse often favoured the latter (Solbakk and Hansen 2006, Dunfjeld-Aagård 2005). Thus, while there is little to suggest that an outright process of colonisation was initiated during the Viking Age, I do think it is fair to say that there is already a slow advance of a colonial interest at this time. The question then, is when said interest was realized as an actual advance.

COLONIZING SÁPMI

The treaty of Novgorod is crucial when trying to decipher the early

---

15 Though it is the prevailing interpretation, there are still some that dispute it (e.g., Nordmark 2014).

colonial history of Sápmi. Signed in 1326, the treaty marked the end of ongoing border skirmishes between what is today Finnmark on the Norwegian side of the border and the republic of Novgorod, which is the area of modern Russia that shares its borders with Scandinavia. The latter had settled with the Nation of Sweden only three years earlier, relinquishing their claim to what is now Finland. Contrary to what might be expected, neither treaty worked to delineate the borders. Rather, they stipulated which parts of the Sámi homelands, and by extension who of the Sámi people, would pay tribute to which country. As such, the treaties confirmed a defined common taxation area (Gallén and Lind 1968). The treaties, which remained in effect until the 19th century, though they were somewhat reduced after the redrawing of borders in the 18th century, caused a situation in which the Sámi were freely exploited and at times were even forced to pay taxes to all surrounding powers at the same time (Hansen 2011:298-9). In the span of 300 years, sources thus paint an altogether more insidious picture of the relationship between the Sámi and their surrounding neighbours.

In his book on the sea Sámi communities on the Norwegian side of the border from 1950, Anders Larsen writes that the Sámi...

> [...] have many stories of the stállu [...]. It is likely [...] that stállu was originally the name given to the tax collectors by the Sámi. The former were oppressors who brutally raided the Sámi dwellings. [...] Today [...] some Sámi believe that stállu is a mean spirit sent by bad people to trouble others (Larsen [1950] 1979:40, my own translation).

It is noteworthy that the impact of tax collectors has made its way into the Sámi language as an established character who even today is called upon as a "bogeyman" to get children to behave. "*If you don't do so and so*" it is often said, "*then Stállu will come get you*". If nothing else, it is a clear indication of how pivotal an event levying of taxes upon the Sámi is, and thus its importance when trying to untangle the complexities of the colonial history. The tax collectors were agents of Nations,

> [...] who refer to our land as theirs, [...] And who consider our homeland theirs. We never sold this land on which our ancestors lived for thousands of years without even leaving a trace behind them, and who did not comprehend that it could be sold for money (Utsi 1993:4).

Here, the philosophy of the gift becomes relevant. As mentioned, there is no evidence that the Sámi actually agreed to have taxes levied at them. Rather, as the "tribute" in early sources is associated with trade and bartering, it is most likely an expression of *"symbolic gifts, with the function of confirming a mutually useful and esteemed relationship"* (Hansen 2011:296). It is as such highly likely that the gift was actually formalized as tax in the treaty of Novgorod, which shows how the Sámi philosophy of gift-giving was perverted.

By the 14th century, it is safe to say that Sápmi had been largely colonized. Yet, to establish an exact dating of the colonial expansion into Sápmi is still difficult, if not impossible. Some 800 years after Tacitus first made mention of the Sámi, others had slowly begun to make their home in Sápmi (Kent 2014:11). Admittedly, the first settlers were small in numbers and they primarily consisted of traders, trappers and hunters that had been drawn by the rich bounties of the land. To explain the infrequent presence of settlers at this time, Norwegian archaeologist Jørn Henriksen (1996) points to the political agendas of the wealthy Norse lords. By word of Othere, we know that a large majority of wealth amongst the North's Norse ruling class was due to the commodities provided by the Sámi. The continued flow of these commodities relied on the Sámi having a stable access to their hunting grounds and other areas for sourcing raw materials.

Allowing for an increased population by way of settling these areas would decrease the hunting grounds and thus jeopardize the supply of goods (Odner 1983:116-7). Hence, at this time, it is likely that the financial interests of the Norse elite actually worked to prohibit a large-scale expansion and ensured that this first colonial wave remained almost inconsequential (Henriksen 1996:79).

NATION-BUILDING AND THE PROCESS OF CONSOLIDATION.

No matter the incentive, by the 13th century, colonists from both Scandinavia and elsewhere in Europe had reached significant numbers (Kent 2014). In all likelihood, this change was triggered by the political climate of the 10th and 11th century (Storli 2006).

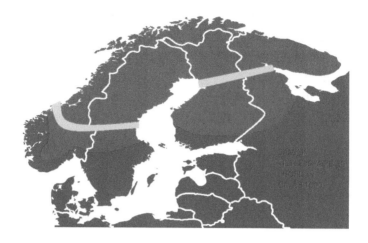

FIGURE 2-2 MAP THAT SHOWS THE PRESENCE OF THE SÁMI IN THE VIKING AGE OUTLINED IN RED. THE YELLOW BANDS ARE THE PERCEIVED BORDERS OF A "TRADITIONAL" SÁPMI. THE DIFFERENT NATION STATES BORDERS HAVE BEEN OUTLINED IN WHITE. THE MAP WAS MADE BY SÁMI SCHOLAR MIKKEL BERG-NORDLIE.

In a Scandinavian reckoning, the Viking Age ends during the 11th century, which coincides with the official formation of the previous Norse chiefdoms into the Christian Kingdoms that would eventually make up Scandinavia. A long time in coming, the previous centuries had been strongly characterized by a process of consolidation. Inger Storli (2016), for instance, argues that one of the largest chieftain farms in North Norway—Borg in Lofoten—was actually abandoned due to conflicts related to this process. She goes on to link this process to Norwegian nation-building.

Admittedly, the abandoning of Borg happened during the 10th century.[16] It serves, however, as an example of the long-time political agenda to unify, in this case, a Norwegian Nation and how this process worked to depose the local Norse chieftains in the Northern areas.

With the removal of the Norse chieftains from their seats of power came a shift in motivation with regards to the settling of Sápmi. Whereas before it was in the interest of the leaders to keep the sojourners to a bare minimum, with an autocratic king, it would be far more beneficial to increase the presence of loyal subjects. "*The colonization by farmers was often encouraged since a permanent population increased the nation's claim to the territory*" (Kuoljok and Utsi 1993:30).

---

16 Borg can be split into three periods of settlements; Borg I during the Migration (400-550 C.E.) and Early Merovingian Period (550 -793 C.E.), Borg II during late Merovingian Period and Viking Age (793-1066) and last, Borg III belonging to the Early Middle Ages (1066-1130) (Munch and Johansen 2003). Storli's argument is as such primarily based on the settlement history of Borg II.

In other words, during the course of the 11th century, the Scandinavian Kings was able to seize control of the Northern areas that until then had been under the control of Norse chieftains and warlords. The political security of the fledgling states was well served by an increasement of non-Sámi settlements as this allowed the Kings to, firstly, lay claim to parts of Sápmi, and second, levy their own tribute on the Sámi (Hansen 2011:296).

There are some interesting commentaries that could be made on the process of unification and the Sámi if one looks to later sources, amongst them the sagas of the Norwegian Viking Kings. In the sagas, or *Heimskringla* as they are jointly named, one story, in particular, stands out. Written down by the Icelandic poet Snorre Sturlason in 1220, Heimskringla make specific mention of the marriage between Harald Fairhair and the South Sámi woman named Snøfrid. To add some context; Fairhair, who is thought to have lived and ruled until 931 or 932 C.E., is considered to be the first Norwegian King to conquer and rule over a majority of Western Norway. During his lifetime, Fairhair was joined in matrimony with six different women. Of those six, Snøfrid is, as I see it, perhaps the most interesting, politically speaking. Snøfrid was the daughter of Svåse, whom sources describe as a Sámi king. As the Sámi do not hold to such traditions of leadership, it is unlikely that Svåse was a king in the true sense of the word.[17] Nonetheless, he was presumably a man of high social status (Hansen and Olsen 2004:66), perhaps even a leader in his *sijte*[18], or community.

As Storli, who is referenced above, has argued, intermarriage was quite common between trading relations at this time. As such, Snorre does not describe an unprecedented occurrence. What makes the marriage between Fairhair and Snøfrid important, however, is the context in which it happens. Not only is Fairhair considered to be the first Norwegian King, additionally his marriage to a Sámi woman is set in a period where efforts to unify a Norwegian Nation was well underway. It has been suggested that the story of Harald and Snøfrid is a Norwegian origin myth detailing, not only the royal lines divine right to rule Norway, but also the rightful annexing of the Sámi homelands

---

17 King was used in relation to Sámi people and persons on several occasions, and it is likely that it was a well-known concept during the Viking Age, and possibly used to put Sámi representatives on equal footing with Norse leaders and kings (Bratrein 2001:2)

18 This is the South Sámi spelling, which I use to reflect that Svåse and Snøfrid by all accounts were South Sámi. In North Sámi sijte is spelled siida.

into the new nation (Mundal 1997, e.g., Odner 1983:27-8). This is an especially important point, because it indicates that at the time of its writing, there was a common perception of there being a Sámi homeland, under Sámi "ruling".

Scholars are doubtful that there ever was a marriage between Fairhair and Snøfrid, but that does not really matter. What matters is the perception of such a narrative. When Heimskringla was written in the 13th century, it was done by request of the Norwegian King whose aim it was to create a divine origin myth establishing the right of rule granted to his lineage (Hedeager 1999:25), and also to establish a legitimate claim to Sámi homelands (Mundal 1996:111). The idea that a mortal man may establish his claim to land by matrimony is a concept that is well established with regards to Norwegian/Swedish and Sámi relations; materialized as *hieros gamos*, meaning a holy matrimony, which signify a union between a mortal king and a woman who personify the land he wishes to conquer (Steinsland 1989).[19] There is as such explicit political designs of a colonial nature on Sámi homelands from the 10th and 11th centuries.

FIGURE 2-3 IN 2018 THE POSTAL SERVICES OF NORWAY COMMISSIONED A SERIES OF STAMPS THAT TOOK THEIR INSPIRATION FROM NORSE MYTHOLOGY. THIS IMAGE DEPICTS THE MARRIAGE OF FAIRHAIR AND SNØFRID, WHICH INDICATE THE IMPORTANCE OF THE MYTH THAT TELLS OF THE PEACEFUL TRANSACTION WHERE THE NORWEGIAN KING THROUGH MARRIAGE PEACEFULLY ANNEX SÁPMI. ©POSTEN.NO

---

19 The two largest ruling lines of Scandinavia in the Viking Age, the Earls of Lade [Ladejarlene] and the Ynglings [ynglinge ætten], Fairhair being associated with the latter, are both associated with myths of hieros gamos where the Gods Odin and Frey respectively married Skade and Gerd. Both are Jötunn females who has been interpreted to represent the land and both have also been suggested to be representatives of the Sámi (Steinsland 1989).

In conclusion, I think it fair to say that a colonial expansion began in the 11th century at the latest and that it was initiated by Norwegian, or what would in time become Norwegian, interests. As time went by, the other three Nations whose borders today cross Sápmi, also sought their 'piece of the cake'. By the 13th century, settlers from all of the above had thus made great inroads into the Sámi homelands. Of course, the increasing number of settlers had several consequences, the heightened presence of both missionaries and church buildings being one, and the pressure on a Sámi way of life was another. I will discuss both, beginning with the former.

GOABDESÁJGGE - THE DRUMTIME

Scattered church buildings and missionaries had already appeared in Sápmi from the start of the colonial expansion in the 11th century. In the early years, the Church's focus lay primarily on the coastal areas and the missionaries as such contended themselves mainly with the Sámi that lived in close proximity to the newly established colonial settlements. There was a genuine interest in converting the Sámi from their blasphemous beliefs, but the political undercurrents aimed at the establishing of Nations was probably more of an ambition (Hansen and Olsen 2004:220). The Sámi homelands were considered strategic points, both financially, but also in regard to deciding on the placement of borders. That is to say, if the Church was able to count amongst their parishioners the Sámi people, then it would be far easier to count them amongst their Countrymen. The first missionaries, as such, "worked [...] to gain [...] political control over the Sámi" (Baer 1982:13).

Up until the reformation, which in the North happened in 1536/7, attempts to christen the Sámi was not uniform, nor was it equally distributed in all areas and communities. The result being that the Sámi religion continued to live beside Christianity for centuries (Mundal 2007, Hansen 2012). However, from the late 16th century, efforts to convert the Sámi intensified (Pedersen 2016:51), and this time the real drive was the negation of a religion believed to be a worship of the Devil and steeped in witchcraft (Pollan 2007). While true that the Church did not facilitate the practice of the Sámi religion beforehand, during the 17th century came a ban on the practice.

FIGURE 2-4 THIS GÅBDÁ, WHICH IS THE LULE-SÁMI SPELLING OF THE WORD, IS A DRUM FROM THE UME SÁMI AREA. IT WAS MADE BY DUOJÁR FREDRIK PROST FROM VIIKUSJÄRVI, A SMALL COMMUNITY IN THE NORTH OF WHAT IS TODAY SWEDEN. FREDRIK IS ONE OF FEW DUOJÁRS THAT CONTINUES THE PRACTICE OF DRUM MAKING, AND THE DRUMS HE HAVE MADE HAS BEEN BOTH EXHIBITED AND SOLD. DO TAKE NOTE HOWEVER, THAT HE ONLY SELL HIS DRUMS TO OTHER SÁMI. © DAVID NUTTI

If found to be in breach, punishment included fines, flogging, imprisonment or at worst, death (e.g., Rydving 1991:32). At this time, the Church authorities initiated a massive effort to collect the *goavddis*[20], the ritual drum that was used by the *noaidi*[21], the men and women that served as the spiritual mediators, guides and leaders of the Sámi people (Porsanger 2012:42).

According to the sources, it is clear that the Church authorities considered the drums to be "*the explicit nucleus of the elusive Saami 'paganism'—i.e., 'the evil' that had to be annihilated*".[22] As turning points go, the 17th century was an especially brutal one. The impact of it is such that within Sámi language it is expressed as a time before, the

---

20 There are different names and types of drums. I use the North Sámi designation, but I have looked at sources detailing all the types and from all areas.

21 Many have translated noaidi with shaman. A shaman, or šamán, is a word originating from the Tungusic Peoples' that are Native to Siberia and Northeast Asia. Its use is related to a spiritual practice and its spiritual leaders. It is not however, a Sámi word. To use shaman is, I believe, a cultural appropriation and should be avoided.

22 The drums taken during this process is today spread throughout Europe as they after confiscation were aquisitioned to private collections and museums.

goabdesájgge meaning the drum time, and an after, referred to as *"the time when one had to hide the drums"* (Rydving 1991:29, 28). In my opinion, this reveals, firstly the immense value of the goavddis, but also the deep impact of this process.

THE FIRST EPISTEMICIDE

As might be expected, the goavddis was used as a means to come into contact with the spirit world, its inscription a mapping, *"not only of the spirit world… it maps the land as well"* (Sáje 23.11.2019), including the multiple realities of the Sámi world, both the physical reality of human presence but also a spiritual dimension (Gothóni and Pentikäinen 1987). It would not be wrong then, to consider the goavddis as a collection of scripture in a society where written sources were not commonplace (e.g., Storm 2017:69). In this capacity, the goavddis was part of Sámi ritual life and a vital part of the noaidi's toolkit. Aside from its use by the noaidi, the goavddis was relevant in everyday life, used more commonly to divine portents, foresee possible dooms or anticipate good fortune. It was, in this sense, also a communication device used to seek advice with regards to most aspects of life (Jernsletten 2009:47, 49). If, for instance, someone was accused of abusing the trust of others, the truth of it could be sought out by using the drum (Kappfjell 1998:46). The goavddis, in other words, was a key element, not only in Sámi religious life, but also of the Sámi way of life.

In Sámi cosmology, *vuoiŋŋalašvuohta* [spirituality] the spirits, other beings, and ancestors is a natural part of life, present in everything surrounding a person. The goavddis was the bridge connecting all of these elements. To prohibit its use was as such, not only an attack on the *noaiddesvuohta* [religious Sámi knowledge] related to the practices of the noaidi, but also on Sámi spirituality on a more general level (Kaikkonen 2019). As I see it then, the banning of the goavddis and the consequent 'time when one had to hide the drums', loudly announce a colonial act of killing knowledge.

TJAALEHTJIMMIE—THE LANGUAGE OF OLD.

The destruction and banning of the goavddis is, in my opinion, the most visible example of epistemicide to occur in Sápmi; in fact, I would claim as examples go, this is textbook. By removing the tools and scripture as it were, of the knowledge keepers and forcing them to go into hiding, much of the knowledge of spiritual matters were lost, sometimes never to be regained in full. Yet, the role of the noaidi persisted, and so too did the drum. [23] Sources from the latter half of the 19th century, for instance, discuss contemporary noaidis' by name (Jacobsen 1987, Hætta, Bergsland, and Bær [1869]1958), whereas others actually caution that knowledge of the noaidi must not be said aloud to outsiders lest they immediately *"reported to those that are not themselves Sámi"* (Pettersson, Bäckman, and Kjellström 1979:95, my own translation). What this proves is that the noaidi, and the knowledge of the drum was kept alive, if secret, up until the 19th century (Kalstad 1997). Duodji has likely played a pivotal role in keeping this knowledge alive.

This I extrapolate from, among other, a recent study on the Sámi ládjogáhpir, or hornhat, that Finnish archaeologist Eeva-Kristiina Harlin and Sámi dáiddar [artist] Outi Pieski has collaborated on. In it, the two assert the likelihood of religious practices and knowledge[s] having survived for far longer amongst women, and from this they convincingly argue the important ritual role of the ládjogáhpir in society related to a female sphere of cosmology (2020:79). We know from other sources that contact between Sámi women and colonial officials was limited, not as a result of Sámi preferences but more to do with the latter's view on women as not suited for public life or important roles (e.g., Storm 2015:216-7). By extension, women were not viewed to figure in the religious life of the Sámi, and so they were not initially targeted to the same degree or as early as their male counterparts. Meaning that the practices and beliefs associated with Sámi women may have survived longer (Price 2002:257)

An interesting commentary on the goavddis in relation to gender is found if we look to one of the noaidi that has been named in historical sources. In the 1830s, a male noaidi, Njaarke-Næjla, used his gievrie, which is the South Sámi spelling of the goavddis, to ask advice on which route his herd was best served taking in the Winter. Having received the advice, he decided to move his herd over the mountains and towards the coast. This proved to be a bad decision as Njaarke-Næjla

---

23 The noaidi either 'inherited' their role from elder relatives, or they were called to the practice by personal experiences with the spirits (Bäckman and Hultkrantz 1978). In my own family on the paternal side, the role as noaidi was passed down the generations. In fact, the last noaidi to be called was my fathers' younger sister, but she did not feel that such a role suited her, and so the knowledge of the noaidi largely disappeared.

lost a significant number of his herd. After, he explained the bad advice with the possibility of his drum having been made unclean by the touch of a woman's hand, and thus unreliable (Olsen 1997). There are a number of sources that cite restrictions on Sámi women's access to religious tools such as the drum (Leem [1767]1975:444). On the other hand, there are equally a number of sources that cite Sámi womens' use of the drum (Hallström 1911:37). Looking to archaeological sources as well as language-based concepts and terms, there is ample evidence that women performed a wide range of functions within a spiritual sphere (Price 2002:260-4). Thus, the contradictory sources may be an indication of the heteropatriarchy enforced upon Sámi society following colonisation. Another suggestion is related to the practice of duodji.

Harlin and Pieski's suggestion on the ritual function of the ládjogáhpir is one example of such. Another example would be the Sámi practice of knitting protection into garments (Falck 2018:82), for instance, with the use of one's hair as I was taught to do by my *aahka* [grandmother, South Sámi spelling]. Another example, which I discuss in more detail in riessat, is the gapta, or gákti.

As previously stated, the gákti is a piece of clothing that embeds important Sámi values, meanings, and concepts. Together with its various accessories, it consists of a silent, yet very visual language expressed for instance, on the South Sámi *boengeskuvmie*, a breast cloth decorated with pewter, beads, or yarn. This language, says the Sámi duojár and scholar Maja Dunfjeld, include in its expression the *tjaalehtjimmie* [ornaments, decoration] of Sámi religious beliefs (Dunfjeld Aagård 1989:153), which probably accounts for the very strict regulations set by elders on who is allowed to learn this practice and its language (Jernsletten 2009:124).

The Sámi scholar Jorunn Jernsletten has noted that the knowledge found in and on the *gievrie* seems to demonstrate "*a continuity between the symbols on the drums and the symbols used with regards to the gapta, taking into account both the shape and decoration*" (Jernsletten 2009:33, my own translation). This likely accounts for how the knowledge of the gievrie could survive for so long after the initial banning.

FIGURE 2-5 THE SYMBOLS AND ICONOGRAPHY OF SÁMI DUODJI PRESENTS A WAY OF LIFE, IDEOLOGY AND COSMOLOGY. IN THE EMBROIDERY OF PEWTER FOR INSTANCE, THERE IS A 'SECRET' LANGUAGE, OR THE TJAALEHTJIMMIE. AFTER THE GIEVRIE – THE HOLY DRUM – WAS BANNED AND CONFISCATED, OFTEN QUITE VICIOUSLY, THE ICONOGRAPHY ASSOCIATED WITH ITS USE WAS PRESERVED IN THIS LANGUAGE. ON THE GIEVRIE, THE DAUGHTERS OF MADTERAAHKA, THE MOTHER GODDESS, APPEARED IN GROUPS OF THREE, OFTEN AS SIMPLIFIED CROSSES. SIMILARLY, IN THE TJAALEHTJIMMIE, JOEKSAAHKA, SAARAAHKA, AND OKSAAHKA ARE PRESENT IN PATTERNS OF THREE CROSSES. THESE GODDESSES WERE, AND STILL ARE, SIGNIFICANT AS THEY, AMONG OTHER TASKS, PROTECT HUMANS IN ALL STAGES OF LIFE. WHAT I HAVE EMBROIDERED IN THIS PICTURE, THUS CARRIES THE RELIGIOUS SIGNIFICANCE OF CALLING UPON THEIR PROTECTION FOR THE CARRIER.

More to the point, female duojárs, by adapting the language of the gievrie to their tjaalehtjimmie was able to ensure that vital knowledge of Sámi cosmology survived in the practices of duodji up until present day. But even the knowledge in duodji was eventually targeted. In large this may correlate to the missionary work to convert the Sámi.

Much has been written about the coming of Lars Levi Læstadius and the extremely pietistic Lutheran movement named for him that began in the mid-19th century (Thulin 1949, Elgvin 2010). Læstadius, who was himself of South Sámi descent owes much of his success to the syncretism of his preaching; not immediately banning the Sámi deities, he instead adapted them to a Christian context. To be fair, in Læstadius' time the movement could be considered emancipatory for women (Nilsson 1988). This I think, significantly contributed to the success of the movement because the heteropatriarchy enforced by colonialism would at this time have been deeply rooted in society, slowly eroding the position and status of women.

Not only did Læstadius regard women as special mediums of grace, he also supported their active presence within the Church (Valkonen and Wallenius-Korkalo 2015:4). It is possible that this attitude reflects his Sámi origin and consequent knowledge of female relevance in a Sámi ritual sphere. Additionally, his knowledge of duodji as a practice that incorporated spirituality might explain his strongly worded opposition to women's *"excessive embellishments"*. This greatly influenced and changed the way woman dressed; silver belts were burned, silk items disappeared from female apparel, and most adornments of the gákti was removed (Harlin and Pieski 2020:89), until all that was left was a *"black dress, which was called 'Dorres reformkjole"* (Gunn 15.05.2020). The ládjogáhpir, too, was a victim of the Laestadian movement, and disappeared during the last part of the 19th century, and *"thus knowledge regarding the hat did not transfer to new generations"* (Harlin and Pieski 2020:79).

Here then, is another example of epistemicide. Only, as opposed to the confiscation of the Sámi drums, this is an epistemicide that is silent, and as such, it is more efficient. Where the targeting of the goavddis made the drums into symbols of resistance (Rydving 1991:29), the Laestadian movement greatly benefited from the already established foundation of a 'colonial wall'. Calling on women to meet the Laestadian concepts of female piety and humility for instance had a great impact on the practice of duodji as an Indigenous knowledge (Kuokkanen 2007a:76). It is this form of epistemicide I will discuss next, when I look at the increased wave of settlers that by the 13th century appeared in Sápmi.

BIRGEJUPMI—THE 'MAINTENANCE OF LIFE'

Just as the Norse lords of the Viking Age had feared, the increased influx of settlers during the 13th century put an increased pressure on the resources, and by extension the Sámi way of life. Prior to the colonisation of Sápmi, the social structure of Sámi society was organized within the system of the sijte or *siida*. Today, siida simply means community or home[24], albeit many would consider its use slightly old-fashioned, especially in communities where Sámi is the primary language (Sara 2015:13). Though no decisive

---

24 Though the siida as a concept is well known, it is siidas with reindeerherding as their unifying elelment that today represent the practice as was (Sara 2015).

definition should be made and regional varieties should be assumed (Solem 1933:94) the siida of old referred to a specific area reserved for the use of one group made up of several families related by kinship or intermarriage (Rydving 2003). The right of fishing, hunting, gathering and making a livelihood within the siida was ensured by rights of inheritance from preceding generations or adoption (Ween 2005:19). Within the siida, there would have been a migratory movement between as many as five locations depending on the season and resources (Sara 2015).[25] By living in and off the area in the siida, people gradually learned to manage said area without exhausting the natural resources (Guttorm 2011:60). In Sámi, this state of being is called *birgejupmi*, which is a concept born from understanding the relationship with one's surroundings holistically. In essence then, the success of the siida depended on birgejupmi as the ´maintenance of life`, meaning to manage and have a good life, socially, economically, spiritually and with respect to health (Porsanger 2012:39).

The incoming settlers had little to no knowledge of the structure of the siida, and even less awareness of the geographical locations of each. Nor did they hold with the concept of birgejupmi. As a consequence, the new settlers greatly disturbed the carefully maintained balance within the siidas, making it difficult to continue this way of life in a sustainable manner (Pedersen 2016:51), and *"[w]ith the appearance of the colonizers the siida system was destroyed"* (Somby 1991:2). While the quote above is drastic, it is also true. Albeit the dismantling of the siidas took time, eventually the colonisation into Sápmi forced a great change. Presumably, the very structure of the siida actually worked against the Sámi. In the face of new settlers, rather than fight over land, it is likely that the Sámi chose to withdraw themselves from potential conflict by simply moving on to another seasonal settlement. While this would indeed keep conflict at a minimum, it also reduced the access to natural resources, which over time forced a structural change in Sámi society.

The authority on the subject, Sámi professor Israel Ruong, was of the opinion that the old siida-system began to erode sometime during the 17th century (Ruong 1937:17-21). There is much to suggest that he is correct. The previous century, that is the 1500s, was one marked by the Nation States increased management to benefit from Sámi trade, and while there were different considerations at play

---

25 A more precise outline of the siida-structure is found in "Lappiske rettsstudier" by Erik Solem (1933)

the end result was the same, leading to a heightened use of natural resources (Hansen and Olsen 2004:248). The resources took another hit when silver was found at Nasafjäll, on what is now the Swedish side of the border, in the first half of the 17th century (Somby 1991:2). With the discovery of such valuable minerals, Swedish authority saw it necessary to increase their presence in these areas. The solution was the Lappmark Proclamation of 1673 that stipulated that any Swede who settled in Sámi areas were to be exempted from paying taxes for 15 years and excused the duty of serving as a soldier in case of war. While it is true that the proclamation stipulated settlers to live by farming alone, leaving the hunting, fishing, and herding to the Sámi,[26] the reality was quite different. The climate was not suitable to farming and so the settlers slowly encroached on the livelihood reserved for the Sámi. Despite the latter's complaints to Swedish authorities, the Sámi were slowly driven further North and away from their homelands (Kuoljok and Utsi 1993:30).

Still, archaeological evidence suggests that the switch from the old siida structure to one which was characterized by herding reindeer as we today know it happened even earlier. In the coastal areas of what is today Norway, and in the South Sámi areas further South, where non-Sámi settlements were at their most plentiful, the Sámi livelihoods of hunting and gathering had during the 16th century been forced to give way to agriculture and hunting of wild animals was adapted into nomadic reindeer herding (Andersen 2002:64, Sommerseth 2009:279, Fjellheim 2012). To be clear, Sámi agriculture existed prior to such adaption. Archaeological evidence suggest the existence of Sámi homesteads as far back as the 5th century (Hansen and Olsen 2004:176). In the Torne Sámi area[27], evidence of Sámi agriculture dates even earlier, placing it to the 2nd century (Andersen 2002:5, 172-82, 422-4).

Agriculture, in other words, was a Sámi livelihood before the colonial expansion. Nevertheless, after the increased pressure caused by settlers during the 16th century, Sámi homesteads increased in numbers. Interestingly, at this time there is also a wave of previously Sámi residencies being entered into the list of non-Sámi farms. This wave

---

26 This was most likely because the high taxes the Sámi paid depended on them keeping up their supply of game and fur.

27 Troms and Nordland on the Norwegian side and the farmost North on the Swedish side. It also includes some areas on the Finnish side.

coincides with new Sámi homesteads being registered further inland in the hills and mountainous areas that had previously not been permanently settled. Some scholars interpret this chain of events to mean that the Sámi of the old homesteads, due to increased wave of settlers, were forced into higher ground (e.g., Hansen 1986:117-8, Storm 1990:163-9). The Sámi archaeologist Oddmund Andersen (2002:168, 462-3) has a different take on it, believing that the transition is due to a shift in ethnicity from Sámi to Norwegian, indicating that what we are seeing is really the first documented cases of assimilation. Which brings me to the next significant manifestation of epistemicide.

THE SECOND EPISTEMICIDE

In the early hours of January 21st in 1821, readers of the British "Times" were informed that one Karen Christiansdatter, despite her *"Lappish origin"* appeared almost *"gracious"* before the audience at London Museum of Natural History and Pantherion, where Karen, alongside her husband and child, was displayed in a living exhibition (Times, London 21. January 1822, quoted in Altick 1978:27). As mentions go, this one seems pretty mild as there should be little to criticize about appearing to be gracious. Nonetheless, this review of a living exhibition reveals, I think, that being a "Lapp" and being gracious at that time was considered contradictory, and herein lies the root of the problem.

If we take a deeper dive into other characteristics of Sámi people from the same century, we find some more explicit descriptions. Including 'degenerate', 'primitive', 'filthy', 'ugly', not to mention the added comparisons to animals, devils, and beasts (Gjessing 1973:78, Eriksen and Niemi 1981:258, Gjestrum 1995:103). In other words, far from being gracious, most contemporaries perceived the Sámi people to be far inferior to the civilized Westerners, and in fact more likely to be related to animals, or at best a race of beings that had once—in the Stone Age—populated the entirety of Europe. As the far more advanced *Homo sapiens* appeared, however, what was left of this ancient human race had been driven further and further North, into the Arctic (e.g., Rygh 1867:100). But to understand the relevance of these characteristics and narratives, we need to return to the process of colonisation.

During the colonial expansion of the West, not only did the colonizing forces create narratives to justify the annexing of lands and incapacitation of people (Henare 2005:60-70). Racial categories were also created to ensure that the White Europeans appeared superior in all areas, and colonial standards were invented and imposed unto all (Painter 2011). There are many ways in which this was achieved. As I have already mentioned, colonisation is a process that typically comes with a set of tools—or strategies if you will—to help ease the transition between colonial force to nation-state (Short 2003, Minde 2005, Zeldenryk and Yalmambirra 2006). Focused on the simple absorbing of one culture into another, the process of assimilation is one. Though it appears harmless, as the story of a grandmother living her life mired in self-hatred shows, assimilation is anything but. If I return briefly to my initial definition of epistemicide, in extension of such, assimilation should be understood as nothing less than the *"deliberate destruction"* of cultures, which in turn makes the act of assimilation, *"an act of genocide"* (Schimmel 2005:50). I will be the first to admit that such wording is dramatic, but it is true, nonetheless. The intent behind assimilation, whichever way one looks at it, is nothing less than the total conversion of languages, worldviews, knowledges, and ways of being. It is in essence, the complete erasure of people and of their civilization.

The longevity of assimilation in a Sámi context, is fairly unique (Minde 2005:5). From the first documented cases and up until the official repeal of a Norwegian policy of assimilation in the mid-20th century, close to 500 years would pass. We can add some decades to that timeline considering the fact that assimilating practices continued well into the 1980s (Minde 2005:11), and, some would claim, even further (Josefsen 2006). Throughout this timeline, the logistics of assimilation differed greatly, and so too did the motivation. Even so, there has been a tendency amongst researchers to associate assimilation with the Norwegianization policy that was put into effect in 1851 (Minde 2005:6-7). In turn, assimilation is more often than not, explained with an increased nationalism during a period of Norwegian nation-building (e.g., Hesjedal 2000). By no means is this assumption wrong, but it is at the same time overly simplistic as both politics and religious, as well as civilizing, motivations applied. [28]

---

28 The first doumented cases in the 16th century, for instance, reveals how assimilation may be caused by political currencies. The political conditions of a colonized Sápmi during the 16th, 17th, - and 18th century was, as I briefly explain above, incredibly tense. The various Nation states were concerned with the financial profits from both Sámi trade as well as the income from taxes levied against the Sámi. In addition, several sites that appeared suitable for the extraction of natural minerals and valuables caused an increase in national governance of areas that were part of the Sámi homeland (Hansen and Olsen 2004:247). Often, the recurring

In her analysis of the policy of Norwegianization for instance, the Sámi scholar Bente Persen (2008) demonstrates how assimilation had a religious element. In relation to the strong missionary period, which was initiated with the banning of the drums in the 17th century, the Church and the Sámi mission viewed the Sámi as, on the one hand, savage devil worshipers, that needed the help of the faith to become good citizens of the states (Pollan 2007, e.g., Kaikkonen 2019:545). At the same time, it was also thought that the Sámi was a childlike people, in need of proper guidance so as to not stray from the right path (e.g., Fur 2006:499). This belief would become so entrenched in the colonial gaze upon the Sámi that years later it was a founding argument in justifying the launch of an official policy of assimilation (Persen 2008:38, 57-8).

Elsewhere, the Sámi historian Henry Minde (2005) has likewise argued how a similar view on the Sámi influenced the early stages of the Norwegianization policy to such a degree that it was primarily focused on civilizing the Sámi; the *"Lappish people"* were *"a childlike people, [...] naive and undeveloped"*, and as such, they were in need of assimilation to reach the *"maturity of Man"* (Gjølme 1886, quoted in Eriksen and Niemi 1981:57). This correlation is made quite explicit, if we look to some of the common perceptions reinforced during the Age of Enlightenment about the perceived "primitive" peoples of the world, amongst which the Sámi was counted.

FROM NOBLE SAVAGE TO INVADER FROM THE FAR EAST.

Late in the 18th century, the intellectual and philosophical movement known as the Enlightenment made a powerful impact on all of Europe. Though some national varieties did exist, the marked preference for empiricism and rational thought was held in common. Conse-

---

disputes over land claims that resulted, used the presence of the Sámi as justification—i.e., citing the Sámi living or moving within the areas in question to be subjects of either state. In an ironic twist, when the disputes had been settled, the prior claim to Sámi as subjects of state was often waived. Instead, the Sámi began to be viewed with suspicion being as they could very well be, at least this was the view of the states at that time, possible agents of a foreign Nation. It is very likely that the suspicion and attached negative view on the Sámi, was eventually adapted by the local authorities and non-Sámi population. In time, this encouraged a massive shift of ethnicity for the Sámi living in more permanent dwellings on the coastlines (Andersen 2002:168, 462-3). The significance of these first cases is simply that assimilation, whilst not executed with intent, did effectively take place befor any official policy to such end.

quently, knowledge was believed to come from a sensory experience, which meant that objects and living things, rather than written text, where the primary sources of knowledge (Livingstone and Withers 1999, Bennett 2004). Within the movement it was thought that religious doctrine with its preoccupation of faith had corrupted the Western civilization. Many of the more prominent philosophers of Enlightenment, among them Jean-Jaques Rosseau, James Dugbar and John Gregory, as such, felt that there was a need to look to more 'primitive' societies that were, to their thinking at least, unspoiled and pure (Henare 2005:70). The naive and childlike quality of the people living within these societies, conceptualized as "Bons Savages" or "noble savage", equally represented the unspoiled quality said thinkers so admired.

The missionaries' imagery of the Sámi as childlike and naive was in many ways continued in the Enlightenment thinker's characterization of "primitive" people (e.g., Mathisen 2020:12). Without further ado, the Sámi people were consequently shifted into the categorization of noble savages, and their origin consequently explained with them being the last remains of the first people to inhabit Scandinavia after the ice retracted. This image was also reinforced in museological displays of that time (see Gjestrum 1995:96), as well as in the 'living exhibitions' mentioned above (Baglo 2011:53). [29] As the far more developed people of Western civilization advanced, however, the "primitive" Sámi had sadly failed to keep up and so they had slowly been forced to retreat to the 'North' (Baglo 2001:33, Hesjedal 2000:22, e.g., Falsen 1821:95, Nilsson 1988:10-2).[30] In the beginning, "primitive" simply held the meaning of first, or original. Even so, the characteristics of "primitive" still implied undeveloped or backward (Mathisen 2004:9). From here, it is a relatively short way to recontextualize the noble savage as someone in need of education and civilizing influences. And who better at providing these things than the very people that initially judged the noble savage in need of such?

In the mid-19th century then, a growing number of people called for the "primitives" of the world to be educated and enlightened as to help bring them into civilized society (Zeldenryk and Yalmambirra

---

29 The Egyptologist Saphinaz-Amal Naguib (2007:9) defines this as "didactic descriptive museology".
30 Quick comment on the use of the word 'North'; principally I don't like to use North in connection with the Sámi as I believe it produces a binary opposition between the two, which eventually results in a delimitation of Sámi presence in the historical Fenno-Scandinavia as seen, for instance, in Figure 2-2.

2006). For the Sámi, this naturally meant that it was necessary to learn either Norwegian, Swedish, Finnish, or Russian and to adapt to the societies of these nation-states. At this time it was believed that "primitive" people were able to evolve past their present 'stage'; if someone classified as "primitive" learned to speak a European language, began to dress in European clothes and converted to Christianity, they would, in essence, become European (Qureshi 2011:189). Assimilation, in accordance with this perspective, was a kindness and an act of social responsibility.

Similar to the initial colonial expansion centuries earlier, it was once more, at least on the Norwegian side, the coastal districts that were primarily targeted. On the Swedish side, while not directed towards any specific areas, assimilation rather depended on whether or not you were affiliated with the nomadic herding of reindeers (Minde 2005:8, also see Lundmark 2008). But that is arguably the case on the Norwegian side as well as the Sámi coastal communities primarily consisted of permanent settlements. It is likely that the difference in which of the Sámi people were targeted was due to the contemporary perception of reindeer herders as the authentic Sámi.

Already in the border treaty of 1752, between Denmark-Norway and Sweden-Finland, a Lapp codicil was added to the agreement in which the right of Sámi reindeer herders to cross borders alongside their herds where formalized, on account of it being "*quite necessary*" to ensure the "*Lappish Nations survival*"(Hielmstierne & Stame [1750]1806, quoted in Hansen and Olsen 2004:278, Ravna 2010). Whereas all others of "*Lappish origin*" had degenerated and now found themselves on the brink of extinction, the authentic Lapp, which still persisted as an expression of the noble savage, was the reindeer herder (Baglo 2001:115). This perspective, famously articulated as "*Lapp will be Lapp*", meant that reindeer herders were to be segregated rather than assimilated (Lundmark 2008:155, my own translation). Of course, the ardour for disseminating reindeer herding as the original livelihood of the Sámi was very much shaped by political machinations. In the words of the well-known Norwegian historian, P. A. Munch, no matter if the "Lapps" were the original population of the Sámi homelands, it was "*only settled with the coming of our Ancestors. And it is the first settlement, with which the history of a Country truly begins*" (Munch 1852:4, my own translation).[31]

In his articulation, I am slightly reminded of the justifications worded by the British to legitimize their colonialization of Australia (Short 2003:491-2, Henare 2005:68-70). As Australia was home to "nomadic"[32] groups of people, it had never been properly settled, making the entirety of the land *terra nullius*, which basically means 'nobody's land'. The application of the terra nullius doctrine is such that any uninhabited land is eligible for the pursuit of territorial ownership by those that first discover it. In the event of lands already being inhabited by nomadic "primitives", as was the case with both Australia and Sápmi, the Lockean ownership principles where thought to apply. That is to say, following the argument of John Locke, who was a noted Enlightenment thinker, "primitive" communities, if they are nomadic, do not have property rights to the areas they use (Ravna 2002:76). This removed the moral obstacle to the annexing of populated lands and thus allowed colonial advancement to begin.

In his wording then, Munch is basically offering a justification for the continued colonisation of the Sámi homelands (Gjestrum 1995:102). Sámi livelihoods, such as agriculture, were in this regard highly problematic. Agriculture was associated with permanent settlements, and if the Sámi were permanently settled, then they would have property rights. The solution was to create an image of the authentic "Lapp" as being a reindeer herder and force assimilation onto all other Sámi (Lundmark 2008). In the ethnographical museums of that time, this eventually became a common trope in the representations of the Sámi (Mathisen 2012:61).

In the latter half of the century, a new narrative on the origin of the Sámi emerged, which continued the process of limiting Sámi presence in Sámi homelands, and which would have far-reaching consequences for the Sámi on all sides of the borders.[33] This new narrative

31 Variations of said argument are still being used presently in order to discredit the Sámi as an Indigenous Nation, which only goes to show the power of academia to write history, and creating narratives (e.g., Eira 2013:340, Nordmark 2014)

32 Though it is taught as a fact, the Indigenous peoples of Australia were in fact, not all nomadic. The majority of them were actually not.

33 Between these two narratives there was a third, wherein the Sámi came to be known as a Stone-Age people that had lived within the arctic (e.g., Rygh 1867:100). This particular turn of events owes much to nationalistic agendas, the purpose of which was to create a common and unifying national identity within the various Scandinavian states (Hesjedal 2000). The Sámi cultures, so profoundly different, was too disruptive for such an enterprise to be successful and the solution was to marginalize the Sámi people, so that their presence in Scandinavian history was lessened allowing them to be distanced from the equation (Minde 2005:5). Soon after, total removal would follow.

owes much to the advance in theories on biology and evolution during the latter half of the 19th century. Most ground-breaking of these was the 1859 publication, *On the Origin of the Species*, in which Charles Darwin presented human evolution as a branching of multiple species from one common starting point (e.g., Darwin [1859]1909). Even if Darwin's theory did not encourage a structuring system of hierarchy for the development of humanity, several chose to regard the 'survival of the species' as a selective process where some races of humanity were biologically lesser while others were more advanced. Not surprisingly, "primitive" people were examples of the former and White Europe served as representatives of the latter (Jølle 2000:33). With this, primitive became synonymous with being in "*an arrested stage of development*" (Bennett 2004:59), which in turn created a scientific basis for the viewing of "primitive" people, including the Sámi, as lesser, and incapable of developing past their present state, far less being able to govern themselves. (Gjessing 1973:102, Gjestrum 1995:103).

As a result of the changing meaning of primitive, contemporary academics soon called for a complete rewrite of Scandinavian history (Rygh 1867:100). The Sámi, unrefined and "primitive" as they were thought to be, could hardly be credited with any of the prehistoric remains that had previously been ascribed to them (Brøgger 1909:165). After all, "*when ever did the Lapps become master builders?*" (von Düben [1873]1977:369, my own translation), as was commented by one Swedish archaeologist. Thus, it seemed for many self-evident that the Sámi culture, far from being Nordic, had to have come from somewhere else. Consequently, Sámi presence was explained as the result of a late migration in the Roman Age from somewhere in Eastern Russia, Eastern Asia, or Southeastern Asia. Within the span of 50 years then, the Sámi went from Europe's Indigenous noble savage to "primitive" invader from the far East (Hallström 1929:56).

RACIAL BIOLOGY AND RESIDENTIAL SCHOOLS

The new narrative found its reasoning, partly in a biological racism. Brought on by the exceedingly increasing contact with different cultures and peoples, as well as the newly developed theories of human origins during the latter half of the 19th century, an unprecedented interest in 'race' manifested itself in a large international movement focused on eugenics. Within the early decades of the 20th century, this interest had resulted in a number of research institutions being established. One of these was the Swedish State Institute for Race Biology (hence SIRB).

Founded in 1922, SIRB was especially focused on mapping the Nordic races, amongst them the biological inferior "Lapps" (Broberg 1995, Kjellman 2013, 2014). By enforcing measurements of skulls and bones, taking unsolicited pictures of men, women and children that had been forced to undress, and mapping dentistry, the SIBR eventually produced a published description of racial characteristics. These studies were aimed at making racialized and biological categorizations of, among others, the Sámi. The Sámi, or as they were called by the institute, the "Lapps" had some very distinguished and racial features. Among others they had,

> [s]hort broad skull; brownish skin; straight, coarse, black hair; brown, narrow eyes, [34]; feeble, straggling beard growth; broad forehead; broad jaw-bones and projecting cheek-bones; small pug-nose, quite narrow and very feebly developed; narrow lower jaw with a pointed chin. Viewed from the front the head is egg-shaped with the small end down—in some cases nearly pear-shaped. The frame is slender and the stature very low: seldom over 160 cm (Linders and Lundborg 1926:40).

Their dark complexion, for instance, was indicative that they belonged in the *"inferiority of darker races"* (Kjellman 2013:190). Here then, SIRB and their racial biology were a great help in justifying the increasingly brutal practices of assimilation. Although the SIRB, in its later years during the 1950s and 1960s, argued against racial discrimination (Ericsson 2020:16), there is no escaping the fact that the institute in its earliest years worked to prove that as:

> "some skin colours, skull shapes, or face features were signs of limited mental and cognitive capacities, it seemed rational to argue that races showing those features could not be entitled to the same rights and responsibilities in society as 'superior races' enjoy. And, most importantly, those inferior races—showing these features—were not to reproduce if the Swedish stock was to be improved" (Kjellman 2013:190)

Starting in the late 19th century then, and until the official repeal, assimilation policies partly found its justification in a biological racism

---

34 I was once asked if I was really Sámi as I had such large eyes, and everyone, "after all, knows that Lapps have squinty eyes".

founded on the "scientific truth" that the Sámi were biologically infe-rior and closer kin to animals than White Europeans. With the new narrative, and the changed meaning of primitive, to civilize all Sámi was still a matter of some concern, but it was now considered almost impossible to save the "*Lappish race*" as they had become so,

> [...] degenerate as to have little hope of any change for the better. They are hopeless, and are the most retarded and lowest of people, and from them, we see the majority of inmates to our asylums and schools for mentally retarded (Brygfjeld 1933, quoted in Eriksen and Niemi 1981:258, my own translation).

This quote is from a letter that was written in 1933, and its intend-ed recipient was the Norwegian Ministry of Church and Education. The author, Christian Andreas Brygfjeld, was at this time the school director in charge of the system of residential schools established in the early 20th century to educate Sámi children. The intent of these schools, and I use the term lightly, was to isolate Sámi children from their original environment, which often involved a forceful removal from their homes and families (Minde 2005:11-2). This, of course, had the intended effect of depriving the children from their language and disrupting the transfer of Sámi knowledge[s], such as duodji, and ways of being from their parents and other elders of their communi-ties.

Brygfjeld's point-of-view was challenged by some (Aarseth 2006:166), but it is nonetheless a fairly good indicator of how the Sámi were viewed in the first half of the 20th century. Another in-dication is found in the children's testimony, which states that their everyday school life consisted of being "*told how little value their lan-guage and culture had*" (Jensen 2007:141) and that they were "*simple*", not to mention how they were "*bullied*" and "*mocked*" by their teachers on account of their ethnicity (Minde 2005:15). The Sámi teacher Per Fokstad, who was himself taken away from his home to a residential school, described his experience as:

> [...] [s]omething inside me is screaming; don't strangle me. Something inside me needs air, wants out, wants to live. But we were branded. We were stepped on and I can never forget it. Never forget how it was. Everything was taken from us. Our mother tongue was banned. No one would listen (quoted in Dahl 1970:10, my own translation).

Other Sámi would describe the loss of language and knowledges differently as there was a question of its value. An one expressed it, *"[w]hat is there to preserve? Only the old farts that can't even walk still speak Sámi. [...] working to revitalize Sámi, that's nonsense"* (quoted in Minde 2005:17).

A SHIFT IN ETHNICITY

The devaluation of Sámi languages and knowledge[s] that in due time seem to have occurred is perhaps, from contemporary perspectives difficult to grasp. But as one friend shared with me when we discussed her father's decision to not speak Sámi to her and her siblings,

> It wasn't evil or bad will that made him decide not to give us the language or the knowledge of the culture. It was, on the contrary, love. He wanted us to succeed in the modern world, and how could we do that if we had Sámi as our first language and acted as Sámi? (Mia 08.11.2017)

To understand the motivation of her father, I have found a quote from the Nigerian novelist Chimamanda Ngozi Adichie (2009) to be an eloquent explanation. When you *"show a people as one thing, as only one thing, over and over again, [...] that is what they become"*. Representation of Peoples' and their cultures, which is what Adichie is here referring to, are almost always embedded in structures of power, and they all too often rest on the authority of *"the mainstream critical centre to the marginalised native[s]"* (Blaeser 1993:56). The classification of the Sámi has historically been about essentializing; creating stereotypes or myths about who they are (Baglo 2001:115), which has worked to homogenize them, reducing them to only one thing (e.g., Comaroff and Comaroff 1992:53, Mennel 1994:182).

In a study from a Sea Sámi community in Western Finnmark on the Norwegian side of the border, the Norwegian anthropologist Harald Eidheim (1971) demonstrated precisely how the essentialization of the Sámi had impacted the Sámi themselves. Due to the assemblage of negative attributes associated with a Sámi ethnicity, a social stigma developed over time, in which being Sámi was analogous with being degenerate, stupid, inferior, and frozen in time. Said characteristics, ensured that being Sámi was a social obstacle, a mark of shame and a category of ill repute. At best, anything that pointed to a Sámi association was thus banished to the private sphere (Hansen 2015:83). It was often completely erased (e.g., Eidheim 1961:38, Minde 2005:9,

Eyþórsson 2008:11-20). The success of said stigma in erasing a Sámi ethnicity is perhaps best illustrated by School director Brygfjeld. In an ironic twist of fate, Brygfjeld was himself of Sámi descent, hailing from the South Sámi communities of Vaapste, or Vefsn in Nordland on the Norwegian side of the border. Nonetheless, as indicated by his less than generous descriptions of the Sámi in his communication with the authorities, he become one of the most ardent advocates of assimilation. Demonstrating the immense success of assimilation as an epistemicide as it encouraged the Sámi themselves to destroy what made them Sámi.

In time, the social stigma attached to Sámi ethnicity caused a massive ethnic shift. Henry Minde (2005:9), defines this shift as an 'ethnic cleansing'. He argues that it was at its peak during the interwar period, affecting many Sámi communities or areas with a high Sámi population density. He refers, for instance, to the municipality of Kvænangen, in Troms County at the Norwegian side of the border, and the result of the census of 1930 compared with 1950. In the first census, 44% of the population defined themselves as being Sámi, but two decades later, there were none left (Bjørklund 1985:12). This, he continues, illustrate how many Sámi, in the span of 20 years, would stop admitting to their Sámi heritage.[35]

In conclusion, the combination of residential schooling which removed children from their home communities, and the social stigma attached to being Sámi, would cause a massive epistemicide. Though the official policy of assimilation was repealed after World War 2, after centuries of assimilation, the damage, or success depending on the point of view, had already been done. Though there is still no full overview available, and the exact number is unknown, the years of assimilation caused a large part of the Sámi population, including the grandmother in the prologue, to reject their Sámi identity, and with it the knowledge of Sámi languages, cultures, knowledge[s] and traditional arts.[36] This also ensured that much of the knowledge pertaining to duodji, *"was erased in our [Sámi] communities [...] we are still strug-*

---

35 I do feel the need to point out that in the mentioned census of 1930 and 1950, the question that was used to define one's ethnicity was language. Meaning that in the span of 20 years it is likely that many had stopped speaking Sámi or was no longer able to do so.

36 Hopefully, the Norwegian Truth and-Reconciliation Commission that is stipulated to be completed by 2023 will provide a full overview, albeit only for the Norwegian side of the border. A similar commission is also in the work on the Finnish side, and the Swedish side has also begun tor structure such a commission, which will contribute to the complete picture.

gling to regain this knowledge" (Ása 07.01.2018).

The initial task set for this chapter was to provide a context for understanding the relevance of identity, sovereignty, duodji and museums. This I believe have been achieved as the coming discussions will explore how these four aspects work together to extract Sámi practices and knowledge[s] from the suspension of epistemicide. To do so, not only was it necessary to discuss the historical process of epistemicide, but it is also vital to connect history with present. Which is what I attempt to do next in my discussion of methodology and theory, respectively.

CHAPTER 3: RUVDEN

GROW YOUR ROOTS DEEP

DEFINING THE SÁMI WAYS OF BEING, OF DOING, AND OF KNOWING AS A CRITICAL METHODOLOGY

AND NOW YOU TAKE OUR STORIES—A PROLOGUE

A while back, I attended a social gathering intended to celebrate Indigenous storytelling. My reason for being there was mainly that one of the speakers had invited me personally seeing as we shared a common Indigenous belonging in Sámi culture, and an interest in storytelling. Whilst still at the reception, a woman approached me. We began talking and at first, we indulged the societal niceties and engaged in small talk: Who are you, what do you do and how did you come to be here at the gathering? The woman exceeded my age by quite some decades, and she had thus witnessed firsthand the beginning of "post-colonialism" in her chosen field of anthropology. I asked her, both from a professional, but also personal curiosity, how she felt about Indigenous storytelling. The woman, not being Indigenous herself, answered with a powerful story.

In her early years as an academic, she had attended a conference discussing research on Indigenous cultures. One session included a panel debate on the topic of Inuit culture and ritual practice. All participants were middle-aged, white men. For her, this was not noteworthy at all—simply the prevailing. Nevertheless, after some time listening to the men speaking, something extraordinary happened; a voice, gnarly but clear, cut above all others. Sitting some ways to the back an old woman of Inuk descent had stood up and started to speak. "First you came, and you took Our land. Then you came, and you took Our language. Then you came, and you took Our culture. And now, you come, and you take Our stories." She then turned her back on the panel, and as she left her voice carried in the silence, "No more"!

Having shared this memory with me, the woman answered my question: "This is what I think of Indigenous storytelling: It does not belong to the researchers of that panel debate and it doesn't belong to me, but to those that share them. We [the researchers] simply make use of them for a time, but after we need to return them in the same shape as when it was given to us" (Solfrid 03.05.2018).

INTRODUCTION

In the wake of post-colonialism,[1] which refers to the historical period or state of affairs representing the aftermath of a Western colonialism, a call for the decolonization of academia has been issued, citing the necessity of theorising Indigenous perspectives and to combat epistemic ignorance. To decolonize however, is not tantamount with the rejection of existing research paradigms and conceptual frameworks of Western thinking and academia. More than an outright dismissal, to decolonize is the process of deconstructing colonial ideologies and the privilege of Western thinking. It is as such a process centred within the colonial structures that perpetuate the existing conditions of academia. This means that the term is problematic, as it, to quote the Sámi dáiddar [artist] Joar Nango, promotes a *"language that continues to polarise an already polarised debate, on the terms set by colonialism"* (quoted in Breivik 2020).

Alongside many other Indigenous researchers, I think we should instead be talking about a process that focus attention on concepts and worldviews operating within Indigenous cultures, making their ontologies, epistemologies and axiologies the core of methodological frameworks (Smith [1999]2012:41, Gaski 2017:179). To clarify my use of these terms, I understand ontology to be the belief in the nature of reality, the basic categories of being and their relations. Epistemology, on the other hand, I consider the rationality of your ontological

---

1   I find using post with colonial to be a strange practice; after all, colonialism is still the reality for most In-digenous communities. In fact, the very definition of Indigenous as: *"a distinctive culture descendent from the populations which inhabited a country, or a geographical region to which a country belongs, at the time of conquest or colonization or the establishment of present state boundaries"* (ILO-169 1989: § 1) imply that colonization has no end. It is as Linda Tuhiwai Smith, in her groundbreaking book, *Decolonizing Methodologies* note: *[n] aming the world as post-colonial is, from indigenous perspectives, to name colonialism as finished business"* (Smith *[1999]2012:101*). However, the term may be used to conceptualize a reaction to or a departure from the aca-demic standards characteristic to the periods of history where colonialism and imperialism were policies that European countries actively pursued.

belief, or how you think about and understand reality, and lastly, axiology is the moral and ethical values of your reality. This, to me, is a process of Indigenization, whereby the significance and application of Indigenous knowledge is asserted into academia, but from a place of Indigenous sovereignty, and centred in Indigenous values, practices, and knowledge systems. The following chapter, and indeed this book in its entirety, is my attempt to Indigenize the field of museology by making Sámi epistemology, ontology, and axiology the core of a methodological framework.

Being Sámi, this in truth means that I am simply employing the Sámi worldview that I have been raised within. Still, I recognize that many have not been fostered to have the same core values that said viewpoint implies. Accordingly, this chapter maps the fundamental principles that went into creating the analytical foundation for researching and understanding the queries in the present work; the methods of inquiry and observation in my empirical approach; and, the verbal unfolding of an analytical tool kit that hopefully is accessible across borders of time, communities, cultures, and cosmology. Before I continue, I would like to offer a note of clarification. I use both knowledge and epistemology in the discussions ahead, and while they at first glance might seem to be synonymous, they are not intended to be so. I use epistemology to denote a knowledge system, the total of making and disseminating knowledges plural. Knowledge, on the other hand I use to convey a justified truth, a category for axioms and postulates so evident and established as to be accepted as true without doubt or controversy.

To create a frame for research that has been conceived in a Sámi context is important, but I do not mean for it to be exclusively used to understand phenomena in Sámi cultures and communities. On the contrary, I think that aspects of my framework and concepts may prove applicable to a broader academic community, as seen with the talking circle (Graveline 2000, e.g., Mannell, Ahmad, and Ahmad 2018), and not only to the original and specific field of reference. Nor is it my intent to advocate the Sámi concepts that I am working with to be reserved for Sámi researchers alone. Nonetheless, it is important to grant Indigenous People the space needed to share their stories, to discuss, and to create discourses based on their knowledge systems. In a way, this chapter is me making the space for said discourses, in the hopes

of opening up a conversation for others to join. As the Sámi scholar, Kristin Jernsletten (2011:9) has answered when asked if there was
room for Sámi knowledge systems, our epistemology, within Western
academia; "*we assume that there is (room), if we make it ourselves*". The
prologue, though not seemingly so at first glance, is a fitting prelude
to the articulated ambitions in this chapter.

Traditional sources are most likely to reflect andro-and Eurocentric values at the expense of diversity. Storytelling and stories offer
researchers the possibility of reintegrating these diversities; contesting
the tendency to interpret the world in terms of both Western and
hetero-patriarchal values (Sangster 1994, Cruikshank 1998, Hirvonen
1999). As such, storytelling is not only an empirical approach of worth.
Stories and storytelling also establish themselves as the natural choice
of methods for my exploration. There are two important reasons for
making this choice, and the prologue indicates what they are.

Firstly, the prologue aims attention at the fact that all too often, a
dominant and non-Indigenous perspective has assumed the right "*to
tell the stories of the colonized and the oppressed*" which has then been
"*re-interpreted, re-presented, and re-told through their own lens*" without
any regard for the actual source communities (Smith 2019:xi). Secondly, in the prologue it is presumed that the significance and shape of
stories might differ from an Indigenous to a non-Indigenous context
(See Triumf 2011). Together, these two presuppositions make the basic premise for the following chapter.

The first premise is almost self-evident. As I navigate the intricacies and vulnerabilities inherent in identity-issues, which are all the
more prominent when the identities in question belong to a people
that for centuries have been oppressed and subjugated to highly de-
meaning practices by both government and academics (Minde 2005,
e.g., Rygh 1867:100, Brøgger 1909:165, Hallström 1929:56), the
matter of control, and in whose hands it is, becomes one of principal
importance. Whose stories are shared, who interprets those stories,
and in which manner are the stories used? I am in no way implying
that stories and storytelling is the end-all of creating empirical material about Indigenous issues, but as a research tool, "*storytelling is a
useful and culturally appropriate way of representing the ´ diversities of
truth` within which the storyteller rather than the researcher retains control*"
(Smith [1999]2012:146). Consequently, stories as well as the act of

storytelling is as I see it suitable as an empirical approach. The second premise is equally as apparent as it encourages an understanding of stories as more than simple oral renderings.

In Indigenous societies, where written materials have been the exemption rather than the rule, it is the stories that serve as literature (Hirvonen 1999). As bodies of living cultural knowledge stories are not only spoken, they are also inscribed onto objects (Guttorm 2001a:15), as documents of law, archival repositories and records of history, and into practices (e.g., Guttorm 2018). *"Luohtán ahte it bilit mu muitalusaid. Don fertet bissut mu duohtavuođas, it ge lasihit maidige"*, 'I trust that you do not destroy my stories. Keep to my truth and add nothing more' (Somby 2016:iii), is perhaps the quote of one person, but it carries a collective understanding that the spoken word is truth, and so it is not for others to change as they please. This is quite different from how stories are perceived in the cultural tradition of the Western thought. Which makes it strikingly evident that in order to understand the relevance of stories and storytelling, or indeed any cultural phenomena, I believe it is of utmost importance to situate it in the culture whence it originally occurred.[2] To do otherwise is a disregard of culturally derived knowledge and thus, in my opinion, an assimilation.[3] As I try to grasp processes of Sámi Indigeneity and sovereign acts, for this reason I have chosen to apply an Indigenous Sámi methodology as the fundamental principle.

In their book on the protection of Indigenous heritage and knowledge, Marie Battiste, a pedagogue of Mi'kmaq[4] descent, and human rights lawyer James (Sákéj) Youngblood Henderson, born to the

---

2   To understand the meaning of a šamán for instance, it is necessary to look to the Tungusic Peoples' that are native to Siberia and Northeast Asia (Kehoe 2000), rather then Mircea Eliade's reinterpretation and consequent academic use as an analytical term.

3   When signing the Waitangi treaty in 1840, Māori chieftains and sovereigns having or possessing "rangatiratanga" allowed New Zealand to become a British sovereignty, whilst still maintaining Māori ownership of land, forests and other properties. With time, it was felt that the Crown had breached the treaty on several occasions, and the Māori demanded that action be taken. Established in 1975, the Waitangi tribunal was to handle these claims and any future accusations of impeachments. Amongst the claimants was a group of prominent Māori woman, but before they were allowed to appear before the tribunall they had to argue their right to do so. The gist of their argument was that the word Rangatiratanga was gender neutral. However, it had in the past been translated with chiefly or sovereignty which in Western knowledge tradition was a male domain and consequently only men could be Rangatiratanga (Smith [1999]2012:48). In this case, both language and social structure was translated from a Western standpoint, resulting in the alienation of Rangatiratanga from where it originally came.

4   A First Nations people Indigenous to Turtle Island, in what is today known as Canada´s Atlantic Provinces and the Gaspé Peninsula of Quebec as well as the norteastern region of Maine in USA.

Chickasaw Nation[5] of Turtle Island[6], warn against *"universal defini-tions of Indigenous knowledge"* as it is always deeply personal and par-ticular (2000:36). Speaking from a Sámi perspective, just because something is true for Cree society on Turtle Island, does not mean it is for Sámi communities in Sápmi, regardless of both cultures being Indigenous (Hirvonen 2009). Nor should it be expected that Sámi society is one of homogenised character as multiple perspectives do exist. Thus, while I use Indigenous and Sámi intermittently, and the work at hand refers to issues that are common to Indigenous Peo-ples' as a whole, I am in truth working from a place of personal Sámi understanding; implementing a methodology that is based on Sámi ontologies, epistemology and axiology, and juxtaposed with the voices of my Sámi collaborators, or verdde as I call them, as well as authors of Sámi literature. It is with these distinctions in mind that I begin to unravel the specifics of my methodology and the methods therein.

TO RUVDEN—MAPPING MY STRUCTURE

Fitting the theme of my book, I envision the structure of the work ahead by imagining it in the shape of duodji. Using the metaphor of braiding, I visualize the methodology as a structure of images by artic-ulating four lines of thought; each one individual, yet still connected, as if I were making a *ruvdu*. The technique involved in making a ruvdu as seen in Figure 3-1, to *ruvdet*, is one of many Sámi braiding proce-dures. It is created through the interlocking of four or more strands, though the total number must be divisible by four.[7]

---

5   Indigenous to Turtle Island, in what is today known as the territories of Southeastern United States of Mis-sisippi, Alabama and Tennesse.

6   The term Turtle Island has its origin in First Nation oral tradition, referencing one story of creation. It has now become a common term used to refer to the continent of North America, rather than referring to the land by the colonial terms that have been enforced and which breaks up tribes and families with arbitrary borders. Using Turtle Island thus unifies the continent and reject colonial rule in a peaceful way (Porter 2008, Pajunen 2020). I have chosen to use the term Turtle Island in consultation with members of First Nation communities on Turtle Island in deference to their chosen terminology.

7   This specific quality of the technique has been associated with its use as a way of teaching mathematics. A Sámi string of numbers do not follow the same logic as does the Norwegian one. Without exception, the Sámi system of numbers is one of ten. Eleven for instance is stated as "oktanuppelohkai", meaning "one towards the second ten". Some researchers have argued that this way of thinking about numbers, is more pedagogic in that children grasps the logic of numbers more easily. Though mathematics has long been thought of as a universal and objective system, it may be considered a cultural system of knowledge that is origin specific as seen for instance, with the existence of the Inuit system of mathematics, or the Māori system of Mathematics (Fyhn et al. 2015).

FIGURE 3-1 THE RUVDU IS AN OLD PRACTICE IN DUODJI. THE RUVDU THAT IS PIC-
TURED HERE COMES FROM A LUHKKA, A HOODED CAPE, I MADE FOR MY BROTHER
5 YEARS AGO. I BROUGHT IT WITH ME TO SHOW AS AN EXAMPLE AT A DUODJEB-
ÁDJI, OR WORKSHOP, IN OSLO THAT WAS FOCUSED ON THE DIVERSITIES OF SUCH
GARMENTS. THIS PICTURE WAS TAKEN BY SÁMI DÁIDDAR ARNHILD HAAGENSEN

In this chapter then, I ruvden my understanding of an Indigenous
methodology and the methods therein by connecting four elements,
beginning with an introduction of Indigenous methodology as a concept.

By no means is it my intent to argue one final definition of Indigenous methodology. As previously stated, to universally define an Indigenous methodology would involve the *"practice of homogenising and
universalising the Indigenous"* (Nakata et al. 2011), which is precisely
what I am trying to avoid. Instead, I will attempt to give a slightly
conversational exploration of the ways in which an Indigenous-led
methodology offers choices that are perhaps more in tune with an
Indigenous holistic approach. Having readied the ground so to speak,
I transition into the second strand, where I discuss my chosen method
of storytelling as an empirical approach founded on Indigenous values, meanings, and norms.

I start my interlocking of the first two strands by referencing some
common Indigenous values of storytelling for one reason alone. As argued by Chadwick Allen (2014:378), who is a professor of Indigenous
and Native American literature, there is a need for a Trans-Indige-
nous approach, a methodology of *"emerging practices designed explicitly
to privilege reading across, through and beyond [...] specific Indigenous
texts and contexts"*. In following his point, which I think is a valid one,
I establish storytelling as a common Indigenous approach of empiric

value before I specify a practice of Sámi storytelling. Reflecting the initial statement of ambition to Indigenize the field in which my book is situated, I hope that this makes my methodological framework accessible to multiple Indigenous communities, but without sacrificing its Sámi context.

To this end, the second strand of my ruvdu presents storytelling as a constituent aspect of Indigenous epistemologies, as ways of producing and disseminating knowledge. Mapping the similarities of storytelling across borders of space and time, helps identify the connective points in what might be a Sámi, but also a more general Indigenous method—if only as abstract ideas. The next objective then, involves a move from the potentially jarring terrain of abstractions into solidifying the pathways of practical implementation. This is when my third strand joins the ruvdu and engage with the first two.

Reflecting the very real conflict that Indigenous Peoples' and communities have felt in their interactions with Western researchers, the third strand is an account of my methodological choices, both before, during, and after fieldwork. It is a highly personal account, which details my battles with reconciling the methodologies and methods designed within a Western research paradigm, to the actual needs and particularities of a Sámi context. At certain places, it almost reads as a diary, and yet it is scientifically relevant for understanding the development of my methodological tools and perspectives. Thus, if at times I take small detours from the established language and vernaculars of my academic community, it serves both a meaning and a purpose that I hope will reveal itself by the end of this discussion.

My struggles with controversies do not end with the methods. The relations that have helped me gain the knowledge that this book hopefully articulate and disseminate, are equally moored in said complexities. As a follow-up to this fact, my fourth and last strand focus on the relationship between "researcher" and "informant". There should be little wonder at the relations of people within a research context being affected by a shift to an Indigenous methodology. Just as stories and storytelling must be perceived in a different manner, so should the connection between myself and the people that inform this book. To that end, my last strand relates the process of redefining said relationship in terms of a Sámi practice by introducing *verddevuohtta*, an old Sámi concept of a reciprocal friendship. More to the point, verddevuohtta is conceptualized anew as the relation between "informant" and "researcher" as *verdde*.

Making transparent the relation between the verdde and myself also makes clear the need for me to externalize for the reader what in Indigenous terms is often related as *self-in-relation*. A Sámi way of expressing this is found in the often-asked question, *'gean don leat'*? The phrasing is generally translated to mean 'who are you', but 'gean' also means 'whose'. In other words, what is really being asked is 'who do you belong to'; which family lines claim you for their own and to which siida/sijte or community do you belong. 'Gean don leat', in many ways, becomes a protocol that reflect the Sámi experience of the world as one that is relational, and the answer to that question, in short, is how you relate yourself, or your self-in-relation (e.g., Jernsletten 2009:47) In the context of an Indigenous methodology, self-in-relation is as such how you define your place in society (Graveline 1998:52). In materializing my self-in-relation, not only do I situate myself, but I also situate my research firmly in a Sámi methodology. With this final strand, my ruvdu will be complete and equally so will the discussion of methodology and methods. To start however, I begin with the first strand, or Indigenous methodology as a research paradigm.

INDIGENOUS METHODOLOGY

In the post-colonial debate of academia, there has emerged what seems to be an ontological conflict between a supposed Indigenous versus Western epistemology (e.g., Øgård and Olsen 08.10.2018). The latter conceived as being the norm, whereas the former, is offered up as an alternative route to accessing knowledge (e.g., Nunn and Reid 2015, Nymo 2015). In that way Indigenous ways of knowing are intended to act as a counterbalance to Western epistemologies and paradigms. By saying so, I do not mean to put forward an image of these different knowledge traditions as either binary or as conflicting or competing, though they are often presented exactly so (Hendry and Fitznor 2012), which I find deeply problematic. Firstly, because homogenizing Indigenous knowledge, and for that matter Western, is not, I believe, sustainable of the contextual circumstances in which knowledge is produced (Hooper-Greenhill 1992), and tend to: "*collectivize many distinct populations whose experience under imperialism have been vastly different*" (Smith [1999]2012:6).

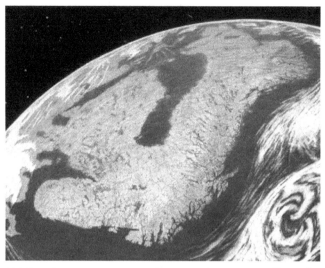

FIGURE 3-2 THIS IMAGE WAS DRAWN BY ELLE-HANSA, THE SÁMI DÁIDDAR HANS RAGNAR MATHISEN. ON IT YOU SEE A MAP OF WHAT APPEAR TO BE AN IMAGINARY LANDMASS BUT, THIS IS A DRAWING OF THE SÁMI HOMELANDS. ORDINARILY, THESE MAPS ARE DRAWN FROM THE PERSPECTIVE OF THE SOUTH GAZING NORTH, OR THE COLONIAL POWERS LOOKING TO THEIR COLONIES. ELLE-HANSA SWITCHES THIS AND DRAW THE MAP FROM A SÁMI PERSPECTIVE LOOKING SOUTH FROM THE VIEWPOINT OF THE NORTH. IT PERFECTLY ILLUSTRATES HOW TWO PERSPECTIVES ON ONE THING MAY CREATE TWO VERY DIFFERENT PERSPECTIVES © HANS RAGNAR MATHISEN/BONO

Secondly, to arrange these different knowledge systems as opponents curbs our ability to bridge them. In the context of Indigenization, the goal should not be to replace one system with another, nor should it be to merge several into one. As I see it, to Indigenize rather means to weave together the many different systems of knowledge so that what emerge is a synergic core that allows for multiple understandings and perspectives. This enables an understanding and a dialogue whilst still maintaining the distinctiveness, and diversity, of Indigenous ways of being, doing, and knowing. Thus, impressing that while there is difference, this does not mean that there is a matter of better or worse (Wangoola 2012:39). In this sense, although it is not the primary objective of the following text, I still hope to give the reader a look at how it is possible to bridge the distance between Indigenous and non-Indigenous scholars and communities. A tall order to be sure, but not, I think, an impossible one.

As I initially stated, it is not my intention to define Indigenous methodology. Indeed, I wonder at the prospect of actually doing so as the concept of Indigenous methodology has different meanings depending on perspective. But for the sake of better contextualizing my research, I will give a short presentation of how I conceptualize and understand Indigenous methodology.

AN INDIGENOUS RESEARCH PARADIGM?

Sharing in the perspective offered by Shawn Wilson (2001:175), a scholar of the Opaskwayak Cree[8] , Indigenous methodology simply means to do research *"from an Indigenous paradigm"* whilst guided by a specific *"set of beliefs"*, or better yet, by ontology, epistemology, and axiology. As I read Wilson, his paradigm is similar to what noted Māori professor of Indigenous research, Linda Tuhiwai Smith, has identified as an Indigenous research agenda: the conceptualisation of both a programme and set of approaches prioritising Indigenous language, social and spiritual practices, and social relations (Smith [1999]2012:120). The noted Cree scholar of Indigenous methodologies, Margaret Kovach (2009:56), also share in the view that research from the perspective of Indigenous methodologies, naturally centers itself within an Indigenous paradigm, as do the Sámi scholars Nils Oskal (2007:163), Rauna Kuokkanen (2000:412) and Harald Gaski (2017a:187) in their respective discussions on Sámi methodology. In this, both Wilson, Smith, and Kovach run parallel to what Oskal, Kuokkanen and Gaski believe a Sámi perspective on research would mean. That is to say, Indigenous Sámi ontology, epistemology and axiology form the guiding principles of an Indigenous Sámi methodology.

A methodology, in this way, becomes the researchers *embodied truth*, or what Donna Haraway, American professor of feminist studies, in her groundbreaking article on situated knowledges terms the sum of our subjective experiences, and thus the specific and particular embodiments of our ontology, epistemology and axiology (Haraway 1988). To me, this indicates that the main focus in an Indigenous methodology is the embodied truth in which the research problems and lines of inquiries are conceptualized and articulated (Smith [1999]2012:ix). This also means that the specific methods that might be employed, needs to be equally grounded in an embodied truth. As Smith points out, *"it is important to have a critical understanding of [...] the tools of research—not just the obvious technical tools [methods] but the*

---

8   First Nation with traditional lands in northern Manitoba, Canada.

conceptual tools [methodology]" (Smith [1999]2012:41).

In this quote, Smith cleverly articulates that while research methods such as focus group discussions or talking circles[9] (e.g., Iversen 2008:29), and oral transmission, or storytelling (e.g., Mannell, Ahmad, and Ahmad 2018:92), may be easily interchangeable between Indigenous and non-Indigenous methodologies, there are still fundamental differences in the ideologies belonging to each (Porsanger 2004:107).[10] Consider the performance of a talking circle; whenever one is enacted, there is a protocol, which means that there are rules and guidelines that caters to the specific needs and cultural demands of the perspectives of those involved (Graveline 1998). These needs and demands are dependent on and among other ontological perspectives. And while the dominant and Euro-centric way of doing research—i.e., western methodologies—conceive of only one physical reality[11] or ontology, most Indigenous worldviews believe in the existence of several (Wilson 2001:176), and these realities are almost always inter-relational (Porsanger 2012:38). In its most basic description, Indigenous ontologies is as such structured around meanings and ways of being, of doing and of knowing; connected to cosmological perspectives and acknowledging nature and the world as living systems in which humans are only one small part (Kincheloe 2011:335).[12]

When considering Indigenous ontologies then, *"reality is relationships, or sets of relationships"* (Wilson 2008:73).[13] Looking to Sámi ontologies, for instance, teaches us that we share the land and waters with other beings such as the *ulddát* [North Sámi] and the *saajveh* [South Sámi]—the underworld people, whom live in a parallel world beneath the surface of the earth and in mountains, invisible to us unless they

---

9   Though using a talking circle in a non-Indigenous context can be a hurtful thing. The worry being that non-Indigenous perspectives transmute the Indigenous ones (Graveline 2000:365).

10 It is important to note that Indigenous methodology often is a combination of, on one hand, existing methodological approaches and on the other of local Indigenous practice (Smith [1999]2012:145).

11 Critical theorists often do their work on the assumption that reality is fluid and dependent on sex, gender, race/ethnicity, culture, and social class. In that way, their epistemology is contextual. Still, the ontological foundation has only one reality.

12 In most literature written by Indigenous scholars and thinkers, *cosmo-vision* sometimes replace ontology to better suit the totality of the bricolage that is an Indigenous worldview (e.g., Åhrén 2010:3, Sara 2018:144)

13 There are however theories which operate on there being more than one ontological reality within the same sphere of understanding or research paradigm. Annemarie Mol is one. In her work on "the body multiple: ontology in medical practice", Mol suggest that *"objects come into being—and disappear—with the practices in which they are manipulated. And since the object of manipulation tends to differ from one practice to another, reality multiplies"* (2002:5). The difference however is that realities are created continuously through human practices, whereas in an Indigenous ontological perspective, different realities already exist regardless of human interaction.

themselves wish to be seen (Bäckman 1975, Porsanger 2012).[14] As children we are taught to respect these beings, and to be aware of their presence so as to live in harmony (Sara 2018:145, Porsanger 2012:39, Jernsletten 2009:94). I remember quite well being told by my aahka never to pour liquid directly onto the ground unless I first stomped so as to warn the ulddát and saajveh less they be soaked. This, she said, was good practice because it ensured that we could live peacefully together. To this day, I stomp before pouring water on the ground, as do many of my relatives.

Within Sámi ontologies, then, what matters is not the entities that are the ulddát and saajveh alone, but the relationship one has with them. To both my aahka, many Sámi communities, and myself, the ulddát and saajveh are as such not *"fairy tales in the western sense of the term, but rather parts of a complex"* worldview that make up the ontologies, epistemologies and axiologies that together form a Sámi whole (Sara 2018:144, e.g., Finbog 2015:99). What would be considered mythical beings outside of a Sámi conception, as such *"still have a place within the [Sámi] worldview"* (Jernsletten 2009:105, Jernsletten 2011:169). Yet, in a non-Indigenous methodology, there is seldom room for understanding the ulddát as more than legends and fantasy. Moreover, this is not a singular problem. When I explained some of the beliefs that my verddes' had shared with me to non-Indigenous colleagues[15], they would sometimes judge it to be *"imagination"*, *"not really scientifically valid"*, and similar to *"new-age superstitions"*. Granted, their judgement comes from their ontological understanding of the world—the belief in an external and assessable truth. The stories and the storytellers responsible for my findings, however, experience their world very differently. The point of employing an Indigenous Sámi methodology, in other words, is being able to do research that acknowledge and understand the existence of the ulddát and saajveh and whatever else Sámi ontologies might have to offer—without defining it as fairy tales, imagination and non-scientific. To me, this lies at the heart of any Indigenous methodology (e.g., Remme 2013:12).

---

14 It should however, be noted that the stories of ulddát is as varied and different as there are varied and different Sámi communities (Pollan 2017). Sápmi is a large and widespread territory, and it just isn´t realistic to expect that the entirety of our communities are the same.

15 Primarily the results that will be discussed in čuoldit, "Weaving Stories: Biographies of becoming, the memory of blood and the practice of duodji"

SÁMI METHODOLOGY AS ONTO-EPISTEMOLOGY.

When adopting an Indigenous ontological perspective, inevitably comes the consequent need of employing the attached knowledge system, or epistemology. In the established vernacular of Western research paradigms, epistemology is regarded as a codified and "*cognitive canon law*" (Haraway 1988:575), which govern how knowledge is created and disseminated. Indigenous epistemologies on the other hand, are plural and they can never be "*standardized, for they are in relation to place and person*" (Kovach 2009:56); there is never only one way of creating knowledge, nor is there a singular method of disseminating it. As a result, Indigenous epistemologies have far too often been disregarded as valid knowledge systems. Instead, the practice within academia has been to define them as traditional knowledges, gained through a process of social learning and sharing that is customary to each Indigenous culture (Four Directions Council 1996).[16] As Indigenous knowledges are likely to be place-based, they have also tended to be treated as valid only in so far as they are localized to specific territories and areas (Virtanen and Seurujärvi-Kari 2019:4). Indigenous epistemologies have consequently been thought to exist besides, but not equal to the epistemological knowledge systems of the West.

Of course, many Indigenous scholars have in later years argued that Indigenous cultures possess their own epistemologies (Wilson 2001, 2008, Kovach 2009, Kuokkanen 2009, Smith [1999]2012). Often, these systems are also intimately linked with ontologies. In many ways, "*an Indigenous ontology is actually the equivalent of an Indigenous epistemology*" (Wilson 2008:73). Which in turn means that many methodologies of an Indigenous nature operate with onto-epistemologies (Wilson 2001, Barrett 2015), demonstrating how the realities of the world intersect with the creation of knowledges. By implementing the definition of onto-epistemology, the relational qualities of both Indigenous epistemologies and ontologies are, I would argue, combined into a relational network from which a holistic understanding may be reached.

Non-Indigenous research paradigms, or methodologies, according to Wilson (2001:176), rest on the belief that knowledge is individual; "*the researcher is an individual in search of knowledge, knowledge is some-*

---

16 Such distinction is, in part, due to the view on Indigenous cultures as static and deprived of the ability to evolve (Porsanger 2011:231, Bennett 2004).

thing that is gained, and therefore knowledge may be owned by an individual". Within an Indigenous research paradigm, however, knowledge is relational (Wilson 2001:177). That is, similar to how Indigenous ontologies often focus on relations, so too do their attached epistemologies. The latter then, is built on relationships, not only with people and objects, but also with the environment—be it nature, other realities or worlds, cosmology, and more (Kuokkanen 2005). Wilson (2008:80-97) divides these relations into those found between people, with the environment or land, within the cosmos, and lastly, with ideas. This emphasise that Indigenous epistemologies is a process of being that has been shaped by integrating relationships and holistic perspectives (Kovach 2009:67). This is also true in a Sámi context.

Jelena Porsanger (2012:42), a Sámi scholar of methodologies from the Russian side of the border, states in her research that "*[e]verything in the [Sámi] world [is] interrelated*". In other words, how someone acts and lives in the world is deeply entangled within a nexus of reciprocal relationships—to people, to things and objects, to non-human beings and entities[17], to cosmology, to lands and to nature[18] (e.g., Kuokkanen 2007b:258). To conceptualize this world of relations, I borrow the term *world in relation* from the Martinique-born writer and thinker Édouard Glissant (2006), who wrote and published on a world made up of relations. There are many ways in which a Sámi *world-in-relation* may be expressed (e.g., Gaski 2017:187). One is the idea of parallel worlds populated by other beings and entities that I earlier made mention of.

Conceiving of the world as one of relations, as a "*world of many worlds*" as it were (de la Cadena and Blaser 2018:4), is also expressed in Sámi languages with the previously discussed concept of *birgejupmi*, which is a way of thinking about the maintenance of life, and which has evolved into a practice, or a way of being, that still effect many living in Sámi communities today (Nymo 2011:275). Another way in which the Sámi world-in-relation is communicated through

---

17 This also include entities such as the ulddát, spirits, ancestors, Gods and Goddesses to name a few.

18 There is no single word in Sámi that is equivalent to the Western concept of nature. Instead, a variety of terms are used depending on context and relation. The term *luondu* for example, implies nature as in the character of something or someone; *olbmo luondu* meaning the nature of a human, or the environment being expressed as *luonddubiras*. On the other hand, when speaking of a geographical area or territories the word *meahcci* is used. And even then, the meaning of meahcci depends on which practice the area is associated with (Joks, Østmo, and Law 2020). Sámi concept of ´nature` is as such relational, defining relationships rather than any one definitive thing (Porsanger 2012:38)

language and practice, is by way of árbediehtu.

Admittedly the term árbediehtu is quite recent in academic circles, as it was first used in 2003 by the Sámi scholar Harald Gaski (2003) to describe the oral passing of knowledge between generations. Since then, however, árbediehtu has been incorporated into academic vernacular as Sámi traditional knowledge (e.g., Guttorm 2011:60, Porsanger 2011:239), or what I term a system of knowledge. Regardless of its designation, the idea of árbediehtu is long-standing. Made up of *árbi*, meaning inheritance, and *diehtu*, meaning knowledge, the term árbediehtu refers to a shared, or collective, and relational knowledge that of old is

> the collective wisdom and skills of the Sámi people used to enhance their livelihood for centuries. It has been passed down from generation to generation both orally and through work and practical experience. Through this continuity, the concept of árbediehtu ties the past, present and future together (Guttorm and Porsanger 2011:18)

Here, the relational quality of árbediehtu materialize as a knowledge that is made by different connections linking ancestor with descendant, past with present, and human with non-human. Árbediehtu, as such, "*is about the sharing of knowledge. How we learn and teach across ages, disciplines, nature, beings and objects*" (Ilse 09.07.2018). This also support the initial suggestion that árbediehtu is a system of knowledge or an epistemology. But as the Sámi scholar of methodology, Rauna Kuokkanen (2007b:254), remarks, it is important that we differentiate between a system of knowledge that is rooted in a collective experience and accumulated for generations and one's individual experience. As an epistemology, árbediehtu is as such made up of what Marie Battiste (1998:18) refers to as "*a cognitive collective experience*". If accepted as such, árbediehtu explicitly illustrate the foundation of onto-epistemology, both the product and the system which created said product. But this I will discuss at greater length in the next chapter.

Within a Sámi onto-epistemology then, knowledge is created by a collective, meaning that an individual cannot monopolise knowledge.[19] To do so would be both inappropriate and contrary to custom-

---

19 In 2019, a social media campaign was launched by several duojárs and Sámi artists after the news broke that Tana Gold and Silver [hence TSG] forge on the Norwegian side of the border had sent several letters of cease and desist threathening lawsuits. The issue was use of the symbol for sun in art and duodji. In 2006, TSG had

ary Sámi practice (Åhrén 2010:3). Nonetheless, if we look to history, Sámi academics have been judged unfairly if working within a Sámi epistemology by those embedded in a Western epistemology. Henrik Kvandahl is a case in point. The Sámi schoolteacher was born in what is now the municipality of Áhkánjárga, or Narvik, on the Norwegian side of the border in 1865. In his academic practice, Kvandahl was a champion of Sámi language and history, which culminated in his publication of "Samefolkets historie"—a historical account of the Sámi people in four parts, published between 1925 and 1947. Evaluating the books of Kvandahl, Henry Minde notes that their scientific value was significantly reduced because it cited various sources juxtaposed with the authors' own comments and reflections, but without making a clear separation between the two (Minde 1995). The reduction of value is dependent, however, on Kvandahl works being viewed from a place of non-Indigenous knowledge tradition. If looked at from within a Sámi epistemology, the reference system employed by Kvandahl is, in my opinion, culturally appropriate to the understanding of Sámi knowledge and knowledge systems as relational concepts. Yet this way of creating and disseminating knowledge have been both ridiculed and deemed non-scientific.

It is from understanding the backdrop of an Indigenous and Sámi onto-epistemology that the choice of methodological framework and the selection of empirical approaches, should be understood. At least in theory. But how does the theory become practice? In answer to this question, I will in the following engage in a discussion on the specific methods employed in my book as well as my reason for choosing them.

INDIGENOUS STORYTELLING

Stories, it is often agreed, are memories; they are the manifestations of lived lives, the memoirs of both individuals and the narrations of historical and political events. In short, stories are the embodied re-

---

copyrighted their design of the sun, which they had reworked from a symbol on a noaide-drum. The sun has an unrivaled position in Sámi cosmology as the father of all, and the symbol and colours of the sun is as such heavily used in duodji and art. The shape of the sun was suddenly the intellectual property of one company, and what is more they were actively working to stop others fom using similar designs. Several Sámi communities worked together to send a petition to the patent office of Norway claiming that to copyright the Sun goes against Sámi traditions and the copyright of TSG should therefor be repealed. In late December of that year the response came, and TSG's copyright was repealed (Utsi 03.12.2019).

cords of the passage of time come to life in, and through, the spoken word and cultural practices. Because they are memories, stories are as such made up of experiences, belongings, and relationships—past, present and even future (Graveline 2000:361). In that way, stories act as vessels, passing along the teachings, practices, and knowledge of the storyteller, and through them, the collective. Born "*of connections within the world, and [...] recounted relationally*" (Kovach 2009:94), stories are a gateway to the holistic perspectives specific to the communities in which the stories were conceived and shared (Cocq 2008:14, Kovach 2009:95-6). Consequently, stories are an invaluable source for, and component of, Indigenous knowledge systems (e.g., Nunn and Reid 2015), reflecting both epistemological, ontological, and axiological perspectives and values. This means that stories are not only told, recounted and passed down: they are also intended as tools of teaching, and of learning (e.g., Triumf 2011:82, Joks 2015:27).

From an Indigenous perspective, stories and storytelling are also important acts of agency (Sium and Ritskes 2013). The Kamillaroi[20] professor of Indigenous research, Larissa Behrendt (2019:175), has described storytelling as "*a transformative practice*" and "*an act of sovereignty*". Her reasoning is that storytelling is one of the ways in which Indigenous people may reassert "*our stories on our land*" which in turn assert "*our ownership*" (Behrendt 2019:177). As I understand her argument, Behrendt is actually saying that to create space for Indigenous stories and the act of storytelling also makes a space for a re-appropriation of Indigenous autonomy (e.g., Clifford 1997:189, Buijs 2016:550). I will try explaining my meaning by referencing the American interdisciplinary scholar James Clifford (1997), and his work on museums as *contact zones*.

Though now part of the museological vernacular, the concept of contact zone was first developed by Mary Louise Pratt (1992:6), an American pedagogue writing on the space of colonial encounters in literature, and where contact zone is defined as

> the space in which peoples geographically and historically separated come into contact with each other and establish ongoing relations, usually involving conditions of coercion, radical equality, and intractable conflict.

In what has today become, it seems, a permanent part of a museolog-

---

20 Indigenous people in Australia whose land extended from New South Wales to Southern Queensland (I am not unaware of the irony that territory is here measured in the language of the colonizers).

ical syllabus, Clifford implemented the concept of contact zone when he described how Tlingit-elders, from the Pacific Northwest Coast on Turtle Island, in the late 1980s came to the Portland Museum of Art by invitation to look at Tlingit objects acquisitioned by the museum in the early 20th century. On the museum's part, the intent was no doubt to increase their knowledge of the objects (Clifford 1997:188). The Tlingit elders' intent, on the other hand, was somewhat different. Taking this opportunity, they used the objects as an entry point to speak of their current political struggles of sovereignty. Though the stories in question where long-established and had been recounted for generations, the elders still managed to relate them to the present (Clifford 1997:191), which to me indicate the value of their stories as both timeless, but also as oral records of history and judicial rights. [21] For this reason, I would claim that Clifford witnessed a performance of embodied sovereignty, though he himself might not describe it as such.

"*Our sovereignty is embodied*", says scholar Aileen Moreton-Robinson of the Goenpul tribe, which is part of the Quandamooka nation in Australia; "*it is ontological (our being) and epistemological (our way of knowing), and it is grounded within complex relations derived from [...] ancestral beings, humans and land*" (Moreton-Robinson 2007:2). The personal and communal autonomy of Indigenous Peoples', in other words, comes from the sustaining, and in some cases retaining, of cultural knowledges and from forging links with communities, ancestors and homelands (Barrett 2015:112, Virtanen and Seurujärvi-Kari 2019:2). It would be accurate to say that these relationships shape our ways of being, our ways of doing, and our ways of knowing. And it is these very relations that are embedded in our stories.

But in the wake of colonialism, with its forced relocations, assimilation, epistemicide and more, these relations are in danger of being destroyed. How then is it possible to maintain these links? I will not pretend that there is a clear-cut answer to this question, but as I have already discussed, an oral rendition may be both a personal narrative, as well as a communal memory. In both cases, stories have the capacity to remind us of who we are and where we belong (Kovach 2009:94); its powers are founded on its relational abilities, re-forging the link

---

21 A common aspect of Indigenous storytelling is that their narrative quality express discourses that, while specific to the community in which they were performed, are often removed from a specific timeframe so as to be equally relevant whether set in the past, the present or the future (Hymes 1992:113).

between people, community, land (Meggitt 1965, Lefale 2010, Myrvoll et al. 2013, Heikkilä 2014), history, past, language, culture (e.g.,
Clifford 1997:188, Buijs 2010:18) and identity (Antze 1996:xxi, e.g.,
Finbog 2015:99). Therefore, stories help create safe spaces in which
the community and the individuals therein, present their history, culture, ethnicity, and cultural identities[22]—both internally, as well as ex-
ternally—as they experience it.

In short, storytelling has the capacity of shifting power from the
researcher, whom for so long defined everything Indigenous, to individual and community, allowing the latter two to re-appropriate
control of their past, present and future (e.g., Buijs 2016:548). Both
stories and storytelling is thus "the *counter-narrative of colonization*"
(Smith 2019:2, e.g., Jernsletten 2011:162). Considering all these facts,
perhaps it is no wonder that in the prologue to this chapter, the old
Inuk woman put so much importance on stories. Next, I discuss how
that might translate into a Sámi context.

STORYTELLING AS A WAY OF INDIGENIZING THE PRODUCTION OF KNOWLEDGE.

In a beautiful work on theorizing Sámi practices and knowledges, the
Sámi scholar Kristin Jernsletten has written that stories are:

> "like place-names; archaeological findings; sacred sites; and a history of in-
> dustrial use of land (such as hunting and gathering)—potential proof of land
> rights, and the people who tell (of) them are often unsummoned witnesses,
> duođašteaddjis" (2011:137).

To me, this quote highlights that in many Indigenous societies where
a literary tradition[23]—or what in Western thought passes as literary—
is recent, literature has nonetheless existed for a long time. In a Sámi
context, "*njálmmálaš árbevierut leat meroštallon girjjálašvuohtan*", 'oral
traditions should be thought of as literature', says the Sámi professor of
literature, Vuokko Hirvonen (2009:93, my own translation). The Sámi
cultures are oral cultures, meaning that our stories survive by being
told verbally or in practices or aesthetics (e.g., Guttorm 2001:49, Virtanen and Seurujärvi-Kari 2019:2, Guttorm, Kantonen, and Kramvig

---

22 This is true regardless of the participants being Indigenous as illustrated by museologist Anne Eriksen (1995)
in her work with veterans of World War II where she found that storytelling was used to make a collective
memory of the war.

23 I use the term literary tradition in the sense of the accumulative process of handing down a body of written
text as opposed to oral literature or non-written process of handing down verbal prose.

2019:153). In fact, the first Sámi publication to put stories into writ-ing, *Muitalus Sámiid Birra*[24] by Johan Turi—being both written in, and by a, Sámi—only came in 1910 (Turi [1910]1987). There were of course, Sámi authors prior to that, but these did not publish in a Sámi language (e.g., Renberg 1904), nor did they follow the vocal and cultural qualities of Sámi storytelling (Gaski 2011).

The qualities in question might be summarized as follows; orality is collective, meaning that it is the spoken word, practices and objects that become the point of reference, and where knowledge is found (Jernsletten 2011:55). This involves an interrelational point of view that teaches one how to listen and gather information from multiple sources, and more importantly, to value these sources equally.[25] Turi, although his work is in a written format, did manage to stay true to these qualities (e.g., Gaski 2011:603), for instance in his artistic pictures which accompanied his written words. Even in his choice of title, the deep roots of the oral customs of Sámi storytelling are visible. In Sámi, the word for story is *muitalus*[26]. It has its etymological origin in the verb *muitit*, meaning to remember (Cocq 2008:41). In fact, muitalus is considered to be "*an account which is factual*" and "*truthful*" (Gaski 2011:594). In Sámi communities then, telling a story is closely related to remembering, meaning that muitalus is both a way of tell-ing stories that is particular to Sámi tradition, and, I would argue, an important component of Sámi epistemology.

The much-loved Sámi multi-artist and scholar, Áillohaš (Nils-Asla-Valkeapää), once said that Sámi literature distinguishes itself because,

> [...] we do not have, as far as literature goes, established norms and con-ventions, not even a written literature as our literary background [...] our literature is based upon oral knowledge that has been handed down through generations and it thus is not very easy to convert into a literary medium. (1998:91)

As is typical of oral cultures (see Cruikshank 1998), Sámi storytelling has long been the preferred means of passing knowledge—both on

---

24 *Muitalus Sámiid birra* simply means "stories of the Sámi people".

25 There is a word for this in Sámi, *gulahallat*, meaning 'communication', which I discuss in the next chapter, where I detail the theory of my book.

26 In Sámi, fairytales are not considered part of muitalus. Rather they have their own category, máinnas. So telling stories imply that you connect to a communal memory whereas telling fairytales means something completely different. Sámi scholar, and elder, Harald Gaski (2019:263) distinguis between muitalus as "*a true-story*" opposite máinnas, which is a "*made-up story*".

an intergenerational level as well as between peers (Balto 1997:70, Triumf 2011:82). *"I learn so much from the stories—sometimes I listen to what the elders talk about, and other times stories are told in conversations with those of my own age. Even then I learn"*, says Sanna, a Sámi woman I once met at a duodji-workshop (02.07.2018).

Raised in a family heavily afflicted by assimilation, Sanna had little exposure to Sámi knowledge systems and culturally derived knowledge when growing up. Today, when she is trying to regain what her family lost, she feels that much knowledge is found in the stories of those around her. Listening to the stories told and sharing her own, she is reminded of who she is and where she comes from, and at the same time she is slowly asserting herself within a Sámi ontology and epistemology. From my own childhood, I too clearly remember that simple questions often received stories in reply. Even today, when I am an adult, my older relatives still convey information to me in the shape of stories. In Sámi society then, *"'epistemological truth' is created and restored by storytelling"* (Kuokkanen 2000:421). But is it an act of sovereignty?

An answer to that question may be found in the publication *Revoicing Sámi Narratives* by Coppélie Cocq (2008). Though not herself of Indigenous decent, Cocq has long focused her interest on Indigenous and Sámi matters. Reflecting said interest, her doctoral thesis makes use of *Muitalus Sámiid Birra* to argue the importance of Sámi storytelling. Based on her research, Cocq claims that storytelling is essential to the positioning of self as it materializes personal experience (Cocq 2008:18). For me this was made clear during one of my conversations with Ása, a duojár from a small Sámi coastal community on the Norwegian side of the border. When finishing our last conversation, Ása thanked me, which I found peculiar because it was, after all, I that had gained the most from our conversations. I forgot, however, to consider the powerful effect of stories when positioning self.

When sharing a story, you create an imaginative landscape in which you become the cartographer. As storytellers, the *muitaleaddji*, you map that landscape, and by doing so you create an emotional, symbolic, historical, spiritual, and cultural significance. To tell a story is in essence a transformative act that help situate yourself in your world (Graveline 2000:361), but only so far as it is relational; told to someone, in connection to, and shared with, others.

FIGURE 3-3 MUITALUSMEANNU" IS A GATHERING OF PEOPLE WITH THE EXPRESS PURPOSE OF STORYTELLING. IT IS AN EVENT ARRANGED FOR THE BENEFIT OF SÁMI STORYTELLERS AND LISTENERS TO LEARN OF THEIR HISTORY THROUGH IN-DIGENOUS STORIES RATHER THAN THE HISTORY BOOKS WRITTEN FROM NON-IN-DIGENOUS PERSPECTIVES. THIS PICTURE WAS TAKEN BY RÁMAVUOL ELLE BIGGE, ELLEN BERIT NYMO DALBAKK, ONE OF THIS EVENTS FACILITATORS, WHO HAS KINDLY ALLOWED ME ITS USE.

A story told with no one to listen, has no effect. Never managing to find its place in a larger whole, the unheard story disappears with its storyteller. If, on the other hand, a story is heard, it manages to display the connections you make and relate them to others, enabling them to understand your story, and to see you as you wish to be seen (Iseke 2013:568). This is what Åsa conveyed in her thanks, when she told me: *"It's not often that people like me [Sámi that are in the process of reclaiming their heritage] are given a voice, so what you are doing matters. It matters that you care and that you want to listen to my stories"* (Åsa 07.01.2018).

In her dissertation, Cocq (2008:77) also argues that stories owe their relevance to them being *"extract[s] from a broader pool of knowl-edge"*. What she means is that stories, once told, are entered into a communal repository—a collection of knowledge that becomes com-mon property. Moreover, everytime the stories are re-told and shared, it has *"served the purpose of passing on [...] knowledge"* (Sara 2018:146). My *siessá*, my father's older sister, is an accomplished storyteller. Once, she told me a story about an experience she had during a walk in the mountains. Having taken a small break, she had used her knife to carve some meat for eating. When she was done, rather than putting the knife back in its sheath, she stabbed it into the ground. Her friend, whom she was walking with, told her not to do that. I asked my siessá if she knew what her friends reasoning had been, and she replied that it was likely due to her action potentially blunting the knife, making it useless. Nevertheless, as our discussion progressed another possibility divulged itself.

I remembered having witnessed a similar thing as a child once, on a walk in the mountain with my aahka, my *gåeskie* [mother's older sister] and her husband. We had stopped for a small break and my uncle used his knife to cut a piece of cheese to go with his loaf of bread. Afterwards, he stabbed the knife into the ground, presumably to have his hands free and still have easy access to the knife. When aahka saw this, she reprimanded him. Her reason was that the iron in the knife was harmful to the people living in the ground—the ulddát, or Saajve.[27] At that point, I had a moment of clarity. I asked her after she reprimanded uncle if the necessity of me stomping on the ground, which I related earlier in the text, was due to the people living in the earth. Her reply was something along the lines of, "*Well, do you like to be wet? Nor do the people living in the ground. You stomp to warn them that water is coming so they can escape it. This is good because it ensures that we live peacefully together*".

To my aahka, it was important that we always have good relations to the people living underground. This she had learned from listening to the stories of her aahka and tjidtjie. In the same way, after our trip to the mountains, I began to learn by listening to hers. When I shared what I had learned from aahka with siessá, she told me that her friend hailed from the same community as aahka. And though she could neither confirm nor deny that her friends reasoning was similar to that of aahka, she was nevertheless intrigued by the possibility. Thus, even if the fear of siessá blunting the knife was very much a valid possibility, an equally valid possibility was to have a good relation to the ulddát and saajveh. Sámi storytelling in this sense,

> [...] teach people to respect their ancestors, to honor the Sun and the planets and to feel the unity of life. Stories teach the ways of the culture and help each person find his or her place in society. They teach the harmony and balance of the universe that maintains good health. They connect the elements of the upper and lower worlds (Helander 1995:7).

In a very visual way, my story of the knife in the ground confirms what Cocq states in her dissertation; that stories take part in a collective and communal repertoire that is contextual as well as being a memorial of

---

27 Only later did I consider that her reaction might also be because placing a knife in the ground could be misconstrued by the others to initiate contact with the gifting of a sjiele.

the discourses and social currents in both past and present, making Sámi stories part of an epistemological system and storytelling a way of practicing knowledge.

While the findings of Cocq are based on a text that was written a century ago, it is no less valid for the present time (Cocq 2008:236). Indeed, as both Sanna, my siessá and I can attest, oral tradition is still an important part of Sámi reality on a day-to-day basis (Nergård and Eriksen 2006, Heil 2014:49). In fact, among young Sámi learners in Sámi-speaking communities, Sámi languages are considered to have more value and fluidity when spoken as opposed to being written down (Outakoski 2015) Which only goes to show that in language, the aspect of Sámi culture as one that is mainly oral is still very much prominent. As Sámi author Kerttu Vuolab (1995:27), from the Finnish side of Sápmi puts it, *"we still have a very rich oral storytelling tradition, and this is still connecting the generations"*. Not to say that written Sámi may not contain a similar fluidity as is evidenced by the work of Turi, for instance.

Still, stories maintain their importance in Sámi communities— both as a way of reasserting yourself and expressing your sovereignty while negating colonial discourses and narratives, but also to manifest and maintain Sámi knowledges—in essence performing a Sámi epistemology.

Storytelling, however, and its place in a Sámi epistemology, should not be confined to oral renditions alone. In fact, as I initially mentioned, there are good indications that both objects and practices can function as stories and storytelling, respectively (e.g., Blaser 2009). Duodji, I believe, is one example of such (e.g., Aagård-Dunfjeld 1991, Guttorm 2018). As a practice, duodji is constituted in complex cultural contexts, and within specific social and material circumstances. It is related to Sámi customs of crafting and aesthetic expressions, and as such, reflects specific values as well as the immaterial knowledge of processes and experiences of materiality.

As is the case with oral storytelling, duodji too takes part in an intergenerational exchange of wisdoms and skills, learned by seeing and reproducing (Balto 1997:70, Triumf 2011:82). This enables a sharing, not only of the practice, but also of deeply rooted collective values, embedded in the relational quality of people, objects, land, nature, other beings, seasonal knowledge and spiritual beliefs (Guttorm 2001:13).

FIGURE 3-4 EMBROIDERY WITH PEWTER IS AN OLD SÁMI TECHNIQUE. IT IS DEEP-LY EMBEDDED IN A SYSTEM OF KNOWLEDGE, ITS ARRAY OF ORNAMENTAL DE-SIGNS AN ACT OF STORYTELLING FOR THE INITIATED READER/LISTENER. THE EMBROIDERY IN THIS WORK IS MADE BY DUOJÁR INA OMMA, FROM A SOUTH SÁMI COMMUNITY ON THE SWEDISH SIDE OF THE BORDER. SHE INITIALLY SHARED THE IMAGE ON HER INSTAGRAM ACCOUNT, @INANIILAOMMA.

It would be fair to say then, that duodji conceptualize a representation of Sámi ontologies and axiology (e.g., Lehtola 2006), and by doing so it also becomes an important aspect of Sámi epistemology (Balto 1996, 1997). I consequently argue that duodji—in both practice and product—convey stories and memories.

I will expand more on this in my next chapter, which concerns the theoretical framework of this book, but for now this will have to suffice as a provisional introduction. It is, however, one that is needed as my argument that duodji is a way of storytelling have some important implications on the implementation of my methods.

MUITALUSAT

If telling stories, and practicing duodji, account for an onto-episte-mological way of creating and disseminating knowledge, as I have thus far argued, then it naturally follows that collecting stories and observing practices is one of the ways in which I may assemble said knowledge. When I began to research and develop my project, my empirical approach was based on this assumption and was as such qualitative in definition; consisting of several planned in-depth interviews with chosen "informants" and intended observations of their practice as duojárs. My reasoning was two-fold. In an in-depth interview, the intent is to create a comfortable space for the "informant" to reflect upon specific subjects (Tjora 2012:104-5). Somewhat naïvely perhaps, I assumed that this method would suit my needs. I did not, however, adequately consider the convoluted response that the word research still awakens in many Sámi. Due to the previous indignities suffered at the hands of scholars[28], Sámi "informants" often under communicate or withhold relevant information when meeting academic researchers. Which resulted in the second assumption that my own Indigeneity would somehow counteract such negative associations. During my first bout of fieldwork or the first two interviews to be precise, I quickly realized that what on paper had seemed suitable, proved to be anything but—which is not an unusual turn of events (e.g., Thorbjørnsrud 2005:21).

SÁMI METHOD/S IN PRACTICE

My journey of empirical entanglement began when I, following the guidelines for ethical approved research, notified the Norwegian Research Centre (NSD) of my project, complete with an interview guide and an information letter with an accompanying consent form. To be clear, the guidelines in question do not account for possible issues related to research in an Indigenous context. And so, the different expectations of Indigenous research are not covered by NSD's guidelines (Drugge 2016). Still, the general practice of research meant that I had to go through them. Having received the go-ahead from NSD in late November of 2017, I had my very first interview shortly after, on December 5th. It should be noted that in advance of these first interviews I had done little to establish an Indigenous framework—i.e., methodology and methods –which in part account for the result, I suspect.

The first two interviews were with Emmy and Stina, young duojárs, from adjacent Sámi communities on the Norwegian and the Swedish side of the border, respectively. I had previously collaborated

---

28 One example would be the forced race biological research performed on the Sámi, which continued long into the 1950s.

with Emmy on another project related to duodji, and when the time came to think of possible verdde, she was one of the first I considered. Through her, I also became acquainted with Stina and her work as a duojár.

During an interview, it is important to create a safe space, allowing for the person/s being interviewed to feel comfortable and in control. This is key, especially when considering the complexities of Indigenous identities, that far too often is still struggling with contexts of colonialism and oppression. To that end location is crucial, with most to-do guides advising that the choice of location be left up to the interviewee, citing their home or workplace as preferable (Tjora 2012:120). In a perfect world, I agree that this is paramount, but, when working within Sámi communities, not always conceivable. Sápmi is large, and thus the parameter of available verdde is excessive. No matter how much I focus on communities on the Norwegian and Swedish side of the border, we are still talking about a sizable area. This means that there are large travel distances between each community. The financial repercussions are such that it has been impossible for me to travel to the homes of each duojár. Which was why I made sure to arrange a meet-up with both Emmy and Stina whilst they were both in Oslo on other business. Per the textbooks, I left the choice of location up to them, but because of the delicate issues we would be discussing, they both preferred my place to a busy coffeehouse in town. In hindsight, it is easy to understand that this choice of location was not conducive to a relaxed and comfortable interview. At least this was the case for Stina. Emmy, because of our past association, was already familiar with my apartment and thus visibly more relaxed. Nonetheless, both interviews were valuable in that they gave me much to work with in terms of what to do, and what not to do when conducting my next interviews.

I think the most important lesson that my interviews with Emmy and Stina imparted in me was the growing awareness that perhaps, in the context of my project, to work within the established guidelines of qualitative research—i.e., interviews and participatory observation—would be difficult. Maybe even contrary to what I hoped to achieve. I base this on two facts: Stina seemed uncomfortable during the interview, and though we had a long conversation, it is quite revealing that she has not approached me afterward for continued talks. Especially since all the other people I have spoken with, have done so. Though at that time, this fact had not yet been established, I still took guidance from my first experience to alter my approach for the next rounds of interviews. To that end, I set out to identify a possible set of strategies or principles through which I could discuss and research the issues highlighted in my book.

THE SEVEN PRINCIPLES OF STORYTELLING.

As the pool of academic writings in Indigenous methodology and methods increase, sources on theorizing and utilizing Indigenous empirical practices, such as storytelling, have reached quite respectable quantities (Cruikshank 1998, Hirvonen 1999, Archibald 2008, Kovach 2009, Iseke 2013, Cocq 2013). This offers multiple choices as to how research may be enacted in contexts of Indigeneity, but with various degrees of importance as to locating and constituting empirical approaches centred on Indigenous worldviews and perspectives. Focalizing said fundamentals, the Sto:lo scholar of Turtle Island, Jo-Ann Archibald, or Q'uo Q'um Xiiem (2008), has conceived of the term *Indigenous storywork*. Here, she manages to encompass the sheer breadth of ways in which Indigenous storytelling serves as a communal memory, as a way of teaching and learning, as well as an expression of Indigenous sovereignty. In adherence to this incredible depth and the diversity of Indigenous storytelling, she has devised seven guiding principles for what a culturally appropriate act of storytelling should be. These are respect, responsibility, reciprocity, reverence, holism, interrelatedness, and synergy.

The first principle, respect, relates to ways of approaching and handling the stories shared (Smith [1999]2012:125). A good way of illustrating this, is in the language of deliverance. Stories come to in a certain context, but when they are written down or translated into another language, sometimes meanings, values, and format become lost in translation (Archibald 2008:26, e.g., Joks, Østmo, and Law 2020). As one of my verdde shared with me: *"once I spoke to someone who came into our community to do research. She didn't understand what we told her and so her work did not represent us truthfully"* (Berit 30.05.2018). When translating stories, whether by language or context, it is important that the storyteller approve. Ideally, between the first storytelling session and up until you hand in your work, the storyteller should always have the opportunity to check your translations. Continuous feedback with all research participants is thus a respectful way of ensuring the authenticity and credibility of a project (Wilson 2008:121).

The next principle refers to the responsibility of keeping and guarding the knowledge inferred from stories (2008:43). Sometimes a story that has been shared is not meant to be translated. Nor is it meant to be shared outside of the source community. As Thomas King, a novelist of Cherokee descent, warns; *"once a story is told, it is loose in the world. So you have to be careful with the stories you tell. And you have to watch out for the stories that you are told"* (King 2005:10). One of my verdde firmly stated: *"Listen, this is just for you because you can understand it, but it's not for others [non-Sámi] to know"* (Sara 29.05.2018). Engaging with Indigenous storytelling should ideally motivate responsibility, not only to the established ethical guidelines of academia (e.g., Kalleberg 2006). It also urges Indigenous researchers to be accountable for their treatment of the stories they collect. Ensuring that how their acquired stories are processed, align with the established practices and expectations of their source communities as well as the verdde that gifted them.

As an empirical approach, storytelling also relies on reciprocity (Archibald 2008:49). Looking to the epistemological character of storytelling, much of what is meant by this principle may be linked to stories ability of passing on knowledge. Telling a story, to reiterate, is to enter it into a collective repository of knowledge. A listener contributes to this ongoing loop of transmittance by re-telling the story, which keeps it alive. As earlier stated, most Indigenous societies, the Sámi included, have traditionally not acknowledged claims to property rights of knowledge. Instead the expectation is that knowledge, once given, should filter back into the community. Of course, the expectancy of disseminating research, as is canonized in established ethical guidelines, already exists (Kalleberg 2006:36). Nonetheless, in an Indigenous society this expectancy is governed on all levels of society. Reciprocity, in other words, plays a regulatory role because it sets up an expectation that everything given or taken requires a return of some kind. This ensures that similar acts of continued generosity are performed, which in turn help maintain harmony and balance.

The next three principles—reverence, holism, and interrelatedness—though separate, are still connected to such a degree that it is best to discuss them as one. Beginning with the first, reverence may have multiple meanings. Even in the case of Indigenous storytelling, reverence may refer to a deference awarded the storyteller, the message of the story[29], or even to the epistemological function of stories in society as a whole. Though all three are equally important, I will focus on the latter implication. "*The communal principle of storytelling implies that a listener is or becomes a member of the community*" (Archibald 2008:26). Stories are the entrance into a holistic understanding of the world, expressing for instance, both spiritual beliefs and the interrelatedness of a Sámi world-in-relation. As such, stories are a patchwork of cultural meanings and practices, rich in both expression and quantity. However, if they are told and received without the elements of reverence, holism and interrelatedness, the likelihood of meanings and practices being ignored, or worse, silenced is almost certain.

This brings me to the last principle, synergy. Adding synergy into the seven principles of storytelling implies that there is a need for a union between storyteller and listener. Earlier I discussed synergy, although at that time I did not define it as such. I refer, of course, to my experience with Ása, who made me very aware that her story came alive only as it was told. This implies that storytelling, in a sense, is a performance that must be performed to or for someone (Archibald 2008:88). This means that the listener becomes an active participant, without whom the act of storytelling does not reach its purpose (Archibald 2008:33).

My assessment of these seven principles as Indigenous practice and method is thus concluded, but by no means is this a final review. The particularities of the principles change meaning dependent on the context in which they are applied. In that way, my reading of Archibald is that when Indigenous storytelling is the primary source of empirical ´data`, the researcher needs to be aware of and work within the boundaries of respect, responsibility, reciprocity, holism, interrelatedness and synergy—working out what those principles should really mean to oneself, and to one's study. To do otherwise is to disengage the stories from the communities they belong to, removing them from their "situatedness" and thus their interpretative framework. Though I have adapted Archibald's principles in my own work, they are still implemented according to the specificities of Sámi storytelling. In or-

---

29 Origin stories, or stories of Creation are examples of stories which are revered for their content.

der to do so, I have tried to determine a strategy for working in Sámi communities—a protocol, if you will. This protocol, for lack of a better word, motivated me to incorporate the seven principles of good storytelling during my next three interviews. More to the point perhaps, these three were a work-in-progress, the aim of which was to create an approach to storytelling that suited both my study and the verddes'. In the aftermath of these three interviews, I developed a systematic approach of three steps that was invariably used in every following interview.

THE THREE STEPS OF SÁMI STORYTELLING - A PROTOCOL.

After my first two interviews with Emmy and Stina, I had planned for another three, hereafter referred to as sessions of storytelling, to be conducted in January of 2018. The three potential verdde, Ása, Aile and Sunna, are all duojárs from the Norwegian side of the border, who make their living from their duodji. I had never met any of the three before my initial approach, but I had heard of them on account of their proficiency as duojárs. When I first made contact, I made sure to keep the conversation casual, discussing everything from recent duodji-projects, both theirs and mine, to more general subjects. These conversations were not part of the storytelling sessions but rather worked to build an amenable relation between us. In her work with life stories from Sámi women, the Sámi journalist Liv Inger Somby (2016:25) refer to this process as *negotiation time*, which I think suits here as well.

During initial contact, the verdde-to-be were also given a thorough description of my project and my aim. At this stage, it was also important for me to explain "*who I am doing this for*", "*why am I doing this,*" and "*what do I hope to achieve*". It was equally crucial that the potential verddes were given insurances that even if they consented at present time, they could withdraw their consent at any later date. This had the potential of creating difficulties later on, supposing that a verdde might negate their participation. I found it more important, however, that the verddes' retained their autonomy in whether or not to be a part of the project at all times.

Assuming they were responsive on first contact, a second conversation would follow a few days later wherein talk revolved around family and kin, as well as our communities. This second conversation was also initiated outside of the storytelling sessions, although it did provide me a frame of reference for each verdde that helped me when I embarked on the sessions themselves. The reason for such lengthy preparation is simple. By engaging in multiple and long conversations, both the verddes and I could establish and make clear our relations to place and people, in essence situating ourselves in a Sámi world-in-relation. Only after this fact, did we arrange for a place and date to do the actual sessions. We also decided on if the storytelling-sessions should be recorded on tape, or if simple notes would have to suffice. Choice of language was left up to the verddes; most spoke in either Norwegian or Swedish, but some wanted their sessions to happen in Sámi, albeit I could only accommodate them if the Sámi language in question was North Sámi. In either case, all my notes were done in English as that has been my general working language, which is why most quotes from the verddes are directly written in said language. This process is the first step.

The differences between the storytelling sessions in January, and the interview with Stina in December, was staggering. The extensive work we had done before the sessions of storytelling ensured that we were comfortable in each other's presence. Nonetheless, it was only when the third of the three, Sunna, reached out to me a few weeks later that I realized how different. In late January, Sunna called me because she had more questions about my project. She also wanted to put me in touch with another duojár because: "*I think he'd be really interesting for you to talk with. He's...really, as a duojár he's absolutely amazing...he's seen it all, you know, and he really understands what we [she and I] talked about*" (26.01.2018). In other words, the amount of time I spent preparing for the storytelling session, with both an initial and a follow-up conversation, allowed her to relate herself to my work. Instead of it being about the project, or about me as a researcher, it was about her relationship to both. I think that this really made a difference, because it embedded in Sunna a small sense of ownership to my project and to the knowledge produced therein.

Ása, the first of the three, confirms this assumption. In the closing of our first storytelling session, she ended our conversation by stating that: "*it's really important that this [our conversation] gets known, there is little information on us and our struggles*[30], *but this project is one way*

---

30 Here she was speaking of coastal Sámi communities, where assimilation hit hardest (Minde 2005).

we can change that" (07.01.2018). Again, instead of it being me as a researcher with my project, it had during our talk evolved into our project—jointly owned by us both. The first step of my protocol then relates to the *before* of a storytelling session. It is here that I lay the groundwork for my empirical approach; encouraging the creation of a safe space in which the storytelling-sessions may be enacted and inducing a pleasant ambience that help me develop a relationship to my verddes of both congeniality and equality, focused on respect and reciprocity.

The next step in my protocol is the storytelling itself. As opposed to what is recommended in a more traditional in-depth interview, there is no list of pre-arranged themes for discussions. Nor do I pre-pare any questions beforehand (Tjora 2012:104). Firstly, because the first step has already made the verdde aware of the focus in the project, my experience is that introducing themes may make the verdde feel constricted in their choice of topics. I would sooner encourage the verdde to set the pace as this allows them to feel in control, taking on the role of collaborator rather than participant. In hindsight, I see that this favour the Sámi way of storytelling as it *"tells a lot of sto-ries simultaneously—one digression leading into another one into another one and so on. But you can rest assured that a Sámi story always returns to its original point*" (Gaski 1997:199). To encourage this, instead of pre-arranged questions and lists I would always bring with me to the sessions whichever small duodji-project that I was working on at that time.[31] It might seem inconsequential, but by doing so, I was able to help ease the verddes' into a conversation with small talk of techniques and experiences within our practice of duodji. Of course, this element is only possible if your verddes are duojárs themselves or at least pro-ficient in the practice of duodji. Though alternatively, depending on the subject of a study, duodji may be substituted by other things and objects.[32] This, at least for me, was a major point of significance as it allowed my verddes to feel in control by giving them something safe to talk about. An added benefit was that it also levelled the power structures between us, equalizing us as verdde.

Another important element of this step was to not keep time. In

---

31 Other researchers that have interviewed duojárs remarked on the presence of duodji—i.e., in practice, seemed to relax the interviewees making it easier to speak with them (e.g., Guttorm 2001:142).

32 If, for instance, you were to speak on spirituality perhaps you could bring a personal object related to that subject.

Sámi there is a saying that "*áigi ii manna, dat boahtá*", or time doesn't pass us by, but comes our way. This goes to the Sámi holistic understanding that time cannot be forced, and that everything has its own pace, which we need to respect (Gaski 1997:167-78). The effect of this is very profound. For one, it detracts from a sense of formality. Additionally, it works to create a safe space. I once spoke with a verdde, Berit, for such a long time that her husband had to come get her and remind her that she had another engagement. This incident caused much laughter on our part, and indulgent humming from her husband. Despite having agreed beforehand on only one meeting, before leaving we made additional arrangements to continue my visit with her the next day. Having spent a night to think it over, she decided to share the stories of her ancestors the next day, stating that: "*it was so good yesterday, and I thought, ´here is one that understands. I can trust her with them [the stories]*" (30.05.2018). This incident also helped me realize the importance of maintaining lines of communications. This is also important in the next and final step.

The final step is the *after* of a session, and while it might not be as vigorous as the other two, it is no less important. Keeping the lines of communication open is not simply something to be said at the end of the second step. It is also something to live by. It encourages your verdde to reach out if they have questions, which is what Sunna did, or if they have additional information or new stories to tell as was the case with Berit. At its best, this step brings a nuanced depth to your research. When two of my verdde realized that I was writing an article on duodji and repatriation, using material related to this project, both asked to read and comment.[33] The end result was that I gained a much stronger position of authority in my claims and conclusions, while reassuring the two verdde of their value to my research.

What characterize all the steps in this protocol, is first and foremost, the seven principles of storytelling. But the steps are also adaptive, flexible enough to be adjusted dependant on verdde and situation. My insistence on this flexibility stems from two specific cases in which I had to adjust the protocol. The first time was when I visited Ájtte with duojárs to look at objects in the museum collection. There was no space to work on our own duodji projects, so step two instead focused on objects found at the museums similar to what Clifford

---

33 I had posted the title and an abstract on one of my social media accounts which they both follow.

describes in his work on museums as contact zones. The second time was during an event that I afterward defined as duodjebádji, and that I eventually developed into a specific method of storytelling but located in the practice of duodji.

DUODJEBÁDJI—CREATING SAFE SPACES.

A duodjebádji is no more or less than what the name implies, which is a workshop gathering people that are dedicated to the practice of duodji. It is based on the principle of relations; between duojárs, between objects, between generations and across borders of time and place. Contrary to the storytelling sessions described in step two of my protocol, a duodjebádji is thus founded on a collective session. There is no one-to-one interaction but rather an open conversation in which many are able to join. In such a way, a duodjebádji may be imagined *"dego gođus, laktit duodji ja muitalusat"* (Ilse 09.07.2018), as a 'weave connecting duodji with stories', created by multiple strands that come together within a specific frame. As a method then, duodjebádji relies on community, each voice acknowledged, but still united as one. It thus reflects the relational and collective feature so prominent within a Sámi onto-epistemology.

I first conceived of this method after having joined a gathering of duojárs in Báddådjo, on the Norwegian side of the border, during a revitalization-project that intended to revive the use of the Pite Sámi gappta. During our stay, in the midst of conversations on duodji, we also found the time to share our stories. It is far too easy to imagine such sharing made possible by the spoken word alone, but our practices were equally important in facilitating our exchange. Through our beading, sewing, and weaving, we worked entire days, sharing experiences and techniques—tricks of the trade, as it were—interspaced with personal stories told in between bouts of laughter as well as tears. As one of the duojárs explained it, we created a safe space *"where some strong stories of both joy and hurt [is] told and shared"* (12.04.2018).

In part, this sense of security is likely to do with the way that coming together in a social setting to practice duodji as a way of creating a safe space for difficult conversations to be had has deep roots in our communities (e.g., Harlin and Pieski 2020:115).

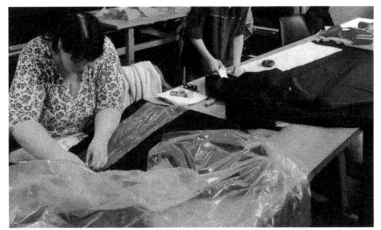

FIGURE 3-5 : I TOOK THIS PICTURE DURING A DUODJEBÁDJI THAT I HELPED HOST
IN THE SPRING OF 2018. THE THEME OF THE WORKSHOP WAS GÁKTIS. ALONGSIDE
A FEW OTHERS, I PARTICIPATED AS A MENTOR TO HELP THOSE THAT HAD NEVER
BEFORE MADE A GÁKTI WITH TECHNICAL SKILLS AND CULTURAL KNOWLEDGE.

During the 1970s and 1980s, for instance, there was a strong political
formation in Indigenous communities worldwide that sought Indigenous sovereignty, including, but not limited to rights to land and
waters, of languages, as well as cultural practices (Minde et al. 2008).
In Sápmi, said social movement was, among others, focused on the
practice of duodji as a means of countering assimilation and colonial narratives (Guttorm 2001a:30, 135-6). From my own childhood,
I remember tjidtjie bringing me with her to such gatherings where
she and other Sámi women would come together for their practice of
duodji.

To me it seemed almost magical, and I was excited every time that
I was allowed to join. Armed with whatever poor attempt at duodji
I was currently struggling with, I would sit at the feet of the women
and listen to their conversations. Delighting in the sense of secrecy
and of being initiated into another world I would listen to talk of customs, and of techniques, as well as stories about families and relations.
Sometimes humorous and "naughty" stories were told, though to be
frank, I did not always understand them, and other times one of the
ladies would yoik. I attended these gatherings, curious and excited, yet
completely unaware of the wealth of knowledge I was made party to.
What I do remember however, is the feeling of safety and of unity, and
the comfort I felt in simply listening. Incorporating these memories
with my experiences from Båddådjo, the method of duodjebádji as an
empirical approach was established.

FIGURE 3-6 DURING A DUODJEBÁDJI DEDICATED TO THE PRACTICE OF WEAVING,
A FEW OF THE PARTICIPANTS DECIDED TO GO OUT IN THE SUN AND WORK.

In a recent publication, the association between safe space and duodji workshop was reinforced. Initiated as part of a project with a focus on the restitution of Sámi heritage objects,[34] the associated workshops were defined as safe spaces where "*all participants would feel free to express themselves*" (Harlin and Pieski 2020:113). These particular workshops were termed *craftivism* as they were initiated to facilitate the re-appropriation of museum objects through crafting. [35] Despite the difference in initial aim, both the method of duodjebádji and craftivism as such have in common that they work to establish safe spaces that encourage participants to share their stories.

Viewed as such, a duodjebádji is similar, I think, to talking circles (also see Boine et al. 2014). As an empirical approach, the talking circle has deep roots in the cultural practices of several communities Indigenous to Turtle Island. Being that it is a method of problem solving, the talking circle is meant to encourage a levelling of participants. There is as such no hierarchy, and power in speaking is shared between the members of the circle. Within the circle, all are thus given an equal sense of "*worthiness, of being valued and listened to, and respected*" (Graveline 1998:176). This helps foster a solidary relation between participants (Graveline 2000:368), which speaks to the cultural locations of the talking circle (e.g., Graveline 2000:361) and the necessity of the participants establishing their self-in-relation; who participates, for what purpose, and from within which ontologies are

---

34 I define the concept of heritage object in giisá.
35 This process is similar to what I have elsewhere termed a symbolic repatriation and wherein duojárs become agents of repatriation through their crafting of objects whose templates are found in museums outside of their Sámi source communities (Finbog 2019).

they located? The talking circle, in other words, is characterized by a sense of belonging and being situated within specific ontologies, epistemologies and axiologies. Touching upon deeply complex issues and in reference to a need to deal with the trauma inflicted by colonialism, the American psychiatrist Laurence Kirmayer (1996), has argued for the necessity of developing specific spaces for a collective re-telling of past, as well as present or future; events that prioritize the collective memories of Indigenous communities. It is my belief that just as a talking circle arguably fills such a space, so too does the duodjebádji—only, it is specifically Sámi, and relates to Sámi practices, ontologies, epistemology, and axiology. This impression of the duodjebádji was only strengthened with time.

During the time period of 2018 and 2019, I organized and participated in numerous duodjebádjis. Most were located in Oslo, but I also travelled to Sámi communities both on the Norwegian and Swedish side of the border. The conduct was similar every time. To start, all participants were given space to present their current projects and if wanted, give a summary of the history behind its practice. In this way another aspect of the duodjebádjis was made clear. Within Indigenous methodologies, there is a heavy focus on elders. Elders are what one might term, *"repositories of cultural and philosophical knowledge and are transmitters of such information"* (Medicine 1987:142). It is not however, your age, but your knowledge and experience that grants you such esteemed designation (Archibald 2008:37, Gaski 2019:260).

Here, I would like to make a distinction. In a Sámi context, an elder might be considered an *eallilan*, which is someone that has lived for a long time and thus reached a certain age and competency. Thus, *"[e]allilan olbmot"* has acquired *"dovdet báikkálaš historjjá, doalahit di-htolágan eallinoainnu ja vuoiŋŋalaš- ja sosiála struktuvrraid"*, a sense of history of place, a specific worldview as well as knowledge of spiritual and social structures' (Pieski 2019:36, my own translation). Nonetheless, within the context of duodji rather than age it is the competency that reflect your role as an elder. To distinguish from the eallilan, I have thus chosen to use the term árbečeahpi[36], or keeper of inherited knowledge. In most of the duodjebádjis I convened, one or more of the participants were árbečeahpis. They could also be eallilan, but

---

36 Another term that might be used is čalbmi, which means 'eye', referencing someone that has reached the level of elder, or knowledge bearer that has developed a particular gaze (Spein 2004).

strictly speaking, their presence was always on account of their role as árbečeahpi. This was very much a conscious decision on my part, as I needed someone with authority within the practice of duodji to be present to appraise the knowledge and stories being shared. Discussions of patterns, both ornamental and of shape, the history of the specific practices and techniques, as well as the impact of the practices in our home communities followed. These conversations ranged from personal narratives[37] to collective memories. Just as I remembered from my childhood, these gatherings became a unifying experience. At the same time, they also offered the participants the opportunity to assert their sovereignty as Sámi, while also embracing Sámi ways of being, doing and knowing.

Both the method of storytelling session as well as duodjebádji put much at stake in terms of the equality of myself and the person I speak with. One verdde, that graciously agreed to be árbečeahpi at one duodjebádji, jokingly stated that "*now I am the teacher, and you are the student*" (Áile 19.09.2019). With humour, she thus articulated how our relation could no longer be defined as that of researcher and what traditional academia would define as "informant". In this, she also provides a good entry point into the next section in which I discuss my adaption of verddevuohtta to define the role of myself and the duojárs and other storytellers I worked with.

VERDDEVUOHTTA–AN EXPRESSION OF A WORLD-IN-RELATION.

Within Indigenous methodologies, or even within Indigenous communities, there is a sense of ill will associated with the word "*informant*". As Linda Tuhiwai Smith ([1999]2012:1) has noted; research is one of the "*dirtiest words in the Indigenous world's vocabulary*", and equally so, I would say, has the word "informant" been marked with a sense of antagonism. While writing this chapter, I was reminded of a story that I have often heard, albeit in slightly different variations:

> Studies of Sámi made by outsiders are often studies of "nameless people". We have been subjects for so long that research is tantamount to work for us; we are said to be among the most studied indigenous peoples on earth. A 1930's

---

37 This is actually very different from talking circles, where the focus is on stripping all speakers of their personal identities and eliminate all personal narratives (Graveline 2000:366).

anecdote describes a Skolt Sámi family as having five members: father, mother, two children, and researcher. But where the photographers and researchers are identified by name—underscoring their authority—the Sámi are usually listed as "Lapps from Enontekiö" or "Lapp types", who convey "traditional Lapp knowledge" or sing "traditional Lapp yoiks" (Lehtola 1996:61).

In recent years, both Indigenous communities and Indigenous researchers have heavily criticised the dominant and Western academia for not being aware of, or worse, not caring about the specific challenges that Indigenous communities have and still face in regards to developing their own methodologies and research paradigms (Battiste and Henderson 2000, Wilson 2008, Archibald 2008, Kuokkanen 2009, Kovach 2009, Smith [1999]2012). The decades of discourse have resulted in many of the Western countries developing ethical research guidelines that profess to be especially aware of Indigenous concerns and needs.[38] This is not the case in the Scandinavian countries, and so there are no commonly applied ethical guidelines for research within Sámi communities (Stordahl et al. 2015). Still, ethical concerns relating to research on and amongst Sámi communities have been raised (Kuokkanen 2008b)[39] and suggestions for some disciplines have consequently been offered (e.g., Guttorm 2008, Drugge 2016).

Centuries of being under the loop of others who have often served both colonial and nationalistic interests have nonetheless left the Sámi with a deep-seated suspicion towards researchers and academia in general (e.g., Hesjedal 2000).[40] Being studied, measured, categorized, and represented—whether dead or alive—has left its wounds. This is expressed in different ways. The saying "*mas amas diehtá maid oarri birrá*[41]" for instance, which asks how anyone can know the minds of others is simply one reflection of these wounds that have survived in Sámi languages (Gaski 2003:34). There is even a specific term, *guoktelussat*, that conceptualize the distrust many Sámi feel towards those

---

38 E.g., Guidelines for Ethical Research in Australian Indigenous Studies, https://aiatsis.gov.au/research/ethical-research/guidelines-ethical-research-australian-indigenous-studies.

39 There is, it should be said, an intention from the Norwegian Sámi Parliament that such guidelines are to be created, however that has yet to have happened.

40 My siessá often tells a funny story about this. My boaresáhčči had little need for museums, but once my siessá brought him with her to a local Noregian museum that was supposed to exhibit Sámi culture. While browsing through the exhibition, boaresáhčči suddenly exclaimed that "*here is my gápmagat—shoes—*". Sometime before he had set out a pair of old Sámi shoes, which had then gone missing. The story continues with boaresáhčči loudly proclaiming something along the lines of; "*didn't I say, what use are museums. Even old rubbish like this they exhibit*".

41 The direct translation is: "How would someone know what the squirrel eats".

wanting to do research on Sámi matters. Meaning 'two tongues', the deeper implication of the term is to withhold or even give false information when in the context of research (Nymo 2011:103). Nevertheless, I do think that *guoktelussat* could also be an expression of customary Sámi communication where it is expected that the listener understands *geažideami*, or context as the Sámi way seldom states things directly. Typically then, the storyteller encourages listeners to interact with the story, asking them to think and judge for themselves by not revealing everything, which would be neither proper nor polite (e.g., Jernsletten 2011:22).

Far too often, the meeting between researcher and Indigenous "informant", has reduced the latter to a means to an end. Exploited for their knowledge, but without ever getting anything in return (West 2018). I´m not trying to argue that this is always the case, but enough of those I have spoken with have indicated a sense of discomfort in the idea of becoming "informants". One of these is Asta, a woman who only learned of her Sámi ancestry in her 40s and whom I have spoken with on several occasions. On our fourth meeting, she nicely captured the sentiment I allude to above: "*In the beginning I was unsure if I should talk to you*". Nonetheless, after several meetings and conversations, she began to feel as if "*we´re [her and I] friends, [...] I could call you when next I´m in Oslo and we can just grab coffee—or something stronger—and chat, gossiping about this and that*" (Asta 21.02.2019). This concern is a common occurrence. Liv Inger Somby (2016:25) also seemed to have experienced this as one of her "informants" stated that "*[i]n lean gal vaikko geasa miehtat muitalit iežan birra, muhto go don nu čábbát ja vuohkkasit jearat, de luohttán ahte it bilit mu muitalusaid*", 'I would not tell my story to some random people. But you asked in a kind and in a beautiful way if I would like to share my story. This is about trust and now I trust you.'

The valuable lesson that one might take from Asta, and for that matter the latter example from Somby's fieldwork, is the very real struggle that many Sámi feel in the face of research. It details the absolute need for mutual trust to exist, which also reflects why it was so necessary for the protocol to have such an extended time of negotiation.

FIGURE 3-7 THE RELATIONSHIP BETWEEN MYSELF AND THE DUOJÁRS I HAVE SPO-
KEN WITH AND VISITED IS HARD TO DEFINE. BUT VERDDE IS PERHAPS WHAT TO
ME COMES CLOSEST AS BEING A GOOD DESCRIPTIVE CONCEPT. HER I AM TO-
GETHER WITH ONE DUOJÁR AND VERDDE WALKING HER DOG IN THE EARLY
MORNING WHILE WAITING FOR THE COFFEE TO GET READY. THIS WAS TAKEN
DURING A WEEKEND VISIT.

At the same time, by dedicating so much time and care to encourage the growth of a reciprocal relation, the depth of said connection
inevitably expand beyond the traditional academic designations of
"researcher" and "informant". In time, I found that these words no
longer suited and were consequently left behind as relationships were
fostered and cared for. But, if not "informant", in what capacity had
I spoken with Asta and the others? A quick glance at other scholars'
work with Indigenous source communities shows many and varied
terms implemented, co-author and collaborator, being some of the
examples. I recognize the validity of these terms as they allow for
Indigenous people and their knowledges to assume a central position.
And yet, I did not see them working on describing the relationship
between myself and my conversational partners. Additionally, I wanted to anchor our relation within a Sámi context as it was important
that the language and concepts I use to explain and/or analyse the
empirical material be Sámi in origin. Then, in late autumn of 2018, I
remembered the concept of *verddevuohtta*.

At its most basic, verddevuohtta simply means ´friendship`, but
the system of verdde, was, and still is, so much more. In times past,
the verdde-system was a relationship between Sámi communities, or
siidas, and people. Characterized by a spirit of give-and-take, the phi-

losophy of the gift as it were, verddevuohtta was a relationship based on the trading of goods and services without there ever being money exchanged. The different parties were *verdde* to each other, and there is ample evidence that the relationship was equal and suited the needs of all involved (Andresen 2001:80). Harald Eidheim, who was briefly introduced in bárket, has written about the system of verddevuohtta as a regulated collaboration between reindeer herders bringing their animals to the Summerland, or the grazing areas used in the summer season, and those living in it permanently (Eidheim 1971:27). Though such arrangements likely had local variables (Andersen 2005:38), the essence of verddevuohtta was similar in that it designates an ecosystem founded on the relational qualities of a Sámi ontology.

Though namely cited in research focused on the relationship between reindeer herders and permanent residents, verddevuohtta is also applicable in several contexts where collaboration or interconnection is significant. Today, the concept of verdde is used both in academic collaborations across the Arctic[42], in municipalities to promote collaboration[43], and even in arts and films[44]. In these cases, verdde is the meeting of equal partners that work together to achieve something. Verdde then, describes a relation of mutual respect, responsibility, reciprocity, and commitment. In this, it mirrors some of the principles that are crucial in Indigenous storytelling, and it was these similarities that first made me consider if my relationship with the duojárs I had spoken with might be defined as verddevuohtta and us—the duojárs and myself—as *verdde*. The times I have discussed the implementation of the term, those defined as such have unanimously agreed on it as fitting.

Relatively little has been written on contemporary expressions of verddevuohtta, at least academically. At a personal level, however, both my parents have spoken of verddevuohtta referencing stories from their parents and grandparents. My knowledge of the system mainly comes from said stories. I have also extensively consulted on the term and its use with áhčči. We spoke at some length, and he did eventually agree with me that verdde might be suitable. He also suggested that the relationship between duojárs and objects might similarly be defined within the spirit of verddevuohtta. Thus, instead of "informant"

---

42 https://samas.no/nb/node/840
43 http://www.kvanangen.kommune.no/verdde-prosjektet.163213.no.html
44 https://www.nordkappkino.no/article1306885.ece

this book applies the term verdde.

As for the specifics of my verddes, I would refer the reader to Appendix 1, where I list all my verdde. All are anonymous and have been given fictive names. I have conflicting feelings about anonymising my verddes as I very much agree with the Botswanan post-colonial scholar, Bagele Chilisa, that a story might lose validity if removed from context (Chilisa 2012:203-9, 223). From the point of view of a critical Sámi methodology, the Sámi worldview depends on relations, and by anonymizing my verddes' I am in essence disguising their relations which do precisely that. In a doctoral thesis from 2015, Sámi scholar Solveig Joks (2015:77) also argues against anonymising your Indigenous sources because doing so runs the risk of *"weakening"* their stories. Nonetheless, my primary concern has been to adhere to the wishes of my verddes. Because of the very personal and painful subjects we touch upon in this work, most have wanted to be anonymous. To honour their wishes and with the consent of those few that were not opposed to being named, I have thus chosen to anonymise everyone.

Having made clear and accounted for both the relation between myself and my verdde, I now turn to the next and last stage of my methodology, which concerns my own situatedness.

SELF-IN-RELATION

As I briefly discussed in giisá, my role as researcher has been heavily impacted by my own ethnic identity as Sámi and my own practice of duodji. In any circumstance where research is being done, it is important to follow the ethical regulations of professional conduct. One of these regulations concerns being self-reflexive (Thorbjørnsrud 2005:20). Reflecting on one's place in research is not unique to Indigenous researchers. Indeed, the act of situating self has during the last 30 or 40 decades taken point in developing a *"budding sense of collective historical subjectivity and agency"* (Haraway 1988:578), which has helped reveal that the world is experienced in different ways, and through different gazes. Professor of museum studies Eilean Hooper-Greenhill, conceptualize this need in her discussion of interpretative communities. These communities, she states, are best understood as *"common frameworks of intelligibility, interpretative repertoires, knowledge, and intellectual skills"* (Hooper-Greenhill 2007:79). What I earlier termed embodied truth is thus the foundation for any ontological, epistemological, and axiological concerns within the methodology of a research project.

However, being an Indigenous researcher also adds to your responsibility. Margaret Kovach (2009:110), when discussing how to situate yourself as an Indigenous scholar states that "*self-location means cultural identification*". To situate self in an Indigenous context is thus a matter of establishing one's place in the world-in-relation. Shawn Wilson has discussed a similar understanding, suggesting that Indigenous research is about *relational accountability*, and that as an Indigenous researcher, "*you are answering to all your relations when [...] doing research*" (2001:177). I interpret his meaning to be twofold: First, in the context of Indigenous research, relational accountability means to make visible one's experience of the world (Meyer 2003), including the relations to and within your community as well as the communities you work within. I take this to mean that as a researcher, I need to take responsibility for how I relate my research, but most importantly, I must be accountable to the people who have given me their stories, their time, and their trust. Although this, to some degree, has been covered in the seven principles of storytelling, responsibility, and respect. I would especially like to expand my understanding by returning to the discussion of ulddát.

The stories of ulddát that were told by my aahka were never meant to be a moral guide teaching me the do's and don'ts of everyday life. Instead, they were aimed at providing me with respect for and an awareness of my surroundings, acknowledging that as a people we are not alone in the universe and that our actions, no matter how seemingly inconsequential, have impact (Sara 2018:145). When doing research within an Indigenous paradigm, as a researcher you need to make similar considerations. Who does your research impact? In what way? Who gains from your research? What is your role as a researcher, and how do you fulfil that role? There are numerous ways in which I could answer these questions, and many would perhaps expect me to make a choice between the Sámi communities I belong to or the academic community that I have adopted for my own. I am not going to make that choice. As I have argued on several occasions, I believe in the value of creating bridges and combining the many ways of knowing rather than just one.

In that sense, I believe that the research presented in the following chapters may be of value to both Sámi communities as well as academia. Beginning with the latter, this book aims to discuss how the relation between museums and Sámi communities is expressed in the practice of duodji. As will be made quite evident in later chapters this relation shifts the core values that we might recognize from a standardized museological syllabus into ones that are founded on Indigenous and Sámi ways of being, doing and knowing. In this, I hope to articulate more clearly the needs of Indigenous and Sámi source communities and furthermore how museums may work to meet said needs. In this intent, I also demonstrate the value of my research in Sámi communities. As we continue to untangle the deep complexities of our colonial history and present, which are very much embedded in museological structures, it is important to keep in mind that we are inevitably hoping to initiate processes of both decolonization and Indigenization. My hope is that the works and research presented in the pages of this book benefit those that are on that journey and working to make such initiatives happen. This is the first aspect of relational accountability.

The second meaning to relational accountability concerns, as I see it the act of situating one's knowledge, or to reveal ones embodied truth. As Donna Haraway, arguably one of our times greatest thinkers, puts it, situating your knowledge is reflecting or thinking about your thinking when doing scholarly research. This, she further states, is a way to position oneself within a pool of knowledge; thus becoming aware of your own interpretative frame (Haraway 1988). In the context of any Indigenous culture, meaning, content and use is gained through an intimate interconnection to a larger whole—or, to rely on Hooper-Greenhills concept, through an interpretive community. Only in reference to that whole, are they—meaning, content, and use—explicable. As an Indigenous researcher working within an Indigenous research paradigm, there will naturally be an innate knowledge of the Indigenous ontology, epistemology, and axiology at work. This knowledge might be shared with your Indigenous community, but not necessarily your academic one. This is why it is important to acknowledge the existence of *silent knowledge*, or knowledge that is imminent yet implicit (Thorbjørnsrud 2005:20). There, but not easily apparent or verbalized.

Having silent knowledge is in many ways a double-edged sword.

To explain my meaning, I will discuss the *insider* position. To be an insider implies that a researcher shares a similar background, or in this case ethnicity, with the group they are studying. In this context, having silent knowledge means that, as a researcher you run the risks of not understanding that something that is obvious to yourself, might not be so to someone outside of your community. I experienced this when presenting a paper on storytelling for a class on methodology. Whereas I implicitly understood the relevance of stories in a Sámi context, those reading my paper, all of whom were non-Indigenous, did not. Thus, when I argued that as researchers our jobs were to safeguard stories and return ownership after the conclusion of a study, some vehemently disagreed stating that stories once given, left the ownership of the storytellers becoming the intellectual property of the researcher. Quite contrary, in other words, to what was expressed in the quote I shared earlier stating that *"[l] uohtán ahte it bilit mu muit-alusaid"*, I trust that you do not destroy my stories. In this articulation lies the implicit understanding of stories not leaving the ownership of their narrator. As an Indigenous researcher, I am very much aware of said fact, and have correspondingly adapted my practice to suit. Here then, is evidenced the necessity of making one's relations, by way of interpretive community, visible.

Another drawback[45] to the insider position is that studies of ethnicity have tended to define the insider position as those that share an ethnic identity with participants, which in turn have worked to homogenize ethnic groups, consequently essentializing identities treating them as distinct and static categories. Writings by academics of insider status, however, draws attention to the multitudes of identities within one singular ethnic group, referencing different life experiences and context in the process (Amit-Talai 2000). I faced an example of this when I, referencing research on Sámi ethnicity (e.g., Bjørklund 2000:32), reiterated the assumption that Sámi language was a primary marker of Sámi ethnicity. The verdde I was in conversation with at that time took objection to such a claim, stating that *"language did not always survive [during assimilation], but it does not make us any less*

---

45 A third potential drawback is the danger of closeness to a research project induce a lack of perspective or an emotive investment that blurs the line between fact and wishful thinking (Turnbull 2010). I don't think though, that this is dependant on ethnicity alone. It may in fact prove true for any project regardless of subject matter (Shelton 2009). Furthermore, I think that by entering into a research project fully aware of the issues I have just described, significantly lessens the danger of it happening, or having to big of an effect.

Sámi. Our markers of identity are maybe different, but they are equal to language and just as important" (Ása 07.01.2018). A notion that is felt by many who, despite being Sámi and proud of their heritage, have not mastered the language (Hansen 2015:81).

Still, the insider position is not all bad. As,

> […] [t]he experiences, which people (including researchers) have amassed, constitute their horizons of understanding. It is easier to understand people with the same language, culture and environmental background and it is easier to communicate and carry out research in what is expected to be one's own cultural complex (Hætta 1996:15).

As important as it is to critically reflect on the aspects of having an insider position, I need to consider the positive aspects. In her work on Sámi women's life stories, Liv Inger Somby (Somby 2016:34) reflects on how learning the cultural codes of a people may take years. Being an insider means that many of these codes are already at play, and you may better recognize processes, practices, and concepts. This is what has allowed me to centre myself and my work in a critical Indigenous methodology and be able to articulate what that means. To some degree, by defining my methodology—ontology, epistemology, and axiology—I have thus already positioned myself within my research, and stating what my embodied truth is. Although this positioning bases itself on a general level, and less on a personal one, it is actually quite appropriate within an Indigenous and Sámi way of thinking. After all, though I do my research as an individual, my context is collective and shaped by many.

It is with these considerations in mind that I turn my discussion now to the theoretical framework of my work.

CHAPTER 4: RIESSAT

PUTTING ONE'S EAR TO THE GROUND

THEORIZING DUODJI AS THE CORE OF A SÁMI INDIGENOUS KNOWLEDGE SYSTEM.

THE SIEIDI AT ÁJTTE—A PROLOGUE

At Sieberboullda in the Sámi community of Sirges, located to Northern Lapland on the Swedish side of the border, there used to be a sieidi—a sacred stone. In the old days, the sieidis where places and objects of worship; stones, or places in nature of a peculiar formation. Sieidis are sites for giving thanks, honouring the bounties of the land, or waters, and giving back to the spirits and beings that guards specific activities or spheres of life. Giving thanks often involved an offering to the sieidi in order to cultivate good relations with the spirit world, ensuring a 'maintenance of life', or birgejupmi which means ways to manage and have a good life, socially, economically, spiritually and in respect to health.

Usually, a sieidi was shared between the surrounding families or siidas—communities. In some cases, a sieidi was strictly shared by specific families, and people of specific kinship. The sieidi at Sieberboullda is of the latter variety. It was removed from its location in 1900 by two young Swedish nobles who had arranged for a guided tour of the mountains in Northern Sweden. Their guide was Sámi, and he knew well where to find the sieidi. The official story goes that the nobles paid the guide to help them remove the sieidi and bring it with them when they left Sápmi to return to Stockholm (Manker 1957:170). The Sámi from the community of Sirges, tells it differently. They claim that the Sámi guide was plied with alcohol to reveal the location of the sieidi. After he sobered up, he was forced to help with the removal, although handsomely paid (Ahlström 12.11.2018).

Regardless of which story that is told, the undeniable fact is that the sieidi, after its removal, was brought south. First to a private collection. Later, in 1905, the sieidi was donated to the Ethnographic Museum in Stockholm, until deposited in Nordiska Museet. Here the sieidi remained until it was finally repatriated to Ájtte in the early years of the millennium

I first saw the sieidi during a visit to Ájtte. I was initially there to meet with some of my verdde. Beforehand, I had also arranged with Eva Ahlström, who is the conservator of the museum's collection, to spend some time at the museum. I was fortunate enough to have the opportunity of following Eva in her daily work. I also spent some time in the various exhibitions at the museum, and I walked through one of them, "Drum-Time", accompanied by Eva and one of the interns at the museum. This exhibition is about the old Sámi religion, and it exhibits sacred objects such as the drums of the noaidi, the spiritual leaders, as well as the sieidi from Sieberboullda. As I passed it, I noticed that it was surrounded by small coins. I asked Eva of their function, thinking, naturally, that they were intentionally placed with the sieidi to stage the ritual context of the stone.

In the old ways of giving offerings, or gifts, it was customary for a reindeer to be taken to the sieidi to be slaughtered, its meat boiled and then eaten. The bones of the slaughtered animal, and sometimes its fat, would be left by the sieidi. Regularly the blood of the animal would also be used to anoint the sieidi. In other siidas, where the primary livelihood was not reindeer herding, other animals was used. Communities located alongside the coastline for instance, would use fish and fish oil. Today the sieidis are honoured in different ways. Most often, coins are left, as is the case at Ájtte. At other sieidis that are still in their original location, the offerings come in a much broader range; small bones, cups with drinks, and other tokens may be found. Sometimes children will leave their deeply loved toys, or small pieces of chocolate and candy, sacrificing what to them holds most value.

Eva was quick to dissuade me from thinking that the coins surrounding the sieidi at Ájtte had been placed there intentionally. "Oh those," she laughed. "No, no. It's not us who place them [the coins] there"(Ahlström 12.11.2018). Further conversation revealed that from time to time, people from Sirges would visit the museum to make gifts to the sieidi.[1]

---

1   This surprised me somewhat as sieidis are made holy by their placement in specific places. Removing them should disrupt the connections of the sieidi to place, spirits, and communities. Talking about sieidis with some verdde, also gave me this impression (Anna 23.04.2020). This was also the case when the sieidi from Gárgovárri, in Guovdageaidnu, that had been removed to the Ethnographic Museum in Oslo in 1906, was repatriated and returned to the same spot in 1999.

INTRODUCTION

Within the scope of academia, a theory is presumed to be a body of knowledge; the generalized thinking about a phenomenon that has been formalized into a set of principles. If, in ruvdet, I described the ways, methods and perspectives by which I examine the world, then this chapter focuses on how I think through my findings, as well as the expression of concepts and articulations to help me make sense of what I have seen and experienced during my research. The following is an attempt to visualize said approach by introducing the analytical framework for my book—the boundary, as it were, in which I assemble and discuss my empirical material.

There is no clear-cut path before me, no easy way for *"dan ođđa bálga, mun guoran"*, this new path to trace, as Niko Valkeapää sings it. For those not well-versed in the intricacies of Indigenous ways of being, doing and knowing, the question of how to theorize Indigenous knowledge[s] might seem superfluous. As a deeper grounding in critical Indigenous methodology is seeded, however, the means of theorizing Indigenous knowledge[s] slowly reveal themselves to be as exhausting as they are complex (Rosiek, Snyder, and Pratt 2020, Virtanen and Seurujärvi-Kari 2019). More to the point, the foundation for theorizing Indigenous knowledges is divulged in the methodology. Though I think this to be almost self-evident, I fully recognize that for those that are not themselves centred in a critical Indigenous methodology, it might not be quite as apparent that theory is born from methodology.

In large, this is due to the *epistemic ignorance* discussed in giisá. Enforced, in part, by the epistemicide that followed in the wake of colonialism and expanded both Western ideologies as well as the attached knowledge systems[2] (Goduka 1999), an epistemic ignorance continues to exclude epistemic and intellectual traditions outside of Western

---

2   It would make sense to talk about a process of othering of Indigenous knowledge systems (Smith [1999]2012:52, Kuokkanen 2009:6). To be understood, *othering* needs to be properly framed: In 1807 Georg W. F. Hegel published "Phenomenology of Spirit" where he wrote about the binary opposition of master and slave. The master-slave dialectic occures when one person (the master) through meeting another (the slave) defines his or her consciousness, but in doing so the Master also sublates the slave thus impressing his or her will on the Other (Hegel [1807]1977:179). As such the reality of oneself as self-conscious is achived only through the recognition and/or creation of a contrasting "Other". This is, broadly put, a process of "Othering". Othering Indigenous knowledge systems created a view in which Western scientific knowledge was considered the norm and thus far superior to any Other knowledge system (Buijs 2016:539). Eventually Western knowledge was superposed on local and traditional knowledge systems (Smith [1999]2012:67)

thought from academic practices and discourses.[3] If we lift this veil of ignorance, however, what notion of theory would emerge? Although it is not my intent to advocate one answer, in particular, I do believe the first step is to traverse the cartesian dualism evidenced by the separation of method and theory (Goduka 1999:27), or what Indigenous philosopher Anne Waters (2004:97) terms a *"dualist binary ontology"*. Within most Indigenous cultures, the theory has rarely been differentiated from practice (Gaski 2019:260). This is certainly the case in a Sámi context (Guttorm, Kantonen, and Kramvig, 2019:153), where the concept of árbediehtu, for instance, emphasizes theory (diehtu) as embedded in practice (máhttu), thus asserting that theories derive their validation from methods. To be fair, theory is almost always embedded in empirical studies anyway; forming *"sets of questions, proclivities and sensibilities, in the context of empirical work"* (Law 2012:225).

Still, I believe that to encourage the Indigenization of research, and by extension, prioritizing Indigenous ideas and ways of being, one needs to engage critically with the concepts and ideas that draw from Indigenous experiences and perspectives. This includes, but is not limited to, a view on theory as something that is not distinguished from methods but rather shaped by them. As such, the following chapter theorize different ways of enacting storytelling with duodji as the primary focus; attempting, as it were, to demonstrate how method and theory are always interdependent.

TO RIESSAT—MAPPING MY STRUCTURE

Following the example of previous chapters, I envision the coming discussions on theory by way of the imagery provided by duodji. Specifically, I structure my discussion using the practice of *riessat* as a metaphor. To riessat, as seen in the figure 4-1 is a practice of fringing where multiple silk threads are knotted together in intricate patterns to form a whole.

In the past, to riessat held qualities of storytelling, and the way in which one shaped the knots and the patterns could convey entreaties of protection, messages, or stories (Guttorm 2013a:913).

---

3   I have also heard epistemic ignorance being referred to as an epistemic violence, which enable "ways of knowing - and the disabling of others" that legitimize or endorse the practices of dominance and subjugation (Harlin and Pieski 2020:143). 'Epistemic injustice' is also used in literature, but more to refer to the harm that Indigenous peoples suffer on account of "domestic" justice systems, and whereby foreign values are made the norm they are judged by (Tsosie 2012:1136)

FIGURE 4-1 TO RIESSAT IS OFTEN SEEN AS A PURELY DECORATIVE ELEMENT. IT IS HOWEVER, DEEPLY EMBEDDED IN A SYSTEM OF KNOWLEDGE; ITS ARRAY OF ORNAMENTAL DESIGNS AND THE PARTICULARITIES OF KNOTS AN ACT OF STORY-TELLING, CONVEYING MESSAGES AND STORIES FOR THE INITIATED TO READ AND LISTEN TO. THIS PICTURE WAS SHARED ON MARIT HELENE EIRA'S INSTAGRAM AC-COUNT, @MARHEIRA

Today, this aspect of the practice is no longer as common, and to ries-sat is, for the most part, used decoratively to make *liidni*, the silken shawls that are often used with the gákti.[4] In my imaginary imple-mentation of the practice however, I focus on the ability of storytelling present within the system of knots. In that sense, just as the multiple threads are moved between knots to tell a story, so too are multiple concepts of duodji brought to the front and united into a theoretical framework, by which I analyse and understand the stories that I have collected from verdde, from practices, and from objects.

Before I can begin my riessat, I feel the need to lay down some important points of clarification. First off, while duodji has been dis-cussed as a possible theoretical frame of reference in other works (e.g., Guttorm 2013b, 2014, Mellegård and Boonstra 2020), there is still no established or fixed framework. I am not really surprised as duodji is a collective practice, and as such it is acted upon and decided collectively within communities and between duojárs (Guttorm 2007). No doubt there is an individual element to one's practice, but there are still spe-cific regulations in place to protect it as a collective heritage (Magga 2014). As such, even if I analyse, construct, and critique on the basis

---

4   The almost co-dependent relation between riessat and liidni is preserved in the combination of the two in the word liidneriessan.

of my own practice of duodji, my duddjot as it were, I still frame my discussion within the collective metaphors, ideas and languages that are embedded in the practice. This imposes certain demands; meaning that, in the coming I present duodji as a conversation between relations—to land, surroundings, other non-human beings, and cosmology as well as the verdde cited in the chapter, many of which have been kind enough to read and comment. It is perhaps, not the most conventional way of presenting a theoretic framework, but it is one that adheres, I think, to Sámi ways of being, doing and knowing.

This brings me to the next point of clarification. In the writing of books, one might ordinarily expect to see a definitive structure whereby chapters are clearly delineated. This has proven nigh on impossible with this work where the theory is concerned. The concepts and articulations that I present in the following, are not only developed within the present chapter. Their evolvement continues throughout, informed by opinions and experiences introduced in conversations. The chapter should thus be viewed not as a complete framework, but rather the starting point that introduces the idea of duodji as theory.

The third point of clarification I should address concerns my use of language. When theorizing Indigenous knowledge[s], it is *"crucial to use Indigenous concepts"* (Virtanen and Seurujärvi-Kari 2019:10). Here, I find myself to be in complete agreement with Kristin Jernsletten (2011:8), when she states that one cannot simply transfer and translate a frame from a Western school of thought, expecting it to be instantly applicable to a Sámi, or for that matter, any Indigenous context, or indeed, the reverse. In the last few decades, a wealth of linguistic and anthropological literature has highlighted the fact that the language one learns has a major impact on how one thinks (Bloom and Keil 2001, Boroditsky 2018). Our language is not only,

> [...] the language of the heart' to those for whom it is a mother tongue, but it is also one of the most developed languages in the world when it comes to describing arctic nature and conditions of life in the North. Sámi descriptions of landscape can function as maps, in which are incorporated topography, geography and information as to which routes are best to take (Gaski 1997:13).

The same applies, as I see it, to duodji, where descriptions of specific practices and techniques also function as a map, in which context, skills, and knowledge is incorporated. Any attempt at translating these concepts might make the map, if not worthless, then at least difficult to use. As one duojár remarked when asked about the language of her practice,

> [...] many things in duodji doesn´t really have a counterpart in Norwegian or Swedish cultures. Look at ´ruvdet`! When I say to you that I will [use] rudvet to finish this belt, I know exactly what that means, and so do you. If I had to explain with many words what I was doing, maybe I would be confused, and you too (29.05.2018).

Consequently, although I recognize that there is a need to make Sámi words and expressions available to a broader audience, I will, for the most part, work within the context of Sámi language. As such, while I give the corresponding, in lack of a better term, names in English, I do focus on discussing the concepts as is, in a Sámi terminology. I think this is important, because even outside of Indigenous methodologies, Indigenous knowledge[s] deserve their interrelated languages to be incorporated. If not, as I already pointed out in the previous chapter, we are really looking at a process of assimilation. Having laid my concerns, hopefully, to rest, I am content to begin laying out the threads, or concepts that I will riessat.

I begin to riessat with threads that are born from a question I was asked when a colleague read some of my methodological reflections, on whether or not I was thinking of implementing Actor-Network Theory (hence ANT) as my theoretical framework. I understand why the question was asked as ANT is meant to facilitate a study of relations that far expand those concerned with individual humans alone (Latour 2005). Considering that the methodology of this work is framed in a Sámi world-in-relation, it seems a logical conclusion. I had already considered ANT at that point in time and decided against its implementation. Still, the question is valid, and I should anticipate it being asked by others as well. As such, the first knot discuss ANT and why it is not at the centre of my work.

The second knot is built on the multiple threads from the concepts and articulations of duodji that I have considered relevant. To be clear, there are many more, but I have singled out those that have proven relevant to analyse conversations with my verdde, or that verdde has brought up themselves. The first thread, or concept, is gulahallat, which deals with the necessity and ability to listen to all voices that are present within the practice of duodji. In this I lay the foundation for understanding the following concepts, not only as determined individually but defined by a collective.

The next thread I will discuss relates to the aesthetics of duodji, the vuogas, by way of *dåajmijes vuekie*. The term is difficult to translate, but *vuekie* relates to customs or traditions. Dåajmijes, on the other hand, is slightly more difficult. Directly translated, it means courtly, but the essence of the word expands such meaning. The correlation of the concept to duodji, however, is one that is made explicit by looking at beauty from a Sámi perspective; what decides beauty, and how is this impacted by the practice of duodji?

From dåajmijes vuekie, I transition into the next concept, which is surroundings or biras. In this thread, I reflect on how Indigenous knowledge[s] arise from landscapes, and how places conversely become repositories of information about relationships and stories; connected to everyday practices, livelihood, and management—or birgejupmi.

Knowledge[s] contained in and of the landscape, is transferred in a continuous process of learning through generations and time. This leads to a new thread focused on how knowledge[s] is/are inherited and the concept of árbediehtu. This thread naturally transitions into another one, that of sámáidahttin, or samification, where I discuss whether there are specific codes—meanings, values, and norms—attached to duodji that are activated when learning the practice.

The third knot that I will riessat, deals with the museological context of my theory. It might not exclusively deal with Sámi concepts of duodji, but it is important nonetheless because it introduce the specific context of dealing with duodji, not as a practice and in relation to function, but to its museification as a result of being entered into museum collections. Here, rematriation, as in the return of objects and the associated practices, knowledges, and protocols, becomes an important concept.

To be more specific, rematriation is a concept that was introduced in the 1990s to discuss what happens after repatriation (Newcomb 1995). It is meant to convey that restoration to Indigenous communities far exceeds the simple return of material culture, which is the implication in repatriation. Rematriation, on the other hand, means returning to "*eana eannážan, to our mother earth*", restoring the balance of relations within our worlds (Harlin and Pieski 2020:127).

In this discussion, I have chosen to explore the gákti, as an expression of the materiality of duodji. Exploring dimensions of knowledge, interrelatedness, and spiritual belief, the gákti, which is the Sámi customary clothing and, some would argue, regalia, is approached as an extension of duodji and its many dimensions is extrapolated to underscore the difference in duodji within its source community and within museums. With this, I conclude my practice of riessat. Before I can do so, however, I begin with looking into the theorizing of relations within a Western context.

THEORIZING RELATIONS—A NORMATIVE APPROACH.

During the early days of museums, in the 18th and 19th centuries, the philosophy of Enlightenment encouraged a preoccupation with material culture, objects and things (Bennett 2004:31, Henare 2005:64-6). Nonetheless, with the advance of sociological theories that favoured structure, symbolism, and semiotics as the mechanisms of ordering the material world, objects and things soon fell out of fashion. For a long time, it was thus commonplace to think of meaning, values, and ideas about the material world as dependent on human and subjective agency alone, relegating all other life forms and materialities to a secondary and much inferior position (Gosden and Marshall 1999, Hooper Greenhill 2000, Lyons 2002, Nordin and Ojala 2018).

In the latter decades of the 20th century, however, the ´material turn`[5] refocused attention on the material world, and more to the point on materiality, which broadly speaking conceptualize the implication of the physical properties of matter in the making of meanings about the social world or the sociality of materialities; what objects and things do, rather than their possible symbolism and semiotics as interpreted by man (Latour 2005, Dudley 2010).[6] In accordance with this interpretation, the material world emerge from its entanglement with sociality and within social fields of multiple actors without distinctions between human and non-human origins (Damsholt, Mord-

---

5 Coined with the argument of post-modernist scholars that the human and non-human dichotomy is misleading, and that social studies should to a larger degree consider the social driving forces of the material world. Gadamer, Merleau-Ponty and Sartre were some important voices in this argument.
6 The referenced 'material turn' has in literature been given multiple names, such as 'new materialism', (Barad 2007), 'new feminist materialism' (Hekman and Alaimo 2008), and 'new empiricism' (Ticineto Clough 2009).

horst, and Gert Simonsen 2009, Geismar 2009).[7]

Implicit in the scope of sociomaterial dynamics—what might be referred to as the sociality of materialities— some scholars believe that movements between social relations, materiality and practice accounts for assemblages of meaning (Fenwick 2010), which assumes that within the networks of relations that constitute the world, specific practices create specific material expressions, or objects and things (e.g., Silliman 2001:195, Fenwick 2010:105, also see Olli and Harliin 2014, Varutti 2015). Engaging with the social dimensions of materiality, would thus imply that objects and things feature heavily in sociomaterial processes from which meaning about the world is construed (Latour 2005). Materiality as a concept, at least to my understanding, as such stimulate a view on the material world in which meaning, values, and norms do not precede, but rather emerges from a reciprocal and relational association with other things; traversing a never-ending process *in which people make objects and objects make people*" (Geismar 2011:210).

Increasingly then, it is assumed that understanding how identities are formed runs parallel to understanding the social significance of the material world (Silliman 2009, Pezzarossi 2014, Varutti 2015). This view has some serious implications for how agency is understood. That is to say, at its crux, even if *"purposeful action and intentionality may not be properties of objects [...] they are not properties of humans either"* (Latour 1999:192). The French sociologist and anthropologist Bruno Latour is renowned for his critique of the disregard of objects and materiality. Challenging how we understand agency in social studies, he argues that we must *"turn away from an exclusive concern with social [human] relations and weave them into a fabric that includes non–human actants"* (Latour 1990:102). This perspective is at the core of his work with ANT; in which everything in the social and natural world exists in constantly shifting networks of relationships—where no one thing is more or less than any other, and where everything has the capacity of agency (Latour 2005). This capacity, he continues, is embedded in actors who take the shape that they do by virtue of their relations to one another. At first glance, ANT seems remarkably similar to how a Sámi world-in-relation could be perceived, which in turn adds to the

---

7   Though there are ways of distinguishing actors, but this is not the result of a presupposed hierarchy but rather emerge from the actors movement in the network of relations (Latour 2005).

presumed relevance of ANT in this study.

Still, I question whether it is possible that the interrelatedness of Latour´s actors reflects the interrelatedness that make up the Sámi world-in-relation. I don't have a definitive answer, and while I do think the relational quality of Latour´s actants extend their original frame of reference[8], I am unsure whether the perspectives found in ANT make space for all the ontologies that would be present in a Sámi world-in-relation (Cordella and Shaik 2006).

In a recent article, a *"pervasive context of settler colonialism"*, what I earlier referred to as the dualist binary ontology of Western research, is made, in part at least, responsible for disregarding the subjectivity of non-human beings in a world perceived to be sociomaterial (Rosiek, Snyder, and Pratt 2020:3). The idea that agency extends not only to humans and objects but also non-human beings is a quality that manifests in most Indigenous perspectives on reality. There are, of course, non-Indigenous scholars that offer options more in line with an Indigenous view on materiality and agency. In this, the British social anthropologist Alfred Gell comes to mind. Gell's (1998) work provides a way of inferring efficacy on materiality without ascribing life force, or personhood, onto objects. Similar, I believe, to what the Istanbul-born social anthropologist, Yael Navaro-Yashin, terms as affect (2012).[9] Still, to quote another professor of anthropology, Heidy Geismar (2011:213), Gell's *"[o]bjects may have an impact (like falling meteorites), but in order to have agency, they must be entangled within social relations and indeed within our own humanity"*.

As the story I earlier shared of my aahka and her belief in ulddát and sajveh highlight, in a Sámi world-in-relation, the interrelatedness of the world does not depend on humans taking part. Other beings have their own ontological reality that exists and impacts the ontological reality of our own world. In the anthology, *A World of Many Worlds*, the editors Marisol de la Cadena and Mario Blaser (2018:4), offer an alternative way of defining such beings as *"other-than-human persons"*, citing both animals and landscapes to have a subjective will equal to that of humans, and more importantly for the present discussion, regardless of humans. The many ontologies present in a Sámi

---

8   This is evidenced for instance, in the work of Annemarie Mol's (1999) on 'ontological politics', in which she argues that since realities change with practices, so too does ontologies.

9   Similar to Gell, Navaro-Yashin (2012:14) believes that *"[o]bjects and a material environment can generate affect, then, but only as they get entangled in forms of human mediation"*

world-in-relation is, in other words, difficult to grasp when working within the boundaries of ANT. To conclude then, rather than importing a framework, which I would need to reshape, I have chosen duodji as a theoretical frame because it already exists within a Sámi world-in-relation and thus it does not need to be adapted, simply introduced. Which is what I do next.

DUODJI AS 'THE SPIRIT OF EVERYTHING'.

I once asked someone how she would explain duodji to someone unfamiliar with the concept. Her answer was that "*[d]uodji is the spirit of everything I am, and everything they [ancestors] were*" (Ása 07.01.2018). Move long enough within circles of duodji, you soon realize that this is not at all a unique perspective. "*Duodji is where I find my past, [...] and those before me [...] which also brings me to my future*" is another way to explain it (Mia 08.11.2017). Another possibility is to articulate duodji as "*everything they [ancestors] were*" (Sanna 02.07.2018). The multiple renderings of reciprocal relations implicated in a Sámi world-in-relation that these quotes, in different ways, bring to mind, are perhaps difficult to envision. Even those of us that are born within these relations, at times, do not know how to perceive them all, and much less point them out for others to see. The sieidi at Ájtte exemplifies this.

As it appears in both local stories, practices, acquisition reports and research papers, the sieidi is constituted in numerous circumstances. It moves from a Sámi ontological, spiritual and relational context to the complexities of colonial narratives, until finally, it settles in the multiple dimensions of ´cultural heritage` [10] and museology (e.g., Mathisen 2009). Entangled within these different narrations, the meanings and values of the sieidi change in an ongoing process of material movement, which emerge, I would say, as an extension of the relations embedded in the stone. What this shows, is that any attempt at interpreting the social significance of the sieidi, rests on its relations becoming visible, not only by word of mouth, but also through practices and materiality.

---

10 Here I am working with the definition offered by the International Cultural Tourism Committee, or ICO-MOS, that states cultural heritage as an expression of the ways of living developed by community and passed on from generation to generation, including customs, practices, places, objects, artistic expressions and values (ICOMOS 2002).

134

In many Indigenous societies, aesthetics are often considered a form of storytelling, or as I briefly discussed in ruvdet, even a way of documentation (Virtanen and Seurujärvi-Kari 2019:2, Guttorm, Kantonen, and Kramvig 2019:153). The practices, stories, and material expressions they produce, often hold sophisticated systems of knowledge that guide how the practitioners move through and relate to the world; how they learn, and how they are taught, the ways in which they experience their world, and how they pass down these experiences to future generations, are all vital parts of said system (e.g., Smith. 2019). The Sámi practice of duodji is no different. In a dissertation on the South Sámi language of symbols, or *tjaalehtjimmie*, the South Sámi scholar and duojár Maja Dunfjeld (2006:16-7) states that duodji is a performance of the body and that its practice (duddjot) is a way of telling a performative story (e.g., Aagård-Dunfjeld 1991:82). The same holds true for the prepared products (e.g., Guttorm 2001:15). Like the practice then, the objects of duodji are also presumed to carry stories (Spein 2019, e.g., Falck 2018:82).[11] As I mentioned in giisá however, far too often, duodji has been relegated to craft and nothing more. Of course, duodji is a craft, but I believe it is also a knowledge system; an epistemology expressed through a relational practice that considers, and is also made up of, knowledge, place, spiritual beliefs, other people, and beings. To articulate all of these is not always straightforward.

Within a Sámi context, stories are created through our experience, our practices, and our communal memories. In my duodji, for instance, I find, not only my stories but also the stories of those that came before and those that will follow. Once, during a visit to my father's home community, his sister—my siessá[12]—who is a duojár, and I went to a museum in a nearby city.

---

11 In many works on Indigenous perspectives and practices, objects are often elevated from mere material into entities themselves; possessing awareness and thus capable of responding to human action, and with whom contemporary people feel kinship (e.g., Clifford 1997, 2004). When conceived of as such, objects are believed to be elders (e.g., Fienup-Riordan 2010:4), part of a living culture within which is the stories and knowledge of said culture (Clavir 2002:xx). In an Indigenous context, elders are approached for their knowledge and wisdom (Jernsletten 2011:13), instructors in the management of values, laws, morals, world-views and stories. Amongst my verdde, many of the duojárs have discussed perspectives on objects that are much the same, citing them as being their "*guides*" (Áile 05.01.2018) or even "*teachers*" (Jane 30.03.2019).

12 This siessá should not be confused with my siessá as mentioned in the chapter on methodology. In North Sámi terminology there are only the word siessá for father's sister, whereas mother's sister is distinguished as *muottá* for the younger and *goaski* for the older.

FIGURE 4-2 WORKING ON ATTACHING A WOVEN BAND TO A BACKING AS TO GIVE ENOUGH SUPPORT IN ITS FUNCTION AS A STRAP ON THE LÁVKA I MADE FOR MY ÁHČČI. THE BAND PICTURED HAS TRADITIONALLY BEEN FASTENED TO HUNTING GEAR OR TO POUCHES MEANT FOR STORING TOBACCO.

At that time, an exhibition showcasing duodji and gáktis from the area was displayed, and my siessá, who had consulted on it, wanted to take a look at the finished result.

While we were there, she pointed out a case that displayed woven bands, telling me that one of the *vuoddagat* [shoe bands] had been woven by her mother, my *áhkku* [grandmother][13]. This was the first time I had seen one of her products, and when I got home that evening, I threaded my *njuikun*, a rigid heddle, using leftover yarn from her [my áhkku] to weave a similar band. While doing so, I reflected on the stories about her that had been shared with me that day, and I remembered my own experiences with her. Through my weaving that evening, the stories of my family for multiple generations became incorporated. The finished band, seen in Figure 4-2, I later added to a *lávka* [bag] that I made for my áhčči, as seen in Figure 4-3.

---

13 North Sámi spelling. Though a grandmother may also be referred to as *boareseadni*, meaning old mother. When I previously mentioned my grandmother on my mother side, I used Aahka, which is the South Sámi spelling of the word.

In this story, I create a weave of relations to signify how the Sámi way of telling stories is an exploration of connections, both past and present, between people and place, and arising from the relation of people and non-human beings. Only as they are narrated, however, do the stories explore these relations, materializing them for others to see (Cruikshank 1998:2, Kovach 2009:94). By way of stories then, storytelling as a practice is a window into the social structure of a society. It is, as we will see, made up of history, law, pedagogics, knowledge, cosmology, memories, and skills—in other words, it is made up by and with a specific [Sámi] onto-epistemology.

FIGURE 4-3 THE LÁVKA I MADE MY ÁHČČI IS A COLLECTION OF STORIES, BUT IT WAS A LONG TIME IN COMING. I HAD LONG PROMISED TO MAKE HIM A PHOTO BAG AS TAKING PICTURES IS ONE OF HIS BEST LOVED HOBBIES. I FINALLY FELT INSPIRED TO MAKE IT WHEN I REDISCOVERED AN OLD HIDE THAT MY TJIDTJIE ONCE PREPARED. THE BAND, AS DISCUSSED, WAS WOVEN USING THE LEFTOVER YARN FROM HIS EATNI, MY ÁHKKUS OWN WEAVING. THE ENAMELS USED ARE LEFTOVERS FROM A TIME WHEN ÁHČČI MADE MY VIELLJAT [BROTHERS] THEIR BELTS. THEY ARE NOW KEPT BY MY VIELLJAŠ [YOUNGEST BROTHER] FOR HIS OWN PRODUCTION, AND IT WAS HE THAT PUT THEM IN.

In stories, worldviews are seeded, and the mapping of them outlined. Theorizing stories thus encourages a commitment to *"becoming involved in one another's lives"*(Haraway 2016:71), enacting the multiple worlding of a Sámi world-in-relation with all its values, meanings and multitudes. These same values, we find in the practice and product of duodji, but how to grasp what they are? There is no clear-cut answer to this question. Yet, learning how to listen to the world-making practices revealed in stories and storytelling is, I think, a good place to start.

When stories are told, performed or enacted in practices and through duodji, they reflect the multitudes of ontologies in which they were conceived; they reveal the many components of the onto-epistemologies that they perpetuate; and, they carry the plural axiological qualities that they were born in. Exploring theory from a place of stories then is, I think, valid in so far as it challenges both myself and my readers to engage with a dense network of relations and connections, 'making kin' as it were (Haraway 2016), of the ontologies that they [the stories] come with. In this sense, storytelling should be considered a *"mediation between many different voices"* (Jernsletten 2011:164). But then, if it is a case of bringing the stories together, knotting them [riessan] in patterns, what is needed is also the ability to observe, take notice and listen. In this, I am reminded of the story of the heart that beats within *Eana*, the Earth.

GULAHALLAT—LEARNING TO LISTEN.

When the Creator had shaped the land and made a dwelling for the People of the Sun [the Sámi], Jubmel placed the still-beating heart of a reindeer doe at the centre of the Earth so that the Sámi, if lost or threatened could put their ears to the ground and listen. As long as the heart continues to beat, and we continue to listen to it, there is life and a future. *"The essential ability to listen in order to hear the message that is being expressed goes back to [this] muitalus"*, says Harald Gaski, a Sámi literary scholar who is himself *"approaching the age of an Elder [eallilan olmmoš]"*, in an essay on the role of the Sámi elder and storytelling (Gaski 2019:263, 262). He goes on to conceptualize this approach as *guldalit*, which in the Sámi language simply means to listen to or for. In his conceptualization however, Gaski redefines guldalit as an act of listening to or for *"messages from Nature, from our fellow creatures, animals, birds, winds, sky, and the Earth"* (Gaski 2019:262). He thus centers the act of listening within the onto-epistemology revealed in and by stories, which is as crucial, I would claim, as the act of telling; so too is the act of listening. As the story of the heart that beats illustrates, how we listen or how we comprehend information, how we communicate is vital if we want to achieve understanding. This is where gulahallat, in my opinion, becomes relevant.

Made up by *gullat*, meaning to listen, and the suffix -*hállat*, which is rooted in the Sámi language as speaking, gulahallat highlights the importance of listening in Sámi cultures (Guttorm, Kantonen, and Kramvig 2019). Its translated meaning is communication, and while it is a correct translation, it fails to adequately take into account the deeper meaning of gulahallat. But then again, as Gaski (2006:8) else-where reminds us, *"[t]ranslating is like building bridges between cultures. A literal translation is seldom sufficient"*.

In a Sámi context, gulahallat is communication between people, but also between *"the interdependence of all things" (Jernsletten 2011:123)*. As such, it indeed rests on the idea of dialogue as a collective practice, but more so, it punctuates that knowledge is never achieved alone. In a master thesis on learning and understanding Sámi Indigenous knowl-edge by way of gulahallat, Aura Pieski formulates the following: *"dilis mas ieš dutkin lean oahpahalli ja báikkálaš olbmot leat mu oahpaheaddjit ja ofelaččat"*.[14] What this means is that "as a researcher, I am myself a novice and thus the people I engage with becomes my teachers and pathfinders' (Pieski 2019:41, my own translation). The deeper impli-cation of this is that to gulahallat, encourages you to engage with your relations to reach a place of knowledge. Any form for dialogue thus happens, not only in a symmetrical manner, but also as a reciprocal communication between people, places, entities, and other beings.

> As a way to come to understand the world, gulahallat is connected to hear-ing, listening and following the world (the land, the animals, the plants), and slowly, later, getting the gift to understand, when one has the patience to listen and hear (Guttorm, Kantonen, and Kramvig 2019:157).

To understand and explain duodji as a theoretical framework, work-ing from a place of gulahallat is, I would argue, absolutely necessary as it is one way in which we may *"dovdat, oaidnit ja vásihit oktavuoda eatnamiin"*, know, sense and experience the connection with the land and our surroundings (Pieski 2019:8)

Connected as it is to both *"hearing or listening in–between and hear-ing or listening together, [gulahallat] is basically something one can only practice with others"* (Guttorm, Kantonen, and Kramvig 2019:157). Duodji, as I see it, works in a similar way. Considered a 'commu-nal property', the mediations of what the practice of duodji entails, whether it be aesthetic expressions, material processes, or intellectual endeavours, is never up to the individual alone (Guttorm 2001:170). Rather, the knowledge of and in duodji is very dynamic; it changes over time in an ongoing dialogue about what really becomes tradition (Guttorm 2012b:75); *"[s]ometimes someone gets an idea. Sometimes we*

---

14 The exact translation should be 'in a situation where I as researcher become an apprentice, and the local people [or community] becomes my teachers and pathfinders'.

accept the change, sometimes we don't. That's our way; we negotiate our traditions every day" (Sara 21.01.2018). This dialogue happens in different ways, but always collectively.

This was experienced by Merethe Kuhmunen, whom I briefly mentioned in giisá, when she wanted to make her brother a man's gákti in a bright pink colour with large and abstract flowers printed on cotton. Her choice was controversial, to say the least, as men's gákti ordinarily have been of the monochrome variety and most often in primary colours. As might be expected, some duojárs disagreed with Merethe's project, feeling that it pushed the boundaries of customary gáktimaking to an uncomfortable degree. After all, a flowery and pink men's gákti, at least in their opinion, went against what they knew to be árbediehtu (Kuhmunen 02.12.2017). Still, the public reception of the gákti has been overwhelmingly positive; it has been written about in Sámi media, and it has also been exhibited in several places. Today, Merethe's pink gákti is considered: *"a good development of gákti-traditions"* because even if it *"breaks the norm, it does so with a sound knowledge of duodji-traditions, and negotiations within the community [of duojárs]"* (Eva 24.03.2018).

What the example of the pink gákti demonstrate is the process of defining what is 'good' development in duodji, versus what might be considered 'not so good'—what the Sámi scholar, Sigga-Marja Magga (2014), refers to as the *geahčastat*, or the gaze; a silent look meant to control and regulate both duodji, but also the duojárs in their practice of duodji. This is the opposite of *olgguŝteapmi*, which is *"servoŝa garra kontrollavuohki, mainna duojár ieŝ dahje su duojit hoigaduvvojit servoŝa olggobeallái"*, or 'a hard form of social control where a duojár and their work is shunned because it sits outside' of what has been decided as good duodji (Magga 2014:41, my own translation). As I see it, gulahallat is one way of conceptualizing the collective negotiation that happens in the practice of duodji.

In a discussion on duodji as methodology, duojár and professor of duodji, Gunvor Guttorm, express her understanding of duodji as follows:

[á]rbevirolaŝ duojis leat njuolggadusat, ja estehtalaŝ áddejumit leat hábmejuvvon juohkebeaivválaŝ doaimmain. Go mii dán áiggi hállat duoji birra, de leat mis mánggalágan duodjevásáhusat. Leat sihke duddjon- ja geavahanvuogit mat leat joatkaŝuvvan ja dasto leat práksisat mat leat riegádan individuála jurddašeamis ja duddjomis.

[D]uodji has rules and aesthetics that have been shaped through everyday life. When we talk about duodji, there are many different experiences to take into account. It is both a craft, in practical function, as well as practices born from individual thinking and the experience of the practice [througout generations] (Guttorm 2014:40, my own translation).

In her description, Guttorm highlights that duodji is made up of rules and regulations that have been developed through practice in the span of generations, aesthetic preferences that have been formed in and by everyday life, as well as individual duojárs thinking and subsequent practice. As we all have our own experiences related to the practice, and since we are taught to consider the aesthetics of it in different ways, duodji is understood and articulated in multiple, and sometimes even divergent, ways. These differences relate to, and are shaped by aesthetic perspectives, the duojárs surroundings as well as epistemological conditions. I will discuss all three, but though they have been separated into sections for the ease of reading, they actually work as extensions of one another, feeding into and affecting each other equally. I begin with the concept of aesthetics, or what may be termed *dåajmijes vuekie* (Kappfjell and Gaski 2018).

DÅAJMIJES VUEKIE

In an essay on the traditions of Sámi aesthetics, Harald Gaski (2017b:188), states that "*aesthetics in 'Western' traditions lack the full implication of what Sámi mean when we talk about aesthetics*". At first glance, this articulation might not be immediately understood, but if we look to the different practices of duodji it might be easier to grasp. In duodji, aesthetics is present in many ways, for instance, in the preparation of materials. The process of *bárket* or tanning skin, as described in Chapter Two, is one practice wherein aesthetics is highly influential. Which species of wood you collect bark from and the season in which you do so for instance, is partially dependant on what a community considers most beautiful. In a recent article on craftmanship as the focus of theorizing Indigenous knowledge, one of the Sámi duojárs being interviewed described how she gathered materials to bárket. The birch used, she explained, must be collected,

FIGURE 4-4 THE EMBROIDERY SEEN HERE IS DONE BY ANN KRISTINE BALTO, A DUOJÁR FROM THE NORWEGIAN SIDE OF SÁPMI. IT WAS MADE FOR A SMALL PURSE THAT I ASKED HER TO MAKE FOR ME, BUT THE EMBROIDERY WAS COMPLETELY UP TO HER.

[i]n the summertime if you want the colour [of the skin] to be brown and the softness [of the skin]. In the winter, it will be light green [the birch] … not as brown. You know in this area, we like the dark brown, but in Kautokeino they want to have it white…the fur…inside…they don't like the brown (quoted in Mellegård and Boonstra 2020:6).

Even in the choice of decoration, aesthetics is expressed. In the communities furthest to the South, designs often come in a geometric shape, as seen with the embroidery of pewter in Figure 2-5, whereas the Northernmost communities seem to prefer a more flowery shape, as evidenced in Figure 4-4. How we perceive beauty in our practice of duodji, in other words, differs greatly. But it is all the same, a *"way of presenting the Saami way of life and ideology"* (Hætta and Eira 2006:18, e.g., Dunfjeld Aagård 1989:54).

During a seminar I curated in late 2019[15] on Sámi aesthetics and material expressions, Lena Kappfjell, who is a South Sámi scholar from the Norwegian side of the border, explained that *"[t]he beauty*

15 Lena was one of the participants I invited to the seminar, "Dåajmijes Vuekie—The Material Expressions of Sámi Aesthetics", that was arranged in relation to the Sámi Dáidda festivála (Sámi Art Festival), that took place in Alta from the 21st to the 24th of November in 2019. The seminar was a collaboration with both Sámi Dáiddačehpiid Searvi (Sámi artist union), Office for Contemporary Art - Norway (OCA), Kunst I det Offentlige Rom (KORO) and Nordnorsk Kunstmuseum (NNKM), for more see https://www.daiddafestivala.no/post/seminar-om-samisk-kunst-dåejmijes-vuekie.

in duedtie, was given to me from the time I was a child. She linked her perception of beauty to the South Sámi idea of *dåajmijes vuekie* (Kappfjell and Gaski 2018). While not at all easy to define, as a conceptualized expression, dåajmijes vuekie conveys that beauty is not based on outward appearance so much as it is *"the relations of a thing's form to its intended purpose"* (Gaski 2017:187). Dåajmijes vuekie as such is very much an expression of beauty as relational (Kappfjell and Gaski 2018:16), which actually reflect what is a larger international tendency within Indigenous aesthetics, where the purpose behind creation and presentation is more important than the means of creation or the content of it (Mithlo 2012:192).

A good example of dåajmijes vuekie in practical terms, is found in the *náhppi*, which is a traditional milking bowl for collecting and storing reindeer milk. As seen in Figure 4-5, the náhppi has a distinct shape; rounded with incurved walls.[16] When milking it is important that little is spilled, hence the concave design of the náhppi (Fjellström 1985:465-6). Here then, is one example of the aesthetics of an object being decided by its purpose (Guttorm 2001:64).[17] Reindeer milking has today been mostly abandoned, but the náhppi is still in use. Even if both the style and purpose is slightly altered, the typical shape is still maintained, carrying the stories of old. In this way, the náhppi makes an excellent argument that dåajmijes vuekie, establishes *"forms of evaluation based on [a] historical consciousness and respect for traditions and cultural values"* (Gaski 2017:189). This impression is reinforced in a collection of oral sources from the Northernmost parts of South Sámi homelands on the Swedish side of the border in the early 20th century, which primarily consists of stories that have been told by Kristoffer Sjulsson, who lived between 1828 and 1908. In said collection, dåajmijes vuekie is at great length described in relation to humans, other beings, lands, duodji, colours and more, listing what makes all of these *"tjappies"*[18], or beautiful (Pettersson, Bäckman, and Kjellström 1979:91).

---

16 There are however variations (Guttorm 2001:86-8), but for the present discussion I do not see the need to discuss them all.

17 The shape of the náhppi is no doubt also affected by the choice of materials. Náhppi is made of burls from wood. It is already round in shape, which has in all likelihood also impacted on its distinctive shape. In some areas the náhppi is made without its walls being curved. This characteristic has been explained in the degree of domestication in reindeers. If an animal is suitably domesticated it will know to stand still during milking, abolishing the need of curved walls (Guttorm 2001:71).

18 Čappat in North Sámi.

FIGURE 4-5 NÁHPPI (NFSA 1688) OF BIRCH. IT WAS PURCHASED IN 1962 BY THE THEN SECRETARY OF THE SÁMI MISSION, BERTRAND M. NILSEN. IT WAS ONE OF THE OBJECTS REPATRIATED BY THE BÅÅSTEDE AGREEMENT AND WAS CONSEQUENTLY RETURNED TO RIDDO DUOTTAR MUSEAT IN 2018.

This view on beauty, it may be claimed, comes from «*nature, reindeer and fish—what at all times surround us*" (Fjellheim 27.11.2019), our *birrasat*, which is my next topic of discussion, or concept of relevance.

BIRRASAT

Birrasat, directly translated, means surroundings, and it has a very important function in Sámi society. If we look to the multitudes of Indigenous systems of knowledge[s] from around the world, one of the commonalities that are easily detected is the influence from our surroundings and place (Virtanen and Seurujärvi-Kari 2019). Sámi knowledge[s] are no different, and our birrasat as such help shape how we understand and view the world. Growing up, tjidtjie would each summer send me home to aahka, where I learned of a world far removed from my life in Oslove. Aahka would bring me on walks, show me places and tell me stories about them and the people that had once lived there—and of the beings that still do. Even if they are hidden from our eyes, she would say, it is important to cultivate a good relationship with them. She would introduce me to the land and the waters and teach me that my will was not above them. If I listened to the land and the waters, she said, and collaborated with them, I would always survive on them.

FIGURE 4-6 THIS PICTURE IS TAKEN AT FINNBOGEN, AT ØKSNINGAN, WHICH IS AN ISLAND OUTSIDE OF THE HELGELAND COAST IN NORDLAND ON THE NORWE-GIAN SIDE OF THE BORDER. THIS IS THE HOMEPLACE OF MY MOTHER AND IT WAS HER BIRRASAT, GROWING UP. THROUGH REGULAR VISITS WITH AAHKA, IT ALSO BECAME PART OF MY OWN BIRRASAT. THE PICTURE SHOWS FINNBOGEN IN 2018 AND WAS TAKEN BY MY FATHER ON MY REQUEST.

Though at that time I did not have the means to articulate what was happening, I see now that my aahka gave me knowledge about the land and waters that we came from, but also the different ontologies that had shaped our perspective on them. This knowledge was of, and from the land, the waters and our birrasat.

The *"Indigenous experience"*, says Kristin Jernsletten (2011:43), *"is spatial, connected to places, to Earth, to the ground on what seems almost a personal level"*. Throughout a continuous presence in and on the land, Indigenous Peoples' have for generations developed knowledges that are shaped from their surroundings, based on the experience of seasons and of place. To bárket, once more, embodies this because it demands that the duojár knows which plants are better served to tan the skin in an aesthetically pleasing way. What time of the year the plants should be collected is also important as *"we need the right bark to tan the skin… See, this birch is best to collect in the summertime to get the colour right"* (Hanna 12.02.2019). The purpose of the finished product is also something that must be considered.

> When you plan for a beaska (a pelt) … the fur skin you use … you need to consider the length of the hairs on the calves, and when is the best time to slaughter. The beaska is made with the fur from the animals slaughtered earliest in the Autumn, because the hair is short and thin…it won't be as warm

as the beaska made from skin taken in October or November. But the skin then is not as pretty because the hairs are longer. All of this is important to consider" (Pia 17.11.2018).

To bárket, in other words, relies on the duojárs knowledge of their material. In Sámi, I have heard this expressed as *"ávnnas muitala mo galggat bargat"* or 'the material shows you the way', which I spoke about in my introductory chapter. What is articulated in this expression is nothing more than the surety that the best way to make use of a material is a knowledge that has been shaped by the experience gained from one's birrasat. This experience comes from interactions with how the seasons impact the animals that give the skin, as well as how the preparation of the skin is affected by the local flora and fauna. Again, what we see is a knowledge that comes from the land.

The example above illustrates how individual practice and experience are important in developing your birrasat, but as the story of me being taught by my aahka demonstrates, you also develop your birrasat by learning from your elders (Mellegård and Boonstra 2020:7). Though I have briefly written on the position of the *árbečeahpi* previously, it is expedient to give a small repetition. Much like the elder, an árbečeahpi possesses competencies and knowledges that are imperative in the maintenance of cultural knowledges. It is experience-based over generations, and it is particular to place and birrasat. This wealth of knowledge and skills, which is at once ancestral and individual, invites me to consider another aspect of duodji. More to the point, it encourages a view on duodji as a system of knowledge, and as such, its place within a Sámi epistemology (Balto 1996, 1997), which is what I discuss next, as *árbediehtu*.

ÁRBEDIEHTU

"Máttuid dieđut oidnojit ja leat vurkejuvvon dálá dujiin", 'the knowledge of our ancestors appears and endure in today's duodji' (Guttorm 2007:62, my own translation). This quote is indicative of the importance that lies in knowledge being passed down through the generations. That is not to say that knowledge may not be passed sideways between peers as I briefly discussed in ruvdet. The best example is the fact that the designation as an árbečeahpi is not conferred based on age, but rather on the level of knowledge and experience one possess-

es (Archibald 2008:37, Gaski 2019:260). Still, there seems to be an expectation that the knowledge that lies at the very core of duodji, be inherited (e.g., Guttorm 2007:68). This, I think, goes back to the fact that of old, the knowledge of duodji has been an important part of an intergenerational exchange of wisdom and skills. More to the point, perhaps, the durability of duodji has depended on it being passed between generations.

> At first, the duojár learned by imitation, carefully observing her grandmother at work and copying movements until they became second nature, embodied, and effortless. The duojár is only consciously aware of the ease and familiarity of knowledge and skills that she embodied when she occasionally learns new techniques (Mellegård and Boonstra 2020:7).

In an illustrative—and rather poetically penned I might add—article on duodji and Sámi pedagogy, the Sámi scholar Rauna Triumf gives some very descriptive examples of how seeing and listening is essential in Sámi teaching methods:

> My mother is trimming a leg of a boot, letting the hair fall gradually into the box, and I also feel like trying trimming. My mother gets me a pair of scissors and a few pieces of hide that I can remove hair from, so that I will learn how to hold scissors. She shows how to hold the scissors and edge them under the fur and then cut the hair (Triumf 2011:83)

I recognize the pedagogy behind these examples because I remember them quite well from my own upbringing. And it makes me look back to the time I made my first gákti. Throughout my childhood, I had seen tjidtjie make countless gáktis. But then, I guess getting a husband, three sons, a daughter and herself properly fitted would make for many opportunities for me to do so. At some point however, I realized that if I wanted more gáktis without having to que up with five others, I had to start making them myself. Having observed, as I said, tjidtjie for a long time, I had a fairly good idea of how to proceed—or at least, I thought I did.

Tjidtjie, with her decades of experience, made the entire process seem so amazingly easy, which I soon found was not the case. Nonetheless, I began the process of making one. Tjidtjie circled around me, carefully observing but never speaking a word. At one point, however, I clearly remember her starting to make a gákti of her own.

FIGURE 4-7 OVER THE YEARS, THERE HAVE BEEN MANY GÁKTIS MADE. SOME-
TIMES I WORK ALONE, SOMETIMES I WORK ALONGSIDE OTHERS AT DUODJEBÁD-
JIS, AND SOMETIMES TJIDTJIE AND I WORK TOGETHER. THIS PICTURE WAS TAKEN
SOME YEARS BACK, WHEN TJIDTJIE AND I WORKED TOGETHER TO MAKE ME A
NEW GEASSEGÁKTI, WHICH IS OF COURSE THE VARIETY FROM MY ÁHČCI'S HOME
COMMUNITY, RATHER THAN THE GAPTA THAT IS USED IN TJIDTJIE'S HOME COM-
MUNITY.

Doing so, she placed herself, rather strategically I might add, in clear
view, giving me a direct line of sight to what she was doing—in essence, giving me the opportunity to imitate her if needed, without
actually having to ask for any help. Though, to be completely honest, I
did eventually have to ask. Now, did I make a perfect gákti. Not at all,
but I did make one, even if tjidtjie laughed when she saw the finished
product. In later years, when asked to help younger kin to make gáktis
I have employed this very method myself.

What all of these stories have in common, is a focus on learning
by seeing, followed by doing.[19] In her master on the use of seal skin,
the duojár and curator Gry Fors (2004) have used the term čalbmi in
this context of transmitting knowledge. Čalbmi literally means 'eye',
and as I understand it, the term is meant to indicate that transmitting
knowledge and practices happens through seeing and doing. Aside
from being the collective memories and experiences from birrasat
then, duodji is also the situated practices created from these memories (Mellegård and Boonstra 2020). Or as articulated by Guttorm;
"*[m]uittán olles rupmašiin. Dan maid dál oainnán, gávnnan fas rumašlaš
muittus*", 'I remember in my body. What I see is preserved as a physical
memory' (Guttorm 2013b:33, my own translation)

---

19 This is actually very similar to what Pierre Bourdieu (1977:87) defines as a hexis of the body in his "Outline
of a Theory of Practice". However, I prefer to use a Sámi term.

Of course, we can no longer take for granted that all Sámi children learn duodji in this way. Due to colonialism and the consequent
epistemidices and assimilation processes that I discussed in bárket,
many Sámi families and communities as a whole experienced a rup-
ture in the knowledge of duodji, as well as other Indigenous knowledge[s] (Inga et al. 1986, Fors and Enoksen 1991). After centuries of
said ruptures having an impact, one important strategy of resistance
was to centre the knowledge[s] and practices and establish one`s own
cultural institutions. Not only was this an important step towards
Sámi self-determination, it was also an important strategy to counteract colonial narratives and reclaiming sovereignty (Hansen 2016).
As a result, more and more are today taught the practice of duodji in
schools, which naturally adds an institutional element to the practice
(Guttorm 2012b).

On the one hand, this ensures that duodji as a practice is available
to anyone wanting to learn but does not have the opportunity to do
so at home. On the other hand, concerns have been raised that moving learning to an institutional setting has resulted in a more formalized use of iconography and understanding of aesthetics or dåajmijes
vuekie (Dunfjeld Aagård 1989:154); in essence, encouraging copying
rather than the innovativeness that is essential to duodji. I do understand the concern. At the same time, I have been involved in facilitating institutional learning for many Sámi wanting to reclaim the
practice of duodji. My experience is that what might initially be acts
of copying in time evolves into innovative expressions of knowledge.
And really, do we not as children learn by repeating what we see others doing? (Triumf 2011:86) Why then should this pedagogy change
simply because those learning are older?

Another aspect I would raise is the assumption that even if the
chance is there, every child wants to learn duodji. Because this is not
the case at all. As one duojár shared with me, "*back then [as a child] I
didn't really have an interest in learning*" (Jane 30.03.2019). Another
made a point of how she as a child

"didn't care that much about [duodji]. My mother would sit at the kitchen ta-
ble working alongside my eldest sister. I was busy with other stuff. But today,
I am the duojár and my older sister doesn't really have time anymore to do it"
(Emmy 05.12.2017)

For those that do learn the way it has been taught for generations however, the skills come by seeing and reproducing, emulating, and doing. The knowledge[s] embedded in duodji, is as such made available in a slow process where practice or *máhttu* is a necessary step (Dunfjeld Aagård 1989:154). Elders, or *árbečeahpi*, parents and other caretakers consequently "*teach by living*" (Hanna 12.02.2019)—doing, and sometimes verbally communicating their own experiences (Balto 1997:70, Triumf 2011:82). In this way duodji, as storytelling,

> "works as an educational tool. Let me make the implications more explicit, since it is used extensively, and quite systematically, in child-raising and the transference of knowledge between the generations" (Balto 1997:92, my own translation).

The practice of duodji, as well as the knowledge[s] it contains, should thus be viewed as an inherited and shared knowledge, or *árbediehtu*.

Both as concept, practice, and materiality, duodji is thus constituted of relations, in-between worlds, and throughout place and time. To practice duodji forge these connections, sustaining the world as one-of-relations, between and to other people, lands and waters, nature, beings, and other entities. In this way, duodji becomes more than the simple designation of craft or of objects it so often has been associated with outside of Sámi communities. Rather, duodji, by way of its interrelatedness, becomes, I believe, a way to reference, activate, and consolidate meanings and values through a specific practice. I have chosen to conceptualize this process as *sámáidahttin*, which I discuss next.

SÁMÁIDAHTTIN

Translated to mean samification, sámáidahttin was first introduced as a concept in an evaluation of the School reform of 1997, which was an educational reformation intended for the primary schools in Norway (Hirvonen and Anttonen 2004). Initially, the term was coined to denominate any educational exercise wherein the emphasis lay on Sámi cultural sensitivity and ways of thinking, but in 2009 it was further defined by Asta Balto, a Sámi educator whose contribution to the development of a Sámi pedagogy is second to none, and Liv Østmo, a Sámi social scientist and also one of the founders of the Sámi University of applied sciences, as an act of Indigenization meant to combat

Eurocentric and Western norms of education, institutions and per-spectives through the return to Sámi values and norms (Balto and Østmo 2009:28). Elsewhere, Balto has also made a point of defining sámáidahttin as a collective process (Balto and Sámi 2008:36), thus reflecting the collective character of Sámi knowledge production. The concept of sámáidahttin has in later years been adapted and applied depending on both context and need; for instance, in museological settings. (e.g., Aikio 2017). As such, I take the liberty of using it here to conceptualize how specific codes—meanings, values, and norms—that are relevant for understanding a Sámi onto-epistemology are developed and adapted through the practice of duodji. More to the point, how duodji is an act of Indigenization.

FIGURE 4-8 REPEATING SPECIFIC ACTS, CREATING A PRACTICE OF DUDDJOT AND ASSOCIATED ÁRBEDIEHTU. THIS PICTURE IS FROM A DUODJI WORKSHOP WHERE PARTICIPANTS LEARNT DIFFERENT TIIDAS AND ASSOCIATED PRACTICES. THE PICTURE WAS TAKEN BY ARNHILD HAAGENSEN.

As already discussed, duodji is both a performance (e.g., Dunfjeld 2006:18) and a bodily practice[20] (Guttorm 2001:49). This is, in fact, embedded in Sámi language, where the practice of duodji is expressed as duddjot. Additionally, how duodji engage specific bodily perfor-

---

20 The term bodily practice is introduced by Paul Connerton (1989:72-76) in his book "How societies remember".

mances is also expressed in *tiida*, or *diida*, though I use the former of these. Dictionaries often define tiida as superstition or old wives' tales (Nielsen 1979). The exact meaning is, I agree, difficult to grasp because tiida is expressed in different ways. It may come across both as lore, as spiritual beliefs (e.g., Harlin and Pieski 2020:128), or even as the precursor of specific acts (e.g., Guttorm 2001:58-9). I will return to the first two later, but for now, I would like to focus on the latter. An example of a tiida would be when my aahka taught me to stomp on the ground before pouring water, which I discussed in ruvdet. What this example also illustrate, is that a tiida is often inherited and enforced through a specific and repetitive action.

In a discussion on tiida associated with duodji, Gunvor Guttorm (2001b:58) mentions that tiidas are sometimes forgotten. This would, for instance be the case in the context of epistemicide, where Indigenous practices and knowledge[s], such as duodji, is slowly eroded by politics of assimilation or even confiscation of objects, as was discussed previously. The associated act, on the other hand, does not always stop being performed. If, for a second, I might return to my aahka's tiida, which encouraged us to stomp on the ground, I once asked my cousin if she remembered performing said act. While she could remember being taught to stomp on the ground, she had never been given a reason for doing so. To be fair, as a child, she never thought to question the act, and later on when our aahka died there seemed as if there were no one else she could ask. Nonetheless, having incorporated this specific tiida, however much unaware she was of it being such, she continued the practice. This only goes to show that even if there is no longer a conscious knowledge as to why it is being performed, people continue to act it out. In this sense, a tiida is a form of body memory. As such, I would argue that the practice of duodji is constituent of meanings about the material world through practice. This would then mean that duodji carries with it both knowledge, traditions, beliefs, and stories, shared between duojárs and transferred from one generation to the next.

Nonetheless, as I have already stated, there is no guarantee that duodji as practice is transferred between generations. This is when my last concept, *rematriation*, becomes valid. Before I go into a discussion on this term however, I will need to briefly talk on the topic of museums and more to the point, what happens when objects of duodji, and Indigenous material culture in general, is entered into museum collections.

MUSEUMS AND THE ASSUMED PASSITIVITY OF INDIGENOUS MATERIAL CULTURE.

Although it is the source communities that initially ascribe value to their objects, when said objects are relocated to museums other meanings are attributed—and they often superimpose the original ones (Cameron 2007:54, Deidre 2007:57). A case in point is the fact that throughout the history of museums, and expressed in the 'exhibitionary complex'[21] of society, objects of the cultural Other have generally been appropriated into one of two categories as either ethnographic artefact or "primitive" art (Price 1989). In museum practice, this binary has been crystallized into two specific exhibition strategies. Namely exotification, which focus on exhibiting that which is alien to a Western gaze by way of contrast and assimilation, which does the opposite of contrasting and instead strips the objects of context to present them simply as 'art for art's sake' (Karp and Lavine 1991:375). In a wonderful reflection on the assumed passivity of Indigenous objects as evidenced in these strategies, the Yorta Yorta[22] curator, Kimberly Moulton puts it like this:

> [s]tanding in the museum in the middle of London, I saw over 200 years of taking our objects, writing about our cultures, extracting knowledge and regurgitating it in the white paradigm. My awe at everything around me soon turned to anger and grief (Moulton 2018:207).

The categorization of Indigenous material culture is questionable on several accounts, but I will simply mention the two that strike me as being particularly problematic in the context of duodji. To start, the divide and categorisation into one or the other completely disregard the fact that most objects from Indigenous cultures, as evidenced by the náhppi above, are seldom limited within categorical boundaries (Phillips and Steiner 1999:3). The second issue I take with the museological practice as it relates to Indigenous objects, is that although

---

21 The expression is coined by the sociological theorist Tony Bennett (1995), and basically it defines society as a spectacle, and museological institutions involvement in providing said spectacle, allows for displays of knowledge and narratives which in turn asserts power dynamics.

22 Aboriginal people whose homelands on the continent of Australia is today known as north-eastern Victoria and southern New South Wales.

included in notions of fine art from the mid-20th century, artefacts of a "primitive" origin is nonetheless defined in accordance with the aesthetics of Western scholars (Phillips and Steiner 1999:3), which is far too narrow to be comparable for instance, with all that is implied in the concept of dåajmijes vuekie. As a result, members of source communities often end up feeling alienated from their own cultural heritage—and this is definitely the case of Sámi objects as well (e.g., Olli 2013:87, Buijs 2016:539). Again, Moulton beautifully puts this experience into words when she writes that

> We continue to be designated within the canon of retrospective nostalgia, within the historical past. If you look at major museum collections across Australia and globally, they are primarily based on nineteenth- and early twentieth-century objects, with gaps in contemporary objects. They have been void of First Peoples' voices. Some of these places continue to re-inscribe the colonial 'other' narrative through non-Indigenous curators still holding the key, apparently unlocking our history but in fact, perpetuating three convenient lies: one, that we have suffered irreparable cultural loss (knowledge and craftsmanship); two, that the object is dormant; and three, that the Western/non-Indigenous lens is the right lens (the white way is the right way) (Moulton 2018:208-9).

When duodji moves from the dimension of practice and use in Sámi communities, to the storehouses of museums, it too becomes a victim to these lies and its original function and meaning are changed (Guttorm 2001:13). Thus, the transition from duodji to museum object demonstrate the impact of the power structures inherent in the epistemic ignorance that I initially discussed, and which rests on the authority, not of Indigenous people themselves, but rather those that have studied them, defined them, and historically ordered their rank in the world (Henare 2005). These complexities may be traced back, at least in part, to the early days of [ethnographic] museums and the influence of the Enlightenment (Bennett 2004).

The general consensus of the modern museums has been to educate the masses (Bennett 2004); to civilize and educate.[23] Coinciding with the first ethnographic museums in the West, the philosophical

---

23 In the 18th century the princely collections slowly transformed into museum collections and were made available to the public (Bennett 1995). At least in some sense of the word, but keep in mind that the public of then and the public of now are vastly different (Abt 2006:123-4). In Norway for instance, public only included some parts of society while excluding others (Eriksen 2009:52-7)

and intellectual movement of the Enlightenment was doing victory laps across most of Europe, and as discussed in bárket, this philosophy changed the value and understanding of source materials. Whereas before, when written sources could be relied upon, the corruption of Faith and church meant that literary source material would run the risk of being biased. Material culture on the other hand, was objective, and so it soon came to pass that objects and things became the primary source of knowledge (Bennett 2004:31, Henare 2005:64-6). Such exaltation was not without consequence.

In due course, it became essential for museums to have permanent access to material culture. This, in turn, encouraged European travellers to collect what they came across in their journeys, and upon return, create their own collections—which was willed to museums upon their death—or donate to museums what they had brought back. The result is that *"[o]bject-based epistemologies were developed which fundamentally altered European understandings of the past and other peoples [...]. Museums were instrumental in these transformations"* (Henare 2005:153). The ethnographic museums of the 18th century thus developed a practice of collecting material culture (Bennett 2004:31, Henare 2005:64-6, 73), which would go on to shape the modus operandi of museums (Clavir 2002).

The supposed mandate of museums to collect, conserve and display material culture, has persisted up until the present, but the reasoning of it has differed. As previously discussed, the view on Indigenous people and their cultures changed greatly throughout the 18th, 19th, and 20th century. The initial perception, which had been somewhat benign, if patronizing, would in time become associated with more negative attributes, and not surprisingly, the practice of museums reflected this (Lonetree 2012). In the heyday of colonial and imperial expansion from the West, it quickly became an established fact that Indigenous, or colonized, cultures were evolutionary dead-ends, and its people, lacking the biological imperative and/or the ability for cultural advancement, would in time disappear (Bennett 2004:59, also see Henare 2005:68-70). Correspondingly, their material culture was also, with time, expected to disappear. Acting in their newly established capacity as temples of knowledge, museums were thus dedicated to preserving the material remains of cultures soon to be extinct (e.g., Vorren and Manker 1957)—often without the approval or even knowledge of the cultures in question (Pareli et al. 2012:29, e.g., Westman 2002, Krmpotich 2011). The repercussions of such were, and to this day are, quite serious.

Throughout its period of existence, museums have by necessity needed to maintain some sort of relationship with their source communities. Almost without fail that relationship has been mired in power relations: sometimes benign and at other times ambiguous. In the case of Indigenous source communities, however, the balance of power has at all times been skewed in favour of the museum (e.g., Clifford 1997:191-2). By and large, the asymmetrical power relation is founded on the question of ownership. Consider, for instance, the banished goavddis' that were confiscated from the Sámi during the 17th and 18th centuries. Most of these drums were quickly remanded into the 'safe keeping' of museums or collections outside of our communities (Westman 2002). Despite multiple requests to repatriate the drums, we are *"constantly reminded, politely, that the drums no longer belong to us"*, as one Sámi museum worker remarked (Elle 29.05.2018). This is not, I suspect, unusual in circumstances where museums owe much of their collection to a colonial past (see Lonetree 2012).

When Senegalese academic and writer Felwine Sarr, together with French art historian Benedicte Savoy (2018), presented their rapport on African cultural heritage in French museums, as commissioned by President Emmanuel Macron, they recommended that everything acquired during the colonial period, and prior to 1960 be returned to source communities. The public outcry in France was heard all over the world. Both academics, museums, and institutions of cultural heritage strongly opposed the conclusions of Sarr and Savoy. The French art historian, Didier Rykner, who is also an editor of Le Tribune Del'Art, argued on France 24 that *"the looting of art was legal"* during the colonial period, and thus the objects acquired during that time should remain with *"the French museums where they belong"* (23.11.2018). One might question the ardent opposition of what seems to be quite logical and by that, I mean the return of what was once looted. However, in this I suspect the very real connection between museums and colonialism reveals itself.

As has been so eloquently argued by many before me, museums have the capacity of shaping knowledge (Hooper-Greenhill 1992,

Bennett 1995, Henare 2005).[24] Amongst those that have persuasively argued for such a statement, we find British-born Eilean Hooper-Greenhill, whose doctorate from 1988 was in sociology, but with an emphasis on museum studies. For all that, it is her later work that I find exceedingly helpful as it is focused on material culture and Indigenous representation. In particular, her articulation that the *"establishment of collections [...] is a form of symbolic conquest"* is, I think, a vital recognition when attempting to disentangle the relations between museums and source communities (Hooper-Greenhill 2000:18).

Though there are, of course, multiple factors that contribute to the convoluted relations between museums and source communities, there is, I think, no denying that the appropriation of ownership to material culture is one of the more paramount. When you control the dissemination of a culture, you also gain the power to name and represent that culture (Webb 2006). Establishing a collection therefore grants one the right to decide how specific cultures are to be imagined and portrayed, and thus how they are to be included or excluded from national and official narratives (Hooper-Greenhill 2000, Reid 2002, Rinta-Porkkunen and Ylitalo 2003, Webb 2006, Han 2013). One example of this is the previously discussed dissemination of the reindeer herder as the true and authentic "Lapp", which was so adamantly argued by historians in the 19th and 20th centuries. This narrative was greatly assisted by contemporary museums and their exhibitions. In the museological literature, this exhibition complex has even been conceptualized as the *"Lappish equipage"* by the Norwegian archaeologist Silje Opdahl Mathisen (2012:61). Opdahl Mathisen also traces the complex from its earliest appearance until the present day, remarking that even if there has been shifting meanings attached, its dissemination has helped create an image of the "authentic" Sámi culture as one in which the primary livelihood is reindeer herding. This, in turn, has ensured a general consensus of said narrative (Webb 2001, Mathisen 2014).

---

24 The capacity to name, represent, interpret as well as create meaning, narratives and knowledge of both the past and present is very much a facet of museum practice (Hooper-Greenhill 2000, Bennett 2004, Henare 2005). The power to represent and interpret does not however, lie in any single thing or object. Rather it transpire on account of the protracted and complex entanglement of museums within the sphere of *cultural politics*—a mix of people´s attitudes, beliefs, and perspectives, as well as media and arts, which together help shape social and political opinion (Newell 2014). As a result, at different times and in different ways, museums have been affected by both political and philosophical currents.

As the self-declared custodians of material culture[25] as well as the guardians of innumerable collections from colonized or otherwise subjugated cultures, museums have thus been greatly influential in determining how source communities were, and are, to be perceived by the general public (Webb 2001) and, sociological studies have proven (Comaroff and Comaroff 1992:53, Mennel 1994:182), even by the source communities themselves (e.g., Eidheim 1971:50-62). Again, the "Lappish equipage" exemplifies this as its dissemination reinforced the Sámi homeland as terra nullius, and thus the legality of it being dispossessed. All too often, it seems as if the influence bestowed upon museums by virtue of appropriated cultural heritage, has been in the service of political interests resulting in museums acting to promote, among others, both colonial and imperial agendas; legitimizing the annexing of territories and validating the removal of sovereignty from Indigenous peoples being but some examples (Bennett 2004, Henare 2005). It is from here we see why repatriation, or better yet rematriation, might matter to Indigenous source communities.

REMATRIATON

In their rapport on African cultural heritage and repatriation, Sarr and Fenway state that repatriation,

> Il s'agit cependant de comprendre, en ce qui concerne le patrimoine, que ce ne sont pas seulement des objets qui ont été pris, mais des réserves d'énergies, des ressources créatives, des gisements de potentiels, des forces d'engendrement de figures et de formes alternatives du réel, des puissances de germination; et que cette perte est incommensurable parce qu'elle entraîne un type de rapport et un mode de participation au monde irrémédiablement obérés.

> [...] is about understanding however, that as far as heritage is concerned, it's not simply objects that were taken, but reserves of energy, creative resources, reservoirs of potentials, forces engendering alternative figures and alternate forms of reality, and this loss is incommensurable. Simply giving back these cultural objects will, therefore, not be a proper compensation (Sarr and Savoy

---

25 What better example of this is there than the controversies surrounding the Parthenon marbles, also called the Elgin marbles after the 7th earl of Elgin that removed them from their original placing in Greece in the early 19th century. The legality of this removal have been extensively challenged (Jenkins 2001), but despite multiple calls for them to be repatriated, the British Museum, whose collection the marbles entered in 1816 adamantly refuse to return them, arguing that they are *"part of everyone's shared heritage and transcend political boundaries"* (Trustees of the British Museum 2012)

2018:34, my own translation).

What they so eloquently articulate in this quote is that, while repatriation within a museological context has mostly been about the return of human remains or objects (e.g., Turnbull & Pickering 2010, Svestad 2013), it is so much more. From an Indigenous point of view, for instance, repatriation also deals with symbolic values (Olli & Harliin 2014), ritual practices (Peers, Reinius & Shannon 2017), abstract ideas of cosmological belief (Krmpotich 2011), and human actions and the innovativeness of aesthetic expressions (Olli & Harliin 2014, Varutti 2015). In this sense, repatriation and reclaiming of Indigenous cultural heritage is often about much more than a simple return, moving instead within the territory of *"healing and well-being"* (Atalay 2019:79).

Material culture has been defined as *"systems of recall for persons and social groups that have been threatened or traumatized by loss"* (Hallam and Hockey 2001:7), and this is where rematriation becomes a valuable option. Far exceeding a simple give-back of objects, rematriation take on the meaning of restoring *"a living culture to its rightful place on Mother Earth"*, and *"to restore a people to a spiritual way of life, in sacred relationship with their ancestral lands, without external interference"* (Newcomb 1995:3).[26] Quite reminiscent then, of what I discussed as sovereignty in giisá. Rematriation, in other words, reject the narratives brought on by the epistemic ignorance of Western thought by restoring Indigenous onto-epistemologies and challenging the three lies that Moulton articulates. That is to say, rematriation, indicate that to simply return an object is, as Sarr and Fenway claim, not an adequate compensation. To return an object does not negate the epistemicide that comes with colonisation. To return an object is not the same as returning all that was lost by way of epistemicide. But, even if *"much of the original meaning"* has been lost, to restore material culture to their source communities will, in time, *"embrace and house new meanings"*, and even facilitate for *"its [the object's] memories [to] awaken"* (Harlin and Pieski 2020:124, 127).

If epistemicide is the illness, then rematriation would be the cure as it addresses not only the alienation between people and material cul-

---

26 Rematriation, whilst recently becoming more common in Indigenous studies has been around as a concept since the mid-1990s, when Steve Newcomb (1995), which is of Shawnee/Lenape ancestry from Turtle Island, discussed repatriation and 'rematriation' as healing.

ture, but also the recovery of a healthy emotional relationship between source communities and the objects that was once looted or otherwise remanded into the custody of museums (Peers 2013, Krmpotich et al. 2013, Atalay 2019, Harlin and Pieski 2020). More to the point, rematriation restores Indigenous sovereignty by reinstating practices, knowledges, protocols as well as Indigenous ways of being, doing, and knowing (e.g., Atalay 2019:81, Harlin and Pieski 2020:124-7). I will try to demonstrate what I mean by discussing the gákti as an example of Sámi material culture.

THE GÁKTI AS STORYTELLING

The reason for choosing the gákti is quite simple. During the harshest time of the ethnic stigma experienced by the Sámi, what was first silenced was the external markers of Sámi identity; that is, languages and gáktis. Removing the gákti however is not simply about clothing or regalia disappearing. As I understand the gákti, it is one of, if not the most, striking examples of the Sámi world-in-relation, materialized in duodji. Which perhaps, goes to explain some of the relevance attached to the garment. For many years now, the gákti has had a perceived position as one of the foremost markers of Sámi ethnicity, eclipsed, it is said, only by the ability to speak a Sámi language (Bjørklund 2000:32, also see Dankertsen 2006, Sivertsen 2011). At its most basic, the gákti is simply clothing worn for protection against the environment (Balto 1996:97). Still, the strong affiliation with Sámi identities comes as no surprise considering the longevity of the garment or that of its predecessors, which has been in use for centuries (Solbakk 2000:107).

The earliest mentions of Sámi clothing is found in Tacitus "Germania" (Tacitus [98]1997:94-5). Of course, at this time, not much is said apart from clothes worn by the Sámi being made of leather. Little may as such be concluded from this early historical work. Leather is also mentioned as the primary source of material some 600 years later, when Paulus Diaconus[27], describes Sámi clothing as being in the shape of leather tunics—loose-fitting clothes extending to knee or hip (Gjessing and Gjessing 1940:45). Other literary sources, amongst them Othere of Hålogaland's travel accounts from the 9th century,

---

27 Paulus Diaconus was a Benedictine monk, as well as a scribe and historian who wrote the account of the Lombards, a Germanic people who ruled most of the Italian Peninsula between 568 and 774, beginning with their origin in Scandinavia.

confirm that tunics made of leather from different animals are present in Sámi society at this time (Simonsen 1957:5). As none of the literary sources can be traced to the Sámi themselves, however, all are second-hand and considering the time lap, perhaps not the most reliable authority on Sámi clothing.

Later sources, however, dating from the 16th and 17th century speak of Sámi clothes by the name of *piask* and *modde*[28], both of which are old Sámi words for fur pelt and skin pelt, respectively (Solbakk 2000:107, see Schefferus 1673, Magnus [1555]2010). In its earliest form, the pelt, or *beaska*, was made by laying the hide of two animals flat with the fur facing in and leashing them together from shoulder to shoulder. Historically, this has been quite common when making clothes in most Arctic cultures (e.g., Hatt 1914:60), but in time the beaska nonetheless began to distinguish itself from the common Arctic variety. The new construction relied on cut pieces from 5-7 hides, adding wedges to give both width and more shape to the garment (Gjessing and Gjessing 1940:47). Although it is difficult to establish an exact date for this shift, it is still reasonable to assume that the changed beaska reflects developing cultural markers specific to the Sámi (Guttorm 2013a:895).

Shortly after the first mentions of beaska, in the 17th century, a similar cut of coloured clothing made from cloth appears in the probate registries (Gjessing and Gjessing 1940:14). These are most likely the first documented gáktis, which imply that the beaska is the predecessor of the gákti—which, incidentally, most duojárs would agree on (Dunfjeld 1999:51, Guttorm 2013a:901). The sources available as to the visual expression of the gákti allow for some commonalities to be established. For the male, collars are often described as high and decorated with straight or triangular lines of varied colours. Sometimes they are also said to be embroidered with yarn, threads made of pewter, or mica. The collars on gáktis that are worn by women, with few exceptions, do not have any height but instead lies flat. Similar to the male collar, it is typically edged with colored bands or other decorations.

Coloured bands also seem to be typical at the shoulders and sometimes at the *holbi*—the bottom of the gákti (Guttorm 2013a:902).

---

28 The modde, or *muoddá* is used when the pelts are furless, or the hides come from animals other than reindeer (Larsen [1950]1979:12.3).

Many of these details have been documented in the coloured paintings, drawings and prints that often accompany the written sources. Although these images should be viewed with some apprehension, they still present details that may be recognized from present-day gáktis. This is not to say that the gákti is a static garment. On the contrary, the gákti have been subject to change in numerous ways (Dunfjeld 1999). Both access to materials and fashion have been deeply influential; during the 1980s, for instance, it became quite common to see puffed sleeves added to the gákti (Guttorm 2013a:911). From observing gáktis in museums, one may also notice a successive change happening parallel to the increased supply of coloured bands and other materials. As I discussed briefly in bárket, the gákti also went through several changes during the advent of Laestadianism during the 19th century.

There is then, an obvious sense of aesthetics, or dåajmijes vuekie at play, which takes into account both personal taste, fashion and function. Additionally, it has been known to happen that some elements are added by the gáktimaker depending on the needs of the wearer; *"in the old days it is likely that extra accessories were added to the gáktis of those that held important roles in society, such as the noaidi. Probably the collar would carry a special designation."* (Berit 30.05.2018). Other times, small elements of artistic varieties are added. In fact, it is said that a skilled gáktimaker hones their skill to such a degree that others may see and recognize it in the execution of the garment (Balto 1996:97).

Besides being a source of aesthetics and individual skills, the gákti is also a vessel of knowledge. It embodies a silent, yet visual, language articulated through the cut and the adornments. Both the neck, shoulder, sleeve and holbi act to situate its wearer in society by indicating place of belonging, family descent, gender, relationship status[29], age[30] and sometimes even social standing (Dunfjeld 1999). Many of the elders in South-Sámi communities will, for instance, claim that the colour grey is indicative of poverty (Anta 01.06.2018), which indicates that something as simple as the choice of colour signifies whether someone is of high or low status.[31]

---

29 In some Sámi communities the gákti is slightly altered after marriage.
30 I refer here to the tradition of coming of age tradition. In South-Sámi communities the colored bands at the bottom of the gákti is reversed (Anne-Maja 17.11.2018).
31 Not unlike how red or blue was indicative of high social standing in the Viking Age, as evidenced by burials.

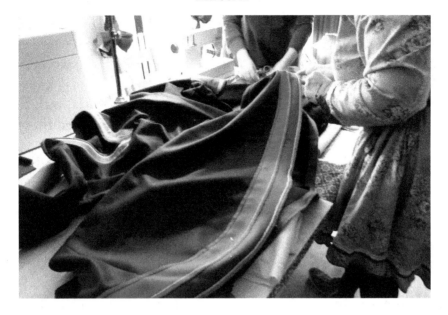

FIGURE 4-9 ASSEMBLING A HOLBI DEMANDS GREAT SKILLS. NOT ONLY IS THE TECHNICAL SKILLS OF THE DUOJÁR IMPORTANT, THEIR KNOWLEDGE OF COLOURS AND PLACEMENT IS EQUALLY CRUCIAL. HERE IS AN EXAMPLE OF THE BOTTOM EDGE OF A PITE SÁMI GAPPTA BEING PREPARED. COLOURED BANDS AS WELL AS THE LISSTO, A NARROW, WOVEN BAND, IS READY TO BE MOUNTED ON THE GAPPTA

In many communities further North, the colour white, amongst elders at least, also bears the meaning of poverty. White fabrics, being as they are not dyed, is often of cheaper make. For this reason, in the past, white fabrics were used for gáktis meant to be everyday wear or workmen's clothes (Silje 15.03.2018). [32] However, for the younger generation, white is increasingly used on gáktis, made for coming-of-age ceremonies and weddings, which indicate that the gákti, to some degree, is slowly adapting to a more Western sphere of influence. This helps to demonstrate that the gákti is anything but a static garment.

Within the specific arrangement of the holbi, or the choice of colours at the back and shoulder, the gákti also possesses the ability to convey its wearers' place of origin, their connection to a specific territory, or siida, and in some cases, even which family the wearer belongs to (Sunna 05.01.2018). [33] This indicates that the relation between place or siida, family, and kin, or *fuolkkit* (Henriksen 1999,

32 On the other hand, when making a beaska white is actually the most valuable color, which is to do with the spiritual value and rareness of the white reindeer (Elsa 13.11.2018)

33 As for designs on the neck, during my visit to Riddo Duottar in Karasjok I had a long conversation with Berit, whom suggested that in the old days specific markings on the neck of the gákti could imply that the wearer had a specific function in society as noaidi, or other leading roles (Berit 30.05.2018)

Labahå 2004), is visually expressed through the materiality of the gákti. In this, the gákti, defined as dipmaduodji and thus very much associated with female duojárs, reflect how it is the Sámi women that *"hálddašit bures sohkavuogádaga dieđuid"*, 'best manage and know the system of kin and clan' (Somby 2016:27, my own translation). In Johannes Schefferus' (1673) "Lapponia" from 1673, it is stated that their gákti-making skills are among the primary arts of Sámi women. This indicates, I would argue, that there was a great value attached to the making of gáktis. Furthermore, I believe that such worth came by way of the gákti communicating complex structures of familial relations and place of descent. The gákti thus conveys the Sámi world-in-relation. It is, I think, highly likely that such an ability, is derived from the past social structure implemented by the Siida system.

Prior to colonisation, as discussed in Chapter Two, the siida referred to a specific stretch of the Sámi homelands, and within this structure, there were strict rules and regulations as to the right of use. Additionally, the siida one belonged to also regulated the spiritual maintenance of the reciprocal relations with the land and the spirits that lived in it (Bäckman 1975). The latter was maintained, either through the sacrificial relationship represented in the sieidies or being aware of and respecting the presence of other beings such as the ulddát (Fonneland 2017). In my opinion, as it so strongly indicates familial and/or geographical belonging, the gákti has served as a document of its wearer's rights of inheritance. Given that the Sámi society relied on either oral or bodily transmittance of knowledge, the relation to land and to people was thus made visible in the materiality of the gákti. This ensured that one would always carry with them a legal document to rights of use. This also suggests, as I see it, that women—being the primary makers of the gákti—had an important role in maintaining and governing the judicial system of Sápmi prior to the epistemicide brought on by colonialism.

Today, when the Sámi no longer live in the Siida structure, at least not in any way that is officially recognized by the different Nation States,[34] the testimony of the gákti might not be needed in the same manner. Still, the interrelatedness and social order of Sámi communities and people are visible in the gákti. Wearing the gákti thus make your relations and your place in the social order, evident for others,

---

34 The exception being reindeerherders whom refer to their specific grazingland as a siida.

thus placing you within the Sámi world-of-relations. This also accounts for the heightened tensions of discussions that relate to the use and making of the gákti, which I discuss in more detail in the next chapter.

The materiality of the gákti also reflects a spiritual dimension, or the tiida. On an individual and collective level, the relationship to an internal and external world is maintained through rituals. These rituals keep the order of life in balance, which is particularly important for the survival of the community. Balance has traditionally been maintained by the Sámi people through rituals, by following normative patterns of behaviour and established practices, by showing respect, and through a dialogue on an individual and collective level (Porsanger 2012:39, Guttorm 2013a:903). Earlier I remarked on the function of tiida as the precursor of specific acts, but a tiida may just as easily be encouraged by the abstinence of action as is the case with the *jijinbelefifer*.

In Sámi duodji, both the guksi, round cups, and the previously mentioned náhppi, are important products. These are made by cultivating *báhkki*, or burls[35] that grow on trees. The jijinbelefifer is the báhkki that grows on the north-facing side of trees, and they are deemed *"unlucky"*[36] and thus not suitable as raw material (Pettersson, Bäckman, and Kjellström 1979:114). Some suggest that the reason is practical as the báhkki facing north has the least exposure to sunlight, which naturally affects the growing rate and quality of wood (Guttorm 2001:54). But I have also heard it said that when making the drums of the noaidi, the goavddis, it is important that the báhkki has had as little sunlight as possible when growing (Násti 13.08.2019). This coincides with the commentary from the previously mentioned Kristoffer Sjulsson, in which he states that some tiida were exclusively for the noaidi to understand (Pettersson, Bäckman, and Kjellström 1979:115).

Though tiidas are not limited to the practice of duodji, they are nonetheless deeply implicated in the material expressions of its practice (e.g., Balto 1996:93 , Guttorm 2001:60). *"[G]o misran lea dat diidastallan, dat diidaárbevierry, go mis lea olu dákkar nu go mu eadni muit-*

---

35 A burl, also known as burr, is a tree growth where grain has grown gnarled, and often in the form of a rounded outhrowth on the trunk of a tree.

36 The exact wording is *"ej ansågos lyxkobringande"*, the exact translation of which is that they were not considered to bring fortune.

alii", as we have this diidastallat, or much tradition of diida, or spells, as my mother has told me' (Harlin and Pieski 2020:128). There is, to my knowledge, no complete syllabus written that details the specific acts, practices, and beliefs regulated by tiidas. Rather, a tiida is passed down the generations and amongst peers, by storytelling and bodily acts (Guttorm 2001:59). The making of a gákti is particularly fraught with these unwritten rules and regulations, even if few are shared out-side of our communities.[37] Several of my verdde have still allowed me to reference one particular tiida pertaining to the use of yellow on the coloured bands used on the gákti.

In the old days, yellow was associated with Beaivi—the sun, who in the Sámi religion is a holy power believed to be the Father of all. Using small amounts of yellow is thus a way of showing Him defer-ence. Too much yellow would mean the opposite (Sávve 06.05.2018), which is why, even today, when so few still follow the old teachings, a gákti made entirely of yellow fabric is not a common sight.[38]

Looking at the different dimensions—tiida, interrelatedness, so-cial standing, aesthetics, and function— involved in the making of the gákti and as such implicated in the practice of duodji, illustrates how values, meanings and expressions of a Sámi world-in-relation appear. In this, practice and interrelated knowledge[s] emerge from the rela-tionship of humans to things, to land, to nature, and to other entities and beings. Meaning about the social world thus emerges from the synergetic movement between material expression, the cultural prac-tice of duodji and the interrelatedness creating the materialities of a Sámi world-in-relation.

The next chapter continues this discussion by looking at how peo-ple and communities have worked to restore Sámi identities and sov-ereignty through the practice of duodji, and furthermore, the specific manner in which such processes happen.

---

37 Exceptions do exist. Konrad Nielsen for instance, share in his writings that pregnant woman had to abstain from decorating themselves with fringed shawls as the knots used to fringe or *riessat* could influence the birth in a negative way (Guttorm 2013a:913)

38 I would still caution against believing this tiida to be universal. One verdde shared with me her belief that the association between yellow and Beaivi is more likely to be a construct of non-Sámi missionaries that believed such a connection existed and some made it their *"business to stop us from wearing yellow"* (Mona 17.08.2019).

CHAPTER 5: ČUOLDIT

WEAVING STORIES

BIOGRAPHIES OF BECOMING, THE MEMORY OF BLOOD AND THE PRACTICE OF DUODJI

ČUOVUN MÁLLE MAN MÁTTUT LEAT MUNNJE OAHPAHAN/ I FOLLOW THE PATTERNS THAT MY ANCESTORS HAVE TAUGHT ME—A PROLOGUE

"I can still remember the very first time that I attended a class to learn duodji. In it we were learning how to make a luhkka[1]. I already knew Sámi knitting and weaving, which I had learned at the feet of my áhkku in early youth. But the gákti and the luhkka, which are both made of cloth, I didn`t know of. You see, there was no trace left of them in my home community". Earlier we had discussed the consequences of assimilation on her home community, and now she referred to that discussion when explaining that while her family always knew that they were Sámi, the social stigma attached to that ethnicity meant that there was little to signify it outside the home. *Still, as a teenager she yearned to connect more to her Sámi heritage, and she decided to leave her home for Guovdageaidnu, a Sámi village located at the Norwegian side of the border, to continue her high school education. Whilst there she took a keen interest in Sámi duodji.* "When I was making that luhkka, something felt very wrong. I can`t really describe it accurately, but when I was attaching the hood something inside me said to me that I was doing it wrong. But I didn`t understand why. Only later, when I was older, did I learn that the luhkka that in the past had been worn in my home community, was without a hood.

I was curious as to what she believed initiated her feelings of wrongness and

---

1   A North Sámi shoulder cape, with an attached hood. The luhkka in the past was exclusively used by men whilst out working. A female variation of similar make is the njálfáhtta, which is both shorter and without a hood.

asked her if she could elaborate. She was quiet for some time before she took a big breath as if she were bracing herself. "Well, I have thought on this many times. Why did it feel wrong to me when I was asked to make something that didn´t, in the past, have a place in my home community? And I think it´s because I somehow knew. Somewhere in my body, I knew that the luhkka that my ancestors wore didn´t have a hood. That it wasn´t right for me". Again, she went quiet for some time before continuing: "I think the knowledge was already in me. My ancestor's knowledge still lives inside me. The old knowledge. It is always there, the memory exists already in my body, but only when I make duodji do I regain a conscious knowledge of it". I took some time to think through her statement before asking what she believed happened when the blood of her ancestors awoke in her a knowledge of her Sámi heritage. She simply replied that "this is how I learn my culture from my ancestors, and it is how I grow to appreciate Sámi culture for what it is without the ugliness that assimilation has caused". Then she turned the tables on me, asking what I thought about her belief. This time I went quiet for a while, taking my time in considering what she had shared with me. After a while, I asked her if she knew or had heard of árbediehtu. She had not heard of the term, but I could sense from her a question of why I brought it up. "Árbediehtu», I told her, "is often translated to mean traditional knowledge, when in fact it directly translates into inherited knowledge". At this point, she interrupted me, "I wondered about my experience, and I even looked at articles on genetic memory, and now you tell me that we already have a word for knowledge that gets passed through our blood. Árbediehtu? Yes, that´s exactly it. Knowledge that you inherit from your ancestors" (Åsa 07.01.2018).

INTRODUCTION

The following chapter looks at the process of regaining Indigenous sovereignty, through the recentering of identities. In our society, and now I am speaking generally, the idea of personal autonomy is meticulously adhered to. So much so, that when the United Nations drafted the declaration of Human Rights in the wake of World War II, they actually declared autonomy to be a basic human right (UDHR 1948). Such, however, has not always been the case. The practice of slavery in the Americas during the 18th and 19th centuries comes to mind as perhaps the most familiar example of autonomy being denied (Bradley 1999).[2] Yet, the lack of sovereignty has been equally long-

---

2 Even when slavery was abolished in the latter part of the 19th century, autonomy was not restored (Hine 2003)

lived, if not more so, for Indigenous communities and peoples. In fact, until very recently Indigenous communities held no true ownership of their land, history, language, culture, identity, and in some extreme cases, even their dead (Hilden 2000, Henare 2005, Cubillo 2010, Smith [1999]2012, Kuokkanen 2019). Despite some recent studies that show Indigenous people surprisingly often found ways of circumventing the absence of autonomy (Murray Li 2000, Baglo 2011), for the most part there was a genuine lack of sovereignty. A lack that some would argue, still exists (Kuhn 2020).

The collective consequences of Indigenous sovereignty being suppressed are too many to list here, but for the purpose of the discussion ahead, I shall focus on the fact that who and what constitutes Indigenous for far too long has been decided by those that are not themselves categorized as such. It should come as no surprise then, that one, if not the greatest project *"of post-colonialism [in] Indigenous societies is the recentering of cultural identity"* (Smith [1999]2012:100).[3] Ása's story is an acute lesson in this respect. Her story is important for a number of reasons, but I have singled out four in particular. First, the relevance of her story lies in how it engages with many of the complex and problematic issues derived from the colonisation of Sápmi; the severing of Sámi knowledges and practices; the disassociation between communities, families and persons; the alienation of the Sámi people from their homelands; and the silencing of Sámi stories and history to name but a few.

Apart from listing how colonialism has impacted on Sámi communities and people, past and present, the relevance of Ása's story also rests upon the fact that it is a surprisingly rich source of individual resilience and resistance in the face of assimilation and colonial narratives. Which in turn, brings me to the third and fourth reason, starting with the fact that relearning Sámi cultural practices and knowledges has been Ása's way of reconnecting with her cultural heritage. From this process, she also came to believe that the power of her ancestors was embodied in her as a genetic memory, or what in the international discourse is referred to as *blood memory* (e.g., Lawrence 2004, Sturm 2011, Watt and Kowal 2019), which she went on to suggest could be conceptualized as an *árbediehtu* related to the practice of duodji.

---

3   To recentre one's identity may of course happen in a multitude of ways (Murray Li 2000, Palmater 2011, Hansen 2015), but each is as valid as the other, and also very much dependent on context.

These four facets will serve as a useful point of entry into the discussions ahead. Consequently, this chapter focus on the following aspects: self-identification, genetic memory, duodji, and árbediehtu. Looking at the interconnectedness of these four within Sámi communities and museums, I will account for, at least in part, how the knowledge of árbediehtu in connection with a practice of duodji, or duddjot, produce a cultural self, which in turn emerges as a Sámi identity.

Before I continue detailing the structure of the chapter ahead, I need to make some clarifications pertaining to terminology. As more and more descendants of Indigenous people of mixed ancestry rediscover and/or reconnect with their ancestry, many have in their later life changed their racial identification, or ethnicity (Watt and Kowal 2019). To researchers of the phenomenon, this group has become known as *reclaimers* (Fitzgerald 2007), *race shifters* (Sturm 2011), *New Identifiers* (Biddle and Markham 2018) or alternatively, people that are or have engaged in *ethnic switching* (Liebler 2004), *ethnic mobility* (Caron-Malenfant et al. 2014), or a *trans of migration* (Brubaker 2016). Ása herself made mention of the term *Ny same*, or *New Sámi* having been applied to her person. I have yet to see the term implemented in an academic context, but I have seen it used on social media. I am sorry to say however, that both Ása and several of my other verdde experienced it as an unfavourable term. In adherence to such, I will in the following use reclaimer and ethnic shift, or *sámáidahttin* (samification) when necessary. With that said, I now return to the structure of the chapter.

TO ČUOLDIT—MAPPING THE STRUCTURE

For the sake of my own as well as the readers' ease, I want to envision my structure as a weave taking place on a njuikun with immeasurable threads. Each thread has its own part to play, but only as the weave comes together does the work unite into one. This analogy is, I think, exceedingly descriptive; on a njuikun, each thread passes through a firm heddle with alternate slots and holes. The resulting warp is threaded in such a way that moving the heddle up, or down for that matter, separates the warp threads into layers while still running parallel. Illustrative then, of the fact that the subjects of this chapter run parallel, but on different levels.

FIGURE 5-1 WHEN I LAST VISITED MY FATHER'S HOME COMMUNITY, A CONSIDER-
ABLE AMOUNT OF TIME WAS SPENT IN MY ÁHKKU'S KITCHEN, WEAVING BANDS
AND EXPERIMENTING WITH COLOUR CHOICES. HERE I AM WEAVING A TRADI-
TIONAL BAND THAT IS SPECIFIC TO THE COMMUNITY.

At first glance, it might be easy to interpret the weave as disorderly, but as any weaver will tell you, there is still structure. To me, the system of distinction in the weave comes from the use of colours and purpose. In this case, three colours for the purpose of the frame also acts as the outline of your weave. Another colour is used for the base thread that passes through the warp threads and binds them together, and one last colour is used to make out the pattern of the weave, thus expressing its imagery.

Mirroring the weave, I have chosen to structure the following chapter into three parts starting with the frame. In this chapter's weave, the frame comes in three colours: árbediehtu, genetic memory and duodji. Though they are separate, in acting as the frame, they blend together to create one lens through which I will analyse the recentering of Sámi identities amongst reclaimers. First, however, I need to expand upon the juxtapose of these three. I do this, by looking into the conventional view on árbediehtu as an inherited and shared knowledge, collective in so far as it is passed down the generations through practice. Following this account, established convention is challenged by adding to the mix the notion of inherent knowledge as a genetic memory and duodji as a practice that unlocks said memory. I do want to add an important note of clarification. It is not my intent to ascertain the scientific possibility of genetic memory as I do not see that as relevant. Rather, what matters is how the belief in such a phenomenon have impacted—or not—on the articulation of Sámi identities.

Having completed the threading of the frame, next I turn to self-identification, which is the last of the four aspects I initially determined, as the pattern of my weave. A pattern may be understood as a regularity, or the way in which something, be it colours, shapes, happenings or more, repeat in a predictable manner—suiting then, as the allegory for a discussion on the formation of Indigenous Sámi identities. As have been shown, Indigenous identities are a breeding ground for controversies and complexities. To think that any process of formation or recentering of identity should happen unheeding of such entanglements is unsound. I have as such chosen to begin the laying of my pattern with a general discussion on the political and social implications that might affect the forming or recentering of Sámi identities.

I continue the discussion by delving deeper into the rich entanglements of becoming Sámi and the corresponding belief in an ancestral memory. This is achieved through the adaptation of sámáidahttin as a constituent concept. Going forward then, I have adapted sámáidahttin to suit my need and will be using it, first, to refer to the act of passing from one ethnic category to a Sámi identity. Additionally, I work with the term as a bodily process in which Sámi cultural codes become incorporated through the practice of duodji. Fresh from this discussion, I turn to the base of my weave.

Just as the base in a weave creates the foundation to see the frame and the pattern, so too does the base of this chapter give room to analyse the process of recentering identity. While it might not be immediately discernible, my base is provided by the role of museums in said process. There are many ways of doing so, but I have chosen to focus on how museums are used by reclaimers in processes where the recentering of identity also includes the revival and restitution, or re-remembrance, of practices and knowledges. By examining the relations between reclaimers and museums, past and present, I thus close this chapter by arguing that museums are a vital part of the knowledge system that is duodji.

Before I go on with my discussion, I would like to remark on my use of re-remembering. I initially adapted this term as an alternative to revitalization. Though the latter is well known in the vernacular of Indigenous acts of restitution and frequently used by my verdde, it is a contested term. Māori scholar of Indigenous methodologies, Linda Tuhiwai Smith ([1999]2012:112), for instance, dislikes it because it *"tends to imply that cultures need[s] rescuing"*. I am inclined to agree, but it is still a term that is implicated when discussing Indigenous processes in which there is an attempt to recover something that has been lost. In his discussion of revitalizing, the historian Robert Archibald (1999:133), suggests that this process instead be coined as an act of re-remembering, which he goes on to explain as a process which brings back knowledge and restores social processes in order to strengthen cultural identity. In the following, I thus use his term as an alternative to revitalization.

BLOOD MEMORY / RECLAIMING SÁMI INDIGENEITY

In a brilliant analysis on why bodies matter, the American philosopher and gender theorist Judith Butler (1993:1) asks: *"Is there a way to link the [...] materiality of the body to the performativity of gender?"*. She thus enters the ranks of prominent thinkers that claim bodies to be sites of production, whether it be gender, cultural meanings, identities, or practices that are propagated and materialized. By no means then, is the idea of the body as a tool through which we experience and make sense of the world, a novel one (Merleau-Ponty [1945]2012, Beauvoir [1949]2000, Bourdieu 1977). Nor is the belief that frequent and nondiscursive practises form the sum of our lived experience, less commonplace (Butler [1990]1999, e.g., Silliman 2001:195). Genetic memory, on the other hand, is not as readily accepted, especially within academia and the subject has consequently gained far less attention. Nonetheless, the notion of an ancestral memory that is genetically inherited has in recent years received some consideration, albeit more in line with the possibility of historical trauma[4] in an intergenerational

---

4   As defined in bárket. Still, to reaffirm, a historical trauma is a generational and collective response to an overwhelming experience and event.

context (Walters et al. 2011).[5]

A brief overview of the studies in question shows that so far, the majority of attention has been on if and how trauma is genetically passed down from one generation to the next (Nagata et al. 1999); or whether trauma may have a greater effect on descendants as opposed to having first-hand experience (Yehuda 1999); or, if gender is significant in perceiving and transmitting trauma (Brave Heart 1999). No doubt these studies are important, but they show a disconcerting tendency to focus on trauma alone, which I find problematic. It is a fact that in many cultures—Indigenous included—there is a real conviction in the existence of genetic memories. And more to the point, that genetic memories pass along much more than trauma (e.g., Hume 2000, Lawrence 2004). Indigenous elders from Anishinaabe[6] communities on Northern Turtle Island, for instance, claim that *"memory is in the blood and bone, [...] our stories are passed not just verbally but through a kind of genetic memory"* (Bombay 2015). In so far as Ása is concerned, this is also true of the Sámi, whose *"bones and blood"*, she believes, holds the *"experiences of [...] ancestors"*. (07.01.2018). Her argument rests, among others, on what might be termed *gamus dovdat* or *čoalit dovdet*, which roughly translates to 'we know by instinct' and 'gut feeling', respectively. As I understand it, these terms materialize in her story as the sense of wrongness she felt when she used the árbediehtu from another community to practice duodji in her home community.

Today, Ása is a highly respected duojár, but as a teen she held little knowledge about her ancestry or Sámi history. Born and raised on the coastline of the Norwegian side of the border, Ása's home community is one that has been greatly afflicted by the assimilation politics of the Norwegian government. Not surprising, if one considers that the coastal communities was amongst those first and most aggressively targeted by said policies (Minde 2005:11, e.g., Eidheim 1971). As a result, Ása grew up being told that *"being Sámi is worthless"*, and that it would serve no purpose for her to be taught *"Sámi cultural expressions"* (07.01.2018). This is not to say that she did not learn any skills at home. On the contrary, her grandmother—herself a duojár of

---

5   If we turn attention to the Sámi context, the shame and ethnic stigma I discussed in bárket is also implied as it is a feeling that many descendants have, and continue to, inherit from their preceding generations (Sikku 03.03.2020).

6   Anishinaabe is an autonym for a group of culturally related Indigenous Peoples' resident in what is now Canada and the United States. These also include the Odawa, Saulteaux, Ojibwe—including Mississaugas—Potawatoi, Oji-Cree and Algonquin Peoples.

note—made sure to pass on what skills she could, but only in so far as they could be labelled and pass as Norwegian.[7] Those skills that were recognizable as Sámi, including language, were not passed on. These skills, Ása explains, "*We made ourselves forget*" (07.01.2018). As statements go, this is exceptionally powerful, and it reflects the discussion of ethnic shifting in bárket, highlighting that forgetting culture and languages was, in truth, a way of surviving.

In her youth this disruption of Sámi practices and knowledge had a high impact, leading her to feel a sense of loss and that "*something's missing even if you don't really know what*" (07.01.2018).

> Knowing that there is a part of your elders' [grandmother] life that you aren't allowed to take part in really hurts […] when you realize how much you lost because of it … I don´t think it´s possible for anyone to understand the sorrow if they haven´t lived it themselves. It´s heart-breaking. Because, when she´s [her grandmother] gone and buried, who else will tell you [about Sámi culture and language]? (07.01.2018).

Short of *árbečeahpis*, or knowledge keepers in her home community, yet wanting to learn, Ása chose as an adolescent to leave for another Sámi community for her secondary schooling. It was here that she first learned about the practice of duodji. In the process, she also learned to access what she believes is a Sámi collective memory. This, in turn, helped assert in her both "*kinship*" and a sense of "*belonging to land, community and culture*". For Ása, duodji became her way of reforging a connection to the Sámi knowledge[s] and practices that had been severed in previous generations.

RE-EMPOWERING SELF THROUGH THE PRACTICE OF DUODJI

Without arguing for or against the validity of Ása's claim to genetic memory, it is true that connections between community, culture, and persons are the foundation of Indigenous worldviews and place of self (Barrett 2015:112). And certainly, as discussed in ruvdet, this is also the case with Sámi cultures (Law 2015). In 2013, a NIKU—Norsk Institutt for Kulturminneforskning—rapport on cultural heritage sites located in North Norway indicated that in Sámi communities, heritage sites are often used to anchor local communities' sense of belonging to their ancestral homelands, and even aid in the survival

---

7   Ása mentions both knitting and weaving as examples of Sámi skills that have been disguised as Norwegian

of collective memories (Myrvoll et al. 2013). This actually followed up some of the findings from an earlier research project that in 2008 was initiated by Sámi allaskuvla, the Sámi university of applied sciences in Guovdageaidnu on the Norwegian side of the border. Árbediehtu, which was the name of the project, found that access to one's ancestral birrasat, or surroundings, helped keep knowledges and practices alive and eased its transmission to descending generations (Guttorm and Porsanger 2011).[8] This, as evidenced by my previous discussion of birrasat [surroundings], also include the practice of duodji.

Linked as it is to a collective life experience, duodji incorporates a common understanding of the landscape, of seasons and materials that is both place-specific and specific to Sámi culture. (Guttorm 2001, e.g., Klokkernes and Olli 2008). Consider for instance, how the long-developed knowledge of the reindeers' anatomy and the local fauna is helpful when preparing and conserving the animals' skin, or bárket. Or how Sámi coastal communities have developed similar techniques related to fish skin, proving that culturally derived processing methods are often influenced by birrasat (Klokkernes and Olli 2008:109). In this capacity, I believe duodji should be considered a nexus, providing a series of connections and relations, including culture, people, land, and communities—both past, present, and future.

To believe that duodji brings one closer to culture, land, and one's ancestors is not at all uncommon. In December of 2018, I attended a talk on the Sámi ládjogáhpir—the hornhat—given by Eeva-Kristiina Harlin, a PhD candidate in archaeology at the University of Oulu, on the Finnish side of the border, who is writing a thesis on, among other subjects, rematriation. The talk was arranged as a brief seminar where Eeva shared her research into the reproduction of museum objects. In her talk, she spoke at great length about Sámi heritage objects, and their migration from everyday objects to museum artefacts and back to everyday objects using the ládjogáhpir as an example (for more see Harlin and Pieski 2020). Her case study is certainly interesting in the context of this book.

For generations, the infamous hornhat was, as discussed in bárket, banned from use. As a result, most surviving hats are today found in museums or private collections (Harlin and Pieski 2020:10).

---

8 It also helped to reinforce birgejupmi. If you recall, this is a concept which describes the maintenance of a good life.

FIGURE 5-2 IN 2019, FOR THE FIRST TIME EVER, THE VENICE BIENNALE HAD SÁMI REPRESENTATION. AT THE FINNISH PAVILION, OUTI PIESKI WAS ONE OF THE ARTISTS REPRESENTED, AND HER PROJECT INCLUDED, AMONG OTHERS THIS LÁDJOGÁHPIR, MADE IN THE SHAPE OF THE ONE HER ANCESTOR HAD ONCE WORN, AND WHICH WAS FOUND IN A MUSEUMS. I WAS FORTUNATE ENOUGH TO BE PRESENT DURING THE OPENING OF THE PAVILION AND WAS ABLE TO TAKE THIS PICTURE.

As part of her Ph.D., however, Eeva has collaborated with the Sámi *dáiddar* Outi Pieski where the latter has created a ládjogáhpir based on one which she found at the National Museum in Helsinki. Outi chose that particular ládjogáhpir because it had once belonged to her ancestor, explaining as she did so, that *"duodji carries knowledge, traditions, history"* and that *"[t]rough duodji a person can get connected with his or her ancestors and be empowered"* (Harlin 2018). I have heard variations of this statement from other Sámi duojárs and makers of duodji, which reflect, I think, that our ancestor's knowledge as sustained in and by duodji is a common perception (Guttorm 2007:63).

Another prominent Sámi duojár that expand on this view is Unni Fjellheim, whom I briefly introduce in giisá. She allowed a glimpse to be shared when, in early 2019, the Norwegian broadcasting corporation (NRK) aired a series of short instalments under the Norwegian title "Arven", meaning heritage. In it, the audience was introduced to an assemblage of craftspeople, amongst them Unni. During her interview, Unni explained what *vætnoe*, the south Sámi equivalent of duodji, means to her on a personal level but also to the Sámi communities as a whole. Vætnoe, she concludes, is something one inherits: "*we learn for generations and we transfer for generations*" (Nøren 2019). When I later spoke with Unni about the broadcast, she told me that what she had wanted to convey was that we learned our vætnoe from those before us, and that we passed on these teachings to those that come after. In doing so, we forge a connection between the past and the present, linking ancestors with descendants (Fjellheim 27.11.2019). As I understand it, what Unni, and for that matter Outi, speaks of is árbediehtu, or shared/inherited knowledge.

Admittedly, the term is, as I have previously mentioned, recent and there is as such no unambiguous definition. What it conceptualizes, however, is not in any way new. That is to say, the act of passing a specialized knowledge—such as duodji—between generations by seeing and doing is both a common and long-lasting way of embedding knowledge in Sámi communities (Balto 1997:70, Triumf 2011:82, Guttorm 2013a:918). Still, if your ancestors were affected by assimilation and other colonial strategies designed to enforce an epistemicide of Sámi practices and knowledges, this way of transferring knowledge no longer applies. But when the continuity of knowledge has been severed, and árbediehtu is no longer a certainty, what then?

WALKING THE ANCESTOR'S PATH

"*Lea nugo sii livččet das mu bálddas*", "*it's as if they are right here, next to me*", explains Cecilie Løvli Korsvoll whilst passing her *giehpa* (shuttle) back and forth between the threads of yarn gathered in her njuikun (Helander 2019, my own translation). In 2019, Cecilie was one of several participants at a course arranged by Oslo Sámiid Duodji and under the skilful guidance of duojár Anna Ciućka-Sjursen to learn Sámi weaving as seen in Figure 5-3.

As a child, Cecilie was unaware that her family was of Sámi descent. Her grandfather was the last generation that spoke the language or was raised within a Sámi culture.

FIGURE 5-3 IN THE WINTER OF 2019, SEVERAL SÁMI CONVENED AT SÁMI HOUSE IN OSLO TO ATTEND A COURSE IN SÁMI WEAVING. IT WAS FACILITATED BY THE LOCAL ORGANIZATION, OSLO SÁMIID DUODJI, OF WHICH I AT THAT TIME WAS THE LEADER.

As an adult, however, he chose to hide all that was Sámi from his son, and consequently, Cecilie never got to learn about her Sámi heritage. Now, as an adult, Cecilie is attempting to reclaim both the culture and the language of her ancestors. Barred as she is from her ancestors árbediehtu, Cecilie has had to look for alternative ways of restoring the severed connection between past and present, as well as the disconnect she feels towards her ancestors. Partly she does so by learning duodji, explaining the reason as being that it embeds in her "*[d]ovdu ahte mus lea oktavuohta iežan máttuide*", or "*the feeling that my ancestors are here with me*" (Helander 2019, my own translation).[9]

The connection that Cecilie speaks of restoring is the same connection that both Outi and Unni touched upon in their stories; a connection granted by árbediehtu, and in extension, by duodji.

---

9   The interview with Cecilie was done by Liisa Helander on November 3rd, 2019 and was subsequently on print in Ávvir the 22nd of that month. It was published in North Sámi, but I translated the entire interview for Cecilie.

FIGURE 5-4 DUOJÁRS GATHERED IN BÅDDÅDJO DISCUSS THE MAKE OF THE PITE SÁMI GAPPTE AND ITS ACCESSORIES BASED ON ORAL AND LOCAL SOURCES, AS WELL AS IMAGES AND ACQUISITION TEXTS FOUND IN ETHNOGRAPHIC AND CULTURAL/HISTORY MUSEUMS.

Nonetheless, there is a marked difference in their stories. Cecilie learnt to weave by attending a session hosted by Oslo Sámiid Duodji, which is a local interest group whose objective includes teaching and sharing knowledge of duodji. In contrast, Unni and Outi learned duodji at the feet of their mothers and grandmothers—seeing, and then doing. This is a significant difference, and I will explain why that is, but first I need to introduce Elly and Sanna.

In the early summer of 2018, alongside several duojárs, I travelled to Båddadjo for a weekend gathering focused on "revitalizing", or better yet, re-remembering the Pite Sámi gappte on the Norwegian side of the border. I was not initially a part of this project, and only joined on the third and last gathering by invitation from the project initiator, Trude Stenhammer.[10] The group was an eclectic one, all with their different area of expertise. One of them, Elly from a small Island community, was a weaver. One evening, whilst weaving *lissto*[11] she told me; *"you know, the knowledge of duodji ... that knowledge lies inside me somewhere. Probably some of my ancestors were great duojárs and now as I work with my hands, their memories come to life in me"* (24.06.2018). Elly's background is surprisingly familiar. Like Ása, Elly never got to learn about her Sámi heritage as a child and had to seek other avenues of learning as an adult. She understands why:

10 My invite came after I contacted her for details on the event.
11 A woven band used at the bottom edge of the Pite Sámi gappta.

180

"My grandparents chose not to teach my parents the Sámi language and culture, and my parents didn't know to teach me. They [her grandparents] knew that being Sámi meant that one was disadvantaged [...] they didn't want that for their children. But that doesn't mean that I don't hurt and feel a great loss, but I can't really blame them either" (Elly 24.06.2018).

But this was not the only familiarity that Elly shared with Ása. She also seemed to share the belief in ancestral memory, but to be sure, I asked her directly, to which she replied that the memories of those that came before her was "*in her blood*" (Elly 25.06.2018). At this point, I outright asked if she was referring to genetic memory. She answered that there was probably a term in Sámi meaning to inherit memories, but as she did not speak her language, she preferred to talk about "*an ancestral memory*" (Elly 25.06.2018).

In a later conversation with Elly, we spoke again on the notion on ancestral memory; "*sometimes you hear about someone who is especially skilled in a particular practice of duodji. I always wonder [...] maybe their skill comes from an ancestor*" (Elly 17.01.2019). This, I think, is associated with the gaze, or *geahčastat*, which I briefly spoke on in riessat. The social control implied in *geahčastat* come into play when duojárs are commended for their *čehppodat* [skill], as in gaining public recognition as a *čeahpes duojár*, or skilled duojár. Implied in this term is an implicit understanding that the person in question has good máhttu, or practical knowledge. Once more, as I understand here, Elly suggests that knowledge of the blood, may be unlocked by practice, and eventually become an expression of ancestor's skill, or máhttu. Here, I believe that *gamus dovdat* or *čoalit dovdet* is relevant once more.

Soon after I returned from Båddadjo, I helped host a duodjebádji in Oslo. It was here that I first met Sanna. Having recently learnt of her Sámi ancestry, Sanna shared with me that she had always sensed that something was missing from her life, "*a loss*", albeit she "*never knew of what*" (Sanna 02.07.2018). For her, attending workshops and gatherings of duojárs, had provided her with an answer; learning duodji had helped her identify that the loss was "*of self, [...] of my history [...] never understanding that I belonged somewhere else*" (02.07.2018). It is of course, never easy to engage in the process of re-remembering. Working collectively, in duodjebádjis, for instance, helps as it reflects the collective feature of Sámi cultures (Harlin and Pieski 2020:116). In as much as she could erase her sense of loss, duodji thus became her way of doing so because it brought her "*closer with my ancestors. It's like I can feel what they felt and know what they knew*" (02.07.2018). When I asked her to elaborate, she added that "*maybe I do […] learn from my ancestors*", and that "*maybe I remember with them*" (02.07.2018). Just as Elly and Ása before her, had done, so too did Sanna express her belief in the possibility of an inherent bodily knowledge determined by the biogenetic and genealogical facts of her Sámi ancestry—a genetic memory inherited from ancestors and unlocked by the practice of duodji.

The shared belief of Ása, Elly and Sanna is interesting for several reasons. Still, there are two that I find to be of particular note, starting with the fact that all three women held no prior knowledge of one another. Nor were they aware of the subjects each had discussed with me. Yet, independent from each other, all three concluded that duodji was not only a learned skill, but also a genetically inherited skill. The second note I want to point out is the fact that both Sanna, Elly and Ása were predominantly raised in non-Sámi environments without knowing, or being actively discouraged from learning, about their Sámi ancestry. Only as adults did the three make a conscious decision to craft their Sámi ancestry into a Sámi identity. This I think, reveals something important because not only did they all at some point decide to pursue a Sámi identity. They did so by correlating their process with the practice of duodji, believing it to awaken their ancestral memories. With these two facts inferred, I now return to the promised explanation of why there is a difference between, on the one hand, how Ása, Elly and Sanna perceive árbediehtu and, on the other hand, how the concept is understood by Outi and Unni.

ÁRBEDIEHTU AS BLOOD MEMORY

When Ása, Elly and Sanna explained their situation, all three remarked upon the fact that when learning duodji, none had a home community or family members to look to. That is to say, in their birrasat, they did not have elders to learn from. On the contrary, they had to travel to other communities and resort to institutional learning by ways of courses. As árbediehtu is conventionally understood, the knowledge of their ancestors was thus lost to them, or at best it was severely fractured. That is not to say that they no longer had any avenues available for learning árbediehtu. As pointed out by Ilse in ruvdet, árbediehtu is not only inherited through descending lines. It is also laterally shared between friends and peers (09.07.2018). Nevertheless, and I think this is the crux of the matter, this would not be an ancestrally inherited knowledge. "*In the traditional knowledge [of duodji], that particular knowledge must be 'inherited'*", says Gunvor Guttorm (2007:68) in a discussion on duodji as concept. To understand what is being said here, I think we need to return to birrasat.

The knowledge of duodji, through a focus on birrasat, is place-based; shaped by the generational experience within specific locations. When that knowledge disappears, there are no guarantee that the exact same knowledge will be available in other communities. Anyone may, of course, learn to practice duodji, and in the same manner, gain árbediehtu. This is evidenced, for instance, by Ása's story, or by Sanna telling of turning to sources such as *Digitalt Museum*[12] as well as "*so many different sources; pictures, and museums, of course, have old [duodji]*" (02.07.2018). Elly likewise speaks of needing to look outside her own community, going to both museums to view their collections and doing courses and travelling to duojárs living in neighbouring communities in order to "*talk and just learn*" (24.06.2018). Even for Outi, the process of re-remembering the ládjogáhpir demanded she turn to the museums. In all of these cases, knowledge was gained in alternative ways.

Nevertheless, in order to inherit the árbediehtu of your ancestors, they must take on an active role in the learning process, and that process must be located to place, or birrasat. Sadly, when knowledge has been lost, there is a "*severance, a broken chain of transmittance*" (Petra 08.06.2020), which makes árbediehtu in its conventional meaning impossible (Guttorm 2001). To bypass this impossibility, I would argue that Ása, Elly and Sanna have conceived of another way to understand árbediehtu. An understanding where diehtu is the knowledge born from a genetic memory and máhttu is the practice that unlocks said memory. Comprehending árbediehtu in this way allows the three to claim their knowledge and practices of duodji as inherited. And it is through this inherited árbediehtu that the three women take part in the living process of being, or becoming, if you will, Sámi.

The notion of an ancestral memory is one that has gained an in-

---

12 Digitalt Museum is an online resource of digitalized collections from museums in both Norway and Sweden. It was established in 2009 and is today run by KulturIT AS which was established two-year prior by the Norwegian Open Air Museum in Oslo and Maihaugen in Lillehammer, in collaboration with ABM-utvikling.

creasing influence in the last few decades, at least in an Indigenous context of re-remembering. On an international level, beliefs about the spirit of one's ancestors being accessible through genetic memory is often articulated as *blood memory*. No doubt, this tendency is related to the fact that more and more, descendants of Indigenous people have rediscovered their ancestry. Alternatively, having always been aware of their ancestry, increasingly, descendants have found themselves becoming invested in reconnecting with their Indigenous roots (Lawrence 2004, Sturm 2011, Hansen 2015, Watt and Kowal 2019).[13] It is in this context, that of reclaimers and a racial shift, blood memory becomes exceedingly relevant. Consequently, a rapidly growing literature shows that thinking in terms of blood memory often appeals to individuals of Indigenous descent that for some reason or another have not been socialized into their source communities' systems of knowledge[s], practices, and beliefs (Watt and Kowal 2019, Sturm 2011). I will explain why that is.

Metaphors of bones and blood are appealing because they imply that Indigenous knowledge[s] and skill[s] are part of one's biological make-up, and as such, they are embodied in reclaimers (Gustavsson and Riley 2018). Bonita Lawrence, who was introduced in bárket, albeit in relation to Indigenous gender systems, suggest that the idea of blood memory is attractive as it implies there being "*a direct link to the lives of our ancestors*", which is "*made manifest in the flesh of their descendants*" (2004:200). Even if there has been a severance and descendants are seemingly assimilated into colonist societies, there is still a way to reclaim the knowledge of ancestors. As a professor of Anthropology, Circe Strum (2011:41), who is of Mississippi Choctaw[14] descent, points out in her research, many believe that their ancestors are "*embodied within […]—and, if listened to, will guide them towards their true path and identity.*" Here then, is revealed the necessity of forging a link between árbediehtu as genetic memory and duodji as a cultural practice.

---

13 A fresh report on the Public health of the Indigenous population and ethnic minorities in Norway, actually estimates that in Finnmark and Troms, two in every five people, or 40%, has Sámi, or Kven, ancestry (Melhus and Broderstad 2020b:16). The findings in Nordland shows that only 13% has Sámi, or Kven ancestry (Melhus and Broderstad 2020a:16).

14 The Choctaw, or Chata, is a First Nation People whose homelands lies to the south on Turtle Island, in what is today known as Alabama, Florida, Mississippi and Louisiana, USA.

THE TRAUMA OF ABSENCE

Both Ása, Elly and Sanna discussed with me the loss that they felt when confronted with their lack of language, cultural knowledge[s], and practices. Their sense of loss, what I would like to define as a *trauma of absence*, is at its very core an "*emptiness*", as well as a perceived insufficient foundation for one's "*authentic self*" to manifest (Karen 15.05.2018). For many reclaimers of Sámi descent, it is this trauma of absence that motivates their shift in ethnicity. Feeling "*empty*" as Lukas, who is from the Swedish side of the border, puts it, to become Sámi was to become a "*more authentic person*" and a return to the "*real [him]*" (02.07.2018). In a discussion on ethno-racial movements, what he refers to as a trans of migration, the American professor of Sociology Rogers Brubaker (2016:48), who is himself of settler descent[15], perceives reclaimers shift of ethnicity to be born because it is "*an enticing alternative to a white identity*" which many experiences as "*culturally and spiritually 'empty*".[16] I actually disagree with Brubaker on this point, at least as far as reclaimers are concerned, which I think is related to their trauma of absence.

Whereas historical trauma, as the cumulative emotional harm caused by traumatic experiences or events, has often impacted in the sense of wanting to forget one's categorization as Indigenous, a trauma of absence is due to the successful dismissal from memory of said experiences or events. More to the point, a trauma of absence affects the descendants of Sámi that experienced a historical trauma, which was then followed by rejecting their ethnicity. That is to say, the trauma experienced by Indigenous individuals that have always been grounded in their heritage reflect their conscious awareness of structural violence, racism, and colonialism. Reclaimers on the other hand, acutely feel a trauma triggered by not knowing, and as such, a consequent sense of lacking proficiency of one's culture and language. "*I always knew that there was something not quite right, I just didn't have the words or the knowledge to actually speak it*", as Karl shared with me when discussing his process of ethnic shifting (13.05.2020). Lukas

---

15 I use settler as it is an international recognized term applied to people of non-Indigenous descent that live in Countries built upon colonial borders.

16 From an Indigenous perspective, one of my Indigenous dialogue partners, Cydd Pajunen, of Ojibwe descent from Turtle Island, pointed out that for many, such and similar articulations often are used to explain and advocate acts of cultural appropriation. Which is, absolutely, a relevant point. It would be too time-consuming to go into the specifics of cultural appropriation, however.

also reflects on how *"I always knew there was something not right. I just never could...I just never knew why. I mean...looking back, now I understand why... but then, I only knew that something wasn't right."* (Lukas 02.07.2018). I would like to make one point of clarity, while I do think that a trauma of absence heavily impacts on reclaimers, that is not to say that Sámi that were raised in the full knowledge of their heritage may not be afflicted by it. But this I will save for my discussions in the next chapter.

Cultures, however,

> [...] do not die easily. Even when many visual representations of a culture are missing, the remaining survivors of a group of [I]ndigenous people often retain a longing for the ways of their ancestors. For some, this is an identifiable feeling, but for others it is a mysterious pain they carry with them with no explanation. They are yearning for something, but they cannot identify what it is. The "something" is often a cultural identity and a connection with ancestors (Pullar 2008:111-2).

To believe in genetic memory is a way of negating the trauma of absence. As Lawrence so eloquently puts it, blood memory allows us to *"claim our ancestors' experience as our own"* and facilitate the belief that it is possible, even in the face of assimilation and consequent epistemicide to *"recreate our cultures based on what we carry in our genes"* (2004:201, also see Hume 2000:130). [17] Indigenous, or in this case, Sámi knowledges and practices have as such not been lost, but are simply waiting to be rediscovered.

Of course, in order to fully understand the need for blood memory as a tool when recentering Sámi identities, we also need to understand the individual stories of ethnic shifting within Sámi communities. As such, I will next turn my attention to the idea of Sámi identity as performative, expressed through modes of subjective identification and cultural repertoires such as árbediehtu and/or duodji and what I have termed a process of *sámáidahttin*, or samification.

---

17 In an almost ironic twist, the racial and ethnic practices of social classification used to exclude Indigenous people from colonial settler populations have as such been adapted. Only now, the biological essentialism is echoed in the strategy used by Indigenous communities to exclude what they perceive to be non-Indigenous individuals (Brubaker 2016:104, Watt and Kowal 2019:68).

RE-REMEMBERING THROUGH THE PRACTICE OF DUODJI

Indigenous historian Taiake Alfred (1995:19), of the Mohawk Nation located in the middle of Turtle Island, argues that Indigenous identities are nested; comprised of several complex layers that form in relation to your local community and your role within it, but also to the Nation-state as well as your profession, gender/s, sexuality and family. Added to this is a history of colonisation, oppression, assimilation, ethnic stigmatization and other trauma, such as one of absence, from which Indigenous identities can never be separated (Weaver 2001). Any Indigenous identity is, in other words, multi-layered and construed in changing, and sometimes even conflicting arrays (e.g., Povinelli 2002:2-3). [18] It should come as no surprise then, that defining Indigenous membership is a subject of controversies worldwide. This is certainly true for Sámi identities.

One of the often-proposed suggestions of Sámi membership is to look to the elective Sámi parliaments and their criteria for Sámi electoral rolls to define who may claim to be Sámi, and conversely, who may not (Hansen 2015:56-7). This is, in my opinion, a flawed solution. From the perspective of electoral rolls, being Sámi is definable, firstly, by a subjective classification within an ethnic category: You must recognize yourself as being Sámi. A second criterion, meant to be objective, demands documented proficiency in a Sámi language either personally or in a parent, a grandparent, or a great-grandparent. Of the 11 Sámi languages that exist today, however, all have been entered onto UNESCO's list of endangered languages and at least two have no native speakers left. All in all, there is about 30% Sámi that are still speaking a Sámi language. Still, it is understandable that such importance is attached to languages.

Language is often cited as a major fact in maintaining ethnic identities (De Vos 1995:23). [19] Perhaps not surprising. In the last few decades, a wealth of linguistic and anthropological literature has dis-

---

18 As Betty Bilaway experienced when her moral obligation to tribal traditions, was contrasted with the financial obligations to her family during a discussion on whether or not mineral exploration should be allowed in her peoples' traditional territories.

19 Much of the discussion in this paragraph is formed by my work together with Office for Contemporary Art—Norway (OCA) and Norwegian Crafts (NC) on curating the seminar, "Båassjoeraejken Tjïrr—Workshops and conversations on Indigenous Languages, Landscape and Aesthetical Practices", which happened in December 2019.

cussed how the language one learns has a major impact on how one thinks (Bloom and Keil 2001, Boroditsky 2018). Each society, Indigenous or not, has its distinctive communication structure, which has evolved over time within the context of specific ontologies (Outakoski 2015). The holistic perspective by which cultures know, learn, and believe, in other words, is very much shaped by language. In Indigenous societies, where written materials have been the exemption rather than the rule, it is as such the spoken language that serves as literature (Hirvonen 2009). What this means, is simply put, that language has the potential to connect speakers with the worldviews and know-hows of their source communities (Archibald 2008:27). A language-based, apparently objective, criterion is, again, not surprising.

Leaving the relevance of language aside, whilst both criteria are "official" in so far as they determine who is recognized as being eligible to vote in Sámi elections (*The Sámi Act*, 1987), the second criteria has nevertheless, and not unduly in my opinion, faced a challenge as it fails to "*adequately take into account the effect of assimilation*" (Niila 13.02.2018). As discussed in bárket, due to assimilation and social discrimination, a large number of Sámi chose, or were forced to do a shift in ethnicity from Sámi to Norwegian or Swedish, and for that matter, Finnish or Russian (e.g., Bjørklund 1985:12). Sámi cultural and language-competencies were consequently hidden away, disguised as non-Sámi or simply forgotten (Ása 07.01.2018, e.g., Hansen 2015:83). Within a generation or two, a break in the continuity of languages, knowledges and practices followed. At the culmination of such a shift, what objectively marks one as being Sámi is thus gone. For all that, many still argue that the language-based criterion is applicable. After all, the scope of time that Sámi languages must have been the primary language in one's family is such that it allows for ruptures to be considered. As such, the argument continues, the criteria for the Sámi electoral rolls should be inclusive enough. Nonetheless, this argument is completely dismantled if you take into account the longevity of assimilation. As I have already pointed out in Chapter Two, assimilatioon has been documented as far back as the 16th century, meaning that there will always be those that cannot claim Sámi as their mother tongue, far less that of their great-grandparents.

There is a third possibility where, if a parent is already on an electoral roll, membership is automatically granted if the child applies when of age.[20] But even this loophole is not perfect. Kajsa is a good example of someone falling between cracks. As she explains it, she is *"not eligible to be on the Sámi electoral roll. My mom is, but she has no interest at all. I've tried to get her to enrol, because then I could as well, but [...] she wants nothing to do with it"* (05.12.2018). Kajsa identifies as Sámi and her local community recognises her as such. According to the formal criteria of the electoral rolls, Kajsa is nevertheless not Sámi enough. Clearly then, enrolment, or at least adherence to its criteria, cannot be obligatory in claiming a Sámi identity. But, equally apparent from my discussions with Ása, Elly and Sanna, neither may genealogical and genetic ancestry be denied as important markers of ethnicity. And here lies the conundrum of Indigenous identity. What then, really decides, who may, and conversely who may not, claim to be Sámi?

Ethnic identities can be a source of great conflict. Especially when ethnic categories have been ranked by "superiority", and where one has been unfavourably compared to a "higher-grade" race, as is the case with the Sámi. The latter of which played the part of the former, and Norwegians, Swedes, Finns and Russians, taking on the role of the latter (e.g., Eidheim 1961:38, 1971:50-6, Eyþórsson 2008:20). The colonial tropes and racial stereotypes—primitive, static, less developed, and unable to progress—enforced by such ranking[21] is largely to blame for the belief that Sámi could never be on par with other ethnicities. If you were Sámi, you could not be anything else. Nor could a Norwegian, a Swede, a Finn, or a Russian, far above the Sámi on the evolutionary ranking, be Sámi (Eidheim 1971:50-62). As one verdde commented:

> [...] in my family we were Norwegian. When I started looking into our genealogy and found that we had Sámi ancestors, my aunt told me that there was no Lapps in our family. We had some links to Norwegian travellers, but that was it. We were true Norwegians! (Ájsa 23.06.2018)

---

20 https://www.sametinget.no/Valg/Innmelding-i-valgmanntallet, https://www.sametinget.se/1061, note that the criteria here discussed are valid only in Norway and Sweden. There is one more criterion that is objective in the Finnish electoral roll, that "he is a descendent of a person who has been entered in a land, taxation or population register as a mountain, forest or fishing Lapp". Additionally, membership is not voluntary. If you fulfil the three criteria, you are automatically added to the electoral roll.

21 Some still argue this point. When the Essand Sijte in North-Trøndelag on the Norwegian side of the border went to court to safeguard their right to commercial fishing in lakes and rivers on the property of Tydal union of landowners in 2008 based on customary precedent, the opposing council argued against citing that *"fishing in motorboats is not part of Sámi culture"* (Larsen and Kalvemo 2008).

This explains why prior to the period of Sámi political rights movement of the 1960s, 1970s, and—1980s, it was not unusual to identify as either one or the other (Nymo 2011:15). After the socio-political movement for Sámi sovereignty, the established pattern of self-identification underwent massive changes. No longer content to remain silent, allowing non-Sámi colonizers to enforce their habitual system of definition: we too, demanded the right of autonomous definition of self. This shift in perspective was soon in effect and far from being a fixed static category, Sámi ethnicity and identity came to be viewed as a continuously evolving social process—both dynamic and flexible, as well as contextually situated (Gaski 2008, Peters and Andersen 2013). In the words of Taiake, Sámi identities became nested.

Understanding identity as nested is of course not unique to Sámi or other Indigenous Peoples' (e.g., Alba 1990:306). Studies nonetheless show that there is a higher probability of someone with Sámi descent to view themselves as such (e.g., Nymo 2011:15, Hansen 2015:83). To quote a friend[22], Sofie, "*I am mostly Sámi, but I am Norwegian too!*" (Finbog 2013:20). Increasingly what I found however, when speaking with several verdde, was that the understanding of nested was slowly changing. Admittedly, the verddes' in question were all reclaimers, and thus have either reconnected with, or discovered, their Sámi heritage late in life. After initiating a shift in ethnicity, these reclaimers for the most part claimed to be in possession of a singular ethnicity. Ájsa, for instance, whose story is shared in the prologue of bárket, explained that she could not "*think of myself as anything other than Sámi*" (23.06.2018). Although born and raised Norwegian, Ájsa chose to "quit" as it were, that part of herself when she discovered that her family had Sámi ancestry. This is in clear opposition to what earlier studies have found, so has something changed? And if so, what has changed.

If I return to my friend, Sofie, whom I quote above, there is a striking difference between her and Ájsa. Raised as Sámi, but with a Norwegian parent, Sofie indeed considers herself both. Like Sofie, Ájsa shares the circumstances of ethnicity in that she too is of mixed heritage. And yet, she has chosen to completely disregard her Norwegian heritage after having rediscovered and re-connected with her Sámi ancestry. It might not be immediately noticeable, but the dif-

---

22 My friend, "Sofie", is actually one of the verdde I got to know when doing my masters in museology on Sámi museums as a contact zone. We have kept in touch, and today consider each other as great friends.

ference is, of course, that Sofie always knew of her ancestry whereas Ájsa did not. The question then, is whether or not a shift in ethnicity involves, according to my verddes' narratives, a complete eradication of non-Sámi heritage? This would certainly seem to be the case. There are of course objections to affirming such a claim; one verdde whose father is of non-European descent still claim his ethnicity as her own. Nonetheless, what she previously thought to be Norwegian descent she has dismissed in favour of a Sámi ethnicity (Emily 08.09.2019). So, rather it might be that reclaimers replace their Norwegian, Swedish, Finnish, or Russian identity with one that is Sámi.

SÁMÁIDAHTTIN—OF BEING AND BECOMING SÁMI

Ájsa's story is, I think, key in understanding this process of ethnic shifting. When she talks about the trauma that her grandmother suffered as a Sámi woman and her own trauma of absence, she states that this trauma "*is what Norwegian heritage gives you*" and that she wants "*no part of that*" (23.06.2018). What is interesting about this statement is that it echoes a larger and parallel trend amongst Indigenous reclaimers on a larger scale. Many of those that reclaim their Indigenous identity often feel that their prior non-Indigenous identity loses its appeal, implicated as it is in the continuation "*of colonial injustice*" (Watt and Kowal 2019:65-6).

Based on the material at hand, I would actually suggest that Ájsa is engaged in a complicated process where the disavowal of a non-Sámi, and Scandinavian ethnicity, stems from the need to remove oneself from the colonial narratives and strategies that caused their initial trauma to occur. This is why, I earlier disagreed with Brubaker's suggestion that Indigenous identities appeal because they are seemingly spiritually richer. Needing to reject their "colonial" ethnicity is, I believe, the reason why so many reclaimers leave their non-Indigenous identities behind. Meaning that reclaimers are actually initiating a process of assimilation. Only this time, it is not with an intent to eradicate what is Sámi, but rather one of samification, or *sámáidahttin*.

Contrary to what might be expected, an act of sámáidahttin does not go wholly uncontested. In his discussion on ethno-racial movements, Brubaker (2016:40-1) warns that in this age of unsettled identities "*we see a sharpened tension*" between given and chosen identity, and with it an increased policing in "*the name of authentic*" self. It seems then, that not only is identity fluid, at times it may also prove to be the opposite and validate the boundaries of ethnicity; the flow of persons across ethnic boundaries, rather than dissolving borders, might, in fact, work to solidify them (as dicussed by Barth 1969:10, 21). Ájsa's experience is a visual illustration of such as she, in choosing to identify as Sámi, could no longer identity as anything other. She is not alone in this.

When sharing her struggles for acceptance within her local Sámi community, Mari explained to me that she never introduced herself as anything other than Sámi and certainly not as Norwegian, even if the latter was her primary ethnic identity for most of her life. Similar to Ájsa, Mari's story is also one detailing a disconnect due to the assimilation of past generations, and the resulting trauma of absence. More so than Ájsa however, Mari spoke of the conflict she had experienced when she "outed myself as Sámi" (03.04.2018). The conflict was not, as one would perhaps assume, due to her Norwegian family alone. Though, as they still refuse to acknowledge their Sámi heritage, they are not exempted from having an important share in it. Even so, much of the conflict stemmed from others in her local Sámi community refusing to acknowledge her as one of them. I think that another reason why reclaimers might prefer to leave behind their non-Sámi ethnicity is due to this struggle. When I asked Mari if she thought her struggle for acceptance within the Sámi community had any bearing on her need to disavowal another ethnicity, she answered that "perhaps it is also that being only Sámi makes it easier for me to come across as Sámi to others?" (03.04.2018).

What I take from Mari's story is that passing into another ethnic category is more than a simple question of personal choice. As Brubaker (2016:106) has stated in his previously referenced study, self-identification does not necessarily mean that others will also identify you as such. Even when backed by ancestry, it does not follow that others will agree with your self-identification: "There is more" says Laara, who hails from a South Sámi community on the Swedish side of the border, "to being Sámi than putting on the gappta and being 'exotic'" (05.04.2018). To him, being Sámi is about more than a verbal statement and visual markers[23]. The point being that having ancestry, while

---

23 It is somewhat ironic that the gákti in academic studies on Sámi Indigeneity has been termed the primary marker of Sámi ethnicity (Bjørklund 2000:32, also see Dankertsen 2006, Sivertsen 2011)

important, is not enough.

Laara's point highlights an important factor in any quest for re-centering identities; namely that subjectivity is never "*ours to craft alone*" (Jones 2015). In a Sámi context, where the world is made up of relations and never based on individuals alone, subjectivity is always a matter of the collective as well. As Linda Tuhiwai Smith ([1999]2012:129), puts it: "*Community is a self-defined space*", and your place in it, at least partly, is defined by said community. Despite a lack of formal policing[24] then, access within an Indigenous boundary is "*not simply who you claim to be, but also who claims you*" as was pointed out in the "Statement on Indigenous Identity Fraud" released by the council of Native American and Indigenous Studies Association in September of 2015[25] (N.A.I.S.A. 2015). It is not, in other words, enough to lay claim to a Sámi identity. Being met and treated as Sámi is an equally constituent factor.

Mari had a relevant remark on reclaimer's subjectively feeling Sámi versus being accepted as such when stating: "*[...] to be accepted as Sámi took [me] 20 years*" (03.04.2018). First and foremost, her statement is of course a very personal reflection on her part. Nonetheless, I also find it to be an incredibly valid observation that even when the individual self may think and/or feel as a Sámi, only when recognised as such by the surrounding community are these feelings confirmed and accepted by the whole. Which begs the question: What is it that the community is supposed to recognise?

DUODJI AS A WAY TO RECONNECT WITH INDIGENOUS KNOWLEDGE[S]

The cultural practices, meanings, and norms attached to being Sámi—the codes of sámáidahttin— are parts of intergenerational transmissions of cultural competency (Boine 2005).

---

24 As in South Africa during apartheid, or in the States until today.

25 The statement was released in the aftermath of the Dolezal affair, where Rachel Anne Dolezal, the then-leader of her local chapter of National Association for the Advancement of Coloured People (NAACP) and Instructor in Africana Studies at Eastern Washington University, received public scrutiny after her parents publicly stated that she was passing as a Black woman while having no verifiable African ancestry.

FIGURE 5-5 A PICTURE OF A MOTHER AND HER CHILD THAT WAS TAKEN DURING A DUODJEBÁDJI. ADMITTEDLY THE CHILD IS STILL TOO YOUNG TO ACTIVELY LEARN, BUT IT ILLUSTRATES THE PRACTICE OF LETTING CHILDREN OBSERVE CULTURAL PRACTICES FROM A VERY EARLY AGE IN PREPARATION OF ATTEMPTING SAID PRACTICES ON THEIR OWN.

As is typical of any society that up until recently was primarily oral, such transmission may happen in one of two ways; either by storytelling, passing knowledge by performing and executing the Sámi epistemology of muitalusat, or through a bodily performance. In Sámi communities, transmitting the codes of sámáidahttin to children thus happens by letting them see and reproduce.

In this setting, not only words, or perhaps in despite of them, facial expressions and bodily acts become important venues of learning; the performative body becoming a source of knowledge, a silent scene of evolving practical skills (Johannessen 1999:26)—communicating a specific onto-epistemology. Learning the codes, in other words, is not simply a matter of obtaining information, the diehtu. It is equally about the process of achieving máhttu, or practical skills. The customary Sámi way of knowledge transfer thus, it must be said, resonates remarkably well with the belief that many reclaimers have in blood memory as diehtu, which they unlock through their acquiring of máhttu, or their practice of duodji.

Though not stated in such a way, in her doctoral thesis on Sámi aesthetics and vætnoe, Maja Dunfjeld (2006), claims that practical skills, or máhttu though she herself does not use that term, is typically transferred either through a profession with a large degree of physical labour, or through the practice of a craft—duodji being an example of the latter. In this process, she continues, it is not only skills that are passed on. Additionally, through the practice of duodji, she claims that a person may also incorporate important socio-cultural aspects of Sámi cultures (2006:18), or what I have defined as the codes of sámáidahttin.

Dunfjeld follows, albeit not intentionally, an earlier thesis delivered by Sámi duojár and professor of duodji, Gunvor Guttorm, in 2001. Here she convincingly argues that duodji—both the practice (duddjot) and the finished product (duodji)—is part of a bodily practice that incorporate not only skills, but also a communal memory of practices, meanings and norms, which I understand to be the codes of sámáidahttin (Guttorm 2001:49). Learning and practicing duodji thus facilitate for the practitioner to be introduced to a Sámi worldview with the attached ontologies and epistemology. Reclaimers that initiate a shift in ethnicity may as such adapt the codes of sámáidahttin by way of duodji. Birthe, whom I first met on a duodji workshop in 2018, may provide an excellent case in point.

DIFFERENT STORIES OF RE-REMEMBERANCE

Born and raised as Norwegian, Birthe had no idea that her family had Sámi ancestry. This changed in the early 1990s when she, after her grandmother's passing, returned home to help clear the estate. Among the many possessions she found was a picture showing her grandmother as a young girl. To her great surprise, her grandmother was wearing what she thought to be a Sámi gákti. This discovery kindled in Birthe "*a draw*" towards Sámi culture, and an eagerness to know more. In time, she would also come to feel the "*emptiness*" that is so prevalent when suffering the trauma of absence. Only as she slowly came to identify as Sámi, beginning her shift of ethnicity, did she feel as if said emptiness began to lessen. After the initial onset, however, Birthe came to realize the marked difference between having Sámi ancestry and being Sámi, the latter having much higher expectations attached than the former.

> ... [B]eing Sámi comes with expectations. You are expected to know things... about history, about your family... who were they and where did they come from... And about Sámi culture, you are expected to know everything. Why is the colour of the gákti this, or what do those symbols [on the gákti] mean? But how am I supposed to know? I never learned this, and there is no one left

in my family to ask. They all [in the Sámi community] expect you to know all this, but they don´t want to teach you. So how was I supposed to know? (Birthe 23.06.2018)

As she describes it, Birthe had little knowledge of Sámi culture, and even less awareness of the cultural practices, meanings, and norms of being Sámi—the codes of sámáidahttin. This lack became glaringly obvious as she approached and interacted with her local Sámi community.

I wanted so badly to take part in Sámi society and culture, but I didn´t really feel welcome. I thought to get myself a gákti, you know... to show... that is, I wanted others to see me as Sámi and I thought if only I had a gákti. So I got [bought] one. And it didn´t make any difference. And then someone told me that I couldn´t just buy gákti. I had to make it myself. But do you think any-one wanted to share their patterns? I had to go to the museums. And I had to find pictures online. Digital Museum. Do you know it? It saved me ... really... And then I also had my grandmother's picture [...]. Years later, when I put on a gákti again, I had made it myself. And then someone asked me who had made it? I admit to feeling pride when I answered that I had made it myself, with help from my grandmothers' picture and the gáktis from a museum. We then started talking about the traditions of the gákti. At the end, she [the woman who had asked the question] smiled at me and said I had done good with making my gákti. That I was a 'čeahpes duojár'. The next time I put it on [the gákti], I don´t know... maybe I wore it different. Maybe I was more confident. But I felt accepted. (Birthe 23.06.2018)

There are, I feel, several points of interest in her story. To start with, Birthe emphasises her difficulties in finding ready-made gákti pat-terns, impressing that no one wanted to help her, which forced her to seek out other venues of information. I will get back to this point, but for now, I wish to focus on the second point of interest, which is that Birthe makes a clear distinction between paying someone to make her a gákti as opposed to making it herself. In my opinion, this distinction reflects the difference of, on the one hand, dressing up in a gákti and, on the other, actually being exposed to the cultural practices, mean-ings and norms of being Sámi through making her own gákti and the practice of duodji. This echos what Laara was saying about how it would be both shallow and unproductive to make the clothes one wears as their only marker of Indigeneity.

This point is also one that may be extrapolated from stories shared by other verdde:

> When I made my first gákti I hardly knew what I was doing. My family suffered years of assimilation and so they hid away. I never knew I was Sámi until recently. And after thinking about it, I decided that I wanted to take back what my ancestors were forced to give up. But no one in my family knew or had any gákti patterns. I had to improvise. I had some help from [other] Sámi in that "koftegruppa"[26], but mostly I had to look at gáktis or old pictures [ed. at museums] and reproduce what I saw in them. I'm not really a duojár, but I knew how to operate a sewing machine and so I tried my best. It was so hard, and in the beginning, I made so many mistakes. But every night I would put my gákti in a chair for the next day when I would resume working. And I swear to you, in the dark, with just me and the gákti something happened. It was alive in some way. It had life and I could see the life. And it seemed to speak to me, telling me that I was on the right path. That I was slowly, with every stitch, becoming Sámi. (Karen 15.05.2018)

This was told to me by Karen, whom I first met in May of 2018, only a few days ahead of the 17th, the National Day of Norway. Our meeting was not pre-arranged, but as it happens, Oslo Sámiid Duodji had arranged an evening where local duojárs would be at hand to answer questions about the gákti: its history, how to wear it correctly and which accessories to choose.

I was initially approached by Karen because she wanted to learn how to correctly lash her gapmagat[27] with vuoddagat. While showing her how, she told me her story, beginning with how this 17th of May would be her first time putting on the gákti. As she spoke, she also confided to me that this made her both excited, and yet, she also felt slightly apprehensive at the thought of wearing her gákti in public. In a low tone of voice, ensuring that the others couldn't hear she explained how *"[e]verything needs to be perfect. I don't want to do anything wrong, you see"* (Karen 15.05.2018). I tried to reassure her that she would look great and that she didn't need to worry. But I understood her trepidation, and I recognized its source.

Karen has Sámi ancestry from her maternal grandmother's side, but this was never spoken of during her childhood or adolescence. On

---

26 This is a reference to an popular facebook group called "Samiske kofter/gákti", which discuss everything related to Sámi gáktis. As of 26th of June 2020, it had 8531 members.

27 Sámi shoes (kommager) traditionally made by leather with a peak at the tip.

the contrary, Karen did not learn that her family had Sámi ancestry until she was an adult. Still, she would reach her 60th decade before she decided to actively attempt to reconnect with her heritage.

FIGURE 5-6 THE LASHING OF VUODDAGAT IS PART OF THE SÁMI TIIDA. HERE SEEN COMPLETED WITH BANDS FROM ČOHKKIRAS, MEANING MEETINGPLACE, OR JUK-KASJÄRVI, WHICH IS THE SWEDISH SPELLING. BUT DIFFERENT COMMUNITIES HAS DIFFERENT PRACTICES; THE PLACEMENT OF THE TASSEL FOR INSTANCE, MIGHT INDICATE DIFFERENT THINGS. HERE THE TASSEL IS CORRECTLY PLACED TO THE SIDE. FURTHER NORTH, IN SOME COMMUNITIES IN FINNMARK ON THE NORWE-GIAN SIDE OF THE BORDER, I HAVE BEEN TOLD THAT PLACING THE TASSEL IN THIS WAY WOULD BE A WAY OF SHOWING DISHONOUR TO THE HOSTS OF THE GATHERING ATTENDED. THIS PARTICULAR PICTURE IS FROM A GATHERING OF DUOJÁRS IN OSLO IN NOVEMBER 2018, AND WAS TAKEN BY ANNE MARTE JOHNSEN WHO HAS KINDLY GRANTED ME PERMISSION TO USE IT.

In this sense, her story is not that different from any of the other reclaimers whose stories I have shared already. Their collective commonality lies in their trauma of absence, born from their ancestors' experiences of degradation and social stigmatization leading to the erasure of their Sámi ethnicity. The stories might have ended there, and no doubt they do for many. For some stories, sequels will appear in time. These follow-ups portray the descendants of the original characters fighting what was imposed on their ancestors' and reclaiming a Sámi ethnicity. So even though the story begins with Karen's grandmother, it does not end with her. Because this story, in a way, also belongs to Karen and, for that matter, to every other reclaimer.

As she told me her story, Karen would sometimes stop me and ask questions: "*Is there a reason why you lash the vuoddagat this way instead of the other?*" (Karen 15.05.2018). Because, I answered her, doing it the other way will only bring you sorrow and misery—part of the *tiida*, associated with the gákti and its accessories that Sámi children learn. I could see that she was intently studying what I was doing, eager to learn. After some time, she stopped me because she wanted to try for herself. After all, she was there to learn how to do it correctly—in line with the tradition and beliefs of the culture which she so desperately wanted to reclaim an affiliation with.

Most studies on recentering Sámi identities show that when shifting ethnicity, reclaimers are very likely to start with the gákti and its accessories (e.g., Dankertsen 2006, Sivertsen 2011). Karen is no different. From old stories within her family, she knew which community her grandmother was likely to originally hail from. This made it easier for her to know which gákti she should use. How it should be made however, the cut, decorations, and colours, was knowledge that her family no longer possessed. In the end she took to social media. Here she was directed by skilled duojárs to museums displays where gáktis was exhibited and digitalized photos—mainly on the platform of *Digitalt Museum*. Combining all of these avenues, she managed to recreate the gákti that her grandmother presumably had used in her youth. It was this reproduction that she, when we first met, was to use for the very first time.

When next I met Karen, in June of 2018, she proudly showed me pictures of her second gákti, a geassegákti[28] that she had made in a lighter fabric meant to be worn in the summertime. The change immediately struck me. A mere month before she had been excited but anxious. Now she was simply excited, and to me it was clear that something had changed. When I asked her about this perceived change, she simply replied that:

> I don't think anyone that hasn't lived this [made a shift in ethnicity] can understand how it feels the first time you put on the gákti. The pride…the joy…it's indescribable, but so powerful… like it's right somehow (Karen 12.06.2018)

For Karen, making and wearing the gákti for the first time had in her mind cemented her place in her local Sámi community. I would say that what she had experienced was the acceptance that is inherent in *geahčastat*, or the gaze.

---

28 Geasse means summer, so geassegákti translate to summergákti. It differs from gákti in that it is often made in lighter fabrics, and also it is usually simplified.

This is in stark contrast to Birthe whose experience was the exact opposite, namely a sense of rejection. Comparing the two stories suggest that the difference chiefly lies in the fact that Birthe bought her first gákti, whereas Karen made hers. At first glance, this difference might seem inconsequential, but the truth is that this is a vital distinction.

Karen's story makes a point of *"they"*, who in this case are the people of the Sámi community she is trying to enter, asking *"about my gákti, and I explained how I had made it from seeing old gáktis in museums and pictures"* (12.06.2018). As she had no pattern to work from, nor a family to rely on, Karen had to look elsewhere for her source material when recreating the gákti of her family and reclaiming her Sámi identity. This process, while painstakingly long and difficult, was also valuable because it forced her to actually learn the cut, the decorations, and the colours of her gákti. Moreover, by attending different workshops and speaking to duojárs, she feels as if she also learnt *"the knowledge behind these choices"* (Karen 08.03.2019). This tells me that Karen, not only proved herself to be a proficient gáktimaker. She also managed to convey that she had begun to grasp the codes of sámáidahttin and that she, for all intents and purposes, had started to conform to some of the cultural practices, meanings and norms needed to become Sámi, thus tapping into an oral foundation as well as a bodily performance as a possible basis for mutual remembrance and knowledge. Karen eventually, like so many other reclaimers, came to recognize this basis as blood memory. Stating that,

> I believe that the essence of my self carries with it the knowledge of my Sámi ancestors… that my blood hosts their [the ancestors] memories. I was transformed when I began doing duodji—no longer am I Norwegian, but I become transformed into [a] Sámi. I am becoming what I always was but didn't consciously know (Karen 08.03.2019).

Quite the opposite, when paying someone to make the gákti in her stead, Birthe received none of the knowledge—the practices, meanings and norms—of gáktimaking, nor did she manage to adapt the codes of sámáidahttin that are so readily available in the practice of duodji. In fact, she herself states that it is only after she gained the skills of gáktimaking and with it, the codes of sámáidahttin inherent in the practice of duodji, that she felt accepted as Sámi.

The link between engaging in a practice of making and the codes of sámáidahttin is, if not made explicit, at least alluded to in previous research. For instance, in the previously mentioned thesis penned by Gunvor Guttorm, some of her verddes' admits to being hesitant to make or sell gáktis to people that do not have the comprehension of its cultural components or the visual language that I discuss in riessat (Guttorm 2001:151), which I here take to mean the codes of sámáidahttin. Again, there is an interesting, if unspoken, resistance against legitimizing entrance into a Sámi ethnic boundary on mere symbolic and external expressions alone. Rather it is the practice or máhttu involved in the making of it that confirms such entrance as being appropriate. This thought has been supported by Hanna, a duojár on the Norwegian side of the border, who often gives courses and workshops in gáktimaking. In one of our conversations, she told me that duodji has become *"a Sámi marker, and if you want to "belong", learning duodji is one way of doing so"* (12.02.2019, also see Helander-Renvall and Markkula 2017:124).

My discussion so far lends itself to my earlier claim that learning and practicing duodji is vital to becoming Sámi and also being accepted as such (e.g., Guttorm 2001a:165). Additionally, there seems to be a conspicuous tendency amongst Sámi reclaimers to develop a belief in blood memory. What is also notable, amongst my verddes' at least, is that reclaimers have a habit of translating blood memory into the Sámi concept of inherited knowledge, where diehtu is the genetic memory of ancestors and where duodji as máhttu, becomes the situated practice that unlocks said knowledge. Having these two factors in common, in many cases, also leads to a third commonality, which is museums. Here, I will return to the other point of interest that I earlier identified in Birthe's story—the need to turn to museums for knowledge and information.

IN THIS HOUSE OF KNOWLEDGE—MUSEUMS AS SITES OF LEARNING

Considering my previous discussion on museums in riessat, there is little wonder why reclaimers would feel a need to turn to museums. When efforts to colonize Sápmi intensified after the 16th century, the consequent epistemicide materialized in different ways, but both the forceful removal of objects as well as the introduction of an official assimilation policy were deemed viable means of implementation. The latter equally ensured that objects were dispossessed as they were quietly disposed of, or alternatively, disguised as non-Sámi (Ása 07.01.2018, e.g., Inga et al. 1986). Coinciding with both the forced removal as well as the dispossession of material culture, Sámi objects were highly sought after by museums from all corners of the world.[29] Indeed, even private collectors, who later bequeathed their collections to various museums, were oftentimes fixated on the "exotic" objects of the Sámi (Gjestrum 1995:103). The result, not surprisingly, being that today most older Indigenous and Sámi heritage objects are in the ownership of museums or other cultural heritage institutions far removed from their source communities (Olli and Harliin 2014:65).

This state of affairs was maintained for an exceedingly long time, but with the ethno-political movement for Indigenous sovereignty and the consequent re-remembering of Sámi languages and cultures, there came a turning point (Gaup 2006). One of which was that issues relating to Indigenous material culture in non-Indigenous institutions were brought to the forefront, including, but not limited to accessibility, collaborative efforts, and repatriation (Inga et al. 1986, Spein and Enoksen 1991)

THE SILENCE OF ERASED KNOWLEDGE[S]

It has long been a common perception that duodji has a positive influence on sustaining not only cultural practices, but also Sámi languages (Lehtola 2006:12). By virtue of their practice of duodji, duojárs as such *"relates to traditions that reflect deeply rooted collective values and norms as well as immaterial knowledge about processes and experience with duodji"* (Snarby 2019). Due to their interaction with material culture and cultural practices, it is highly likely that duojárs had particular awareness of there being a loss. Though, in many cases, it is unlikely that they could pinpoint exactly what had been lost.

---

29 For instance, the Ethnographic Museum of Oslo. The early ethnographical museums were mainly established as colonial institutions to house the "exotic" artefacts travellers had brought home from the colonies (Røkkum 2005:119). The idea was that "primitive" cultures were unable to represent themselves, and the task thus fell to the colonizers from the far more civilized West (Brenna 2002:143). In 1852, British Museum wanted to establish permanent collections housed in the Crystal Palace which had been built for the World Exhibition of that same year. B.M consequently approached the University of Oslo asking for their help in acquiring Sámi objects. The University where quick to acquiesce and began collecting by sets of two. One for the British Museum, and the other for their own collection, which was transferred to the Ethnographic Museum in Oslo in 1857 (Gjestrum 1995:103).

Still, the duojárs in Sápmi would presumably be extra attentive to practices and knowledges lacking in their own or other Sámi communities. Eventually, they began to question this lack and why "*there was seemingly no exterior signs of Sámi culture left in what historically had been Sámi territories*" (Åsa 07.01.2018). Here, I would like to return to Åsa. In our conversations, she explained the loss of knowledge and practices in her community with the following.

> Growing up, we were taught that being Sámi was worthless, so why should we learn Sámi cultural expressions? It's funny, because a lot of what is traditional "Norwegian handicraft", in our area is really Sámi, but we put a different label on it to make it worthwhile [Red: knitting and weaving]. But those arts that we could not disguise as Norwegian, we made ourselves forget. Today, when being Sámi is no longer associated with shame, we want those arts back. You see, we were never not-Sámi, only we didn't display any outward sign of our Sámi heritage. What revitalization has done for our community is learn us how to once more show to everyone that we are Sámi and proud of it. Re-learning the mica-technique even though every object that has it from old is down south [Red: at museums], has been our way of doing that (07.01.2018).

Not only does this quote explain the why. It also explains how duojárs worked to reverse the lack by looking to museums. Hoping to regain the Sámi cultural heritage that was missing from Sámi communities, many duojárs began a slow search for surviving objects and/or other source materials (Inga et al. 1986, Spein and Enoksen 1991, Dunfjeld 1999). Well aware that Sámi objects at the time of assimilation in the 19th and 20th century had been favoured by collectors and museums, the search started in said institutions.

Ove Pettersen, who at that time worked at the Norwegian Folk Museums which, at that time, was home to the largest and oldest collection of Sámi artefacts on the Norwegian side of the border, recalls with great detail how duojárs, both individually and in groups, asked to look at Sámi artefacts that had been collected from their source communities.[30] Some of them were granted permission and thus had the opportunity to study old forgotten Sámi objects and clothes.

Many of the verddes' that I have collaborated with for the last few years have similar recollections; only their point-of-view is slightly

---

30 This was an in-person communication from Ove that happened on the 8th of September in 2017.

different. Hanna, who was introduced earlier, remembers when she in the 1980s took part in a group of duojárs who wanted to look at Sámi heritage objects and had to travel to:

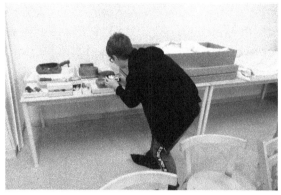

FIGURE 5-7 TAKING PICTURES OF SÁMI HERITAGE OBJECTS FOUND IN THE COLLECTIONS OF ÁJTTE.

Copenhagen. They used to have all our drums...those that were from [..] Norway anyway. The National Museum has a lot of old Sámi objects, and I went there with […] other duojárs, and we took pictures and made patterns from them [the objects] (Hanna 12.02.2019).

Of course, this was before the time of *Recalling Ancestral Voices* (Kuoljok 2007) and *Bååstede* (Pareli et al. 2012), both of which were projects working to return Sámi heritage objects. To most Sámi communities at this time, repatriation was an *"impossible dream"* (Áile 05.01.2018).

If you can't take home the original, a copy is a decent replacement—then at least you have a similar object at hand, and that's the most important thing. Because to learn, you need to see—you need to look at an object and to touch it. Of course it would be best to have the original brought back home, but beggars can't be choosers—at least not yet!" (Áile 05.01.2018).

Duojárs then, took it upon themselves to go where the objects were. Interestingly, many were not satisfied with studying artefacts whose provenience could be traced back to their own communities. They also focused on Sámi objects in general.

Though I briefly touched upon this earlier, I think the point might survive being repeated. In oral communities, the written word is not a conventional source of knowledge. Rather, when written sources are relatively recent, which is the case in Sámi communities, documents of history, judicial practices and narratives are often found elsewhere.

When discussing the gákti in riessat, for instance, I focused on the function of a gákti as a judicial testament of inherited rights in addition to being a garment that clothes you. In other words, our documents are our objects (Guttorm 2001:15). In this sense, I would argue that duojárs are knowledge keepers, reading and disseminating their knowledge through their bodily practice of duodji. I will explain my meaning with the introduction of Naja.

DUODJI AS A REPOSITORY ARCHIVE OF KNOWLEDGE

During my time in Bådedadjo where I first met Elly, I also made the acquaintance of Naja. Born on the Swedish side of the border, and to a reindeer herding family, Naja in her own words states that *"there was never a question about ancestors or where I come from [...] in my duodji, I know. I find everything I am in there [duodji]"* (22.06.2018). Raised with duodji as a natural part of her daily life, she had always felt secure in her identity as Sámi. When we first met, Naja had been a duojár for more than 40 years. This meant that she had worked with duodji during the peak of Sámi re-remembering, which she admitted gave her some peculiar realisations; *"I feel so bad for those that don't know where they came from; where their ancestors bones rests; where their blood belongs. If I can help ease that [lack] in any way..."* (23.06.2018).

Throughout her years as duojár, Naja had helped several reclaimers with researching their ancestor's gáktis. This included *"going to museums"* (23.06.2018). In time, she built an archive of knowledge based upon countless visits to museums where she studied old Sámi artefacts, taking pictures, making patterns, and collecting techniques as well as old ornamental depictions. All of these details she gathered in several blue binders, some of which she brought along to our gathering. During our stay, she allowed me to look through them, and on our last day together, she offered me the opportunity to take pictures and draw the patterns she had brought along if I wanted. Her reasoning was that *"I have so much knowledge in these binders, and it's not right to keep it to myself. They should be shared [...] I really should think about publishing them so that more may have access to their heritage"* (Naja 24.06.2018).[31]

---

31 Based on the discussion so far, it would be very easy to argue that much of Sámi heritage objects has survived

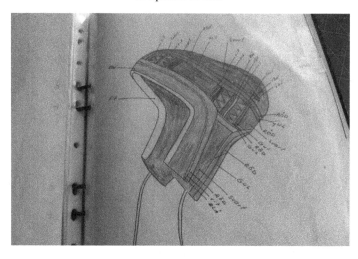

FIGURE 5-8 THIS IS JUST ONE OF THE MANY PICTURES I WAS ALLOWED TO TAKE OF THE CONTENT OF NAJA'S BINDERS. I WAS ALSO ALLOWED TO SHARE IT IN MY BOOK. THE GAHPIR, OR HAT, IS FROM THE COMMUNITIES OF GÁRASAVVON, OR KARESUANDO, ON THE SWEDISH SIDE OF THE BORDER.

Naja's story has several interesting points, amongst them her desire to publicize her archive. I choose to highlight this point as it is very much a rare intent. Admittedly there are duojárs that have published their findings after looking at old Sámi objects in museums (e.g., Inga et al. 1986, Spein and Enoksen 1991, Dunfjeld 2006, Harlin and Pieski 2020). Most, however, while willing to share their findings with others if asked, resist making their archives public. It might be difficult to understand such hesitancy, but it does make perfect sense in the context of Indigenous re-remembering.

Though not herself Indigenous, Diana Taylor (2003:41), an American professor of performance studies, argues that when cultures and people are seeking to undo the harm caused by colonialism and the suppression of Indigenous cultures, it is not archives that offers tools. Rather it is repositories of bodily embedded knowledge and practices and, I should like to add, it is what comes of those practices and performances. In other words, it is the codes of sámáidahttin found and embedded within the practice of duodji. The unwillingness of many duojárs to make their practices and knowledges available in writ-

___

to this day because museums have acquisitioned them, which in turn might be a used to counter appeals to repatriate. The argument, however, is flawed as it fails to consider the fact that when source communities look to museums for heritage objects, they do so simply because colonialism—by which the collecting practices of museums is a by-product—destroyed Indigenous cultures in situ, or at least heavily contributed to such destruction.

ing, I think, stems from this fact. Despite the patterns and drawings that duojárs bought home with them, Sámi techniques, practices and knowledge that had been lost were only brought *"home with duddjot [the practice of duodji]"* (Áile 05.01.2018), and revived through *"their [the duojárs] practice"* (Inga 15.01.2018).[32]

The re-remembering of one particular Sámi technique might drive this point home further—both with regards to the duojárs working in the years of the Sámi re-remembering, and the reclaimers of today. I speak here of riebangolli, or the technique of applying mica to garments and accessories as seen in Figure 5-9. In the following, I will look at both the technique, the process of re-remembering, and the consequences of said revival in Sámi communities.

RIEBANGOLLI—PRACTICE AND KNOWLEDGE RE-GAINED

FIGURE 5-9 THIS PICTURE SHOWS THE DETAILS OF THE RIEBANGOLLI-TECHNIQUE, HERE APPLIED ON A BELT MADE BY DUOJÁR BIRGIT KARLSEN EIRA. SMALL PIECES OF CLOTH HAVE BEEN CUT OUT IN DIFFERENT SHAPES, AND SMALL HOLES HAVE BEEN MADE WHEREIN A SMALL PIECE OF MICA IS INSERTED. THE CLOTH IS THEN FASTENED BY HAND STITCHING.

---

32 Elsewhere, I have put forth an argument that during the re-remembering, duojárs were actively working to repatriate Sámi culture, but without changing the physical location of the objects in question (Finbog 2019). This process is, I would argue, fairly similar to what Cunera Bujis (2016), curator of the arctic collection of Museum Volkenkunde in Leiden, Netherlands, define as visual repatriation. By digitalizing pictures of Inuk, and giving their source communities access, she argues that the images are being visually repatriated, and thus there is no need to return ownership of the actual pictures to the people in them or their decendants (Buijs 2016:548). There are of course, some differences. In the case discussed by Bujis it is the museums initiative to repatriate, whilst the duojárs of the early re-remembering were the sole agents in promoting repatriation—and in a way they did achieve their objective, albeit in a symbolic manner.

Riebangolli, or mica, is a mix of minerals with a tendency to shimmer when it is hit by light. The direct translation of riebangolli is fox gold, but it is more commonly referred to by the alternative name of crow's silver, or poor man's gold. Of old, riebangolli has likely been an important component of Sámi religious practices and presumably, its function has been that of the *šiella*, which is an amulet of luck and/or protection against malevolent powers or spirits (Inga et al. 1986:45, e.g., Turi [1910]1987:158). In this sense, the riebangolli at one point, was likely to be deeply embedded in complex social and cultural relations. Presumably, the same is true of the riebangolli technique.

Written sources, as far back as the 18th century, speak of riebangolli as a technique that is uniquely Sámi, and particular to the coastal communities on the Norwegian side of Sápmi (Gjessing and Gjessing 1940:23-4). Later finds also place the techniques in inland communities, but Gjertrud Gjessing and her husband, Norwegian archaeologist Guttorm Gjessing who would later go on to become the director of the Ethnographic Museum in Oslo, has argued that this was due to said communities "borrowing" the technique from the coast (Gjessing and Gjessing 1940:24). In more recent years, duojár Jorunn Løkvold (2019:15) from one of the technique's source communities, has researched the practice and found that objects with riebangolli were also made on the Russian side of the border. Whether or not this will modify the Gjessing's interpretation has yet to be determined.

Despite the inconsistency of its geographical range, what is certain is that the technique during the years of assimilation disappeared (Larsen [1950]1979:12), and by the 1930s it had largely been forgotten (Løkvold 2017:4). This might have been the end of it if not for the dedicated work of several duojárs in the 1980s and 1990s, when the technique was rediscovered during a large scale re-remembering project set in the municipalities of Kåfjord and Kvænangen in the county of Troms and the municipality of Loppa in the county of Finnmark (Spein and Enoksen 1991). To add some context into the discussion, said communities were amongst those that were first and hardest hit by the Norwegian assimilation policy in the 19th century, and as a result there has been a long-term fracture, ensuring that "*traditions have been broken, and thus partly forgotten*" (Løkvold 2019:7). A project was thus initiated in the 1990s, when several prominent duojárs decided to trace their cultural heritage in museums in an effort to strengthen

Sámi culture and identity in their home communities.

In the beginning, the goal of the project was to find old gáktis for the purpose of restoration and reconstruction. During one of their visits to the Norwegian Museum of Cultural History, the duojárs also came across the riebangolli-technique as it had been implemented on several belts meant to be worn with a gákti. [33] Realising its significance they meticulously documented every discernible detail of these belts and began to make reproductions. Ordinarily, copying objects is frowned on in the practice of duodji. In the creative process, "*ávnnas muitala mo galggat bargat*", the material shows you how to shape it, meaning that the material and the duojár always engage in a dialogue; the former is equally as important as the latter in the shaping of the end product (Guttorm 2012a:55). With copies, however, the voice of the material is drowned, which ends up "*killing the material*" (Ovlla 24.04.2019).

In the case of a re-remembering project, however, the main point is to relearn how something is made. Hoping to "*reclaim the belts for use*" in their source communities (Inga 15.01.2018), the duojárs reproduced every belt and as such managed to take home both a piece of cultural heritage as well as "*the knowledge of making them*" (Áile 05.01.2018). This also reflects the belief that it is through the actual practice that you gain the knowledge of making. As a result, the first belts that were made with the riebangolli technique were exact images of the old belts found at museums. But it was in their making that the starting point for re-learning to decorate using riebangolli lay; the copies allowing the duojárs to "*learn the practice, and understand it*" (Inga 15.01.2018).

Jorunn, whose home community is one of those represented in the aforementioned re-remembering project, offers additional insight through her own work. Having spent three years (2016 –2019) researching the riebangolli-technique, Jorunn speaks of developing her method. She shares that she starts by studying the "*old objects [...] taking measurements, made drawings, examining the ornamental decor and craftsmanship, colours and shape. I then recreated all these by making copies*". Her method is remarkably similar to how the árbediehtu of duodji is transferred in line with Sámi pedagogy, as was discussed in

---

33 Belts decorated with riebangolli had however, become known in other Sámi communities further south in Troms County during a similar re-remembering project (Inga et al. 1986:45-7).

riessat.

The difference is simply that instead of imitating others, you are in fact imitating the practices you are able to observe in the finished products. In her method, she thus embraces the practice of duodji as a vital way of procuring empirical material. Jorunn herself speaks on the necessity of practice which has allowed her to "*know the material, and also the practices behind the belts*" (Løkvold 2019:19). Despite the decades that separate Jorunn's project from the initial re-remembering project, the duojárs involved in the latter employed the same method. The method of making copies to relearn practices, in other words, sets a precedent for efforts of Sámi re-remembering. Not that there are not different ways to revitalize, but as past projects and the stories I have shared indicate, there is a conspicuous pattern to be seen where study is followed by making a copy.

In a recent text on re-remembering, Gunvor Guttorm, discuss how the body remembers movements and that this evolves into an embodied knowledge. Crafting something thus means that the "*maker experiences the action and learns something through the crafting*" (Guttorm 2020:104). This does not necessarily mean that what the maker learns is a knowledge that existed in the past, but rather an interpretation (e.g., Løkvold 2019:9). This was certainly the case with the riebangolli technique. The collective assembly of belts that were reproduced during the re-remembering project of the 1990s displayed a curious tendency. They were either decorated with isolated elements of decor as seen in Figure 5-9, or they displayed a decor that was consistent throughout. Believing this to be of particular significance, the duojárs went back to the museum archives to look at the acquisition texts. Here they learned that the former way of decoration was mostly attributed to female wearers whereas the latter was reserved for men. This allowed them to assume that the belts had been gendered in the past.

As discussed in riessat, it is not unusual for gáktis or its accessories to convey small messages. Duodji, after all, is a language available for those that speak it.[34] In South-Sámi communities, for instance, the tjaalehtjimmie embroidered onto the boengeskvuvmie, or breast cloth and collar of the gappta, impart judicial and ritual messages, respec-

---

34 An example of such language is the decoration on belts in Guovdageaidnu, where round buttons indicated that the wearer is single, and square buttons indicate the opposite.

tively. According to Maja Dunfjeld (1991), decorative elements in the practice of duodji is as such comparable to storytelling. Of the duojárs that today work with the riebangolli technique, one has indeed claimed that the decoration that we see on the belts in question is a *"vocabulary of meaning"* (Áile 05.01.2018).

The duojár in question, Áile, was born and raised in a small coastal community on the Norwegian side, during the years of Sámi re-remembering. She has fond memories of that time.

> I was young then, and so eager to take pride in my Sámi self. We had one gákti then. It was a reproduction, but everyone in my community made use of it. There was only a handful of us who could make the gákti and the belts back then, but we taught ourselves. It was important that we take back that which had been lost and learning the riebangolli-technique was a small, but very important step (Áile 05.01.2018).

As she understands it, a re-remembering process has two steps. First comes the stage of reproduction, or the actual making of an object. Next, and equally important, is the revival of the knowledge found in the object, the rematriation. Of course, such knowledge refers to the making as well, but mainly what she is describing is the language of the object. She exemplifies her meaning by referring to the assumption that the belts decorated with riebangolli are gendered, *"how you put on the riebangolli is [today] decided by the gender of the wearer. To wear a belt with separated elements of decor is indicative of femininity, whereas a complete decor is meant to be worn by men"* (Áile 05.01.2018). Today there is reason to question whether the belts were gendered in the past, as more belts have come to light that deviate from the norm (Áile 05.01.2018). Nonetheless, the riebangolli-technique is not *"a static expression, [...] it continues to evolve"* (Løkvold 2019:19), meaning that when the language of duodji is fractured or damaged new meanings and articulations may emerge. As Áile explains it, *"[t]he Sámi culture is alive and well in our communities, [...] We aren't afraid to push boundaries. We experiment and we make new traditions that are our own"* (Áile 05.01.2018). In conclusion, it does not matter if the belts were gendered in the past. Through the re-remembrance of the riebangolli-technique, the belts have become gendered. Thus, even if it is possible that the gender-specific decoration is in fact not an old knowledge, it has nonetheless evolved into one. This is a key point in understanding reclaimers process of recentering identity.

In a discussion on memory and material culture, the American anthropologists' Jennifer Lorna Hockney and Elisabeth Hallam (2001:48-50), speak on objects as mnemonic tools, referencing their ability to recollect social relations and personal associations.[35] According to the two, any object may evolve into a material cultural expression that function within deeply complex social and cultural relations, acting as the foci of collective memory, narratives and the construction of both community and individual identities.[36] As I see it, the belts decorated with riebangolli may be understood as mnemonic tools. To those that make and wear the belts, the importance of the riebangolli-technique is this:

> [u]sing mica to decorate is our tradition. It belongs to the coastal communities and it is not a tradition in the inland. It is a coast Sámi tradition and knowing that is important because we are a Sámi community with our own traditions and the riebangolli tradition is a sign that we are Sámi as much as the reindeer herder in the inland is Sámi (Ása 24.01.2018)

This quote asserts that duodji, as an extension of the riebangolli technique, contain the memories of a community, not only as visual representations, but because their presence bring forth stories of the past, the present and the future. Imagine if you will a mother making a belt decorated with riebangolli. The belt is meant to be worn by her daughter, who was born after the Sámi had begun to re-remember their cultural heritage. By this time, much of the stigma once attached to Sámi ethnicity, has been removed. The daughter was raised to be proud of her heritage and she has expressed a desire for a local gákti and the belt that goes with it. Going in, the mother has no preconceived notions, but making the belt that she has seen only in museums and picking riebangolli from the playgrounds of her childhood, awakens her memories. The image that comes to life in her mind shows

---

35 The concept shares some similarity to that of inalienable object as it has been defined by Anette Weiner (1992).

36 The recent publicazion on the work of Outi Pieski and Eeva-Kristiina Harlin and the ládjogahpir is one example, I would argue, of an object becoming a mnemonic tool. In their discussion, they have rightly pointed out that colonialism and the assimilation that followed created profound changes in gender roles. Of old, Sámi society regarded women and men as equals; their dynamic characterized by symmetrical and complimentary domains, roles and tasks (Harlin and Pieski 2020, also see Lawrence 2003, Kuokkanen 2007a, 2019). Outi and Eeva have suggested that the ládjogahpir indicate the role of women before heteropatriarchy, which is a constituent of colonialism, was successfully enforced (Harlin and Pieski 2020:124). Due to this process, much of the original meaning of the ládjogahpir is lost. But, making and wearing the hat houses new meanings and narratives of decolonial feminism. The ládjogahpir, in other words, has became the foci for a collective memory.

her walking with her grandmother, who once told her of the time that people used the riebangolli on clothes and showed her how it glimmered when she held it up against the light (Ella 23.06.2019). Taking back this memory, suddenly she is bridging the Sámi culture of the past belonging to her grandmother, with the assimilated Sámi represented by her parents, to herself and her daughter being, of course, the Sámi that are rediscovering their heritage, connecting with and re-learning their culture.

If the objects that have been decorated with riebangolli are understood as mnemonic tools, they are no less than the materialization of their source communities and the Sámi within them. The identities of reclaimers were once side-lined and made inert. In this they reflect the practices and knowledges that had been forgotten or laid dormant. But, reawakening the one, I think, frequently awakens the other. There is a sense of relief in knowing that what *"once was may be again. Nothing is ever truly lost as long as someone remembers"* (Ella 23.06.2019). The memory of ancestors found in the blood of reclaimers re-emerges when uncovering the memory of objects found in museums. Similarly, the memory of objects previously lost to their source communities re-emerges when reclaimers reconnect with their ancestors through their blood memory.

This effect has been described by the Indigenous dancer Sam Mitchell and scholar of drama and theatre Julie Burell (2016) as a re-patriation of memory. Similar, I would argue, to an act of rematriation, the return of objects and the re-remembrance of their making, allows for Sámi communities to create meanings, values, and stories, which in turn allows for a new narrative to be developed that may act as a counter to both colonial narratives as well as the enforced epistemicide of the past. This narrative might not be written down or published in "credible" avenues, but it is no less important or meaningful. Through their practice of duodji, reclaimers thus create a material landscape that mirrors their metaphysical journey of rediscovering their ancestral heritage and recentering of self by producing and reproducing new values, meanings, narratives, and identities.

The next chapter will take a closer look at how this connects to museums, but with a focus on museum artefacts and heritage objects.

CHAPTER 6: BEARALDUODJI

BEADING NEW PATHS OF KNOWLEDGE

LEARNING TO KNOW THE VOICE OF ANCESTOR'S AND THE STORIES OF OBJECTS

VUODJASKÁHPU AND THE WINGSPAN OF AN OCEANBIRD—A PROLOGUE

"There is much knowledge, in this place", says Jovnna. We are standing outside Ájtte Museum in Jåhkåmåhkke waiting to be let into the depot by the museum conservator, Eva. While we wait, Jovnna and I discuss our different practices in duodji. I work primarily with soft materials, whereas his chosen practice relies on wood and bone. Jovnna, is a duojár, born and raised in a Sámi community on the Swedish side of the border, where he was taught at his father and-grandfathers knee. Today, he earns his living by making and selling duodji. This is not his first time visiting Ájtte.

"Many don't get to learn at home anymore. It's not their fault, it's just how it is." Jovnna explains how many today come to Jåhkåmåhkke because they want to learn to duddjot as this is the place where one of the oldest Sámi schools that offers duodji as an education lies. Many of those that come to study "find much help here [in Ájtte]. The museum offers to the students to come into the collection and see the objects ... to learn from them [the artefacts]". Jovnna, though it has been a long time since he himself studied here, is here to make use of the same offer; to study objects, and to learn from and with them.

"This is beautiful [...] I have never seen anything like it" is the comment he makes as he holds on to an old Sámi vuodjaskáhppu a little later, once finally inside the collection. A vuodjaskáhppu is a container of wood, made to store butter. Jovnna turns to Eva and asks whether there is any knowledge

on the object in the databases. She looks up the acquisition number on her computer and replies with the expected information: "It's a vuodjaskáhppu, used to store butter. The precise age is unknown, but we can trace it at least 100 years back." She continues to read for a bit and then she exclaims, "Ah, yes, I remember this one. [Another duojár] saw it when he was last here, and he told us that the seams of the box were made with the wingspan from an ocean bird!" Jovnna is excited by the prospect. Typically, the seams on a vuodjaskáhppu are made by roots, or even animal tendons, and never have he before heard of wingspans being used.

He continues looking at the vuodjaskáhppu, turning it this and that way. "Hmmm, I wonder how it is prepared [the wingspan], I need to call [the other duojár]" he muses to himself. "I wonder if it has some specific significance in the choice of material?" Obviously, he has taken inspiration from the object, and the hitherto unknown technique of using wingspans to sew seams. Even when we continue looking at different items, he goes back to the vuodjaskáhppu to once more look at the object, feel it in his hands and smell it. Before we all leave the depot, he turns back, looking at the vuodjaskáhppu one last time (Jovnna 14.11.2018).

INTRODUCTION

The previous chapter closed off by questioning whether museums take part in a large-scale system of knowledge activated, in particular, by acts of re-remembrance. The following chapter continues this line of thought but shifts the focus to Sámi heritage objects in museums and their interactions with duojárs through the analytical lens of rematriation. If, in čuoldit, my focus was on duojárs and their stories, then this chapter explores the stories that are embedded in objects and how they impact Sámi negotiations of self. More accurately perhaps, in the following, I explore how duojárs make use of museum objects to re-remember and mediate ontological and epistemological knowledge[s], thus making objects, and by extension, museums into important sites of Indigenous sovereignty.

Despite their very real connection with colonialism and imperialism, ethnographical and cultural-historical museums have in recent years worked to improve and transform the relationships between cultural heritage and formerly colonized or Indigenous peoples, whom by their very definition are still colonized (Clifford 1997, Peers 2013). All in an effort to redefine themselves as ethical institutions, positioning

themselves as spaces that promote social equality whilst raising awareness of social and political issues (Sandell 2017, Paul 2018). Especially
in contexts of colonialism and the dispossession of cultural heritage
from Indigenous source communities is such ambition increasingly visible, resulting in museums attempting to become the platform
giving voice to previously silenced groups, and offering source communities the possibility of reconnecting with their heritage objects
(e.g., Clifford 1997, Peers 2013). In Norway, for instance, it has since
2000 been the practice of museums to make their collections of Sámi
cultural heritage accessible to the Sámi population (Østby 2000). Accessibility, however, is not a concise term, and as such it is practiced
differently from museum to museum.

There are three issues that immediately come to mind with regards
to accessibility. To begin, it is an issue of some bearing that the majority of Sámi heritage objects remains in museum collections that are
both physically and spiritually far removed from their source communities (Olli and Harliin 2014:65). Access thus necessitates travel over
long distances, and inevitably many never get to take such a journey.
Another concern is the fact that many museums do not advertise their
collections of Sámi objects. While true that many of today's museums have digitalized the entirety of their collections, this does not
necessarily equate to access, which I was reminded of when a friend
from Japan showed me pictures of Sámi heritage objects displayed in
a Japanese museum of ethnography. If not for her making me aware, I
would not have known of their existence.

Nor is it easy to be allowed within said collections without some
sort of academic credentials, considerably decreasing the number of
people that are allowed access. The third reason for concern thus applies directly to the question of sovereignty. While the present practice may allow, or sometimes even encourage source communities access to their material culture, museums still retain ownership which
does little to change the deeply problematic and asymmetrical power
dynamics embedded in the relationship between museums and source
communities (Finbog 2019, e.g., Moulton 2018, Harlin and Pieski
2020). Even in the case of repatriation, and the return of heritage
objects to source communities, there is still the possibility of non-Indigenous museums and cultural heritage institutions continuing to
assert control over the objects in question, for instance, with regards

to conservation or, once more, the notion of accessibility. The recent repatriation project of *Bååstede* is an example of such.

Meaning 'return' in the South Sámi language, Bååstede names an agreement of repatriation between Norwegian Folk Museum, or Norsk Folkemuseum (hence NFM), the Cultural-Historical Museum in Oslo (hence KHM), and the Sámi museums on the Norwegian side of the border (Pareli et al. 2012). Though the agreement was stipulated in 2012, it was signed much later in 2019. While the initial intent to return should be applauded, I still think it worrisome that the agreement stipulates, firstly, that Sámi museums must conserve and store the objects as regulated by NFM and KHM, and second that museum personnel must be qualified by guidelines set by NFM and KHM (Pareli et al. 2012:53-4).[1] In their defence, NFM and KHM are simply following the standards of ICOM, but it is nonetheless problematic as it makes decisions for how Sámi museums are to develop their practice as Indigenous institutions.

Mainly, my critique of Bååstede rests on two facts; to begin, Sámi árbediehtu details many different ways of conserving material culture that is not as yet accepted practice within the conventional standards of museum conservation (Olli 2013). This means that Bååstede at present prohibits árbediehtu from being practiced within the Sámi museums. *"There is not enough research at this time for us to promote the scientific value of árbediehtu in the practice of conservation"*, as Anne May Olli, the director of Riddo Duottar Museat in Kárášjohka on the Norwegian side of the border explains it (29.05.2018). Furthermore, material culture is viewed very differently in a Sámi context. As such, the treatment of objects might differ. In Sámi museums, for instance, it has long been the practice to allow full access to the entire source community within dedicated spaces. These rooms provide the Sámi with an opportunity for sensory engagement with heritage objects. Sadly, as one verdde stated, *"I'm not sure this [room] will be a possibility when we adapt our present practice in accordance with Bååstede"* (Elle 29.05.2018). In other words, as per the stipulations set forth in the agreement of repatriation, Sámi heritage objects are presumed to be handled in line with a non-Sámi perspective and custom.

As I understand it, this indicates that a Western museological ide-

---

1   In conversations with museum workers, I was told that the first stipulation was mutually agreed upon as the Sámi museums hoped this would force the governments to increase funding, which was needed to build new or adapt existing Sámi museum structures to make them meet the general standards of ICOM.

ology is presumed and thus imposed onto Sámi museums. Not only does this continue the tradition of enforcing non-Sámi values and norms onto Sámi ways of being, doing, and knowing, it also continues the silencing and erasure of Indigenous sovereignty (Simpson 2008:64). How, then, can I claim that museums are sites of sovereignty? The prologue is a good entry point in this regard because the experience of Jovnna, illustrates how *"[e]ach duodji object carries a story"* (Spein 2019), and furthermore how said stories are made accessible to duojárs [and other interested parties] by way of their tangible interaction within Sámi museums.

The idea of objects being containers of knowledge and/or stories is not unusual in Indigenous contexts. In her work with the Yup'ik communities on Turtle Island, for instance, the cultural anthropologist Ann Fienup-Riordan (2010:4) has noted that objects are often seen as entities, possessing awareness and with whom there is a sense of kinship as if they [the objects] where themselves elders, teachers and/or storytellers. This is also, as the following discussion will show, the case of Sámi heritage objects. Still, when heritage objects move from their source communities into the keeping of museums, their aspects and possibilities are diminished. In the following, I discuss the movements of heritage objects from source community to museum artefact, and back to source community through acts of rematriation; how said transition impact on the objects themselves; and lastly, how source communities and the people herein are affected by this transition.

BEARALDUODJI—MAPPING THE STRUCTURE

As in every other chapter of this book, the outline of my structure has been informed by a practice of duodji. For this chapter, I have chosen bearalduodji or beading as my medium. Beading is broadly speaking, the art of attaching beads together by stringing them on the thread and then fasten them to cloth or leather. The iconography that is often presented in beading, follows the tjaalehtjimmie; a language where every element is a word, expressing Sámi philosophy, cosmology, and law. In this chapter, however, I have decided to structure my discussion from a beadwork I did for my muottal [older sisters' daughter]. It derails slightly from what one would normally expect from beading, as what I made was the logo of her favourite band to be attached to an outer pocket of a backpack. The principle is nevertheless similar.

To begin the beading, I outlined the logo with black beads. In the context of the present chapter, the outline is arguably the boundary of discussion. In this chapter the outline is provided by a discussion on museums as memory institutions. It picks up on the discussion on museums from riessat, furthering the notion of objects being silenced and their meanings and values replaced when transitioning from heritage objects to museum artefacts. From a focus on the dispossession of Indigenous cultural heritage, I continue my discussion by filling in the main colour of this chapter's beadwork. Focusing on acts of restitution and renewal, I attempt to demonstrate how sensory access to heritage objects encourage processes that re-establish or interpret the stories, meanings, and values of the past, as heritage objects, and present, as museum objects. To do so, I blend Sámi concepts and contexts with ones that are more general, and yet I am primarily focusing on the various processes of restitution that occur when duojárs and other members of Sámi source communities interact with museum objects to recreate or re-remember knowledges and practices.

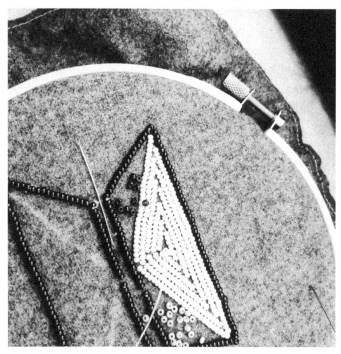

FIGURE 6-1 THE LOGO IN QUESTION BELONG TO THE GROUP BTS OF WHICH MY MUOᵮᵮAL IS A HUGE FAN. IT WAS, I ADMIT, VERY DIFFERENT FROM WHAT I NORMALLY DO, BUT ALSO FUN AS IT INVOLVED ME HAVING TO MAKE SOME DIFFERENT CHOISES AS TO FASTENING THE BEADS. IN THIS IMAGE, THE OUTLINE HAS BEEN COMPLETED AND I AM IN THE PROCESS OF FILLING IN THE MAIN COLOUR.

The shading of the beadwork comes next and last. Here, I expand on previous parts by discussing how acts of rematriation are also acts of sovereignty. To do so, I implement the system of the gift, arguing that the Sámi philosophy of interrelatedness is present in the rematriation acts encouraged by duojárs through their work on re-remembering practices of duodji. In this, I follow up on the initial discussion from giisá on sovereignty as an expression of cultural integrity and systems of interrelatedness. I thus come full circuit, ending with how museums and collections become locations where Sámi source communities not only mediate their identities, but also engages in acts of sovereignty.

MUSEUMS AS MEMORY INSTITUTIONS

However much the early museums of the 18th century were committed to the pursuit of artefact-based knowledge (Henare 2005:49), their focus has expanded in the present day. More accurately, museums have increasingly been compared to archives and libraries as institutions of memory (Dupont 2007, Dempsey 2000, Hedstrom and King 2004). Memory, it seems, has thus become a *"powerful metaphor for the social role of [...] museums"* (Trant 2009:369), which in turn reveal a general assumption that museums are meant to collect and share, not only the objects of our past but also the memories of it (Dupont 2007:13). This inclination is not, however, recent. For some time now, museums have been centred on memories as they have ordered, categorized, preserved, displayed and disseminated them for the public to see (Hooper Greenhill 2000, Padiglione 2016). This is exemplified, for instance, by the "Lappish equipage", discussed in riessat, which had serious repercussions, even in present day, for how Sámi people and their cultures were and are viewed by a mainstream public (Webb 2006, Mathisen 2014).

As 'memory institutions,' it is accepted, or even expected, that museums are to tell stories about objects and things which connect to and help create, not to mention reinforce, larger narratives; reflecting, if nothing else, their ability to shape our understanding of past and current events (e.g., Wolff, Mulholland, and Collins 2012). That is not to say that the power to name and represent, as I discuss in riessat, has gone uncontested (e.g., Hilden 2000, Hooper-Greenhill 2000, Webb 2001, Reid 2002, Deidre 2007, Buijs 2010, Cubillo 2010, Dudley 2010, Mathisen 2012, Kreps 2015). On the contrary, making use of the term 'memory institution' and the narrative powers implied herein has been problematised as it, firstly, generalize the concept of memory (Robinson 2012:414). In the context of Indigeneity, for instance, objects are thought to have memory and also the ability to share their memories with others (e.g., Fienup-Riordan 2010:4, Harlin and Pieski 2020:127). In other words, how memory is perceived varies greatly. In Andean cosmology, for instance,

> [t]he future is behind, and the past is ahead. So, if we 'imagine the future' according to or following the notions of time-space [Pacha] in Andean cosmology, this would be: Remembering the Future (Amaut 24.09.2020).

Looking to Māori understandings also reveals a different perspective in that,

> [t]here is a whakataukī (insight into Māori thought) that echoes across Moana Oceania[2] in various ways—'Ka mua, ka muri'—walking backward into the future—meaning that we must consider what has come beforehand when we go forward (Black 28.09.2020).

If we return to ruvdet and the discussion therein on muitalusat, memory is that which carries the collective history of the Sámi people, as well as being one of our most important sources of sovereignty. Not only is memory complex, it is also expressed and materialized in numerous ways. Still, the restrictive perspective that has so far homogenized memory, thus encouraging its easy governability, is very much evident in museological contexts.

This forces us to consider how, when making museums into the institutions that guard and narrate memories, a priori assumptions are easily made, first, about whose memories are to be preserved, or better yet, which version, and second, on whose terms they should be perpetuated (e.g., Merrill et al. 1993). As memory institutions, museums are deeply implicated in the politics of identity, possessing the *"power to name, to represent [...], to create official versions, to represent the social world and to represent the past"* (Hooper-Greenhill 2000:19). Of course, following the advance of post-colonial theories, the impact of European colonial rule on museological practices has been challenged and so too has the impact of their narrative powers (Hooper-Greenhill 2000, Bennett 2004, Henare 2005). Still, it has proven difficult to change museological structures even in the wake of critique.

---

2   She uses the term, 'Moana Oceania' in place of the imposed and problematic term 'Pacific' to empower and privilege the Indigenous languages and perspectives within said territory.

FIGURE 6-2 THE MOUNTED TEXT BESIDE THE CASE STATES THAT THIS IS A "MAN-TEAUX DE CHASSE INNUS" OR AN INNU HUNTING JACKET BROUGHT TO FRANCE FROM FORT CHINO IN WHAT IS TODAY CANADA. NO MENTION OF THE PRES-ENT-DAY NAME OF KUUJJUAQ. NOR IS THE WAY IT WAS COLLECTED PROBLEMA-TISED AT ALL. THIS IS VERY MUCH AN EXPRESSION OF 'ART FOR ART'S' SAKE, WHICH HAS BECOME INCREASINGLY POPULAR AMONGST ETHNOGRAPHIC MUSEUMS IN LATER DECADES AS IT SILENCE THE CONTEXT OF OBJECT'S ACQUISITION WHICH MEANS THAT THE MUSEUMS MAY AVOID A PUBLIC DEBATE ON THE MORALITY OF PAST COLLECTING PRACTICES

I remember quite well a discussion I had after a seminar that I attended in Paris. The topics of discussion at the seminar were, among others, the question of cultural heritage acquired under colonial rule. In relation to said subject, the organizers arranged for a brief visit to "Musée du quai Branly", whose ethnographic collection numbers more than a million objects from Indigenous cultures and previous colonies. To walk through their various displays and reading the mounted wall texts was, I admit a peculiar experience. The year before, Sarr and Savoy's rapport on African heritage objects in French Museums had demonstrated the various discourses of power and sovereignty attached to many of the narratives encouraged by museums. Among them the thought that as Musée de quai Branly had opened in 2006, the collection, consisting of donations and older collections from other museums, *"isn't really colonial"*. Or this was the sentiment of the museum, as explained by one of the convenors of the seminar, repeating what they had been led to believe by correspondence with the museum.

Throughout the geographical and temporal span of the colonial expansions of the West, entire Nations have been destroyed by invading settlers (Kingston 2015); heteropatriarchy and gender discrimination enforced by foreign systems of value (Lawrence 2003, Kuokkanen 2007a); spiritual beliefs and religious systems dismantled and devalued by zealous missionaries (Rydving 1991); languages destroyed or nearly so by cultural imperialists (Minde 2005); lands and people stolen, and Indigenous sovereignty undermined or outlawed (Comaroff and Comaroff 1992, Westman 2002, Pollan 2007, Nordin and Ojala 2018). While it would be quite easy, and indeed tempting, to assume that the stories of violence born in colonial circumstances no longer apply (e.g., De L'Estoile 2008), or indeed, that they happen elsewhere, they are very much present within an Indigenous context, meaning that they continue to affect people, the Sámi among them, in diverse ways (Josefsen 2006, Harlin and Pieski 2020). They also, I would argue, affect objects because these stories pertain to and survive in them, transforming their materiality into locations of memories and stories (Clifford 2004:16, e.g., Somby 2016:93). I will explain my meaning by problematising the processes of dispossession of objects from their source communities.

THE DISPOSESSION OF CULTURAL HERITAGE

In no way is it my intent to claim that all Indigenous objects in museums have made it there as a result of force or theft. Though the acquisition of some objects is the result of such practice, the Sámi goavddis—our sacred drums being one example of such—many items were purchased from source communities, either for museums or for private collections that were later bequeathed to museums. But even in the context of the latter, we have to take into consideration that consent needs to be informed and unforced, and if consent was given in a colonial context it is, in my opinion, always questionable (e.g., Sarr and Savoy 2018).

Despite the diverse conditions in which Sámi heritage objects have been acquired or, as the case may be, remanded into the custody of museums, I thus think it fair to say that they have done so in a context of 'hybridism'. By this, I do not mean the hybridism that in later years has become a favoured museological strategy where museum artefacts are augmented by digital media to create stories and meanings (Fraser et al. 2004). Rather, I am referring to the fact that heritage objects, once entered into museum collections, in addition to carrying the onto-epistemological values of their source communities, also end up being adapted into the object-based epistemologies of museology.[3] Entered into Western systems of knowledge and value, "*object value becomes mutable*", prone to change and thus subverting the values and meanings attributed to the object in their source communities (Cameron 2007:54). In some cases, these new meanings and attributes even come to impact on the source communities' future perceptions of the objects in question (Barker 2001).

For this reason, the American Associate Professor of Art, John Peffer, has suggested that objects of a non-Western category, which has been absorbed into Western museum collections, should be viewed with a "*diasporic focus*", suggesting that they are "*objects in motion, [...] that articulate between and across disparate cultural histories*" (Peffer 2005:339). Kimberly Moulton, the Yorta Yorta curator whom I first introduced in riessat, seems to follow up this suggestion when she speaks on "*our histories [...] in the form of the diaspora of cultural belongings overseas [in museums]*" (2018:200). What this quote express, at least to my understanding, is that museum artefacts, when viewed as diasporic objects, reveal the vast matrix of stories, meanings, and memories embedded by virtue of their shifting contexts. In other words, they reveal how objects of the cultural 'Other', when displaced, endure a process which the French writer and curator, Lotte Arndt argues,

> [...] inclure la violence infligée à l'objet lui-même, dont les accoutrements sont souvent dépouillés, vernis ou remodelés. Dans le passé, son nom, son identité, sa signification locale et sa fonction ont aussi été arrachés.

> [...] include the violence inflicted to the object itself, whose attributes are often stripped, embellished, or reshaped, and in the end, their names, identities, significations and functions, completely destroyed or altered (2011/2012:70, my own interpretation).

To be fair, both Peffer and Arndt write on African cultural heritage in museums, but as Moulton demonstrates, their findings are equally valid in different contexts of colonialism; objects found in Western

---

3 Not to say that museums are not shifting "*the paradigm of traditional museums space*" (Moulton 2018:201), but insofar as I see it, as long as museums refuse to return objects acquired in contexts that are to put it mildly, dubious, I would argue that museum practice is still governed by an object-based epistemology.

museums, whether they be of Sámi origin or belonging to any other culture marked by colonialism, are thus embedded in a disputative plurality of stories, semantics and symbolic meanings as well as multiple epistemological dimensions. I will return to the latter, but for now I will focus on the changing stories, values, and meanings.

When acquired by museums, the primary qualities of Indigenous objects as well as the context in which they are interpreted, are far more likely to be determined outside of their source communities (Moulton 2018:207-8). As one verdde explained it, when duodji is placed in museums "*I feel as if they're locked up in there [museums]*". This "*is no good. If you can't see and speak with it [the object], then it's really not part of the culture anymore*" (Áile 05.01.2018). What this duojár was trying to convey was not, I think, the sense that museum objects have been abandoned by their source communities, but rather that they have been dispossessed and removed from their rightful place. I would also argue that this feeling is at the heart of the criticism aimed at museums from a Sámi standpoint, in which they are accused of removing objects from a living cultural tradition and transposing them into dead things that are frozen in time (Olli 2013:87).

There are a number of ways to discuss the consequences of such, but for the purpose of the present chapter, the main concern that I would raise is that these objects often become "*signs of some elsewhere and some other time for the mainstream culture*" (Peffer 2005:341), making museums into "*asymmetric spaces of appropriation*" where "*the Others come to perform*" (Boast 2011:63). The experience that was shared with me when I met a duojár who recently returned from abroad and from visiting several museums, illustrate this quite well:

> When I was there, I saw them [Sámi heritage objects], and they were old friends. But I could not speak to them. Nor could I hold them. They were trapped in big cases of glass. They were there and I could see them, but I could not really meet them. Even if I could, I don't know if we could speak. Do they still know the [Sámi] language[s]? Do they still remember our stories? (Sunna 05.01.2018).

Stories made from and about objects in diaspora inevitably put their mark on the collective mainstream memory to the degree that the uprooted objects experience their original stories being subdued and displaced (Sarr and Savoy 2018:49). This begs the question, is it possible to restore these objects to their original communities, and in the process regain their functions, meanings, and protocols as well as their original ontological and epistemological implications? This is the question, around which I next discuss the relation between museums and objects as opposed to the relation between source community and object. To do so, I begin by sharing a personal memory of my own experience of said relations.

THE OLD CRADLE AND ITS MANY STORIES

I was very young when I first understood that my identity as Sámi, though at the time I was unable to articulate it as such, was a battleground for complex political and historical issues reaching back several centuries and across many different nation-states. This realisation came to me after my primary school visited NFM to look, among others, at their permanent exhibition on Sámi culture. Being the only Sámi in my class, at least to my knowledge, I eagerly anticipated the opportunity to demonstrate my advanced knowledge of my people and my culture. Imagine my distress then, when reality did not meet my expectations.

Growing up as I had in an urban environment during the 1980s, the exhibition was far removed from what I knew as Sámi. Besides the focus on reindeer herding, of which I had no practical knowledge, the exhibition to me seemed old-fashioned and more reminiscent of my aahka and áhkku's generation than my own. In this, I think it fair to say that the exhibition displayed what Homi K. Bhabha ([1983]2006:248), the Indian critical theorist famed for his contribution to the post-colonial discussion, has conceptualized as *fixity*, meaning that it appeared static and frozen in time.

At this age, I could not distinguish that there was a difference between the narrative created by the exhibition and the reality that I had lived every day of my life. Thus, at the tender age of eleven, my once uncompromising certainty of who I was, had been irrevocably disturbed. I was distraught, and as children do, sought comfort from my parents. They eased my fears explaining that I came from a people as diverse as the colours of the rainbow and that the museum either did not know of or acknowledged this diversity.

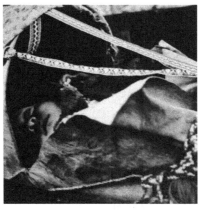

FIGURE 6-3 GIERKAMAS, OR CRADLE BABIES, WAS NOT AT ALL A COMMON SIGHT IN THE 1980S', AS THE SOCIAL STIGMA OF BEING SÁMI AT THAT TIME WAS STILL VERY STRONG. STILL, BEING THE CHILD OF TWO EXTREMELY ENGAGED ACTIVIST WORKING FOR SÁMI POLITICAL RIGHTS SAID STIGMA WAS CONTINUOUSLY DEFIED, HENCE THIS IMAGE OF ME AS A VERY YOUNG CHILD BEING PLACED IN A GIETKKA FOR SLEEP AND PROTECTION.

This I translated into me being far cleverer than any of the museum workers and instead of doubting myself, clearly, I needed to make it my mission in life to educate the poor ignoramuses of the world. Of course, these are the reflections and thoughts of a child, but what the experience had left me with was the understanding that someone had decided to tell the story of my people, but it was a story I felt that I had no part in.

When years later I revisited the exhibition, my experience of it was quite different. My return came about as part of an organized preparation for final exams in a Sámi language class at the Sámi College of applied sciences. The teachers that had accompanied the students to the museum tasked us with finding an object and write about its history—both in general, but also as it related to us on a personal level. I chose a gietkka, a baby cradle because I remembered my mother telling me that I was a *gierkamas*[4] or cradle child, meaning that as a child, I had been placed in one for sleep and protection. Suddenly the exhibition was no longer someone else's story. It had also become my own. And yet, the exhibition in question was largely unchanged, and the objects displayed were the same as when I had previously visited. At this point, I realized that it was not the exhibition or the narrative created by the museum that was different. Rather, what was different was the stories I could hear in the objects and thus how I read the

4   Gierkamas is actually the Sámi dialect spoken in my father's home community, and gietkamánná would be the North Sámi spelling found in books of grammar and in dictionaries.

exhibition and interpreted its narrative.

In her study of museum artefacts, the Danish museologist Camilla Mordhorst (2009) has demonstrated how certain objects carry multiple stories and/or meanings. These variables have been attached to the objects at different times and in different museological contexts, but they continue to exist simultaneously, albeit in a hierarchy. The gietkka illustrates this point, providing as it does, the multiple and different stories told by the museum as well as those shared in their source communities. In the case of the former, the gietkka represented an ethnographic artefact defined by its function and related to Sámi child raising of the past—exotic and in contrast to the mainstream society in Norway. To me, however, the gietkka was a tangible memory of my own childhood, very much present and relatable. Still, my experience was that one story had consumed the other, and only by inserting myself into the narrative with my own personal story did I manage to listen to the stories born when it still resided in its source community.

Being detached from the original frame of reference and given new value and meaning is often the case when objects shift from their context of use to museum objects (Clifford 1988:231). As 'memory institutions', museums constitute various practices in which value and meaning are determined. The result, not surprisingly, is that the other ways of knowing and of remembering, especially those that are Indigenous, have been dispossessed (Cameron 2007:51-2). It follows then that objects that have been implicated in the asymmetrical power relations of museums and Indigenous source communities, also become the site for such dynamics. This is very much evidenced by the fact that there was a third story in circulation, although at that time I was unable to hear it.

This story only came to me when I, for a brief period of time, had an internship at the museum when I was doing my master in museology. During a bout of research for an exhibition[5], I came across the gietkka once more, or more to the point, I came across its acquisition text. Admittedly, the documentation on the gietkka was sparse, which is not at all uncommon and reflects the sometimes morally questionable character of collections (Pareli et al. 2012:29). As such, I was not surprised to discover that the information on the gietkka was limited

---

5   The exhibition was "Finstemte kvinnfok" produced on the occasion of the 100-year jubilee of women's right to vote in 2013, and where I focused on finding Sámi objects that could represent the presence of Sámi interests in the exhibition, represented by, among others, by Elsa Laula Renberg.

to its assumed provenience and the name of the person who gifted the museum with it in the early 20th century. There are examples of other acquisition texts, however, being more specific, and for the sake of argument, I will instead refer to one such story.

This story, for my part at least, began in 2015, when I visited the ethnographic museum of Volkenkunde in Leiden, Netherland. I was initially in Leiden to give a lecture at the nearby university on my research into Sámi museums as contact zones and their implications for the mediation of Sámi identities. After my talk, I was approached by the curator in charge of the Arctic collection at Volkenkunde, a large part of which is Sámi in origin. By her kind invitation, I had the opportunity to visit and look at both their current display as well as their collection. Though not part of the exhibition, one object which immediately stood out to me was an old gietkka. Added to the collection in the mid-19th century, the gietkka had an attached acquisition story that I found very disturbing as it detailed the deliberate theft of the cradle after its owner, a Sámi woman who had carried her newborn child in it, refused to sell it. The story was not previously known, I think, to the curator whose rejoinder when I expressed my discomfort at the story, was that they [museums] thankfully did not hold to such practices anymore.[6] But it hit me then, would this story ever be disseminated if and when the gietkka was put on display? Based on the choice of exhibition strategy for their Sámi display at that time, which was assimilation or art for art's sake, I doubt it.

THE BRUTALITY OF DISPLACEMENT

The two gietkkas at Volkenkunde and NFK serve as a good example of how objects, through their use, acquisition, and consequent museological categorisation become, what the British social anthropologist Elisabeth Edwards (2001:2), terms *"a site of intersecting histories"*, a location for multiple stories, meaning, values, and intentions. Such stories, she continues, are never hidden, only unspoken (Edwards 2015:246). When observing museum objects with a diasporic focus, however, the many simultaneous and intersecting, and at times even disparate stories, embedded in them appear. Dependent on the viewer's context, their embodied truth as it were, the presence, visibility,

---

6   This opens a completely different discussions of whether or not it is morally justifiable for museum to keep objects that so explicitly demonstrate that they have not been acquired in a lawful manner.

and tangibility of an object might as such provoke different reactions. This is clearly illustrated by one story shared by a verdde, who in her capacity as duojár have traveled Europe and visited museum collections quite extensively.

> There I heard the voices of my ancestors in all the [Sámi] things that they [the museums] had. People around me spoke of their beauty. They said they were so interesting to look at. They were happy and pleased. I wanted to cry. I felt that they too [the objects] would cry if they could (Sunna 05.01.2018)

Within the many stories evoked by the movement of Indigenous objects, whether they are lost to, stolen from, or forgotten in their source communities, choosing which stories to listen to also means picking which stories to validate, and conversely, which stories to invalidate. In my opinion, this creates a *hierarchy of stories.*

The hierarchy of stories is not static. Willen H. Willems (2014:107), who was a Dutch professor of archaeological heritage management, has discussed how cultural heritage in many ways revolve around the hierarchy of stories. Use of the past in the present often relates to how the latter is purposely created by ascribing specific value to material culture in response to the needs and desires of stakeholders. An object is, as such often used in contradicting and opposing ways, promoted very much on account of specific needs at specific times. The hierarchy of stories is consequently reproduced in the present day, but always with intent. I am tempted to define this process as a *syndrome of incompleteness.*

Introduced by Sarr and Savoy in their report on repatriation, a syndrome of incompleteness is born from the fact that an absence of cultural heritage in source communities, ostensibly as the result of a dispossession, might *"rendre la mémoire silencieuse"*, or render memory silent (2018:41, 30, my own translation).[7] A syndrome of incompleteness thus argues that many of the stories that are embedded in objects, as well as their meanings and values, become equally displaced from source communities upon the objects' physical removal. As I see it, this is illustrated by the gáktis that were displaced and eventually forgotten in some Sámi communities. As a judicial document detailing individual and collective rights, when displaced and eventually for-

---

7   In the original version of the report, which is in French, the term 'syndrome of incompleteness' is not mentioned. As such, whereas I everywhere else refer to the original report, in relation to this specific term I have had to cite the English translation.

gotten, the judicial practices and knowledge[s] embedded in the gák-tis also disappeared. (e.g., Spein and Enoksen 1991). For this reason, while it is true that displacement historically has been associated with the forced removal and/or relocations of targeted groups of people, as a strategic process of *"systematic deprivation[...]to destroy a group in whole or in part"* (e.g., Basso 2016:6), I would argue that the displacement of objects is equally crucial.

In support of this argument, I would point to the fact that many of the Indigenous heritage objects in non-Indigenous museums,

> [...] are no longer made by First Peoples who have not had access to such items to begin the process of revival. As long as these objects remain dislocated from their peoples, there will be no end to the trauma suffered by First Peoples communities in relation to this displacement and history of stolen goods or traded goods under exploitative social structures. The longer non-Indigenous people continue to have control, and First Peoples cannot engage, the longer this trauma will recycle (Moulton 2018:200).

If I shift the focus back to a Sámi context, as well as the multiple epistemological dimensions implicated that were briefly mentioned above, the epistemicide that took place in Sápmi had multiple consequences. As I discussed in čuoldit, the epistemicides initiated in Sápmi would sometimes force Sámi communities to "forget". Objects are a vital part of such intent. As has been noted by Outi Pieski in a recent discussion on repatriation and decolonization of museums, *"Our objects are our living ancestors"* (Pieski 07.10.2020). The stories, meanings and values embedded in Sámi heritage objects are as such lessons from our eallilan [elders] and dispensed across borders of time and place. As much as people then, objects are equally important components in the Sámi onto-epistemology that I have previously defined as árbediehtu. In other words, the removal of objects from source communities has very much been an integral part of the colonial experience of epistemicide (Peers 2013:142). As one verdde articulated, *"[h]ow do you tell of your life, if the words to express it no longer exist?"*. If there are none left to remember the stories, the meanings and values, how do *"we remember"*? (Elle 29.05.2018)

I would claim it as an indisputable fact that the removal of heritage objects in source communities disrupted, eroded, or destroyed many of the customary tools for maintaining and transmitting knowledge[s] and practices. *"[L]earning traditional practices was not something that [we] were concerned with back then. Today, many of the tradition-bearers [árbečeahpis] in our communities are gone. Now we must learn from duodji [objects]"* (Ása 07.01.2018). Intimately linked with the epistemicide then, I argue that objects, or the forced lack thereof, what I would term the *brutality of displacement*, had an equally crucial role in the process of epistemicide. Furthermore, I would suggest that the brutality of displacement is very much related to the trauma of absence, only this time I use the term to conceptualize a trauma that also afflicts those that are born and raised Sámi.

Nevertheless, the brutality of displacement does not need to be final. Continuing this line of thought, I very much agree with Moulton when she suggests that repatriation is the solution to the dispossession of material culture experienced by Indigenous people worldwide. She continues, however, by stating that *"it is not as simple as just handing them back"* (Moulton 2018:200), which echo the stance of Sarr and Savoy in their discussion of repatriation and, for that matter, the sentiments of source communities where *"returning objects is good, but it is what the objects carry...knowledge and stories..."* that matters (Áile 05.01.2018). As is made painfully clear by the processes that shape and create the brutality of displacement, however, the transformation experienced by objects once they are entered into a museum may be difficult, or at times even impossible to reverse (Barker 2001). That is to say, even when repatriated there is no guarantee that a complete recovery of previous meanings, stories and values is a possibility.

There are several examples of such being the case in Sápmi alone (Inga et al. 1986, Spein and Enoksen 1991, Harlin and Pieski 2020, Guttorm 2020). What most of these examples have in common, however, is their expressed formulation of intent. In the rematriation of the ládjogáhpir, for instance, even if the stories, meanings, and values that it once housed has been lost, by making and wearing the ládjogáhpir in present time, an interpretation and reflection happen which eventually ensures that new stories, meanings and values are created (Guttorm 2020:108). Similarly, as was the case with the riebangolli-technique, new dimensions of meanings and stories were created after they had been re-remembered in the source communities. In my opinion this process of renewal is very closely aligned with a return to Indigenous, or Sámi, philosophies. Next, I explain what I mean by this.

'CEREMONIES OF RENEWAL'

As is the case with many Indigenous philosophies (Wilson 2008:73, Kincheloe 2011:335, Atalay 2019:81-2), the Sámi worldview is one that puts at its core the interrelatedness of existence. Many of the stories, practices, and objects of Sámi source communities, materialize these relations. More than simply returning the tangible expression of a Sámi world-in-relation, objects offer us the possibility of renewing the intangible aspects associated with said world. As a concept, rematriation acknowledges this in a way that repatriation is incapable of doing. In that sense, rematriation is what happens after repatriation and deals with every aspect of objects—tangible as well as intangible—being re-inserted into society. This focus on re-remembering intangible aspects of cultural heritage makes rematriation, to my understanding at least, very similar to what museological literature has referred to as *ceremonies of renewal* (Peers 2013).

The term was initially introduced by Canadian professor of Education, Cynthia M. Chambers, and Indigenous scholar and elder, Narcisse Blood of the Kainai First Nation on Turtle Island in an article discussing the relationship between people and land. As they explain it, a ceremony of renewal is a way of restitution that returns the interrelational balance of the world *"nurtured through unimpeded access, continued exchange of knowledge, and [...] visiting and exchanging gifts and stories"* (Chambers and Blood 2009:267). Admittedly, Blood and Chambers introduced the concept in relation to land, contending the necessity of access to sites of great ceremonial and spiritual value as these places are *"storied"* and thus repositories of knowledge[s], of meanings and of values (Chambers and Blood 2009:259). As has been established, however, objects are similarly storied, and the concept of ceremonial renewal is as such applicable to museum artefacts. Indeed, the large-scale project 'Kaahsinooniksi Aotoksisaawooyal/Our ancestors have come to visit: Reconnections with historic Blackfoot shirts', illustrates such.

In this project, five Blackfoot shirts collected in the 1830s and eventually acquired by the Pitt Rivers museum, was shipped back to what is now Alberta, Canada, on loan to two local museums. Intended to *"encourage the transmission of cultural knowledge within Blackfoot communities by using the provocation of touch to encourage participants discussions"*, a total of 500 source community members handled the shirts during their time back on Turtle Island (2013:136). In the past, museums often used poisonous chemicals in their conservation practice. A lot of the time, museum artefacts are thus harmful to handle without significant protection (Olli 2013:19). The trace amount of pesticides found on the shirts, however, was so small that they could be safely handled using simple gloves (Peers 2013:142).

The initiators of the project soon discovered that there was an unintended consequence. In their interaction with their source communities, the presence of the shirts forged anew crucial connections of social relations; they encouraged the reawakening of kinship between descendants and ancestors; helped restore the link between people and land, to ancestral knowledge and practices as well as between people and other entities. This, in turn, commenced a process of healing which was termed a ceremony of renewal (Peers 2013:146).

As to the question of healing, Robert Yazzie, a former Chief Justice of the Navajo Nation on Turtle Island, has observed that "*we, as Indigenous peoples, must start [...] taking control of our personal lives, our families, our clans and our communities. To do that, we must return to our [...] relationships*" (Yazzie 2000:47). According to Yazzie, healing is both a collective and an individual process asserting spiritual beliefs, but also the knowledge[s] embedded in heritage objects and the relations they take part in. Just as the brutality of displacement once reinforced the strategy of epistemicide, so too does the return of objects—by way of repatriation and rematriation—help with healing and re-remembering stories, meanings, and values, whether they be original or reinterpreted.

Although the project did not include permanent repatriation of the shirts, those involved still managed to engage in the process of rematriation, reclaiming both embodied practices, as well as aspects of emotional and spiritual obligations. But this effect did not stop with the 500 invited to handle the shirts. In an article that connects the repatriation of Indigenous objects with acts of healing, it has been noted that even the stories of engagements provide some form of healing for the listeners (Atalay 2019:81). This is similar to what the duojárs involved in the re-remembrance of the riebangolli-technique that I discussed in čuoldit experienced. Bringing back the knowledge and the practice of riebangolli had an impact on the entire source communities, not only the duojárs involved in the process of re-remembrance.

As Ása explained it, "*[w]hat revitalization has done for our communi-ty is teach us how to once more show to everyone that we are Sámi [...] Re-learning the mica-technique [...]has been our way of doing that*" (Ása 07.01.2018).

The return of the Blackfoot shirts, however brief, demonstrate the importance of repatriation in contexts of Indigeneity, supporting Moulton's proposal that it is the solution to ending the ongoing cycles of trauma brought on by epistemicide and colonial encounters. To begin the healing of the brutality of displacement demands, as such, nothing less than our living elders being returned. This is certainly a viable solution in a Sámi context, as will be demonstrated next.

RE-ESTABLISHING A SÁMI WORLD-IN-RELATION.

The connection between people and objects that is destroyed, or at least greatly disturbed by the brutality of displacement, have long been a subject of discussion in museological literature (Clifford 2004, Pullar 2008, Arndt 2011/2012, Sarr and Savoy 2018). In an article discussing the impact of material culture on processes of recentering Indigenous identities, James Clifford (2004:16-7) argues that heritage objects are sites of both complex stories and layers of meaning. In working with such objects, he continues, the maker may find his or her place in so-ciety by confirming existing traditions and in some cases even permu-tate these, which works to provide fresh ground for negotiating iden-tities—both old and new, single and plural (Jones 2010). His point is strikingly familiar to the argument I presented in čuoldit on the relation between the practice of gáktimaking and the adaption of the codes of sámáidahttin. This makes me consider that said connection could be a ceremony of renewal. The story of one reclaimer, Marte, gives great support to this suggestion.

I met Marte in 2018 when I, for a brief spell, travelled to the North of Norway on what was meant to be a vacation. As I happened to be near one of my verdde's home communities, I reached out asking if she wanted to meet up for a coffee. She ended up inviting me to attend a workshop she was arranging to facilitate the making of gáktis. Driv-ing to the event, I had no intention of working. I was simply looking forward to catching up, spending time doing duodji in her company. During the workshop, however, I was approached by Marte. Although this was our first meeting, she already knew who I was, having heard of me from other verdde, and thus she had a passing familiarity with the research that I was doing. As a reclaimer, Marte was in the process of re-remembering her Sámi heritage, and now she wanted to share her story.

Born and raised in an urban area on the Norwegian side of the border, she had always known that her father's hometown had a large Sámi community. She never knew, however, that her father's family mainly came from the latter. Still, she was incredibly open when she explained that she had always felt that there was a lack in her life, as if something was missing; *"there's this strange vacuum almost, a space inside that's empty"* (Marte 26.6.2018). As she reached adulthood, she began to articulate this trauma of absence into a suspicion that it was related to being Sámi. Eventually, she decided to do research into her ancestry, at which point she discovered that her great-grandmother was counted as Sámi in the census of 1930. As a result, she began the process of reclaiming said ancestry, starting with extrapolating which gákti she held ancestral rights to. Describing her experience, she stated that

> I had no one to turn to because no one in my family that might know was willing to even entertain the idea of us having Sámi ancestry. But I knew her name [the great-grandmother], which meant that I eventually was able to discover which gákti to get (Marte 26.6.2018).

Like so many reclaimers before her, Marte initially turned to different archival sources, which in turn led her to museums. First, *Digitalt Museum* looking up pictures of gáktis. Eventually, she also travelled directly to various museums to look at the sources in person.

It was during one such trip that Marte made an interesting discovery. Looking through multiple acquisition texts, she found a gákti that had belonged to a relative of her great-grandmother. When we first met, it was this gákti that Marte wanted to recreate. It is, she told me, *"a sense of coming home. Making that which my great-grandmother could have used…I don't know, I feel that … I am taking back something that belongs to me"* (Marte 26.6.2018). During the few hours we spent talking, Marte shared with me the stories she had collected on her journey, as they had once been told in a museum, but also how she had reinterpreted them.

I often wondered in the following months how her story continued but was reconciled to never knowing. Nevertheless, six months later, Marte made contact once more to share with me that she had finally completed her gákti. To her, the entirety of the process had been deeply emotional because it had encouraged her to remake the relations of the past and reinterpret them in the present. In her own words, this process had to her been as if an *"ancestor reached through time to teach me, welcoming me back home"* (Marte 13.01.2019). I asked how that had made her feel. Nothing less, she answered, than *"the knowledge that I am Sámi, and the security of being accepted as such"* (Marte 13.01.2019).

Marte's sense of ancestral connection after having worked on the gákti, as if her great-grandmother reached through time and worlds to support and guide her path, invokes what I believe is a relevant aspect of the rematriation-process. To be more precise, the feelings Marte described on the completion of her gákti acknowledge the interrelatedness of a Sámi world-in-relation. *"I know who I am"* (Ása 24.01.2018), *"I know where my ancestors are"* (Laara 05.04.2018), and *"I know my relations"* (Naja 22.06.2018) are all variants of this interrelatedness. As one verdde explicitly expressed it, *"[m]y place in the world…that is from my kin, it comes from the land…it is in my blood"* (Áile 05.01.2018).

When the brutality of displacement occurs, the conscious knowledge of these relations is removed, either in full or partly, which in turn disrupts the interrelatedness of a Sámi world-in-relation, creating a trauma of absence. The ability of objects to re-insert such interrelatedness is evident in how Sámi source communities react upon seeing them as museum artefacts.

> It was wonderful to see them [museum artefacts]…I imagine how they came to be…what stories they carry, I can only wonder…what knowledge[s] do they hold, what can they teach but at the same time, I feel a sense of alienation. Their voices come to me only in whispers and I cannot hear them clearly" (Sunna 05.01.2018).

The severance of objects and things is not simply a question of physical conditions. As the earlier discussion of the brutality of displacement makes evident, there is more to removing objects and things from their source communities; *"The voices are silenced…I cannot hear them whisper…muted behind glass and hidden away…they [objects] are removed from Sámi"* (Áile 05.01.2018).

When Marte, after years of research and questioning, found a gákti that could be traced to her ancestor, she was able to reconnect with her family's past, the stories once silenced by dispossession voiced once more. Not by the museum, which now owned the gákti, but by Marte herself as she slowly came to *"know my ancestors' voice,"* which in turn taught her to *"listen to the stories told by the gákti"* (Marte 13.01.2019). For her, the process of making her own gákti thus became a ceremony of renewal. Relearning the stories in the gákti, reconnecting with her Sámi ancestry, and finding her place within her Sámi community as such helped restore her relations and with it, her place in a Sámi world-in-relation. Demonstrating, quite evidently, that *"access to [...] objects can help rebuild relationships which have been disrupted"* (Conaty and Crane Bear 1998:73), reactivating the world as one of relations.

THE TACTILE TANGIBILITY OF MUSEUM OBJECTS

It would be easy to deem Marte's story as one of success alone. And yet, her story also reveals her struggles. Interacting with her ancestor's gákti was restricted to sight alone, meaning that the level of her interaction was limited to photos or while separated by a wall of glass. Though she herself did not spend much time debating this topic, she did state that the gákti, in her opinion, *"should be where it belongs, at home with us"* because it would allow her and other relatives to *"work with"* it by touch and sense (Marte 13.01.2019). To understand the express need that this quote describes, it is necessary to understand the powerful effect of our senses. To elaborate, I will introduce another verdde, Ella.

Ella was born in the South of Norway to a single mother who is Norwegian. While she always knew that her father was Sámi, she had little contact during her formative years, and so she never managed to connect with him or his family. After she had her first child, however, she began to take an interest in reconnecting with her Sámi ancestry, and eventually, she found the gákti, and by extension, duodji. During the summer of 2019, Eva participated in several courses and workshops that I helped host in Oslo that centred on encouraging proficiency in the Sámi aesthetics of dáajmijes vuekie.

Trained as a dressmaker, her technical skills as a seamstress were extremely sharp, and during the course, she ended up teaching me several tricks of the trade. Meaning that she did not attend the course due to needing help in that department, but because she lacked the árbediehtu of gáktimaking. In conversations, Ella explained how she had been greatly helped along by looking at digitalized Sámi collections in museums in order to make herself and her children gáktis. She nonetheless remarked that,

> [t]he museum [Ájtte] have gáktis on display... I wish I could touch and really work with them [the gáktis]. I´m going back, you know... I...someone told me......you can ask to see them [gáktis] outside of the exhibition...like, really touch and study them, and....I´m doing that...I'm gonna make one myself after. (Ella 23.06.2019)

Mari Rorgemoen (2011:84), who is an expert on the national costumes of Norway [bunad], has discussed how making reproductions is a traditional method used in the transference of knowledge[s]. This is similar to the method discussed in čuoldit, whereby the act of copying is extensively used to retain practices and knowledge[s] in processes of re-remembrance. As explained by Rorgemoen, the point of said method is not to recreate objects of the exact same values and meanings. This, she continues, would be impossible as the copied objects become new objects in their own right and thus associated with new and different values and meanings. Media theorist Sean Cubitt (1998:31) advocates a similar view in his argument that a reproduction is, in fact, as unique as the template. When objects are remade, their definition as a reproduction is simply one of many aspects. The other aspects of the remade object are equally relevant, and these help shape an object that is both new and original. [8]

Marcus Boon, who is a professor of English, expands on this perspective in his book, *In praise of copying*. Here Boon impress upon his readers that the very act of reproducing objects is a unique process, both with regard to the context in which the action takes place, but also as it relates to the feelings and personal experiences evoked in someone when engaged in such an act (Boon 2010:17).

The re-production of heritage objects is thus more than the mere

---

8   From a museological perspective, a copy is generally seen as less than the original. This concern is founded on the fear that a copy may subvert the values and meanings attributed to the original. Though said view first appeared in the late 16th century (Boon 2010:48, also see Nagel and Wood 2010), it has nonetheless made a great impact on traditional museologist practice, and indeed within the Western paradigm as a whole (e.g., Cameron 2007:51, Fyfe 2004:48). The social antrhopologist and museologs, Fiona Cameron, argues that said fear very much rests in the underlying concern that copies leave museum collections obsolete and rendering museums in much the same way (Cameron 2007:50-1).

act of copying. It is a deeply ingrained custom whereby the practitioner learns and develops his or her knowledge of cultural tradition
or árbediehtu through an act of imitation (Dunfjeld 2006:17). Similar then, to the customary practice of knowledge transference in a
Sámi context where one generally learns by seeing followed by doing. Re-remembering Sámi heritage objects through the method of
'crafting', or making, is as such one way in which duojárs may re-learn
"*things through our fingers, bodies and emotions*" (Guttorm 2020:105).
As was explained by one duojár, "*to learn you need to see. You need to
look at an object and to touch it*" (Áile 05.01.2018). The importance that
both Marte and Ella put on the need to touch and interact with the
gáktis they have or wish to remake reflects this way of learning. This
element of tactility in the process of re-remembering is not unusual in
Indigenous contexts.

In her contribution to an anthology on Indigenous representation
in art galleries, Canadian museologist Ruth Phillips (2002:62-3) states
that for many in Indigenous source communities, learning from museum objects is not only about the visible aspects. There is also an emphasis on the emotional, spiritual, and social perceptions embedded in
objects—or the interrelatedness of things. According to Laura Peers
(2013:142), who was the curator in charge of the Americas collection
of Pitt Rivers during the reconnection project with Blackfoot shirts,
Indigenous researchers express such emphasis as they "*often perform
the objects' functions; lifting masks to faces, placing hats on heads, draping
robes over elders to acknowledge their kinship relations, social structure,
clan rights*" which in turn works to ensure that "*the objects are reabsorbed
into social relationships*". As I see it, Peer's researcher is interchangeable
with duojár as the same need and tendency is very much present in the
interaction of the latter with museum artefacts.

The exhibition that I visited with my siessá when we went to look
at gáktis from our source community, which I briefly spoke about in
riessat, is one example of such. We visited quite early in the day, my
siessá having taken the day off to spend it with me visiting people and
places. As a result, the exhibition space was empty of other visitors. The
gáktis that were exhibited were, as expected, kept behind thick ropes
to discourage the audience from getting too close. That did nothing
to stop my siessá from climbing over the ropes to touch the gáktis,
feeling their fabric, studying the seams and the cuts of the garments,

discovering the small details that went into their making. I should add that she did have the presence of mind to ask me to check if we were alone before she did so. Having made sure of our privacy, I joined my siessá behind the rope, equally immersed in the need to touch and feel the gáktis. Interspaced between our tactile explorations, we would call each other's attention to small details, discussing the possible reasons behind specific choices and decorations. This process is a *"repatriation of [...] knowledge,"* as the Sugpiaq[9] professor of Education, Gordon Pullar, puts it (2008:112). And it is a process that is quite common in the practice of duodji. As one verdde explains,

> When I began [to practice duodji], I learned from a book. My áhkku taught me some as a child, but now she is long gone and back then, I didn't really have an interest in learning. Only when I moved away [from a Sámi community] did duodji become important. Eventually I began to look at objects. When I saw something I liked I never asked [the maker] how it was done or if they could show me. I asked to take a closer look at it [the object], and I studied it, and I learned (Jane 30.03.2019)

In this quote, Jane, a young Sámi duojár from a Sámi community on the Swedish side of the border, argues that the knowledge needed to re-remember practices of duodji may be retrieved when one is able to study the tangibility of the objects as well as its visual representation; what materials are used, what is the measurements, how does the object look from every angle? To answer these questions, a picture is not enough, nor is a brief encounter with an object that has been separated by glass or rope sufficient. The need to interact with museum objects in a capacity that expands beyond the act of looking is very much illustrated by both Jane as well as my Siessá and I. But it is also an indicator of how difficult it is to perform said action within the confines of museums where touch is generally discouraged (Susan 1999:28).

In an Indigenous context, the value of touching and handling objects in museums is immense (Clifford 2004, Peers 2013, Harlin and Pieski 2020, Guttorm 2020). And yet, there is a tension between the canon of Western conservation practice and preservation as it is understood from an Indigenous perspective. The former approaches preservation with a view to preserving an object's physical integrity

---

9   An Indigenous people of Turtle Island.

and thus preserve the cultural significance—aesthetic, historical, and contextual—of it (Candlin 2008). From the latter perspective, however, preserving the cultural significance of an object is so much more; it is also the preservation of stories, meanings, and values (Clavir 2002:xvii). While it is true that museums have expanded how Indigenous researchers may interact with objects, the same does not necessarily hold true for the rest of the source communities. The story of one verdde, Násti, illustrates such.

Násti comes from a coastal community on the Norwegian side of the border. Though she has always been comfortably aware of her Sámi identity, she only recently began working to reconnect with Sámi spirituality. The Lenape-Cherokee psychologist, Ann Dapice (2006:257), has argued the necessity of taking cosmological beliefs into account in processes of Indigenous restitution, stating that *"[f]or the spiritual aspect, it is important to encourage reconnection to creation, the earth, the sky and nature—to perceive the beauty, awe, and wonder that surrounds us"*. Meaning that in the treatment of trauma caused by colonialism and epistemicide, it is important to include a spiritual renewal. In *"my journey, I have found a relief in understanding that we are all connected, and those connections is what create life"* (Násti 13.08.2019). An important aspect of this journey for Násti, has been the goavddis.

As discussed in bárket, most of the goavddis from Sápmi today reside far from their source communities and in museums. The consequence of such is that *"its guiding drumming is not reaching into our ears from the museums cellars"*, as Outi Pieski recently stated in her talk on "Decolonizing the Museum and Public Art" (Pieski 07.10.2020). Not a researcher or otherwise connected with a Western academic sphere, Násti experienced some difficulties getting access to drums; having to contend with viewing them in their glass cases at various museums. Their presence, she states, was,

> […] muted. Like their spirits were captive. I could still feel their power and I could hear them whisper, but I couldn't grasp what they were saying. Imagine if I could sit with them and hear them speak loud and clear; what would they say, what would they share (Násti 13.08.2019).

Because she was unable to truly sense the presence of the drums in museums, Násti turned to her ancestors and the realm of their spirits. Pleading for their guidance, Násti explained that she *"needs help. Now you must come to me and you must help me find my way"*. Some nights later, Násti believes that one of her ancestors answered her plea and came to her in a dream giving her the guidance she needed.

> They showed me how to make a drum. They came many nights, giving me knowledge until they told me that I was ready to make one. When I went to find the báhkki [material to make the drum], I was guided there … It felt as if someone reached out from another time and place, guiding my hand. Even when I made the drum, I had someone standing with me who guided me and showed me what to do (Násti 13.08.2019)

As Násti told me this story, she cried. For her the experience had centred her within a place of comfort and security; forging links and making kin of forgotten ancestors, connecting, not only to her culture, but also the people that had lived in that culture before her.

The spiritual dimension that Násti speaks of is not reserved for working with the goavddis alone. In her quest to remake the gákti of her ancestors, Marte also refer to a spiritual dimension. Explaining how she could sense the presence of her ancestors, she too felt as if *"they [her ancestors] came to me, and they spoke to me. At first, I couldn't really understand, but as I continued to work on the gákti…it was as if… I feel… I learnt to know my ancestors voice"* (Marte 13.01.2019). This is also why she expressed her concern that the gákti was encased behind glass, and thus muted. Despite having successfully engaged in a ceremony of renewal, she still felt great sorrow at her ancestor's gákti being kept in a museum far from its source community. Kimberly Moulton (2018:210) expresses a similar concern.

> I wondered, if it [the object] was going to sleep, when would be the next time it might wake up? The notion that all of the objects were sleeping and dormant made me consider their purpose, locked away in the dark halls of these institutions. I believe cultural belongings, whether old or new, are constantly awake, and recharged when they have community with them. There is a reciprocal channel that is opened when community connects.

When Sámi heritage objects are returned to their source communities, they too experience a recharge. Their voices become loud, and their stories are made clearer. On their return, and with a sensory engagement, I believe it is possible for source communities and heritage objects to initiate the process of gulahallat. Next, I explain why that is by returning to Jovnna and the vuodjaskáhppu.

BACK TO THE VUODJASKÁHPPU

FIGURE 6-4 'STUDIE MAGASINET' AT ÁJTTE IS DEDICATED TO SÁMI VISITORS AT THE MUSEUM THAT WANT A SENSORY INTERACTION WITH THE HERITAGE OBJECT FOUND IN THEIR MUSEUM COLLECTION.

When I travelled to Jåhkåmåhkke and Ájtte in the Winter of 2018, I held no preconceived conceptions. My reason for travelling there was that I had been told that I would *"probably find Ájtte of interest. They have a room, you know, where people can ask to go to and there, we are allowed to work with the collection"* (Emmy 05.12.2017). When I reached out to other duojárs who had at some point been at Ájtte, this was also their experience of the museum. As such, I contacted Eva Ahlström, the museum's curator, and asked if it would be possible for me to visit. Eva was happy to welcome me and facilitated a week of access. The first day I spent at Ájtte included a tour of the entire facility, including the dedicated space of 'Studie Magasinet'. She explained how the museum had set aside this space to encourage source communities' sensory interactions with their heritage objects. *"All are welcome here; we simply keep the objects for the community"* (Ahlström 12.11.2018). Being very much aware of the fact that access to Indigenous source communities might mean vastly different things, I asked her; "Who is allowed access"?

> The collection is open to all. It is one of the founding principles that the museum is for the Sámi to use as they need. Interacting with objects falls into that need, and so that is what we facilitate. No matter who ask, as long as they provide a reason, they are allowed access (12.11.2018).

Any museum which represents and serves living cultures must respect and accept their needs, even when these contradict standard museum

245

procedures (Harth 1999:280). More so, I would argue, when the cultures in question are Indigenous. Such a mandate takes on different shapes and forms. One example is the ritual space that some museums with large quantities of Indigenous cultural heritage offer their source communities. That is, some museums restrict access to their collection for the general audience, removing human remains as well as sacred or ceremonial objects from the main collection by giving them a space of their own which may only be entered by museum staff or representatives from the source communities. The objects that have been seconded to such spaces are also not available for research purposes (Kreps 2015:13). Another example is the 'Studie Magasinet' at Ájtte.[10]

Not to be confused with a ritual space, 'Studie Magasinet' is a room dedicated to the sensory interaction between the source community and objects. "*To interact with their objects is an important aspect of the [Sámi] culture. This room is meant to facilitate that*", as Eva puts it (Ahlström 12.11.2018). For anyone wanting to make use of the room, they are first asked to pick out the objects they wish to be present in it by way of Ájtte's digitalized records. List in hand, Eva then collects the objects and places them in the room ready to be studied. And it was this room that Jovnna and I occupied when he found the previous unknown technique, to him at least, of the vuodjaskáhppu.

The time that we spent in this space continued our earlier discussion of duodji. Focused on his own practice, Jovnna explained about the various qualities of the many objects that he had chosen among Ájtte's collection to take a closer look at. At several points, he would hand me objects and explain about their dåajmijes vuekie, or vuogas, demonstrating how beauty and function was combined.

> You see here how there are holes placed in the scabbard [making a pattern]? It's beautiful, right? But it also serves a purpose; if air is not able to circulate within the scabbard, there is a danger of mold appearing and the bone might start to decompose. So the beauty also has a function (Jovnna 14.11.2018)

Sharing specific details of techniques and practices, interspaced with his personal anecdotes, he thus managed to convey the knowledge and stories in the objects laid out in the room, making it accessible to both myself and Eva. This situation is similar to Aura Pieski's experience

---

10 I would be remiss not to mention that many other Sámi museums have similar spaces. Including Riddo Duottar. When I visited the latter however, said room was closed for construction and as such I did not have the opportunity to interact with duojárs in said space.

as described in riessat, where she, as a researcher, and arguably a voice of authority, becomes a student in the face of her verdde's knowledge. The key to gulahallat is the acknowledgment of learning being done collectively, we listen to the in-between and together we thus hear "*the voices of ancestors and the stories of objects*" (Jovnna 14.11.2018).

This resonates well with the experiences of another verdde, Áile, who I introduced in my discussion on the riebangolli-technique.

> You go to reclaim knowledge[s]. I didn't realize before how much had been forgotten in our communities. [We] have forgotten so much...we hardly even know anymore all the knowledge[s] forgotten in our communities. When you go there [Ájtte] you can know again. Together with the objects [we] remember once more (Áile 19.09.2019).

While Jovnna and I spoke, Eva sat in one corner of the room next to an old computer in which she entered the information shared by Jovnna, ensuring that "*we [in the museum] make a record of new knowledge*" (Ahlström 12.11.2018). This was how, on a previous occasion with another duojár, Eva had been able to enter the information about the vuodjaskáhppu that captured Jovnna's interest. This demonstrates what Gordon Pullar (2008) argues in his discussion on repatriation, that knowledge is rarely lost in its entirety. Rather, it is misplaced, waiting to be re-remembered. The knowledge that duojárs share as they study and work with the heritage objects on-site at Ájtte is recorded and made available to the entirety of the Sámi communities. In this way, the process I witnessed was a repatriation of knowledge, but more than that, it was also an exchange. More to the point, the exchange to me seemed to be an expression of the gift.

RETURNING TO THE GIFT

As I have previously discussed, both in bárket but also in riessat, the interrelatedness of the Sámi world-in-relation is expressed, among others, through the gift, which in Sámi is materialized as sjiele or šiella. Rauna Kuokkanen argues that the gift is one of the structuring principles of the Sámi social world. She does distinguish between gifts to the land and those meant to initiate or confirm relations. The former of which is said to reflect the interdependency of land and people, which shapes our birrasat—or surroundings, whereas the latter acknowledge the social ties related "*to everybody and everything*"

(Kuokkanen 2006:256, 258). Whichever categories apply, the gift is nonetheless of a ceremonial character meant to, firstly, acknowledge that the world is made up of relations, and furthermore commit both giver and receiver to honour said relations (Kuokkanen 2007b:65, e.g., Pettersson, Bäckman, and Kjellström 1979:134); even if the latter may sometime misconstrue the value of it as a tribute which I discussed in bárket.

It may be easy to discount the philosophy of the gift as either a romanticised display of Indigenous 'traditions' and an archaic expression of times gone by. No doubt Marcel Mauss' ([1925]2002) discussion on the gift as a social system prior to 'modernity' is owed considerable credit as the reinforcement of, one the one hand, tradition and, on the other, contemporary, thus creating a binary opposition that places Indigenous practices firmly within the boundaries of the former (Kuokkanen 2006:266, also see Porsanger 2011). The gift is neither romanticised nor archaic. It is an expression of an intricate web of connections, extended into the complex relations between people, to land, to spirits and other beings and entities. It is what makes up the social structure of the world, and what defines the place of individual and community. The fact that Sámi visitors continue to leave gifts with the sieidi at Ájtte demonstrates that this perception of the world is not a thing of the past, but in fact continues to characterize the Indigenous and Sámi experience (e.g., Jernsletten 2009:105). How the gift continues to impact Sámi lives is also evident in many of the stories that have been shared in the pages of this work.

In this, I am reminded of the Mohawk scholar Marlene Brant Castellano (2000:23-4), who argues that Indigenous knowledge[s] may be revealed in numerous ways as either dreams, visions, or intuition, which in Sámi would be the *gamus dovdat* or *čoalit dovdet* that I previously discussed in relation to reclaimer's blood memory. These disclosures are presented, she believes, as gifts; as knowable things, as objects reflecting relations, as stories, as memories, as acknowledgements, and more. This is mirrored within Sápmi, where Rauna Kuokkanen, for one, has argued that the inclusion of Sámi, and other Indigenous knowledges and epistemologies in the dominant academia of the West is a gift given to relieve epistemic ignorance. It is also, she claims, a gift that invokes responsibility in the recipient to acknowledge and honour other ways of knowing (Kuokkanen 2008:65).

The gift, in other words, is shaped and presented in multiple and complex ways; Násti's story, for instance, reveals one example of the gift in that her ancestor reached out to her in a dream, gifting her with the knowledge of the goavddis. Another example of the gift, we find in Marte's story when she describes how her interaction with the gákti gifted her with the ability to hear her ancestor's voice and listen to the stories embedded in her ancestor's gákti. I also believe that the stories shared and collected in the giisá are gifts. This opinion is only furthered by the principle of synergy in storytelling that Ása expressed when she emphasised the importance of her story, her gift, being received and honoured by me as a listener in ruvdet.

In an interview, the Syilx[11] educator and artist Jeanette Armstrong explains that *"what you are gifted with, and what you have been given in terms of skills, doesn't only belong to you. It belongs to the community, and it is there for the benefit of the community"* (Isernhagen 1999:162). This reflects, as Kuokkanen has noted, that the system in which the gift takes part is *"circular"* (2006:158). Not in the sense that a gift demands a gift in return. Rather, the circulatory aspect of the gift comes from the responsibility that it encourages.

One of the verdde that I have extensively collaborated with as an árbečeahpi for duodjebádjis is Áile. After the conclusion of one of our earliest duodjebádjis, Áile described the event as a *"safe space where stories were shared"*, and that they [the stories] *"started a process of healing and acceptance [of colonial trauma]"* (Áile 11.09.2018). The stories that had been shared at this event were particularly fraught with grief. One of the verdde, Sanna, had shared a brutal story of how colonialism and assimilation had affected her on a personal level, and several had cried during her story. She concluded the story by saying that being involved with duodji,

> [...] engaging with the practices of my ancestor's... re-remembering their knowledge...taking part in Sámi wisdom and skills...these have helped me to live with everything that has happened and actually feel good about myself (Sanna 11.09.2018).

Having listened to Sanna's story, Áile came to believe that the storytelling engendered in her a responsibility. In broad terms, this responsibility was to continue sharing her knowledge as an árbečeahpi. This

---

11 Indigenous community on Turtle Island.

was a very crucial moment as to the direction of my research because it gave me a particular insight; the connections that had been made between Áile and those that participated in the duodjebádji continued to exist even after the workshop's conclusion. The relations that had been initiated, had grown, and developed until they became embodied. Through their continued interaction, the gift of both stories and knowledge was continually renewed and secured, absorbed into and reproducing a Sámi world-in-relation. From another verdde, who participated in another workshop with Áile as árbečeahpi, these relations were articulated as "*bonds of friendship*" that far exceeded the expected "*obligations of friends*" (Elsa 13.11.2018). It is perhaps not surprising then that in many Indigenous communities—Sámi included—artists and duojárs are considered pillars of their communities, deeply involved in the process of healing the continued trauma of colonial encounters (Robbins and Dewar 2011). A role which I believe comes, in part at least, from their connection to material culture and heritage objects.

THE GIFT AS INDIGENOUS SOVEREIGNTY

My initial discussion of sovereignty in the context of Indigeneity focused on it as an autonomy embedded in the relational qualities, we as a People embody. Within said understanding, the right to centre Sámi ways of being, doing and knowing in everyday life was emphasized both through a spiritual independence, language renewal, cultural revitalization, intellectual property rights, land rights and health and well-being. The gift is an expression of said qualities, as it materializes through "*specific ways of knowing, relating to, and being in the world*", that make kin and reflect the interrelatedness of a Sámi world-in-relation (Kuokkanen 2006:265). Every time a duojár contributes to the collective pool of knowledge found at Ájtte, whether by sharing knowledge, offering their stories, or donating their work, they forge or re-establish these relations. Ájtte, on their part, commit to the system of gift-giving by ensuring that knowledge is stored in a "*nexus of knowledge*", dedicated to sharing that knowledge with Sámi source communities (Sunna 26.01.2018).

FIGURE 6-5 THE DEAVDDAGAHPIR, OR HAT WORN BY FEMALES IN MY ÁHČČI'S HOME COMMUNITY. THIS WAS MADE FOR A YOUNGER RELATIVE SOMETIME AFTER MY VISIT TO ÁJTTE. LOOKING AT HATS IN THE MUSEUM COLLECTION HELPED ME BECOME BETTER ACQUAINTED WITH THE VARIOUS CUSTOMS OF THE HAT IN HER HOME COMMUNITY.

In my time at Ájtte, I was privileged to see this system of gift-giving in practice. Together with Jovnna, for instance. But the duojárs that make use of "Studie Magasinet" have different motivations for entering, and their responses to the room thus vary. Still, one incident stood out to me. In the late afternoon on my fourth day at Ájtte, I was allowed to tag along with a group of four duojárs that had asked to look at different examples of the beaska—the Sámi fur pelt discussed in riessat. I met one of them, Anna, the evening before to walk through the collection to pick out which objects to bring into the room. In a re-enactment of what is the first step in my protocol of storytelling, the time of negotiation, we chatted about our duodji, our communities and our fuolkkit [kin]. It turned out that she was acquainted with some of my family, and this led her to asking whether I wanted to see if we could find a beaska from either of my home communities. I was actually more interested in seeing some hats and we thus picked some of those as well.

The next day we all met up outside Ájtte, and I was introduced to the other three duojárs before we headed into the "Studie Magasinet". In many ways, the sessions that I took part in were similar to the one I had engaged in a few days prior with Jovnna. Anna was by far the most accomplished duojár present, containing immense knowledge. She soon took the lead, speaking on the various practices and knowledge[s] related to the beaskas' we had picked. Sometimes she, or one of the other duojárs would share a personal story about their practice or a beaska they had seen or interacted with previously. Among the four of us, Anna was the only one who had herself made a beaska, and she shared her knowledge of the process. In the corner, Eva was busy recording what was being said. Sometimes she would ask a clarifying question about either the object we were looking at, a specific practice of duodji that had been mentioned, or Sámi terminology. At one point however, Anna stopped speaking. Simply studying one beaska, turning it this or that way, feeling the seams and studying the colour palette of the ribbons. Though I was paying some attention to her movements, I was also in conversation with the other three.

All of us nonetheless focused on Anna when she asked Eva for information on the beaska she was holding at that time; "*[t]ell me, do you know the maker's name*" (Anna 16.11.2018). Eva turned to the computer, entering the inventory number the beaska had been tagged with before she replied that the "*beaska was collected sometime in the 1960s and was previously owned by [name]. She is also said to be the duojár that made the beaska*" (Ahlström 16.11.2018). At this point, Anna turned to one of the others and asked "*isn't [name] a relation of yours*" (Anna 16.11.2018). Sara, the duojár in question, considered for a moment before replying that "*Yes…I think…if I'm not wrong she was my áhkku's sister*" (Sara 16.11.2018).

Before I continue, a small introduction is in order. Sara is a young duojár from a North Sámi community on the Swedish side of the border. The practice of duodji has been a constant in her life and she has never consciously felt the trauma of absence that so many reclaimers struggle with. Due to her home community being adjacent to Jåhkåmåhkke she has always been in close proximity to Ájtte, and the brutality of displacement has thus been somewhat negated. Nevertheless, with the discovery of her áhkku's sister being the previous owner and maker of the beaska in question, a change came upon her. As her áhkku's sister had died young, she had never developed a relation to her. Her memories pertaining to her áhkku's sister being limited to a black and white photo on her áhkku's living room wall.

During her interaction with the beaska however, it was obvious that she was reconnecting to an ancestral voice; "*Oh…look at this seam…it's so neat. She must have had great skill…I wonder how she felt making it and wearing it*" (Sara 16.11.2018). The cut, the seams, the choice of colours was at great length discussed. In between comments,

Sara took multiple pictures, and she wrote down the information that Ájtte had on the beaska. But mostly, she held it; "*I almost want to try it on*", she said (Sara 16.11.2018), but due to the pesticides that are often found on older objects this was not a possibility, and I rather question if it would be possible even in the absence of such harmful chemicals. But the need that Sara expressed is worth noting. This was a desire, not born from the tactile exploration that so often is a prelude to the repatriation of knowledge.

Instead, Sara's express wishes to touch the beaska and to try it on came from her longing to re-engage with her ancestor's practices of duodji and stories, creating new meanings and values of the old, if you will. "*I don't remember hearing much being said about [name], but I think I'll ask áhkku about her when I go home*" (Sara 16.11.2018). It is not unusual for heritage objects to evoke emotions in members of their source community, renewing their intended function and creating new stories, values, and meanings. In the case of Sara and the beaska however, there was also the relation between an ancestral object and its descendant to consider. In Sara's own words, the discovery of the beaska gave her a:

> […] profound sense of presence. Before you told me [directed to Anna] that this was made by my fuolkkit I thought the beaska beautiful, but like any other beaska. Now, knowing that it once was worn by my áhkku's sister, made from the knowledge [árbediehtu] in my family…I can't describe it. But I feel richer somehow (Sara 16.11.2018)

FIGURE 6-6 THERE IS MANY STORIES OF SÁMI DISCOVERING AN OBJECT OF THEIR ANCESTORS MAKE, OR PREVIOUS USE, IN MUSEUMS. I HAD NEVER BEFORE HOW-EVER, WITNESSED THIS HAPPENING IN PERSON. SARA'S REACTION UPON LEARN-ING THAT THE BEASKA WE ARE HERE LOOKING AT HAD ONCE BELONGED TO HER ÁHKKU'S GRANDMOTHER MADE A CLEAR ILLUSTRATION OF HOW RELEVANT THESE HERITAGE OBJECTS ARE TO THEIR DESCENDANTS.

Many Indigenous communities state that when ancestors are removed from their homeland, the community is splintered, and it cannot be made whole again until the ancestors return (Rowley and Hausler 2008:210). In many ways, this is comparable to the feelings associated with a trauma of absence, which help underscore its connection to the brutality of displacement. If Sámi heritage objects, as Outi Pieski claims, are our living ancestors, their removal from source communities means that we lose our ability to listen to their voices. *"We cannot hear our ancestors speak"* (Sunna 26.01.2018)

What Sara's story illustrates is the moment when the voice of ancestor's become distinct once more. The object, in this case, the beaska, was never silent, but simply silenced, muted in museum basements or behind glass cases. Denied the opportunity of activation and with it a presence in a Sámi world-in-relation. By re-connecting with the beaska, Sara had the opportunity of establishing a relation beyond time and space. Not only with the beaska, but also with her áhkku's sister. In this way, heritage objects become an important source of guidance, teaching its source communities how to reconnect with a way of life that is grounded in reciprocity and interrelatedness as expressed in the Sámi world-in-relation. Outi Pieski concludes in her recent talk on repatriation and de-colonization of museums, *"how can we learn back a healthy way of living when we are missing guidance from our ancestors [...] that is why we need to get our belongings back home to Sápmi"*. It is through the accessibility to heritage objects that *"we heal our relations"* (Ovlla 24.04.2019), encouraging the restitution of knowledge[s], and practices and restoring identities and sovereignty.

CHAPTER 7: ŠIELLA

CONCLUSIONS AND PERTINENT THOUGHTS

THE VALUE OF THE GIFT

INTRODUCTION

In the introduction to this work, I set out to discover some of the processes of Sámi identity-formation and acts of sovereignty within the boundaries of museums, and furthermore how objects and things—material culture—and the practice of duodji engage in said processes. Throughout this book, considerable time and effort have been spent discussing this line of inquiry. Not so much to provide a textbook answer to disseminate, but more to introduce the incredible complexities of identities and museums, the sheer breadth that has been revealed in the context of Indigenous identities, material culture, and museums. My strategy for discussing the line of inquiry was to, and I quote,

> disregard the conventional translation of duodji as 'craft' and [...] consequently re-conceptualise the practice with the intent to re-establish it as a Sámi system of knowledge; Second, [...] examine how the practice of duodji may affect the identity of the duojár; and lastly, [...] investigate the role that Sámi museums have come to occupy in the relationship between identity, duodji, material culture and sovereignty

I will attempt to summarize my discussions in response to the three intents in my strategy, starting with my re-conceptualisation of duodji. The need for such rethinking became evident very early in my project as the more I spoke with verddes', the more I realized that the diminishing of duodji and women's role in the practice has been a direct result of colonialism and the strategy of epistemicide.

REVISITING EPISTEMICIDE

If the discussions in this book are proof of one thing, it is that the history of the Sámi People cannot be reduced to the past alone. Our stories live on in our ways of being, doing, and knowing and conversely, our ways of being, doing and knowing continue to survive in our stories. In bárket I refer to many of these stories. As they are not numbered nor lined up in alphabetical order, they exist in the space between the pages, which in Sámi would be *girjelatnja*. Weaved together with sources of a more traditional nature, these stories define the impact that colonisation has had on both Sámi sovereignty and Sámi identities. I imagine bárket to have been a chapter that readers have found difficult. I know that I myself struggled with my articulation of the stories therein. Knowing abstractly the history of one's people and shaping that knowing into descriptive words for others to read are two vastly different things. It was nonetheless a necessary endeavour as it provides a much-needed context. To know the struggles that many are faced with today as they mediate their Sámi self, and in this act, position themselves as sovereign subjects of a Sámi Nation, we must first comprehend the impact of colonisation and of epistemicide on such processes.

But to speak of epistemicide in a Sámi context is often met with counters of invalidation. As a word, epistemicide often brings to mind images of brutal destructions of knowledge; we see it on the news whenever there is a natural disaster impacting on sites of specific cultural relevance. It was seen during world war 2 with the bombing of important monuments and the looting of art. We all saw it in 2018 when *The Museu Nacional* in Rio de Janeiro, Brazil, was devastated by a fire consuming more than 20 million items, many of these Indigenous in character. These are all forms of epistemicide that are recent, and that were undeniably loud. But when the epistemicide in question was initiated 500 years ago and when the epistemicide specifically targeted the intangible qualities of individuals and communities by way of objects and governance, its impact is somehow reduced to historical times or not considered significant. This produces and disseminates an understanding of epistemicide as harmless at present, a linear concept of time once more allowing for a perceived distance, transforming it into nothing more than a word used to describe certain events but without ever considering the personal stories of the peoples whose lives were irrevocably changed.

As I see it, this is similar to how the other strategies that are employed in the process of colonialism rarely ring true to the actual horror they inflict. Assimilation, segregation, and residential schools fail to adequately convey the trauma of colonialism. If I were to replace these terms with more descriptive explanations, however, what we are left with are impressions of cultural genocide; the targeted destruction of languages, knowledge[s], and practices. These ways of explaining the colonial strategies are often much harder to contend with because it is more difficult to reject the notion of deliberate destruction. In bárket, this was the resolve behind the writing.

My hope was to convey that the strategies associated with colonization, even if set within history and no longer overtly practiced, continue to impact Sámi lives. The story chosen for the prologue in bárket is a case in point, reminding us that these processes have not remained in the past. They continue to work and impact lives in the present day by way of lateral and historical trauma, as well as the trauma of absence and the brutality of displacement that I conceptualise in čuoldit and bearalduodji, respectively. That being the case, I do not hesitate to claim that epistemicide is a continued reality for the Sámi, exemplified in the epistemic ignorance I briefly mentioned in giisá and riessat. Nor do I hesitate to argue that the longevity of epistemicide has had an immense impact on duodji, and on duojárs—especially on women practitioners.

This sounds nasty—and indeed it is, as we realize when we stop to think about it. The way that a particular culture formulates its knowledge is intricately bound up with the very identity of its people, their way of making sense of the world and the value system that holds that worldview in place. Epistemicide, as the systematic destruction of rival forms of knowledge, is at its worst nothing less than symbolic genocide.

FROM THE COLONIAL DIMINISHMENT OF DUODJI...

This is made clear when duodji is reconceptualised, the concept removed from its singular association with craft. That is to say, in riessat I demonstrate how duodji is a sophisticated system of knowledge, centred within the interrelatedness of a Sámi world-in-relation. Following this, I argue that duodji is a vital component of a Sámi onto-epistemology, and that this system consists of various practices that create meanings. I make this argument both for the present-day practice, but I also argue that this is the case in historical times. Starting with the latter, I suggest that the particular knowledge of place and family that is embedded in the gákti implies a judicial application. By extension, I also suggest that the gáktimaker, who for the most part were women, were charged with keeping the judicial records of rights of inheritance and that they meticulously documented this in the gákti. Similarly, the value of Sámi women and duodji in relation to cosmology is also established by my discussion in bárket, on women's roles in everyday ritual life, the vuoiŋŋalašvuohta, as well as their mediation of the noaiddesvuohta, which revolved around more specific tasks and roles of the spiritual leaders. In particular, I make a point of how women duojárs, after the goavddis [the holy drum] was banished, referred to its ritual language and thus the function of mapping the Sámi world/s and cosmology into their practices of duodji. Though not explicitly stated at the time, this leads me to believe that the practice of duodji has deep connections with ritual practices, which is an argument I find support for in my discussion of tiida, or the ritual dimension of duodji, in riessat.

By offering up these two examples, not only do I highlight the multiple aspects of duodji as a system of knowledge. In addition, I demonstrate how the heteropatriarchy of colonialism by way of epistemicide took part in devaluing the relevance of duodji and, by doing so, also diminished the social roles and tasks conferred on Sámi women. The present-day hierarchy between dipmaduodji, which is mostly associated with women, and garraduodji, which has been related to men's practice, and that I briefly spoke of in giisá, is evidence of such.

The deep connectivity of artistic practices and Indigenous ways of being, doing, and knowing has immense value in notions of methodology and theory, yet rarely are we as Indigenous researchers, encouraged to look to these practices. As I make clear in riessat, I too began my search for theory in the established core of Western academia. Somewhat ironically, the theoretical framework that truly tempted an exploration was one that created a sense of recognition in its focus on the world as relational, and yet duodji was a far more viable candidate. Was it the familiarity of duodji that stood in the way, the ever so trite experience of not seeing the wood for all the trees at play? Or was it perhaps the unvoiced concern that moving beyond the familiar and documented shores of academia and into the beautiful complexities that guide my practice as a duojár would not be accepted due to epistemic ignorance? I want to say no, but realistically speaking, it is a struggle to make the space needed for Indigenous ways of being, doing and knowing within Western academia. At some point, however, we all need to take into account and realize where our research is leading us, and how best to facilitate the extrapolation of what it is saying.

While it is true that duodji far too often has been defined as nothing more or less than 'craft', this does not mean that we need to accept such limitations. As a theory, duodji demonstrates the ontological, epistemological, and axiological qualities present in a Sámi world-in-relation, materialized as practices and as material culture and heritage objects. It demonstrates the relations that make up our realities, the interrelational bonds with people, past and present; to land; to spirituality and cosmology, and to spirits and other beings. It illustrates how all of these are made kin, but more importantly, duodji teaches us how to follow these relations. This, in my opinion, is the value of duodji as a theory. It guides our analytical gaze and provides us with an invaluable toolkit to understand the many relations deeply embedded in Sámi material culture as well as the practices and interactions that initially embedded them. The gákti, once more, serve as an example of such.

In addition to highlighting the depth of duodji as a practice, the gákti also demonstrates what is lost when it is forgotten. The alienation between people, knowledges and cultural practices that often happen as the result of an epistemicide does not simply remove objects from everyday life. It also removes a way of life and the utter security of one's place in the world, unravelling relations and making strangers of kin; it is in truth the complete erasure of everything one is and ever was. This is what the trauma of absence is born from, and it is what comes of the brutality of displacement. This might sound dramatic, and indeed it is if we stop to think about what an epistemicide entails. The onto-epistemology of a people is bound up in that peoples' very essence of self; how we learn; how we perceive our world; how we put value on things and practices; and the ways in which we recognize and honour our relations are all essential parts of our knowledge systems. When that is destroyed, what is under attack is, in essence, our methodologies and philosophies, and our ways of being in the world.

...TO A 'CEREMONY OF RENEWAL'.

We all come from somewhere; a place of origin and a society that adhere to specific worldviews, and thus follows certain beliefs, practices, and knowledge[s]. As individuals we are shaped by the paradigms born of our worlds, and they set a precedent for how we act in the world, toward one another, and with our relations. The Sámi world-in-relation as such provides a complex terrain, and the map we need to navigate is given through our practices, embedded in our bodies as ways of being, knowing and doing. We rarely need to consciously reflect on such because this is what we know to be the way of things. But what if you were denied such embodied truth. What if the politics of colonialism and the consequent strategies of epistemicide had robbed you of your practices and knowledge[s]. What then? This very question is what I, at least in part, have attempted to answer in čuoldit. It bases itself on the second intent of this work, which is to look at how a practice of duodji may affect the identity of duojárs.

To reconnect with the past and to remember the stories of ancestors is never an easy or straightforward journey. Nor is it one that is taken lightly. The stories of the giisá certainly make this evident, varied as they are in their depictions of the many processes activated when recentering Sámi identities. Nonetheless, there is a peculiar tendency of those that I name reclaimers. Namely, their development of sophisticated systems of practices and concepts to help with the process of connectivity. These include some strongly held beliefs of cultural knowledge[s] and practices being carried in genes, and that these memories call out, demanding to be heard, making their presence known in unconscious ways, expressed for instance in a strong yearning for Sámi culture as was the case with Birthe who described a draw towards Sámi cultures after discovering her own Sámi heritage; a sense of something missing as evidenced by the trauma of absence as Lukas describe; or linked to intuitive senses, as was experienced by Ása. All of these have the possibility of materializing by way of ancestral memory, what the international literature refers to as blood memory, or what in Sámi I would conceptualize as a sense of gamus dovdat or čoalit dovdet.

The value of blood memory, for those that believe in it, is the idea that knowledge[s] and practices never disappear. They are silenced, but not erased. Despite all evidence to the contrary, an epistemicide is within such a train of thought never permanent. Knowledge[s] never die; they simply hide away, forgotten for brief spells of time, waiting to once more be called into practice. Such beliefs are quite persistent in an international context of Indigeneity, but more to the point they prevail in many of the processes described in the stories of the giisá. These processes also have a tendency in a Sámi context to become embedded in certain practices, one of which is duodji.

Duodji takes part in the system of knowledge which includes the concept of árbediehtu, or inherited knowledge. As the materialization of a Sámi onto-epistemology, to move and learn within said knowledge system means that one is also adapting specific meaning and values—what I have termed the codes of sámáidahttin. Such codes are of course, available in multiple avenues, for instance, by way of stories as discussed in ruvdet. As children, we listen to the stories and we learn of and with them, which provides an entry point into the Sámi world-in-relation. But for those raised outside of our communities that have been called home only as adults, duodji is perhaps easier as a way to grasp such codes.

Understanding that the knowledge of duodji collectively survives due to a transfer between generations, reclaimers tap into the idea of árbediehtu but on their own terms by claiming that their blood carries the inherited knowledge of their ancestors, diehtu, and by way of their practice or máhttu, they reactivate their inherited knowledge, thus reproducing relations and situating themselves within a Sámi world-in-relation. Interestingly, this reasoning is not reserved for reclaimers alone. In the case of the ládjogáhpir's rematriation, Outi Pieski also argued the presence of ancestors. Unlike the reclaimers, however, she argued that the ancestors are the objects themselves. As eallilans, or elders, objects must be included in the system of knowledge that is duodji. Not simply as objects of the practice, but as entities in their own right, deeply embedded in the interrelations of the Sámi world-in-relation, carrying their own stories, values, and meanings.

When transferred into museums, however, the voice of the objects is muted and thus, their stories and knowledge[s] become silenced. This is the brutality of displacement, and its connection to reclaimers reveals itself in their trauma of absence. But the trauma of absence may also relate to other contexts, for instance, when knowing the eallilan in museums but still be unable to hear them as they are locked in basements or behind glass. It is the trauma of absence and the brutality of displacement that encourage both reclaimers and duojárs [although these titles may be intermittent] acts of re-remembrance. Here another aspect of árbediehtu is revealed. Namely, how árbediehtu as a system of knowledge has incorporated museums as a vital component.

As I discussed in riessat, we can no longer take for granted that the practice of duodji and the knowledge[s] contained herein is generationally transferred as has been the custom. This is true even in those communities that never experienced a complete break of transference and where the knowledge[s] are maintained. This focuses attention on the value of institutions; among them, museums. With their vast collections of Sámi heritage objects, museums are filled to the brim with sources—objects and things—that make acts of re-remembrance possible. In the process of recording information followed by making reproductions, duojárs and reclaimers make use of museums to re-appropriate knowledge[s], practices and heritage objects. In other words, by way of duojárs and reclaimers, museums have become embedded in the Sámi knowledge system of árbediehtu and, by extension, of duodji.

BY WAY OF THE GIFT

In bearalduodji, when I claim that Jovnna, the vuodjaskáhppu and Ájtte is an expression of the gift, this is not done lightly. Though I connect the Sámi world-in-relation with the gift in ruvdet, in bearalduodji I make an explicit statement that this connection is an expression of Indigenous sovereignty, and furthermore that said expression encourage a cultural integrity by way of accessibility to Sámi heritage objects in museums. In giisá, where I initially broached the subject, I argued that in the context of Indigeneity, sovereignty must be understood as relational. That is, the personal and collective autonomy of the Sámi comes from the sustaining, and in some cases retaining, of cultural knowledges and from making kin with communities, ancestors, and homelands. In this sense, sovereignty is a spiritual process that is continuously maintained by reforging and ensuring the maintenance of all relations and is embodied in people through their Sámi ways of being, doing and knowing.

The brutality of displacement disrupts this continuity and thus works to erode the interrelatedness of the Sámi world-in-relation, removing objects and with them the stories they carry and their presence in a complex network of kin and relations. As these objects are eallilan, they take part in a bigger network that connects the entirety of the world-in-relation. As such, their loss inevitably impacts said world; empty spaces are created, a trauma of absence fuelled, and the spirituality of people wounded. It is not possible to negate this damage; what has been put into effect cannot be undone. But the trauma of silence and the brutality of displacement is something we are able to counteract, working to reduce its force. This is achieved by access to heritage objects, either by way of repatriation, rematriation or 'ceremonies of renewal.'

Restoring objects to source communities invites the disrupted relations back into play, allowing the connections between ancestors and descendants to be restored and the relations to land, cosmology, and other beings to be made anew. In other words, making kin through people, duodji as well as stories, meanings and values are embedded in Sámi heritage objects. When this process is initiated, the voices of ancestors are once more known to source communities, and we learn to listen to the stories of objects. To achieve this, duojárs and reclaimers together with Sámi museums play a vital part. Not only through their sharing of knowledge but by way of its dissemination. Engaging with the knowledge[s] of heritage objects, re-activating these knowledges through practices of duodji, and passing them on to others is nothing less than a system of gift-giving. And by engaging in this system, relations are forged—both those of old as was the case with Sara—as well as creating new ones, which was what Jovnna did when he learned the name of the duojár that had previously shared information on the vuodjaskáhppu. In this way, Sámi heritage objects facilitate the making of kin. This, in turn, helps recreate or restore the interrelatedness that is at the core of Sámi ways of being, doing, and knowing, and thus of Indigenous sovereignty. Inevitably ensuring that Sámi museums and heritage objects become sites of Indigenous sovereignty. This, in turn, enables healing, both spiritually, collectively, and individually of colonial trauma, lateral violence, the trauma of absence and the brutality of displacement.

REFERENCES

Abt, Jeffrey. 2006. "The Origin of the Public Museum." In *A Companion to Museum Studies*, edited by Sharon Macdonald, 122 – 134. Malden: Blackwell Publishing.

Adichie, Chimamanda Ngozi 2009. *The Danger of a Single Story*.

Aikio, Áile. 2017. "Supporting Sámi Identity? Representation of the Sámi People in the Sámi Museum Siida." ECPR General Conference, Oslo.

Alba, Richard D. 1990. *Ethnic identity : the transformation of white America*. New Haven: Yale University Press.

Alfred, Taiaiake G.R. 1995. *Heeding the Voices of Our Ancestors: Kahnawake Mohawk Politics and the Rise of Native Nationalism*. Toronto: Oxford University Press.

Allen, Chadwick. 2014. "Decolonizing Comparison." In *The Oxford Handbook of Indigenous American Literature*, edited by James H Cox and Daniel Heath Justice. Oxford University Press.

Altick, Richard Daniel. 1978. *The shows of London*. Cambridge, Mass: Belknap Press of Harvard University Press.

Amit-Talai, Vered. 2000. *Constructing the field : ethnographic fieldwork in the contemporary world, European Association of Social Anthropologists*. London: Routledge.

Andersen, Oddmund. 2002. "Flyttefolk og bofaste : en studie av samisk bosetting i Sør-Troms og Nordre Nordland." PhD, Tromsø: University of Tromsø

Andersen, Thomas Ole. 2005. Markasamiske kombinasjonsnæringer : en undersøkelse på mikronivå 1860-1920. Hovedfagsoppgave. Tromsø: University of Tromsø

Andresen, Astri. 2001. "Flytting, fødsler og død blant nomadene i Torne lappmark." *Ottar* 2001, nr 3 = Nr 236:36-44.

Antze, Paul & Lambek, Michael. 1996. "Introduction: Forecasting Memory." In *Tense Past : cultural essays in trauma and memory*, edited by Paul & Lambek Antze, Michael, xi - xxxviii. New York: Routledge.

Antze, Paul, and Michael Lambek. 1996. *Tense past : cultural essays in trauma and memory*. New York: Routledge.

Archibald, Jo-ann. 2008. *Indigenous storywork : educating the heart, mind, body, and spirit*. Vancouver B.C.: UBC Press.

Archibald, Robert. 1999. *A place to remember : using history to build community*. AltaMira Press.

Arndt, Lotte 2011/2012. «Réflexions sur le renversement de la charge de la preuve comme levier postcolonial.» *Le journal de Bétonsalon*, pp. 69-77.

Atalay, Sonya. 2019. "Braiding Strands of Wellness: How Repatriation Contributes to Healing through Embodied Practice and Storywork." *The Public Historian* 41 (1), pp. 78-89.

Baer, Lars-Anders 1982. "An Indigenous People in Their Own Land"." In *The Sami National Minority in Sweden*, edited by Birgitta Jahreskog. Stockholm: Almqvist & Wiksell International.

Baglo, Cathrine. 2001. *Vitenskapelige stereotypier: om konstruksjonen av samene som kulturhistorisk enhet i tida fram mot 1910*. Hovedfagsoppgave, Tromsø: University of Tromsø.

Baglo, Cathrine. 2011. *På ville veger? Levende utstillinger av samer i Europa og Amerika*. PhD, Tromsø: University of Tromsø.

Balto, Asta. 1996. *Kunnskap og kompetanse i Sápmi : en samisk skole i emning : forhold fra den samiske utdanningssektoren. Kunnskapsbilder.* Karasjok: Davvi girji.

Balto, Asta. 1997. *Samisk barneoppdragelse i endring.* Oslo: Ad notam Gyldendal.

Balto, Asta, 2008. Sámi oahpaheaddjit sirdet árbevirlaš kultuvrra boahttevaš buolvvaide : dekoloniserema akšuvdnadutkamuš Ruota beale Sámis, in *Dieđut* Vol. 4/ Guovdageaidnu: Sámi allaskuvla.

Balto, Asta, and Liv Østmo. 2009. "Mánggakultuvrralasvuoda oahpu sámáidahttin Sámi allaskuvllas/Indigenizing the study of Multicultural Understanding at the Sámi University College." *Sámi dieđalaš áigecála* 1-2.

Barad, Karen. 2007. *Meeting the universe halfway : quantum physics and the entanglement of matter and meaning.* Durham: Duke University Press.

Barker, John. 2001. "Dangerous Objects: Changing Indigenous Perceptions of Material Culture in a Papua New Guinea Society." *Pacific Science* 55. doi: 10.1353/psc.2001.0028.

Barrett, Estelle. 2015. "Materiality, Language and the Production of Knowledge: Art, Subjectivity and Indigenous Ontology." *Cultural Studies Review* 21 (2), pp. 101-119.

Barth, Fredrik. 1969. *Ethnic groups and boundaries : the social organization of culture difference.* Oslo: Universitetsforlaget.

Basso, Andrew R. 2016. "Towards a Theory of Displacement Atrocities: The Cherokee Trail of Tears, The Herero Genocide, and The Pontic Greek Genocide" *Genocide Studies and Prevention: An International Journal* 10 (1), pp. 5-29.

Battiste, Marie 1998. "Enabling the autumn seed: Toward a decolonized approach to aboriginal knowledge, language, and education.", *Canadian Journal of Native Education* 22 (1):16-27.

Battiste, Marie, and James (Sa´ke´j) Youngblood Henderson. 2000. *Protecting Indigenous Knowledge and Heritage: A Global Challenge.* Saskatoon: Purich.

Beauvoir, Simone de. [1949]2000. *Det annet kjønn.* Edited by Toril Moi and Bente Christensen, *Le deuxième sexe.* Oslo: Pax.

Behrendt, Larissa. 2019. "Decolonizing institutions and assertive self-determination: implications for legal practice." In *Decolonizing Research : Indigenous Storywork as Methodology*, edited by Jo-Ann Archibald, Jenny Lee-Morgan and Jason De Santolo, 175-186. New York: ZED.

Bennett, Tony. 1995. *The birth of the museum : history, theory, politics, Culture : policies and politics.* London: Routledge.

Bennett, Tony. 2004. *Pasts beyond memory : evolution museums colonialism.* London ;,New York: Routledge.

Berg, Edel. 2001. "Arkeologi i grenseland : bruk av (skolte)samisk etnografi i studier av forhistoriske fangstsamfunn." Master, Tromsø: University of Tromsø.

Bergstøl, Jostein. 2008. *Samer i Østerdalen? : en studie av etnisitet i jernalderen og middelalderen i det nordøstre Hedmark.* PhD, Oslo: Kulturhustorisk Museum

Bhabha, Homi K. [1983]2006. "The other question : the stereotype and colonial discourse." In *Visual Culture. Critical concepts in media and cultural studies*, edited by Joanne Marquard Smith Morra, 248-266. London: Routledge.

Biddle, Nicholas, and Francis. Markham. 2018. *Indigenous Identification Change between 2011 and 2016: Evidence from the Australian Census Longitudinal Dataset.* Canberra: Centre for Aboriginal Economic Policy Research, Australian National University.

Bjørklund, Ivar. 1985. *Fjordfolket i Kvænangen : fra samisk samfunn til norsk utkant 1550-1980.* Tromsø: Universitetsforlaget.

Bjørklund, Ivar. 2000. *Sápmi : en nasjon blir til : fremveksten av samenes nasjonale fellesskap.* Tromsø: Tromsø museum.

Blaeser, Kimberly. 1993. "Native literature: Seeking a critical center." In *Looking at the words of our people : First Nations analysis of literature*, edited by Jeannette C. Armstrong, pp. 51 - 62. Penticton, B.C.: Theytus Books.

Blaser, Mario. 2009. "Political Ontology." *Cultural Studies Review* 23 (5-6), pp. 873–896.

Bloom, Paul, and Frank C. Keil. 2001. "Thinking Through Language." *Mind & Language* 16 (4), pp. 351-367.

Boast, Robin. 2011. "Neocolonial Collaboration: Museum as Contact Zone Revisited." *Museum Anthropology* 34, pp. 56-70.

Boine, Else Målfrid, Inger Helen Erstad, Anni-Siiri Länsman, and Merete Saus. 2014. "Diehtobádji Sámis – geahččaleapmi ovddidit sámi fágaolbmuid kulturgealbbu." *Sámi dieđalaš áigecála* 1.

Boine, Else Målfrid. 2005. Trondheim: E.M. Boine. 2005. " Fra far til sønn : kjønnsperspektiv og sosial kompetanse i samisk sammenheng." Hovedfagsoppgave, Trondheim: NTNU.

Bombay, Amy. 2015. Lasting effects of trauma reaches across generations through DNA. In *CBC News*, edited by Roseanna Deer Child.

266

References

Boon, Marcus. 2010. *In praise of copying*. Cambridge, Mass: Harvard University Press.

Boroditsky, Lera. 2018. "Language and the Construction of Time through Space." *Trends Neurosci* 41 (10), pp. 651-653.

Bourdieu, Pierre. 1977. *Outline of a theory of practice*. Vol. 16, *Esquisse d'une théorie de la pratique*. Cambridge: Cambridge University Press.

Bradley, Patricia. 1999. *Slavery, Propaganda, and the American Revolution*: University Press of Mississippi.

Bratrein, Håvard Dahl. 2001. "Finnekongen Martin og rikskongen Håkon den femte." *Håløygminne* B. 21, årg. 82, pp. 1-10.

Brave Heart, Maria Yellow Horse 1999. "Oyate Ptayela: Rebuilding the Lakota Nation Through Addressing Historical Trauma Among Lakota Parents." *Journal of Human Behavior in the Social Environment* 2 (1-2), pp. 109-126.

Breivik, Andreas. 2020. "Where Do We Go From Here?" *Nordic Art Review*, 30.06.

Brenna, Brita. 2002. "Utstillingsteknikk og representasjonspolitikk : på verdensutstilling i Paris i 1889." In *Tingenes tale : innspill til museologi*, edited by Hans-Jakob Ågotnes and Kari Gaarder Losnedahl, Johansen, Anders pp. 133-161. Bergen: Bergen museum.

Broberg, Gunnar. 1995. *Statlig rasforskning: En historik över Rasbiologiska institutet*. Lund: Lund University.

Brown, Deidre. 2007. "Te Ahua Hiko: Digital Cultural Heritage and Indigenous Objects, People, and Environment." In *Theorizing digital cultural heritage : a critical discourse*, edited by Sarah Kenderdine and Fiona Cameron. Pp. 77-91. Cambridge, Mass: MIT Press.

Brubaker, Rogers. 2016. *Trans : gender and race in an age of unsettled identities*. Princeton, NJ: Princeton University Press.

Brøgger, A. W. 1909. *Den arktiske stenalder i Norge*. Vol. 1909 no. 1, *Skrifter (Videnskabsselskapet i Kristiania, Christiania[Oslo]: I kommisjon hos Jacob Dybwad.

Buijs, Cunera. 2010. "Sharing East Greenlandic Material Culture and Photographs." In *Sharing knowledge & cultural heritage, First Nations of the Americas : studies in collaboration with indigenous peoples from Greenland, North and South America : proceedings of an expert meeting, National Museum of Ethnology, Leiden, the Netherlands*, edited by Pieter Hovens, Laura N. K. Van Broekhoven and Cunera Buijs. Leiden: Sidestone Press.

Buijs, Cunera. 2016. "Museum collection decolonization and indigenous cultural heritage in an island community: East Greenland and the 'Roots 2 Share' photo project." *Island Studies Journal* 11 (2), pp. 537-560

Butler, Judith. 1993. *Bodies that matter : on the discursive limits of "sex"*. New York: Routledge.

Butler, Judith. [1990]1999. *Gender trouble : feminism and the subversion of identity*. New York: Routledge.

Bäckman, Louise. 1975. "Sájva : föreställningar om hjälp- och skyddsväsen i heliga fjäll bland samerna." 13, Almqvist & Wiksell.

Bäckman, Louise , and Åke Hultkrantz. 1978. *Studies in Lapp Shamanism. Stockholm Studies in Comparative Religion*. . Stockholm: Almqvist & Wiksell International.

Cameron, Flona. 2007. "Beyond the Cult of the Replicant: Museums and Historical Digital Objects - Traditional Concerns, New Discourses,." In *Theorizing digital cultural heritage : a critical discourse*, edited by Sarah Kenderdine and Fiona Cameron, pp. 49-75. Cambridge, Mass: MIT Press.

Candlin, Fiona. 2008. "Museums, modernity and the class politics of touching objects.", In *Touch in Museums: Policy and Practice in Object Handling*, edited by Chatterjee, H.pp. 9-20, Oxford: Berg

Caron-Malenfant, Éric, Simon Coulombe, Eric Guimond, Chantal Grondin, and André Lebel. 2014. "Ethnic Mobility of Aboriginal Peoples in Canada Between the 2001 and 2006 Censuses." *Population 69* 1 (29).

Castellano, Marlene Brant. . 2000. "Updating Aboriginal Traditions of Knowledge." In *Indigenous Knowledges in Global Contexts: Multiple Readings of Our World*, edited by George J. Sefa Dei, Budd L. Hall and Dorothy Goldin Rosenberg, pp. 1-36. Toronto: Toronto Universty Press.

Chambers, Cynthia, and Narcisse Blood. 2009. "Love Thy Neighbour: Repatriating Precarious Blackfoot Sites." *International Journal of Canadian Studies* 39-40, pp. 253-279.

Chandler, Michael J., and Christopher Lalonde. 1998. "Cultural Continuity as a Hedge against Suicide in Canada's First Nations." *Transcultural Psychiatry* 35 (2), pp. 191-219.

Chilisa, Bagele. 2012. *Indigenous Research Methodologies*. Los Angeles: SAGE Publications.

Clavir, Miriam. 2002. *Preserving what is valued : museums, conservation, and First Nations, UBC Museum of Anthropology Research publication*. Vancouver, B.C: UBC Press.

Clifford, James. 1997. *Routes : travel and translation in the late twentieth century*. Cambridge, Mass: Harvard University Press.

Clifford, James. 2004. "Looking Several Ways. Anthropology and Native Heritage in Alaska." *Current Anthropology* 45 (1), pp. 5-30.

Cocq, Coppélie. 2008. Revoicing Sámi narratives: north Sámi storytelling at the turn of the 20th century. Umeå: University of Umeå

Cocq, Coppélie. 2013. "From the Árran to the Internet: Sami Storytelling in Digital Environments." *Oral Tradition* 28 (1).

Comaroff, Jean, and John Comaroff. 1992. *Ethnography and the Historical Imagination.* Boulder, CO: Westview Press.

Conaty, Gerald, and Clifford Crane Bear. 1998. "History, Connections, and Cultural Renewal." In *Powerful Images: Portrayals of Native America,* edited by S. Boehme, pp. 63–74. Seattle: University of Washington Press.

Connerton, Paul. 1989. *How societies remember, Themes in the social sciences.* Cambridge: Cambridge University Press.

Connerton, Paul. 2011. "The spirit of mourning : history, memory and the body." Cambridge: Cambridge University Press.

Cruikshank, Julie. 1998. *The social life of stories : narrative and knowledge in the Yukon Territory.* Lincoln, Neb: University of Nebraska Press.

Cubillo, Franchesca. 2010. "Repatriating Our Ancestors: Who Will Speak for the Dead." In *The Long way home : the meanings and values of repatriation,* edited by Paul Turnbull and Michael Pickering, pp. 20-26. New York: Berghahn.

Cubitt, Sean. 1998. *Digital aesthetics, Theory, culture & society.* London: Sage.

Dahl, Tor Edvin. 1970. *Samene i dag--og i morgen: En rapport.* Oslo: Gyldendal.

Damsholt, Tine, Camilla Mordhorst, and Dorthe Gert Simonsen. 2009. *Materialiseringer : nye perspektiver på materialitet og kulturanalyse.* Århus: Aarhus Universitetsforlag.

Dankertsen, Astri. 2006. "Men du kan jo snakke frognersamisk" : tradisjon og kulturell innovasjon blant samer i Oslo. Hovedfagsoppgave, Oslo: University of Oslo.

Dankertsen, Astri. 2014. *Samisk artikulasjon : melankoli, tap og forsoning i en (nord)norsk hverdag.* PhD, Bodø: Nord University.

Dapice, Ann. 2006. "The Medicine Wheel." *Journal of transcultural nursing : official journal of the Transcultural Nursing Society / Transcultural Nursing Society* 17, pp. 251-60.

Darwin, Charles. [1859]1909. *On The Origin of Species by means of natural selection : or, the preservation of favored races in the struggle for life.* P. F. Collier.

De L'Estoile, Benoît. 2008. "The past as it lives now: an anthropology of colonial legacies." *Social Anthropology* 16 (3), pp. 267-279.

de la Cadena, Marisol, and Mario Blaser. 2018. *A World of Many Worlds*: Duke University Press.

de Sousa Santos, Boaventura 2008. "Introduction." In *Voices of the World (Reinventing Social Emancipation Toward New Manifestos),* edited by Boaventura de Sousa Santos. Pp. Xv, Verso Books.

De Vos, George A. 1995. "Ethnic pluralism: Conflict and accommodation: The role of ethnicity in social history." In *Ethnic identity: Creation, conflict, and accommodation, 3rd ed.,* pp. 15-47. Walnut Creek: AltaMira Press.

Dempsey, Lorcan. 2000. " Scientific, industrial, and cultural heritage: A shared approach: A research framework for digital libraries, museums and archives." *Ariadne* 22.

Drugge, Anna-Lill. 2016. *Ethics in indigenous research: past experiences - future challenges.* 1 ed, *Samiska studier.* Umeå: University of Umeå.

Dudley, Sandra H. 2010. *Museum materialities : objects, engagements, interpretations.* London: Routledge.

Dunfjeld-Aagård, Lisa. 2005. "Sørsamiske kystområder : tolking av fortidig samisk tilstedeværelse i Ytre Namdal." Hovedfagsoppgave, Tromsø: Universitetet i Tromsø.

Dunfjeld-Aagård, Maja 1989. "Symbolinnhold i Sørsamisk ornamentikk." Hovedfag i duodji/ master in duodji, Statens Lærerhøgskole i forming., Statens Lærerhøgskole i forming.

Dunfjeld, Maja. 1999. "Åarjel-saemien gapta, gåptoe - sørsamekofta." In *Dräkt - rapport från seminarium vid Ájtte,* edited by Inga-Maria Mulk, pp. 51-59. Jokkmokk: Ájtte.

Dunfjeld, Maja. 2006. *Tjaalehtjimmie : form og innhold i sørsamisk ornamentikk.* Snåsa: Saemien sijte.

Dupont, Christian. 2007. "Libraries, Archives, and Museums in the Twenty-First Century: Intersecting Missions, Converging Futures?" *RBM: A Journal of Rare Books, Manuscripts, and Cultural Heritage* 8, pp. 13-19.

Duran, Eduardo. 2006. *Healing the soul wound : counseling with American Indians and other native peoples.* New York: Teachers College Press.

Edwards, Elizabeth. 2001. *Raw histories: photographs, anthropology, and museums.* Oxford: Berg.

Edwards, Elizabeth. 2015. "Anthropology and Photography: A long history of knowledge and affect." *photographies* 8 (3), pp. 235-252.

Eidheim, Harald. 1961. "Samane - nokre aktuelle problem." *Sámi œllin : Sámi sœrvi jakkigir'ji ... = Sameliv : Samisk selskaps årbok ...* Nr. 4 (1959/1960), pp. 34-47.

Eidheim, Harald. 1971. *Aspects of the Lappish minority situation, Scandinavian university books.* Oslo: Univer-

References

sitetsforlaget.

Eikjok, Jorunn, and Gunhild Hoogensen Gjørv. 2007. "Gender, essentialism and feminism in Samiland." In *Making space for indigenous feminism*, edited by Joyce Green, pp. 108-123. Black Point: Fernwood Publ. Zed Books.

Eira, Stine Sand. 2013. "Herrer i eget hus» - Finnmarksloven i media." *Norsk medietidsskrift* 20 (4), pp. 330-346.

Elgvin, Lilly-Anne Østtveit. 2010. "Lars Levi Læstadius' spiritualitet." *Bibliotheca theologiae practicae* 88, Skellefteå: Artos & Norma bokförlag.

Eliassen, Bent-Martin, Marita Melhus, Ketil Hansen, and Ann Broderstad. 2013. "Marginalisation and cardiovascular disease among rural Sami in Northern Norway: a population-based cross-sectional study." *BMC Public Health* 13 (1).

Ericsson, Martin. 2020. "What happened to 'race' in race biology? The Swedish State Institute for Race Biology, 1936−1960." *Scandinavian Journal of History* Vol 46 (1), pp. 1-24.

Eriksen, Anne. 1995. *Det var noe annet under krigen : 2. verdenskrig i norsk kollektivtradisjon*. Oslo: Pax Forlag.

Eriksen, Anne. 2009. *Museum. En kulturhistorie*. Oslo: Pax forlag.

Eriksen, Knut Einar, and Einar Niemi. 1981. *Den finske fare. Sikkerhetsproblemer og minoritetspolitikk i nord 1860-1940*. Oslo: Universitetsforlaget.

Eyþórsson, Einar 2008. *Sjøsamene og kampen om ressursene*. Karasjok: ČállidLágádus.

Falck, Erika Nordvall. 2018. *Aejlegsvaanhts: Thaebpies feegreme vaanhtsi bïjre noerhtedajvesne*. Jokkmokk: Ájtte.

Falsen, Christian Magnus. 1821. *Geografisk beskrivelse over Kongeriget Norge, og udsigt over dette lands ældste historie og forfatning, som en indledning til Norges udførligere historie*. Christiania [Oslo].

Fanon, Frantz. [1963]2007. *The Wretched of the Earth*: Grove Atlantic.

Fanon, Frantz. [1967]2008. *Black Skin, White Masks*: Grove Press.

Fenwick, Tara. 2010. "Re-Thinking the "Thing" Sociomaterial Approaches to Understanding and Researching Learning in Work." *Journal of Workplace Learning* 22 (1-2), pp. 104-116.

Fienup-Riordan, Ann 2010. "From Consultation to Collaboration." In *Sharing Knowledge and Cultural Heritage: First Nations of the Americas. Studies in Collaboration with Indigenous Peoples from Greenlandm North and South America*, edited by Laura van Broekhoven, Cunera Buijs & Pieter Hovens, 1 - 5. Leiden: Sidestone Press.

Finbog, Liisa-Rávná. 2013. "Med nav og eiker. En museologisk analyse av hvordan markesamisk identitet skapes, reforhandles, vedlikeholdes og utvikler seg ved Várdobáiki samisk senter."Master Oslo: University of Oslo.

Finbog, Liisa-Rávná. 2015. "Gákti ja goahti ; heritage work and identity at Várdobáiki Museum." *Nordisk museologi* (2), pp. 95-107.

Finbog, Liisa-Rávná. 2019. "The Duojár: An Agent of the Symbolic Repatriation of Sámi Cultural Heritage." In *Research Journeys In/To Multiple Ways of Knowing*, edited by Jennifer Markides and Laura Forsythe, pp 93-102. Dio Press.

First Nations Constitutional Convention. 2017. *The Ulure Statement of the Heart*.

Fitzgerald, Kathleen J. 2007. *Beyond White Ethnicity: Developing a Sociological Understanding of Native American Identity Reclamation*. Lanham, MD: Rowman & Littlefield.

Fjellheim, Sverre. 2012. *Gåebrien sijte : en sameby i Rørostraktene*. Røros: S. Fjellheim.

Fjellström, Phebe. 1985. *Samernas samhäale i tradition och nutid*. Värnamo: P. A. Nordstedt & Söners Förlag.

Fonneland, Trude. 2017. "Ein sieidi si rolle i religionsutøving i samtida." *Tidsskrift for kulturforskning* 16 (1), pp. 71-84.

Fors, Gry, and Ragnhild Enoksen. 1991. *Vår folkedrakt - sjøsamiske klestradisjoner, Sámi Instituhtta*. Karasjok: Davvi Girjii.

Four Directions Council. 1996. "Forests, indigenous peoples and biodiversity: Contribution of the Four Directions Council." In, edited by Four Directions Council. Secretariat of the Convention of Biological Diversity.

Fraser, Mike, John Bowers, Pat Brundell, Claire O'Malley, Stuart Reeves, Steve Benford, Luigina Ciolfi, Kieran Ferris, Paul Gallagher, Tony Hall, Liam Bannon, Gustav Taxén, and Sten Olof Hellström. 2004. *Re-tracing the Past: Mixing Realities in Museum Settings,*: ACM Press

Freire, Paulo. 1970. *Pedagogy of the Oppressed*, New York: Herder and Herder.

Fur, Gunlög. 2006. "Reading Margins: Colonial Encounters in Sápmi and Lenapehoking in the Seventeenth and Eighteenth Centuries." *Feminist Studies* 32, pp. 491-521.

Fyfe, Gordon. 2004. "Reproductions, cultural capital and museums: aspects of the culture of copies." *Museum and Society* 2 (1), pp. 47-67.

Fyhn, Anne Birgitte, Ylva Jannok Nutti, Ellen J. Sara Eira, Tove Børresen, Svein Ole Sandvik, and Ole Einar Hætta. 2015. "Ruvden as a Basis for the Teaching of Mathematics." In *Indigenous Innovation: Universalities and Peculiarities*, edited by Elizabeth Sumida Huaman and Bharath Sriraman, pp. 169-186. Rotterdam:

SensePublishers.

Gabriel, Mille. 2008. "Introduction: from conflict to partnership." In *Utimut: Past Heritage -- Future Partnerships, Discussions on Repatriation in the 21st Century*, edited by Mille Gabriel and Jens Dahl, pp. 12-21. Copenhagen: International Work Group for Indigenous Affairs and Greenland National Museum & Archives.

Gallén, Jarl, and John Lind. 1968. *Nöteborgsfreden och Finlands medeltida östgräns,* Helsingfors: Svenska litteratursällskapet i Finland.

Gaski, Harald. 1997. *Sami culture in a new era : the Norwegian Sami experience.* Karasjok: Davvi girji.

Gaski, Harald. 2003. "Álbmotviisodat ja árbedieđut: Árgabeaivválaš poesia sátnevádjasiin,dajahusain ja árváductsain." In Árvvut – Árvo – Vierhtie – Samiske verdier, edited by Edel Hætta Eriksen, pp. 33-40. Káráš̌johka: Davvi girji.

Gaski, Harald. 2006. *Time Is A Ship That Never Casts Anchor. Sami Proverbs.* Edited by Harald Gaski. Káráš̌johka: ČálliidLágáduS.

Gaski, Harald. 2011. "More than Meets the Eye: The Indigeneity of Johan Turi's Writing and Artwork." *Scandinavian studies* 83 (4), pp. 591-608.

Gaski, Harald. 2011/12. "Dan maid čalbmi ii oainne – Johan Turi čállima ja dáidaga erenoamáš̌vuohta." *Sámi dieđalaš áigečála* 1/2, pp. 113-132.

Gaski, Harald. 2013. "Indigenism and Cosmopolitanism: A Pan-Sami view of the Indigenous Perspective in Sami Culture and Research." *AlterNative: An International Journal of Indigenous Peoples* 9, pp. 113-124..

Gaski, Harald. 2017. "Indigenous Aesthetics: Add Context to Context." In *Sámi Art and Aesthetics. Contemporary Perspectives*, edited by Aamold. Svein, Elin Haugdal and Ulla Angkjær Jørgensen, pp. 179-193. Aarhus: Aarhus University Press.

Gaski, Harald. 2019. "Indigenous Elders' Perspective and Position.(Nordic Colonialisms and Scandinavian Studies)(Viewpoint essay)." *Scandinavian Studies* 91 (1-2), pp. 259 -268.

Gaski, Lina. 2008. "Sami identity as a discursive formation : essentialism and ambivalence." In *Indigenous peoples: self-determination, knowledge, indigeneity*, edited by Minde, Henry, Harald Gaski, Svein Jentoft & Georges Midré, pp. 219-236. Delft: Eburon

Gaup, Káren Elle. 2006. "Historie, minne og myte i moderne samisk identitetsbygging." *Samisk identitet: Kontinuitet og endring* edited by Vigdis Stordahl pp. 85-98. Guovdageaidniu: Sámi Allaskuvlla.

Geismar, Haidy. 2009. "The Photograph and the Malanggan: Rethinking images on Malakula, Vanuatu." *Australian Journal of Anthropology* 20 (1), pp. 48-73.

Geismar, Haidy. 2011. ""Material Culture Studies" and other Ways to Theorize Objects: A Primer to a Regional Debate." *Comparative Studies in Society and History* 53 (1), pp. 210-218.

Gell, Alfred. 1998. *Art and agency : an anthropological theory.* Oxford: Clarendon Press.

Gjessing, Gjertrud, and Gutorm Gjessing. 1940. *Lappedrakten : en skisse av dens opphav.* Vol. 4:2, *Instituttet for sammenlignende kulturforskning (trykt utg.).* Oslo.

Gjessing, Gutorm. 1973. *Norge i Sameland.* Oslo: Gyldendal.

Gjestrum, John Aage. 1995. "Utstilling av levende mennesker : ei historie om samisk kultur og fremmede blikk." *Dugnad* Vol. 21, nr. 1, pp. 93-108.

Glissant, Édouard. 2006. *une nouvelle région du monde.* Paris: Gallimard.

Goduka, I. N. 1999. "Indigenous epistemologies - ways of knowing: Affirming a legacy." *South African Journal of Higher Education* 13 (3), pp. 26-35.

Gosden, Chris, and Yvonne Marshall. 1999. "The cultural biography of objects." *World Archaeology* 31 (2), pp. 169-178.

Graveline, Fyre Jean. 1998. *Circle Works: Transforming Eurocentric Consciousness.* Fernwood Publishing.

Graveline, Fyre Jean. 2000. "Circle as methodology: Enacting an Aboriginal paradigm." *International Journal of Qualitative Studies in Education* 13 (4), pp. 361-370.

Gustavsson, Madeleine and Mark Riley. 2018. "The Fishing Lifecourse: Exploring the Importance of Social Contexts, Capitals and (More Than) Fishing Identities." *Sociologia Ruralis* 58 (3), pp. 562-582.

Guttorm, Gunvor. 2001a. "Duoji bálgát - en studie i duodji : kunsthåndverk som visuell erfaring hos et urfolk." PhD, Tromsø: University of Tromsø

Guttorm, Gunvor. 2007. "Duodji - árbediehtu ja oapmi = : Duodji - hvem eier kunnskapen og verkene? = Duodji - Sámi handcrafts - who owns the knowledge and the works?" In *Árbevirolaš máhttu ja dahkkivuoigatvuohta / doaim*, edited by John Trygve Solbakk, pp. 62-94. Káráš̌johka Sámikopiija.

Guttorm, Gunvor. 2008. "Duodjedutkama etihkka dieđuid máhcaheamis = Ethics in research on duodji (Sámi handicraft) and the returning of knowledge." In *Sáme- ja álgoálbmotdutkama etihkka : seminára raporta, Káráš̌johka 23.-24.10. 2006 = Ethics in Sámi and Indigenous Research : report from a seminar in Káráš̌johka, Norway, November 23-24, 2006*, pp. 75-80, 81-86.

Guttorm, Gunvor. 2011. "Árbediehtu (Sami traditional knowledge) - as a concept and in practice." In *Working with Traditional Knowledge: Communities, Institutions, Information Systems, Law and Ethics: Writings from the Arbediehtu Pilot Project on Documentation and Protection of Sami Traditional Knowledge* edited by Jelena Porsanger, Gunvor Guttorm pp. 59-76. Guovdageaidnnu: Sámi Allaskuvlla.

Guttorm, Gunvor. 2012a. "Duodji : A New Step for Art Education." *International Journal of Art & Design Education* 31 (2), pp. 180-190.

Guttorm, Gunvor. 2012b. "Paradigm shift in the view of duodji in the 21st century: Higher education in duodji." *WINHEC: International Journal of Indigenous Education Scholarship*, (1), pp. 68-82.

Guttorm, Gunvor. 2013a. "Den samiske drakten i historiens løp." In *Bunad*, edited by Bjørn Sverre Hol Haugen, pp. 888-918. Oslo: Cappelen.

Guttorm, Gunvor. 2013b. "Lánjáid stellen – duddjoma ovdánahttinbargu fenomenologalaš geahčastagas." *Sámi dieđalaš áigečála* 2, pp. 33-48.

Guttorm, Gunvor. 2014. "Sámi duodjemetodologiijat." *Duodji 2012 : riikkaidgaskasaš sámiid ja eará eamiálbmogiid duodje-, dáidda- ja hábmenkonferánsa / [doaimmaheaddjit/editors:] Gunvor Guttorm & Seija Risten Somby*, pp. 35 - 48.

Guttorm, Gunvor. 2017. "The power of natural materials and environmental in contemporary duodji." In, *Sámi Art and Aesthetics: Contemporary Perspectives*, edited by Svein Aamold, Elin Haugdal & Ulla Ankjaer Jørgensen pp. 163-177, Aarhus: Aarhus University Press

Guttorm, Gunvor. 2018. "Stories Created in Stitches." *Afterall: A Journal of Art, Context and Enquiry* 45 (1), pp. 18-23.

Guttorm, Gunvor. 2020. "Historijjálaš Duoji Lahkonit Duddjomiin/ Studying a Historical Craft through Crafting." In *Ládjogahpir – Máttaráhkuid gábagahpir/The Ládjogahpir – The Foremothers` Hat of Pride*, edited by Outi Pieski and Eeva-Kristiina Harliin, pp. 103-10. Kárášjohka: Davvi Girji.

Guttorm, Gunvor and Jelena Porsanger. 2011. *Working with traditional knowledge : communities, institutions, information systems, law and ethics : writings from the Árbediehtu pilot prosject on documentation anf protection of Sami traditional knowledgde*. Vol. 1/2011, *Dieđut (trykt utg.)*. Guovdageaidnu: Sámi allaskuvla.

Guttorm, Hanna Ellen, Lea Kantonen, and Britt Kramvig. 2019. "Pluriversal stories with Indigenous wor(l)ds creating paths to the other side of the mountain." *Dutkansearvvi dieđalaš áigečála* 3 (2), pp. 149 - 172.

Hallam, Elizabeth, and Jennifer Lorna Hockey. 2001. *Death, Memory and Material Culture*. New York: Bloomsbury Academic.

Hallström, Gustaf. 1911. "Traditioner om lapptrumman." *Fataburen 1910*, pp. [20]-48. Fataburen ... : Nordiska museets och Skansens årsbok

Hallström, Gustaf. 1929. *Kan lappernas innvandringstid fixeras? En arkeologisk studie.* . Stockholm.

Han, Le. 2013. "Our Home Is Here: History, Memory, and Identity in the Museum of Chinese in America." *Communication, Culture & Critique* 6 (1), pp. 161-178.

Hansen, Hanna Horsberg. 2016. "Constructing Sami National Heritage: Encounters Between Tradition and Modernity in Sami Art." *Konsthistorisk tidsskrift* 85 (3), pp. 250-255.

Hansen, Klara. 2015. Being Sami: an ethnography of identity through the lens of the Riddu Riđđu festival. PhD, Canberra: The Australian National University.

Hansen, Lars Ivar. 1986. *Samiske rettigheter til jord på 1600-tallet : "finnejorder" i Sør-Troms = Sami title to land in the 17th century : "Finnejorder" in Southern Troms; Norway*. Vol. 20, *Sami title to land in the 17th century "Finnejorder" in Southern Troms; Norway*. Oslo: Novus.

Hansen, Lars Ivar. 2011. "Norwegian, Swedish and Russian "tax lands" in the north." In *Taxes, tributes and tributary lands in the making of Scandinavian kingdoms in the Middle Ages* edited by Steinar Imsen, pp. 295-330. Trondheim: Tapir Academic Press.

Hansen, Lars Ivar. 2012. "Juxta paganos: Th e delineation of the religious frontier in the North." In *'Ecclesia Nidrosiensis' and 'Noregs veldi': The role of the Church in the making of Norwegian domination in the Norse World*, edited by Steinar Imsen, pp. 301–331. Trondheim: Tapir Academic Press.

Hansen, Lars Ivar, and Bjørnar Olsen. 2004. *Fram til 1750*. Vol. [1], *Samenes historie*. Oslo: Cappelen akademisk forl.

Haraway, Donna. 1988. "Situated Knowledges: The Science Question in Feminism and the Privilege of Partial Perspective." *Feminist Studies* 14 (3), pp. 575-599.

Haraway, Donna J. 2016. *Staying with the trouble : making kin in the Chthulucene, Experimental futures: technological lives, scientific arts, anthropological voices*. Durham: Duke University Press.

Harlin, Eeva-Kristiina 2018. "Foremothers: Repatriation and rehabilitation of lost cultural heritage." 05.12.2018.

Harlin, Eeva-Kristiina, and Outi Pieski. 2020. *Ládjogahpir – Máttaráhkuid gábagahpir/The Ládjogahpir – The Foremothers` Hat of Pride*. Kárášjohka: Davvi Girji.

Hatt, Gudmund. 1914. *Arktiske skinddragter i Eurasien og Amerika : en etnografisk studie*. København: J.H. Schultz.

Hedeager, Lotte. 1999. *Skygger av en annen virkelighet : oldnordiske myter, Skygger af en anden virkelighed*. Oslo: Pax.

Hedstrom, Margaret, and John Leslie King. 2004. "On the LAM: Library, archive, and museum collections in the creation and maintenance of knowledge communities " In *Mapping innovation: Six depth studies* Paris: Organization for Economic Co-operation and Development.

Hegel, Georg Wilhelm Friedrich. [1807]1977. *Phenomenology of spirit*. Edited by J. N. Findlay, *Hegel's Phenomenology of spirit*. Oxford: Oxford University Press.

Heikkilä, Karen. 2014. "'The forest is our inheritance': An introduction to Semai Orang Asli place-naming and belonging in the Bukit Tapah Forest Reserve." *Singapore Journal of Tropical Geography* 35 (3), pp. 362-381.

Heil, Gudrun. 2014. "Hverdagslig samhandling og kulturoverføring mellom samiske bestemødre og deres barne-barn." Master, UiT The Arctic University of Norway.

Hekman, Susan J., and Stacy Alaimo. 2008. *Material Feminisms*. Bloomington: Indiana University Press.

Helander-Renvall, Elina, and Inkeri Markkula. 2017. "On Transfer of Sámi Traditional Knowledge: Scientifica-tion, Traditionalization, Secrecy, and Equality." In *Indigenous Peoples' Cultural Heritage*, edited by Alexan-dra Xanthaki, Sanna Valkonen, Leena Heinämäki and Piia Kristiina Nuorgam, pp. 104-129. Brill | Nijhoff.

Helander, Elina. 1995. "Sami medical concepts and healing methods." *Báiki. An American Journal of Sami Living"* 12, pp. 6-7

Helander, Liisa. 2019. "Čuoldimin ođđa ruohtasiis Sámi kultuvrii " Ávvir, 22.11.2019.

Henare, Amiria. 2005. *Museums, Anthropology and Imperial Exchange*: Cambridge University Press.

Hendry, Joy, and Laara Fitznor. 2012. "Introduction." In *Anthropologists, indigenous scholars and the research endeavour : seeking bridges towards mutual respect*, edited by Joy Hendry and Laara Fitznor, pp. 1-18. New York: Routledge.

Henriksen, Jan Erik. 1999. "På lavvotur : om nettverkstradisjoner i det samiske samfunn." *Nordisk sosialt arbeid* Årg. 19, nr. 1, pp. 10-18.

Henriksen, Jørn Erik. 1996. Hellegropene : fornminner fra en funntom periode. Master, Tromsø: University of Tromsø.

Hernes, Maria. 2017. Being Sami Enough – Increasing the Sami Stage of Performance. Master, Oslo: University of Oslo.

Hesjedal, Anders. 2000. "Samisk forhistorie i norsk arkeologi 1900-2000." PhD, Tromsø: University of Tromsø.

Hidle, Johannes, and Johannes Oterbech. 1917. *Fornorskningen i Finnmarken*. Kristiania[Oslo].

Hilden, Patricia Penn. 2000. "Race for Sale: Narratives of Possession in Two 'Ethnic' Museums." *TDR: The Drama Review: A Journal of Performance Studies* 44 (3 [T167]), pp. 11-36.

Hine, Darlene Clark. 2003 "Black professionals and race consciousness : origins of the civil rights movement, 1890-1950." *Journal of American history (trykt utg.)*. 89, pp. 1279-1294.

Hirvonen, Vuokko. 1999. "Sámeeatnama jienat : sápmelaš nissona bálggis girječállin." Guovdugeaidnu: DAT.

Hirvonen, Vuokko. 2009. "Juoiggus uksan sámi njálmmálaš girjjálašvuhtii : bálggis gillii, identitehtii ja iešár-vui". *Sámi dieđalaš áigečála*, 1-2, pp. 90-105.

Hirvonen, Vuokko, and Kaija Anttonen. 2004. *Sámi culture and the school : reflections by Sámi teachers and the realization of the Sámi school : an evaluation study of Reform 97, Mo sámáidahttit skuvlla?* Kautokeino,-Karasjok: ČálliidLágádus.

Hooper-Greenhill, Eilean 1992. *Museums and the Shaping of Knowledge*. London: Routledge.

Hooper-Greenhill, Eilean. 2000. *Museums and the Interpretation of Visual Culture*. London: Routledge.

Hooper-Greenhill, Eilean. 2007. "Interpretive Communities, Strategies and Repertoires." In *Museums and their Communities*, edited by Sheila Watson, pp. 76-94. London: Routledge.

Hume, Lynee. 2000. "The Dreaming in Contemporary Australia." In *Indigenous Religions: A Companion*, edited by Graham Harvey, pp. 125–39. London: Bloomsbury Publishing.

Hymes, Dell. 1992. "Use all there is to use." In *On the translation of Native American literatures*, edited by Brian Swann. Washington: Smithsonian Institution Press.

Hætta, Inga Hermansen, and Máret Gaup Eira. 2006. Sámi duodji/ Samisk håndtverk/ Saami handicraft. In *Fag-trykk Ide Alta*, edited by Duodjeinstituhtta. Alta: Duodjeinstituhtta.

Hætta, Lars Jacobsen, Knut Bergsland, and Anders Pedersen Bær. [1869]1958. *Mui'talusat*. Vol. 7, *Studia septen-trionalia (trykt utg.)*. Oslo: Universitetsforl.

Hætta, Odd Mathis 1996. *Archaeology – a link between past and present?*. Vol. Dieđut *Awakened Voice. The Return of Sami knowledge* edited by Elina Helander, pp. 13-20. Guovdageaidnu: Nordic Sami Institute.

ICOMOS. 2002. International Cultural Tourism Charter. Principles And Guidelines For Managing Tourism At

References

Places Of Cultural And Heritage Significance. ICOMOS International Cultural Tourism Committee.

ILO-169. 1989. "Om Urfolk og stammefolk i selvstendige stater."

Inga, Torbjørg A., Lise Gjesdal Thelle, Ardis Ronte Eriksen, and Elrun Ronte Eriksen. 1986. *Samisk koftebruk : i Ofoten og Sør-Troms*. Tromsø: Universitetsforlaget.

Iseke, Judy. 2013. "Indigenous Storytelling as Research." *International Review of Qualitative Research* 6 (4), pp. 559-577.

Isernhagen, Hartwig. 1999. *Momaday, Vizenor, Armstrong: Conversations on American Indian Writing*. Norman: University of Oklahoma Press.

Iversen, Tobias Buschmann. 2008. Pasientoversikten, personlig men ikke privat? : en tverrfaglig studie av et sentralt støtteverktøy for helsepersonell. Trondheim: T.B. Iversen.

Jacobsen, Kjell 1987. "Njaarke-Næjle: Nils Jonson, Vesterfjella, 1795-1869." In Årbok for Helgeland 18. årg, edited by Øyvind Jenssen. Mosjøen: Helgeland historielag, Rønnes Trykk.

Jenkins, I. 2001. "The Elgin Marbles: questions of accuracy and reliability." *Int J Cult Prop* 10 (1), pp. 55-69.

Jensen, Eivind Bråstad. 2007. "Nord-Norge, en flerkulturell landsdel." *Tidsskrift for psykisk helsearbeid* 4 (1), pp. 15-24.

Jernsletten, Jorunn. 2009. *Bissie dajve : relasjoner mellom folk og landskap i Voengel-Njaarke sijte*. PhD, Tromsø: University of Tromsø.

Jernsletten, Kristin. 2000. "Fra de kolonisertes ståsted – en samisk mot-diskurs." *Kjellerdypet – Tidsskrift for humaniora*, pp. 53-55.

Jernsletten, Kristin. 2011. *The hidden children of Eve : Sámi poetics : guovtti ilmmi gaskkas*. PhD, Tromsø: University of Tromsø.

Johannessen, Kjell S. 1999. *Praxis och tyst kunnande*. Vol. 3, *Filosofi och ingenjörsarbete*. Stockholm: Dialoger.

Joks, Solveig 2015. "Laksen trenger ro, Tilnærming til tradisjonelle kunnskaper gjennom praksiser, begreper og fortellinger fra Sirbmá-området " PhD, Tromsø: University of Tromsø.

Joks, Solveig, Liv Østmo, and John Law. 2020. "Verbing meahcci : Living Sámi lands." *The Sociological Review* 68, pp. 305-321.

Jones, Angela 2015. "Rachel Dolezal is Really Queer: Transracial Politics and Queer Futurity." *Social (In)Queery*. https://socialinqueery.com/2015/06/17/rachel-dolezal-is-really-queer-transracial-politics-and-queer-futurity/.

Jones, Siân. 2010. "Negotiating Authentic Objects and Authentic Selves: Beyond the Deconstruction of Authenticity." *Journal of Material Culture* 15 (2), pp. 181-203.

Josefsen, Eva. 2006. Selvopplevd diskrimminering blant samer i Norge. Alta: Norut NIBR Finnmark.

Jølle, Harald Dag. 2000. "Hvorfor holder jeg eskimoen for stående over europæerne?" : kulturforskeren Fridtjof Nansen og "de arktiske andre". Hovedfagsoppgave, Tromsø: Universitetet i Tromsø.

Kaikkonen, Konsta Ilari. 2019. "From, into, and back: translations of the Sami words noaidi and noaidevuohta in context." *Religion* 49 (4), pp. 539-570.

Kalleberg, Ragnvald. 2006. *Forskningsetiske retningslinjer for samfunnsvitenskap, humaniora, juss og teologi, Retmingslinjer - NESH*. Oslo: Forskningsetiske komiteer.

Kalstad, Johan Albert 1997. "Slutten på trommetida - og tida etter." *Ottar* 4.

Kappfjell, Lena and Harald Gaski. 2018. "Dåajmijes vuekie lea saemien vuekie." Din : tidsskrift for religion og kultur 2, pp. 12-18.

Kappfjell, Tom. 1998. "Slektsbenevnelser - laahkoeh : samisk inndeling av familie og personer man er, og blir knyttet til gjennom livsløpet fra fødsel til død." Åarjel-saemieh = Samer i sør Nr. 6, pp. 39-49.

Karp, Ivan, and Steven D. Lavine. 1991. *Exhibiting cultures : the poetics and politics of museum display*. Washington: Smithsonian Institution Press.

Kehoe, Alice Beck 2000. *Shamans and Religion: An Anthropological Exploration in Critical Thinking*. Waveland Press.

Kent, Neil. 2014. *The Sámi peoples of the North : a social and cultural history*. London: Hurst.

Kincheloe, Joe L. 2011. "Critical Ontology and Indigenous Ways of Being." In *Key Works in Critical Pedagogy*, edited by Kecia Hayes, Shirley R. Steinberg and Kenneth Tobin, pp. 333-349. Rotterdam: SensePublishers.

King, Thomas. 2005. *The truth about stories : a native narrative, Indigenous Americas*. Minneapolis: University of Minnesota Press.

Kingston, Lindsey. 2015. "The Destruction of Identity: Cultural Genocide and Indigenous Peoples." *Journal of Human Rights* 14 (1), pp. 63-83.

Kjellman, Ulrika. 2013. "A Whiter Shade of Pale: Visuality and race in the work of the Swedish State Institute for Race Biology." *Scandinavian Journal of History* 38 (2), pp. 180-201.

Kjellman, Ulrika. 2014. "How to picture race?: The use of photography in the scientific practice of the Swedish State Institute for Race Biology." *Scandinavian Journal of History* 39 (5), pp. 580-611.

Klokkernes, Torunn, and Anne May Olli. 2008. "Understanding Museum Artifacts: The Role of Tradition Bearers and Material Analysis in Investigating Skin Processing Technology." In *Preserving Aboriginal Heritage, Technical and Traditional Approaches: Proceedings of a Conference Symposium 2007 : Preserving Aboriginal Heritage, Technical and Traditional Approaches, Ottawa, Canada, September 24-28, 2007*, edited by Carole Dignard. Canadian Conservation Institute = Institut canadien de conservation.

Kovach, Margaret. 2009. *Indigenous Methodologies: Characteristics, Conversations and Contexts*. Toronto: University of Toronto Press.

Kreps, Christina. 2015. "Appropriate Museology and the "new museum ethics"." *Nordisk museologi* 2, pp. 4 - 16.

Krmpotich, Cara. 2011. "Repatriation and the generation of material culture." *Mortality: Archaeologists on contemporary death* 16 (2), pp. 145-160.

Krmpotich, Cara, Laura Peers, Committee Haida Repatriation, Museum Pitt Rivers, and Museum British. 2013. *This is our life : Haida material heritage and changing museum practice*. Vancouver: UBC Press.

Kuhmunen, Mereth. 12.09.2019. Queer duedtie. In *Panel at Sápmi Pride in 2019*, edited by Liisa-Ravna Finbog.

Kuhn, Gabriel. 2020. *Liberating Sápmi: Indigenous Resistance in Europe's Far North*. Oakland: PM Press.

Kuhn, Thomas S. [1962]1996. *The structure of scientific revolutions*. 3rd ed. ed. Chicago: University of Chicago Press.

Kuokkanen, Rauna. 2000. "Towards an 'Indigenous Paradigm' from a Sami Perspective." *Canadian journal of native studies* 20 (2), pp. 411-436.

Kuokkanen, Rauna. 2005. "Láhi and Attáldat: The Philosophy of the Gift and Sami Education." *The Australian Journal of Indigenous Education* 34, pp. 20-32.

Kuokkanen, Rauna. 2006. "The Logic of the Gift: Reclaiming Indigenous Peoples' Philosophies." In *Re-Ethnicizing the Minds?: Cultural Revival in Contemporary Thought*, edited by Thorsten Botz-Bornstein and Jürgen Hengelbrock, 251-271. Amsterdam & New York: Rodopi.

Kuokkanen, Rauna. 2007a. "Myths and realities of Sami women : a post-colonial feminist analysis for the decolonization and transformation of sami society." *In Making space for indigenous feminism* edited by Joyce Green, pp. 72-92. London: Fernwood Publ. Zed Books,

Kuokkanen, Rauna. 2007b. *Reshaping the University : responsibility, indigenous epistemes, and the logic of the gift*. Vancouver: UBC Press.

Kuokkanen, Rauna. 2008a. "From research as colonialism to reclaiming autonomy : toward a research ethics framework in Sápmi." In *Sáme- ja álgoálbmotdutkama etihkka*, pp. 48-63.

Kuokkanen, Rauna. 2008b. "What is Hospitality in the Academy? Epistemic Ignorance and the (Im)Possible Gift." *Review of Education, Pedagogy, and Cultural Studies* 30 (1), pp. 60-82.

Kuokkanen, Rauna. 2009. *Boaris dego eana: Eamilbmogiid diehtu, filosofijat ja dutkan, Vol. 2, SÁMIacademia* Kárášjohka: ČállidLágádus.

Kuokkanen, Rauna. 2019. *Restructuring relations : indigenous self-determination, governance, and gender*. New York: Oxford University Press.

Kuoljok, Sunna. 2007. *Recalling Ancestral Voices - Repatriation of Sámi Cultural Heritage: rapport från ett interreg-projekt om en databas för samiska föremål på museer i Norden : rapporten avser projektets svenska del*: Johkamokk: Ájtte.

Kuoljok, Sunna, and John E. Utsi. 1993. *The Saami. People of the Sun and Wind*. Johkamohkk: Ájtte

Labahå, Tove-Lill. 2004. "Slektsmønstre i et samisk perspektiv. En samfunnspedagogisk tilnærming." *Kirke og Kultur* 109 (03), pp. 375-385.

Larsen, Anders. [1950]1979. *Mærrasámiid birra*. Vol. 16, *"Om sjøsamene"* og andre skrifter. Tromsø: Tromsø Museum.

Larsen, Dan Robert, and Johannes E. Kalvemo. 2008. ""Vil ha kommersielt fiske på privat grunn." ", 06.11.2008. Accessed 06.11.2008.

Latour, Bruno. 1990. "Technology is Society Made Durable." *The Sociological Review* 38, pp. 103-131.

Latour, Bruno. 1999. *Pandora's hope : essays on the reality of science studies*. Cambridge, Mass: Harvard University Press.

Latour, Bruno. 2005. *Reassembling the social : an introduction to actor-network-theory, Clarendon lectures in management studies*. Oxford: Oxford University Press.

Law, John. 2012. "Notes on fish, ponds and theory." *Norsk antropologisk tidsskrift* 03-04 (23), pp. 225–236.

Law, John. 2015. "What's wrong with a one-world world?" *Distinktion: Scandinavian Journal of Social Theory* 16, pp. 126 - 139.

Lawrence, Bonita. 2003. "Gender, Race, and the Regulation of Native Identity in Canada and the United States: An Overview." *Hypatia* 18 (2), pp. 3-31.

274

References

Lawrence, Bonita. 2004. *"Real" indians and others : mixed-blood urban native peoples and indigenous nation-hood*. Lincoln, Neb: University of Nebraska Press.

Leem, Knud. [1767]1975. *Beskrivelse over Finmarkens lapper : 1767 = Canuti Leemii de lapponibus Fin-marchiæ, eorumqve lingva, vita et religione pristina commentatio, multis tabulis æneis illustrata*. Edited by Asbjørn Nesheim, *Canuti Leemii de lapponibus Finmarchiæ, eorumqve lingva, vita et religione pristina commentatio, multis tabulis æneis illustrata*. København: Rosenkilde og Bagger.

Lefale, Penehuro. 2010. "Ua 'afa le Aso Stormy weather today: traditional ecological knowledge of weather and climate. The Samoa experience." *Climatic Change* 100 (2), pp. 317-335.

Lehtola, Jorma 2006. Sámi Duodji - Sámi duodjesearvvi 30-jagi ávvudančájáhuskataloga. Inari: Sami Siida Museum.

Lehtola, Veli-Pekka 1996. "The Sami: A history of our own." In *Awakened Voice. The Return of Sami knowledge*, edited by Elina Helander. Pp. 72-73. Guovdageaidnu: Nordic Sami Institute,.

Liebler, Carolyn A. 2004. "Ties on the fringes of identity." *Social Science Research* 33 (4), pp. 702-723.

Linders, F. J., and Herman Lundborg. 1926. *The Racial Character of the Swedish Nation*. Uppsala: Almqvist & Wiksell.

Livingstone, David N., and Charles W. J. Withers. 1999. *Geography and Enlightenment*. University of Chicago Press.

Lonetree, Amy. 2012. *Decolonizing Museums: Representing Native America in National and Tribal Museums*: The University of North Carolina Press.

Lundmark, Lennart. 2008. *Stulet land: svensk makt på samisk mark*: Ordfront.

Lyons, Claire L. 2002. *Objects and Identities: Claiming and Reclaiming the Past*. Los Angeles, CA: Los Angeles, CA: Getty Research Institute.

Løkvold, Jorunn. 2017. Sjøsamiske koftebelter med kråkesølvdekor - riebangolleherven. In *Årsrapport - stipendiat i håndverk*: Norsk Håndverksinstitutt.

Løkvold, Jorunn. 2019. Håndverkstradisjoner innenfor samiske klesplagg i Nord-Troms og Vest-Finnmark. In *Sluttrapport - stipendiat i håndverk*: Norsk Håndverksinstitutt.

Magga, Ole Henrik. 1996. "Sami Past and Present and the Sami Picture of the World " In *Awakened Voice. The Return of Sami Knowledge*, edited by Elina Helander. Pp. 74-80. Guovdageaidnu: Nordic Sami Institute.

Magga, Sigga-Marja 2014. "Geahčastagat, olggušteapmi ja albma duoji gáibádus – duodjekontrolla duojáriid vásáhussan/The gaze, shunning and demand of proper duodji – the control of duodji as experienced by Saami craft workers." *Sámi dieđalaš áigečála* 2, pp. 29–46.

Magnus, Olaus. [1555]2010. "Description of the northern peoples, 1555. : Volume III." In *Olaus Magnus, a Description of the Northern Peoples 1555*, ed Peter Foote. Farnham, Surrey, England ;,Burlington, VT: Ashgate Pub.

Manker, Ernst. 1957. *Lapparnas heliga ställen : kultplatser och offerkult i belysning av Nordiska museets och Landsantikvariernas fältundersökningar*. Vol. 13, *Acta Lapponica*. Stockholm: Gebers.

Mannell, Jenevieve, Lida Ahmad, and Ayesha Ahmad. 2018. "Narrative storytelling as mental health support for women experiencing gender-based violence in Afghanistan." *Social Science & Medicine* 214, pp. 91-98.

Mathisen, Silje Opdahl. . 2012. "Northern Borderlands and the Aesthetics of Ethnicity. Intervisuality and the Representations of the Sami in Early Exhibitions at National Cultural Museums in Norway and Sweden." *ARV*, pp. 57 – 72

Mathisen, Silje Opdahl. 2014. "Etnisitetens estetikk : visuelle fortellinger og forhandlinger i samiske museumsut-stillinger." Det humanistiske fakultet, Universitetet i Oslo.

Mathisen, Silje Opdahl. 2020. "A record of ethnographic objects procured for the Crystal Palace exhibition in Sydenham." *Nordisk Museologi* 27 (3), pp. 8-24.

Mathisen, Stein Roar. 2004. "Representasjoner av kulturell forskjell. Fortelling, makt og autoritet i utstillinger av samisk kultur." *Tidsskrift for kulturforskning* 3 (3), pp. 5-25.

Mathisen, Stein Roar. 2009. "Narrated Sámi sieidis : heritage and ownership in ambigious border zones." *Ethnologia Europaea*, pp. 11-25.

Mauss, Marcel. [1925]2002. *The gift : the form and reason for exchange in archaic societies, Essai sur le don*. London: Routledge.

Medicine, Beatrice. 1987. "My elders tell me." In *Indian education in Canada*, edited by Jean Barman, Yvonne Hebert and Don McCaskill, pp. 142-52. Vancouver: UBC Press.

Meggitt, M. J. 1965. *Desert people : a study of the Walbiri aborigines of Central Australia*. Chicago: The University of Chicago Press.

Melhus, Marita, and Ann Ragnhild Broderstad. 2020a. FOLKEHELSEUNDERSØKELSEN I NORDLAND. Tilleggsrapport om samisk og kvensk/norskfinsk befolkning. Tromsø: UiT Arctic University of Norway

Melhus, Marita, and Ann Ragnhild Broderstad. 2020b. FOLKEHELSEUNDERSØKELSEN I TROMS OG FIN-NMARK. Tilleggsrapport om samisk og kvensk/norskfinsk befolkning. Tromsø: UiT Arctic University of Norway

Mellegård, Viveca, and Wiebren J. Boonstra. 2020. "Craftsmanship as a Carrier of Indigenous and Local Ecological Knowledge: Photographic Insights from Sámi Duodji and Archipelago Fishing." Society & Natural Resources, pp. 1-21.

Mennel, Stephen. 1994. "The Formation of We-Images: A Process Theory." In Social theory and the politics of identity, edited by Craig Calhoun, pp.175-197. Oxford: Blackwell.

Merleau-Ponty, Maurice. [1945]2012. Phenomenology of perception. Edited by Donald A. Landes, Taylor Carman and Claude Lefort, Phénoménologie de la perception. London: Routledge.

Merrill, William L., Edmund J. Ladd, T. J. Ferguson, Elizabeth Cruwys, Alan S. Downer, Christian F. Feest, Charlotte J. Frisbie, Joyce Herold, Schuyler Jones, Robert Layton, and Larry J. Zimmerman. 1993. "The Return of the Ahayu: da: Lessons for Repatriation from Zuni Pueblo and the Smithsonian Institution [and Comments and Replies]." Current Anthropology 34 (5), pp. 523-567.

Meyer, Manulani Aiulani. 2003. Ho'oulu: Our Time of Becoming : Collected Early Writings of Manulani Meyer: 'Ai Pōhaku Press.

Minde, Henry. 1995. ""Dagen er kommet" : Henrik Kvandahl og hans verk: Samenes historie I-III." Hammarn Årg. 2, nr. 4 (1995), pp. 40-44.

Minde, Henry 2005. "Fornorskina av samene - hvorfor, hvordan og hvilke følger." Gáldu čála - tidsskrift for urfolks rettigheter (3).

Minde, Henry, Harald Gaski, Svein Jentoft, and Georges Midré. 2008. Indigenous peoples : self-determination, knowledge, indigeneity. Delft: Eburon.

Mitchell, S., and J. Burelle. 2016. "Dee(a)r Spine: Dance, Dramaturgy, and the Repatriation of Indigenous Memory." Dance Res. J. 48 (1), pp. 41-54.

Mithlo, Nancy Marie. 2012. "Silly Little Things": Framing Global Self- Appropriations in Native Arts." In No Deal! Indigenous Arts and the Politics of Possession, edited by Tressa Berman, pp. 188–206. . Santa Fe: School for Advanced Research Global Indigenous Politics Series.

Mol, Annemarie. 1999. "Ontological politics: a word and some questions." In Actor network theory and after, edited by John Law and John Hassard, pp 74–89. Oxford Blackwell.

Mol, Annemarie. 2002. The body multiple : ontology in medical practice, Science and cultural theory. Durham: Duke University Press.

Mordhorst, Camilla. 2009. Genstandsfortællinger : fra Museum Wormianum til de moderne museer. Vol. b. 7, Tidlig moderne. København: Museum Tusculanum.

Moreton-Robinson, Aileen. 2007. Sovereign subjects : indigenous sovereignty matters, Cultural studies. Crows Nest, N.S.W: Allen & Unwin.

Moulton, Kimberley. 2018. "I Can Still Hear Them Calling. Echoes of My Ancestors." In Sovereign Words. Indigenous Art, Curation and Criticism, edited by Katya García-Antón, pp. 197–214. Oslo/Amsterdam: OCA/Valiz.

Munch, Gerd Stamsø, and Olav Sverre Johansen. 2003. "C-dates." In Borg in Lofoten : a chieftain's farm in North Norway, edited by Gerd Stamsø Munch, Olav Sverre Johansen and Else Roesdahl. Bøstad, Trondheim: Lofotr - Vikingmuséet på Borg Tapir Academic Press.

Munch, Peter Andreas 1852. Det Norske Folks Historie. Christiania [Olso].

Mundal, Else. 1996. "The perception of the Saamis and their religion in Old Norse sources." Shamanism and northern ecology. Pp. 97-116. Berlin: Mouton de Gruyter, 1996.

Mundal, Else. 1997. "Kong Harald Hårfagre og samejenta Snøfrid : samefolket sin plass i den norske rikssamlingsmyten." Temahefte i norrøn filologi, pp. 39-53.

Mundal, Else. 2007. "Kristninga av samane i lærebøker og faglitteratur Sijte – og kva kjeldene frå mellomalder seier", In Om sørsamisk historie. Foredrag fra seminar på Røros 2006 og Trondheim 2007, edited by Susanne Lyngman, pp. 110-125. Snåsa: Stiftelsen Saemien.

Murray Li, Tania. 2000. "Articulating Indigenous Identity in Indonesia: Resource Politics and the Tribal Slot." Comparative Studies in Society and History 42 (1), pp.149-179.

Myrvoll, Elin Rose, Tone Magnussen, Thomas Johansen, Brigt Dale, Alma Elizabeth Thuestad, and Stine Barlindhaug. 2013. Kulturminner og verdiskaping i Nord-Norge : kunnskapsinnhenting - verdiskaping i nord. Oslo: NIKU, Norsk institutt for kulturminneforskning.

N.A.I.S.A. 2015. Statement on Indigenous Identity Fraud. https://www.naisa.org/: Native American and Indigenous Studies Association.

Nagata, D. K., S. J. Trierweiler, R. Talbot, and D. K. Nagata. 1999. "Long-term effects of internment during

References

early childhood on third-generation Japanese Americans." *The American journal of orthopsychiatry* 69 (1), pp. 19-29.

Nagel, Alexander, and Christopher S. Wood. 2010. *Anachronic Renaissance*. New York: Zone Books.

Naguib, Saphinaz-Amal. 2007. 2007. "The One, the Many and the Other: Revisiting Cultural Diversity in Museums of Cultural History." In *National Museums in a Global World – NaMu III*, edited by Arne Bugge Amundsen and Andreas Nyholm. Linköping: Linköping University Electronic Press.

Nakata, Martin, Victoria Nakata, Sarah Keech, and Reuben Bolt. 2011. *Decolonial Goals and Pedagogies for Indigenous Studies*. Vol. 1.

Navaro-Yashin, Yael. 2012. *The make-believe space : affective geography in a postwar polity*. Durham, N.C: Duke University Press.

Nergård, Jens-Ivar, and Jan Eriksen. 2006. *Den levende erfaring : en studie i samisk kunnskapstradisjon*. Oslo: Cappelen akademisk.

Newcomb, Steven. 1995. "Perspectives: Healing, Restoration, and Rematriation." *Indigenous Law Institute News & Notes* Spring/Summer, pp. 3.

Newell, Stephanie. 2014. "What is meant by "Cultural Politics"." *DirtPol*, 14.01.2019. https://blogs.sussex.ac.uk/dirtpol/2014/04/01/what-is-meant-by-cultural-politics-by-prof-steph-newell/.

Nielsen, Konrad. 1979. Lappisk (samisk) ordbok. edited by Konrad Nielsen. Oslo: Gyldendal.

Nielssen, Alf Ragnar. [2012]2019. *Landnåm fra nord : utvandringa fra det nordlige Norge til Island i vikingtid*. 2. opplag. ed. Stamsund: Orkana akademisk.

Nilsson, Kristina. 1988. *Den himmelska föräldern : ett studium av kvinnans betydelse i och för Lars Levi Laestadius' teologi och förkunnelse*. , Almqvist & Wiksell.

Nordin, Jonas M., and Carl-Gösta Ojala. 2018. "Collecting, connecting, constructing: Early modern commodification and globalization of Sámi material culture." *Journal of Material Culture* 23 (1), pp. 58-82.

Nordmark, Ingrid. 2014. "Samer er ikke Norges urfolk. Debattinnlegg av Ingrid Nordmark, adjunkt med tilleggsutdanning." *iTromsø*, 25.06.2014. Accessed 16.01.2019. https://www.itromso.no/nyheter/article9850265.ece.

Nunn, Patrick D., and Nicholas J. Reid. 2015. "Aboriginal Memories of Inundation of the Australian Coast Dating from More than 7000 Years Ago." *Australian Geographer*, pp. 1-37.

Nymo, Randi. 2011. Helseomsorgssystemer i samiske markebygder i nordre Nordland og Sør-Troms: praksiser i hverdagslivet: "En ska ikkje gje sæ over og en ska ta tida til hjelp". PhD, Tromsø: University of Tromsø.

Nymo, Randi. 2015. "Everyday Life Between Knowledge Systems in the Markebygd Areas." In *Idioms of Sámi health and healing*, edited by Stein R. Mathisen and Barbara Helen Miller, pp. 157 - 182. Edmonton, Alberta: Polynya Press, an imprint of The University of Alberta Press.

Nøren, Mali Finborud. 2019. The Heritage. Norway: Ladybird Film AS.

Odner, Knut. 1983. *Finner og terfinner : etniske prosesser i det nordlige Fenno-Skandinavia*. Vol. 9, *Oslo occasional papers in social anthropology (trykt utg.)*. Oslo: Department of Social Anthropology, University of Oslo.

Odner, Knut. 1989. *The Varanger Saami. Haboitation and economy 1200-1900*. Oslo: A. D. Institute of Social Anthropology.

Olli, Anne May. 2013. Pesticider i samisk gjenstandsmateriale. Master, Oslo: University of Oslo.

Olli, Anne May, and Eeva-Kristiina Harliin. 2014. "Repatriation: Political Will and Museum Facilities." In *Museums and restitution : new practices, new approaches*, edited by Louise Tythacott and Kostas Arvanitis, pp. 55-70. Farnham: Ashgate.

Olsen, Bjørnar. 1984. Stabilitet og endring : produksjon og samfunn i Varanger, 800 f.Kr.-1700 e.Kr. Master, Tromsø: University of Tromsø.

Olsen, Bjørnar. 2004. "Hva er samisk forhistorie?" *Samisk forhistorie* edited by Mia Krogh and Kjersti Schanche, pp. 20-30. Varangerbotn: Varanger Samiske Museum.

Olsen, Lars. 1997. "Om runebommen (1885)." *Ottar* 4, pp. 4-7.

Oskal, Nils. 2007. "Muhtin dieđafilosofalaš váttisvuođat vuođđudit earenoamáš álgoálbmotmetodologiija." *Sámi dieđalaš áigečála* 1 (2), pp. 161-180.

Outakoski, Hanna 2015. "Davvisámegielat čálamáhtu konteaksta/The context of North Sámi literacy." *Sámi dieđalaš áigečála* 1, pp. 29-59.

Padiglione, Vincenzo. 2016. " Fazer falar o silêncio da história : a virada narrativa dos museus." *Fractal: Revista de Psicologia* 28, pp. 181-186.

Painter, Nell Irvin. 2011. *The History of White People*. W. W. Norton & Company.

Pajunen, Cydd Siniikwe 2020. "On racism and Indigenous terminology." Facebook, 11.05.2020.

Palmater, Pamela D. 2011. *Beyond Blood: Rethinking Indigenous Identity*: UBC Press.

Pareli, Leif, Sissel Ann Mikkelsen, Anne May Olli, and Stein Storsul. 2012. Bååstede - tilbakeføring av samisk kulturarv. Norsk Folkemuseum, Sametinget, Norsk Kulturhistorisk Museum.

Paul, Jarrad W. 2018. "Not my ancestors! The importance of communication in the display of human remains: a case study from Australia." *Museums & Social Issues* 13 (2), pp. 94-106.

Pedersen, Bård Magn et al. 2016. NOU 2016:18. In *Hjertespråket : forslag til lovverk, tiltak og ordninger for samiske språk : utredning fra utvalg oppnevnt ved kongelig resolusjon 19. september 2014 : avgitt til Kommunal- og moderniseringsdepartementet 10. oktober 2016*edited by Kommunal- og moderniseringsdepartementet. Oslo: Departementenes sikkerhets- og serviceorganisasjon, Informasjonsforvaltning.

Peers, Laura. 2013. "'Ceremonies of Renewal': Visits, Relationships, and Healing in the Museum Space." *Museum Worlds* 1 (1), pp. 136-152.

Peers, Laura, and Alison K. Brown. 2003. "Introduction." In *Museums and source communities : a Routledge reader*, edited by Laura Peers and Alison K. Brown, 1-16. London: Routledge.

Peffer, John. 2005. "Africa's Diasporas of Images." *Third Text* 19 (4), pp. 339-355.

Pentikäinen, Juha. 1987. "The shamanic drum as a cognitive map : the historical and semiotic study of the saami drum in Rome". In *Mythology and Cosmic Order* edited by Gothóni, Rene, and Juha Pentikäinen, pp. 17-36 Helsinki: Finnish Literature Society, Finland.

Persen, Bente. 2008. "At bringe dem fram til mands modenhet" : en studie av fornorskningen av samene i Porsanger, 1880-1980. Master, Oslo: University of Oslo.

Peters, Evelyn, and Chris Andersen. 2013. *Indigenous in the City: Contemporary Identities and Cultural Innovation*: UBC Press.

Pettersen, Bjørg. 2011. ""Mind the digital gap: Questions and possible solutions for design of databases and information systems for Sami traditional knowledge."." In *Working with traditional knowledge*, edited by Jelena Porsanger, Gunvor Guttorm, pp. 163-193. Guovdageaidnu : Sámi Allaskuvla

Pettersson, O. P., Louise Bäckman, and Rolf Kjellström. 1979. *Kristoffer Sjulssons minnen : om Vapstenlapparna i början af 1800-talet / upptecknade af O. P. Pettersson ; red. av Louise Bäckman och Rolf Kjellström*. Vol. 20, *Acta Lapponica*. Stockholm.

Pezzarossi, Heather Law. 2014. "Assembling indigeneity: Rethinking innovation, tradition and indigenous materiality in a 19th-century native toolkit." *Journal of Social Archaeology* 14 (3), pp. 340-360.

Phillips, Ruth. 2002. "A Proper Place for Art or the Proper Arts of Place? Native North American Objects and the Hierarchies of Art, Craft and Souvenir." In *On Aboriginal Representation in the Gallery*, edited by Lynda Jessup and Shannon Bagg, pp. 45–72. Hull: Canadian Museum of Civilization.

Phillips, Ruth B., and Christopher B. Steiner. 1999. "Art, Authenticity, and the Baggage of Cultural Encounter." In *Unpacking Culture : Art and Commodity in Colonial and Postcolonial Worlds*, edited by Ruth B. Phillips and Christopher B. Steiner, pp. 3-19. Berkeley: University of California Press.

Pieski, Aura. 2019. "Gulahallat eatnamiin ja čáziin: Muitalusat eamiálbmot oahppan- ja gulahallanvugiin Deanuleagis." Master. Guovdageaidnu:Sámi allaskuvla/ Sámi University of Applied Sciences.

Pieski, Outi. 07.10.2020. *New Directions – Decolonising the Museum and Public Art*: Nordiska Museet Statens konstråd.

Pollan, Brita. 2007. *For djevelen er alt mulig : kristne historier om samene*. Vol. 158, *NFL*. Kristiansand: Høyskoleforl.

Pollan, Brita. 2017. *Slik den ene samen har fortalt til den andre samen : stemmer fra den gamle kulturen*. Vøyenenga: Emilia.

Porsanger, Jelena. 2004. "An Essay about Indigenous Methodology." *Nordlit: Tidsskrift i litteratur og kultur* 8 (1), pp. 105-120.

Porsanger, Jelena. 2011. "The problematisation of the dichotomy of modernity and tradition in indigenous and Sami contexts." *Working with traditional knowledge*, edited by Jelena Porsanger, Gunvor Guttorm, pp. 225-252. Guovdageaidnu : Sámi Allaskuvla

Porsanger, Jelena. 2012. "Indigenous Sámi religion : general considerations about relationship. In *The Diversity of Sacred Lands*, edited by Josep-Maria Mallarach, Thymio Papayannis and Rauno Väisänen in Europe, pp. 37-45. Gland: IUCN,

Porter, Tom. 2008. *And Grandma Said--Iroquois Teachings: As Passed Down Through the Oral Tradition*: Xlibris Corporation.

Povinelli, Elizabeth A. 2002. *The cunning of recognition : indigenous alterities and the making of Australian multiculturalism, Politics, history, and culture*. Durham, N.C: Duke University Press.

Pratt, Mary Louise. 1992. *Imperial eyes : travel writing and transculturation*. London: Routledge.

Price, Neil S. 2002. *The Viking way : religion and war in late Iron Age Scandinavia*. PhD, Uppsala: Uppsala University.

References

Price, Sally. 1989. *Primitive Art in Civilized Places*: University of Chicago Press.

Pullar, Gordon L. . 2008. "Repatriation, cultural revitalization and indigenous healing in Alaska." In *Utimut: Past Heritage -- Future Partnerships, Discussions on Repatriation in the 21st Century*, edited by Mille Gabriel and Jens Dahl, pp. 108-16. Copenhagen: International Work Group for Indigenous Affairs and Greenland National Museum & Archives.

Qureshi, Sadiah. 2011. *Peoples on parade : exhibitions, empire, and anthropology in nineteenth-century Britain.* Chicago: University of Chicago Press.

Ravna, Øyvind. 2002. " Rettsvernet for samiske rettigheter fram til siste halvdel av 1700-tallet – og betydningen av dette i dag " *Kritisk Juss* (29), pp. 75-90.

Ravna, Øyvind. 2010. "Lappekodisillen av 1751 og dens rettslige betydning i dag." *Lov og rett* 49 (7), pp. 392-406.

Reid, Donald Malcolm. 2002. *Whose pharaohs? : archaeology, museums, and Egyptian national identity from Napoleon to World War I*. Berkeley: University of California Press.

Remme, Jon Henrik Ziegler. 2013. "Den ontologiske vendingen i antropologien." *Norsk antropologisk tidsskrift* 24 (1), pp. 6-24.

Renberg, Elsa Laula. 1904. *Inför lif eller död? : sanningsord i de lappska förhållandena*. Stockholm.

Rinta-Porkkunen, Nina, and Saija Ylitalo. 2003. "If we do not know our past, we have no future : the importance of a museum and a home district for local identity." *Nordisk museologi* 1, pp. 111-128.

Robbins, Julian A., and Jonathan Dewar. 2011. "Traditional Indigenous Approaches to Healing and the modern welfare of Traditional Knowledge, Spirituality and Lands: A critical reflection on practices and policies taken from the Canadian Indigenous Example." *International indigenous policy journal* 2 (4), p. 2.

Robinson, Helena. 2012. "Remembering things differently: museums, libraries and archives as memory institutions and the implications for convergence." *Museum Management and Curatorship* 27 (4), pp. 413-429.

Rorgemoen, Mari. 2011. "Kopiering av tradisjonskunst som læringsmetode." *Formakademisk* 4 (1).

Rosiek, Jerry Lee, Jimmy Snyder, and Scott L. Pratt. 2020. "The New Materialisms and Indigenous Theories of Non-Human Agency: Making the Case for Respectful Anti-Colonial Engagement." *Qualitative Inquiry* 26 (3-4), pp. 331-346.

Rowley, Susan , and Kristin Hausler. 2008. "The Journey Home: A Case Study in Proactive Repatriation." In *Utimut: Past Heritage -- Future Partnerships, Discussions on Repatriation in the 21st Century*, edited by Mille Gabriel and Jens Dahl, 202-12. Copenhagen: International Work Group for Indigenous Affairs and Greenland National Museum & Archives.

Ruong, Israel. 1937. *Fjällapperna i Jukkasjärvvi socken*. Vol. 3, *Geographica, Skrifter från Universitetens geografiske Institution*. Uppsala: Universitetet i Uppsala.

Rydving, Håkan. 2003. "Innledning." In *Mytisk landskap : ved dansende skog og susende fjell*, edited by Arvid Sveen, pp. 9-23. Stamsund: Orkana.

Rydving, Håkan 1991. "The Saami Drums and the Religious Encounter in the 17th and 18th Centuries. ." In *The Saami Shaman Drum*, edited by Tore Ahlback and Jan Bergman, pp. 28-51. Åbo: The Donner Institute for Research in Religious and Cultural History.

Rygh, Oluf. 1867. *Aarsberetning for 1866*. Kristiania: Foreningen til Norske Fortidsmindesmerke Bevaring.

Rykner, Didier. 23.11.2018. Art Repatriation: Who do African art treasures belong to? In *France24*, edited by François Picard.

Røkkum, Arne. 2005. "Nært, vilt og skjønt ; typer og karakterer i etnografiske utstillinger og forestillinger." *Norsk antropologisk tidsskrift* 16 (2-3), pp. 119-178.

Sandell, Richard. 2017. *Museums, moralities and human rights, Museum meanings*. London: Routledge.

Sangster, Joan. 1994. "Telling our stories: feminist debates and the use of oral history." *Women's History Review* 3 (1), pp. 5-28.

Santos, Boaventura de Sousa. 2014. *Epistemologies of the South : justice against epistemicide*: Routledge.

Sara, Máret Anne. 2018. "Indigenous Stories, Indigenous to Global Survival." In *Sovereign words : indigenous art, curation and criticism*, edited by Katya García-Antón. Pp. 141-50. Oslo, Amsterdam: Office for Contemporary Art Norway Valiz.

Sara, Mikkel Nils Mikkelsen. 2015. Siida ja siiddastallan Å være en siida – om forholdet mellom siidatradisjoner og videreføringen av siidasystemet Being siida – on the relationship between siida tradition and continuation of the siida system. PhD, Tromsø: UiT Norges arktiske universitet.

Sarr, Felwine, and Bénédicte Savoy. 2018. Rapport sur la restitution du patrimoine culturel africain. Vers une nouvelle éthique relationnelle. Paris.

Schanche, Audhild. 1995. "Det symbolske landskapet – landskap og identitet i samisk kultu." *Ottar* Menneske og landskap (4), pp. 38-47.

Schanche, Audhild. 2000. *Graver i ur og berg: samisk gravskikk og religion fra forhistorisk til nyere tid*: Davvi Girji OS.

Schanche, Kjersti. 1994. "Gressbakkentuftene i Varanger : boliger og sosial struktur rundt 2000 f.Kr." PhD, Tromsø, University of Tromsø.

Schefferus, Johannes. 1673. *The history of Lapland : wherein are shewed the original, manners, habits, marriages, conjurations, &c. of that people, Lapponia*. Oxford:

Schimmel, Jessica, 2005. "Killing Without Murder: Aboriginal Assimilation Policy as Genocide." *The Lehigh Review - a Student Journal of the Arts and Sciences* 13, pp. 35-54.

Shelton, Anthony Alan. 2009. "The Public Sphere as Wilderness: Le Musée du quai Branly." *Museum Anthropology* 32 (1), pp. 1-16. doi:

Short, Damien. 2003. "Reconciliation, Assimilation, and the Indigenous Peoples of Australia." *International Political Science Review - INT POLIT SCI REV* 24, pp. 491-513.

Sikku, Karolina Pirak. 03.03.2020. Katarina Pirak Sikku - i rasbiologernas spor. In *Kulturreportaget i P1*, edited by Helen Alm. Sveriges Radio.

Silliman, Stephen. 2001. "Agency, practical politics and the archaeology of culture contact." *Journal of Social Archaeology - J SOC ARCHAEOL* 1, pp. 190-209.

Silliman, Stephen W. 2009. "Change and Continuity, Practice and Memory: Native American Persistence in Colonial New England." *American Antiquity* 74 (2), pp- 211-230.

Simonsen, Povl. 1957. *Ottar fra Hålogaland*. Tromsø: Tromsø museum.

Simpson, Audra. 2014. Mohawk Interruptus. Political Life Across the Borders of Settler States. Durham and London: Duke University Press.

Simpson, Moira G. 2008. "Indigenous Heritage and Repatriation - A Stimulus for Cultural Renewal " In *Utimut: Past Heritage -- Future Partnerships, Discussions on Repatriation in the 21st Century*, edited by Mille Gabriel and Jens Dahl, pp. 64-77. Copenhagen: International Work Group for Indigenous Affairs and Greenland National Museum & Archives.

Sium, Aman, and Erik Ritskes. 2013. "Speaking truth to power: Indigenous storytelling as an act of living resistance." *Decolonization: Indigeneity, Education & Society* 2 (1), pp. I-X.

Sivertsen, Elin Anita. 2011. ""Jeg er same, og jeg bærer det med stolthet": Identitet, ambivalens og tradisjon blant unge samer." In *Kulturell kompleksitet i det nye Norge*, edited by Thomas Hylland Eriksen og Hans Erik Næss pp 147-157. Oslo: Unipub.

Smith, Linda Tuhiwai. 2019. "Foreword." In *Decolonizing Research : Indigenous Storywork as Methodology*, edited by Jo-Ann Archibald, Jenny Lee-Morgan and Jason De Santolo, pp. XI-XII. London: Zed Books Ltd.

Smith, Linda Tuhiwai. [1999]2012. *Decolonizing methodologies : research and indigenous peoples*. 2nd ed. ed. London: Zed Books.

Smith., Hinekura. 2019. "Whatuora: Theorizing "New" Indigenous Research Methodology from "Old" Indigenous Weaving Practice." *Art/Research International: A Transdisciplinary Journal* 4, pp. 1-27.

Snarby, Irene. 2019. "Duodji as Indigenous Contemporary Art Practice." *Norwegian Crafts*, 25.04.2019.

Solbakk, John Trygve, and Britt Hansen. 2006. *"The Sámi people : a handbook"*, Samene en håndbok. Karasjok: Davvi girji.

Solbakk, Aage. 2000. Ávjovári-Kárášjoga historjá : 1553-1900. Vol. 1. Kárášjohka: Davvi Girji.

Solem, Erik. 1933. Lappiske rettsstudier, *Instituttet for sammenlignende kulturforskning* Vol. 24. Oslo: Aschehoug.

Somby, Liv Inger. 2016. "Mus lea ollu muitalit, muhto dus nu unnán áigi : Life-stories told by elder Sámi women - A critical social analysis." Master, Guovdugeaidnu: Sámi allaskuvla/Sámi University of Applied Science.

Somby, Niilas A. 1991. "Colonization " *Báiki. An American Journal of Sami Living"* (1).

Sommerseth, Ingrid. 2009. *Villreinfangst og tamreindrift i indre Troms : belyst ved samiske boplasser mellom 650 og 1923*. PhD, Tromsø: University of Tromsø,

Spein, Gry-Kristina Fors. 2004. Selskinn som en mulig ressurs : bruk av sel i Finnmark, Grønland og Island. Hovedfagsoppgave. Guovdageaidnu: Sámi allaskuvla/ Sámi University of Applied Science.

Spein, Gry-Kristina Fors. 2019. "Duodji as a Starting Point for Artistic Practice." *Norwegian Crafts*, 07.05.2019

Spein, Gry-Kristina Fors, and Ragnhild Enoksen. 1991. *Vår folkedrakt : sjøsamiske klestradisjoner*. Kárášjohka: Davvi girji.

St. Germain, Brenda 2014. "Behind the colonial wall: The chains that bind resistance." Master of Social Work, BSW, University of Victoria.

Steinsland, Gro. 1989. "Det hellige bryllup og norrøn kongeideologi : en undersøkelse av hierogami-myten i Skírnismál, Ynglingatal, Háleygjatal og Hyndluljóð." PhD, Oslo: University of Oslo.

References

Stordahl, Vigdis. 1996. *Same i den moderne verden : endring og kontinuitet i et samisk lokalsamfunn.* Karasjok: Davvi Girji.

Stordahl, Vigdis, Grete Tørres, Snefrid Møllersen, and Inger-Marit Eira-Åhren. 2015. "Ethical guidelines for Sami research: the issue that disappeared from the Norwegian Sami Parliament's agenda?" *International Journal of Circumpolar Health* 74 (1), pp. 1-8.

Storli, Inger. 1991. "De østlige smykkene fra vikingtid og tidlig middelalder." *Viking* 54, pp. 89-104.

Storli, Inger. 1994. *"Stallo"-boplassene : spor etter de første fjellsamer?* " Oslo: Novus forl.

Storli, Inger. 2006. *Hålogaland før rikssamlingen : politiske prosesser i perioden 200-900 e.Kr.* Oslo: Novus forl.

Storli, Inger. 2016. "Borg - mellom høvdingdømme og kongemakt." *Viking* 79, pp. 75-94.

Storm, Dikka. 1990. *Kystsamisk bosetning i Sør-Troms : etableringen av en markebygd og ressursutnyttingen i området : en undersøkelse i Gressmyrskogen på Senja.* Hovedfagsoppgave, Bergen: University of Bergen.

Storm, Dikka. 2015. "Reindrift, hushold og kjønn: Sør-Troms på 1700-tallet, i historisk kildemateriale." *Nordlit 36*, pp. 211-228.

Storm, Dikka. 2017. "The Church, Pietist Mission and The Sámi. - An Account of a Northern Norwegian Mission District in the Early Eighteenth Century." *Norsk tidsskrift for misjonsvitenskap 3*, pp. 59-75.

Strompdal, K 1954. *Samene i helg og yrkje fortalde av dei sjølve og andre. Frå Helgeland og Namdal, Norsk Folkeminnesamling Nr. 18.* Oslo.

Sturm, Circe. 2011. *Becoming Indian: The Struggle Over Cherokee Identity in the Twenty-first Century.* Sar Press.

Susan, Stewart. 1999. "Prologue: From the Museum of Touch." In *Material Memories: Design and Evocation*, edited by Marius Kwint, Christopher Breward and Jeremy Aynsley, pp. 17-36. Oxford: Berg Publishers.

Tacitus, Cornelius. [98]1997. *Agricola og Germania.* Edited by Trygve Width, *Thorleif Dahls kulturbibliotek.* Oslo: Aschehoug i samarbeid med Fondet for Thorleif Dahls kulturbibliotek og Det norske akademi for sprog og litteratur.

Tallbear, Kim. 2016. «The US-Dakota War and Failed Settler Kinship", *Anthropology News, sfaa.net*

Taylor, Diana. 2003. *The Archive and the Repertoire: Performing Cultural Memory in the Americas*: Duke University Press.

The Sámi Act. 1987. The Sámi Act - Act of 12 June 1987 No. 56 concerning the Sameting (the Sami parliament) and other Sami legal matters (the Sami Act). edited by Ministry of Local Government. regjeringen.no.

Thorbjørnsrud, Berit. 2005. "Feltarbeid: En personlig reise til økt innsikt." In *Kulturvitenskap i felt: Metodiske og pedagogiske erfaringer*, edited by Anders Gustavsson, pp. 19 - 48. Kristiansand: Høyskoleforlaget.

Thulin, Henning. 1949. *Lars Levi Læstadius och hans förkunnelse.* Stockholm: Filadelfia.

Ticineto Clough, Patricia. 2009. "The New Empiricism: Affect and Sociological Method." *European Journal of Social Theory* 12 (1), pp. 43-61.

Tjora, Aksel Hagen. 2012. *Kvalitative forskningsmetoder i praksis.* 2. utg. ed. Oslo: Gyldendal akademisk.

Trant, Jennifer. 2009. "Emerging convergence? Thoughts on museums, archives, libraries, and professional training." *Museum Management and Curatorship* 24 (4), pp. 369-387.

Triumf, Rauna. 2011. "Small stories: A guide to learning and teaching Sámi arts and crafts." WINHEC: International Journal of Indigenous Education Scholarship, (1), pp. 77-86.

Trustees of the British Museum. 2012. "The Parthenon sculptures: The Trustees' statement." accessed 07.07.2020. https://www.britishmuseum.org/parthenon-sculptures-trustees-statement.

Tsosie, Rebecca. 2012. "Indigenous peoples and epistemic injustice: science, ethics, and human rights." *Washington Law Review* 87 (4), pp. 1164-1201.

Turi, Johan. [1910]1987. *Muitalus sámiid birra.* Jokkmokk: Sámi Girjit.

Turnbull, Paul. 2010. "Introduction." In *The Long Way Home: The Meaning and Values of repatriation*, edited by Paul Turnbull and Michael Pickering, 1 - 14. New York: Berghahn.

UDHR. 1948. United Nations Declaration on Human Rights. edited by United Nations.

Utsi, Johan Ante. 03.12.2019. "Sølvsmie mister eneretten til sol-designet." *NRK Sapmi.* Accessed 30.09.2020. https://www.nrk.no/sapmi/tana-gull-og-solvsmie-mister-eneretten-til-sol-designet-1.14805358.

Utsi, John E. 1993. "We Are Still Alive." In *The Saami. People of the Sun and Wind*, edited by Sunna kuoljok and John E. Utsi. Johkamohkki: Ájtte

Valkeapää, Nils-Aslak. 1998. "I have no beginning, no end " In *No Beginning, No End. The Sami speak up*, edited by Elina Helander and Kaarina Kailo. Alberta/Guovdageaidnu: Canadian Circumpolar Institute/ Nordic Sami Institute.

Valkonen, Sanna, and Sandra Wallenius-Korkalo. 2015. "Embodying religious control: an intersectional approach to Sámi women in Laestadianism." *Culture and Religion* 16 (1), pp. 1-16.

Varutti, Marzia. 2015. "Crafting heritage: artisans and the making of Indigenous heritage in contemporary Taiwan." *International Journal of Heritage Studies* 21 (10), pp. 1-14.

Virtanen, Pirjo Kristiina, and Irja Seurujärvi-Kari. 2019. "Introduction : Theorizing Indigenous Knowledge(s) " *Dutkansearvvi dieđalaš áigečála* 3 (2), pp. 1-19.

von Düben, Gustaf. [1873]1977. *Om lappland och lapparna*. Tofter: Östervåla.

Vorren, Ørnulv, and Ernst Manker. 1957. *Samekulturen : en oversikt*. Vol. 5, *Tromsø museums skrifter (trykt utg.)*. Tromsø: Tromsø museum.

Vuolab, Kerttu. 1995. *café boddu: Riggodagaid botnehis gáldu- maidnasiid mearihis mearkkašupmi*. Kárášjohka: Davvi Girji.

Walters, Karina L., Selina A. Mohammed, Teresa Evans-Campbell, Ramona E. Beltrán, David H. Chae, Bonnie Duran, and Karina L. Walters. 2011. "BODIES DON'T JUST TELL STORIES, THEY TELL HISTORIES: Embodiment of Historical Trauma among American Indians and Alaska Natives." *Du Bois review : social science research on race* 8 (1), pp. 179-189.

Wangoola, Paulo. 2012. "Mpambo Afrikan Multiversity, Dialogue and Building Bridges Across Worldviews, Cultures and Languages." In *Anthropologists, Indigenous Scholars and the Research Endeavour. Seeking Bridges Towards Mutual Respect*, edited by Joy Hendry and Laara Fitznoor, pp. 28 - 43. New York: Routledge.

Waters, Anne. 2004. *Language Matters: Nondiscrete Nonbinary Dualism*. Malden: Blackwell.

Watt, Elizabeth, and Emma Kowal. 2019. "To be or not to be Indigenous? Understanding the rise of Australia's Indigenous population since 1971." *Ethnic and Racial Studies* 42 (16), pp. 63-82.

Weaver, Hilary. 2001. "Indigenous Identity: What Is It and Who Really Has It?" *The American Indian Quarterly* 25, pp. 240-255.

Webb, Sharon. 2001. "Contested Histories of Multiple Pasts?: The representation of the archaeological past in the museum." Phd Cambridge: University of Cambridge.

Webb, Sharon. 2006. "Making museums, making people : the representation of the Sámi through material culture." *Public archaeology* 5(2006)No. 3, pp. 167-183.

Ween, Gro. 2005. "Inför lif eller död? : om kulturell kontinuitet og et sørsamisk verdensbilde." *Sørsamiske sedvaner* 5, pp. 12-34.

Weiner, Annette B. 1992. *Inalienable Possessions : The Paradox of Keeping-While Giving, Inalienable Possessions: The Paradox of Keeping-While Giving*. Berkeley: University of California Press.

West, Helga. 2018. "Mitäs me väsyneet saamelaiset, maailman tutkituin kansa." 09.11.2018. https://helgawest.com/2018/11/09/mitas-me-vasyneet-saamelaiset-maailman-tutkituin-kansa/?fbclid=IwAR0DbaZ5mcu7RoculX80gBdjtCRZN1Oz7eSJb5zUhVuHuVOrNM6NusM32lU.

Westman, Anna. 2002. "Samiska trummor, vilken är deras betydelse idag?" In, *Vem äger kulturarvet? : anföranden vid konferens om återföringsfrågor vid Ájtte, Svenskt Fjäll- och Samemuseum 6-8 juni 2000*, pp. 55-59. Jokkmokk: Ájtte.

Willems, W. J. H. 2014. "The Future of World Heritage and the Emergence of Transnational Heritage Regimes." *Heritage & Society* Vol 7 (2), pp. 105-120.

Wilson, Shawn. 2001. "What Is an Indigenous Research Methodology?" "*Canadian journal of native education*, Vol.25 (2), pp. 161-178.

Wilson, Shawn. 2008. *Research is ceremony : indigenous research methods*. Halifax, N.S: Fernwood Publ.

Wolff, Annika, Paul Mulholland, and Trevor Collins. 2012. "Storyspace: a Story-driven Approach for Creating Museum Narratives." In *Proceedings of the 23rd ACM conference on hypertext and social media*, pp .89-98

Yazzie, Robert. 2000. "Indigenous Peoples and Postcolonial Colonialism." In *Reclaiming Indigenous Voice and Vision*, edited by Marie Battiste, pp. 39-49. Vancouver and Toronto: UBC Press.

Yehuda, R. 1999. *Risk Factors for Posttraumatic Stress Disorder*. American Psychiatric Press.

Zachrisson, Inger. 1984. "De samiska metalldepåerna år 1000-1350 : i ljuset av fyndet från Mörtträsket, Lappland = The saami metal deposits A.D. 1000-1350 in the light of the find from Mörtträsket, Lapland." PhD, Umeå: The University of Umeå.

Zeldenryk, Lynne Michelle, and Yalmambirra. 2006. "Occupational Deprivation: A Consequence of Australia's Policy of Assimilation." *Australian Occupational Therapy Journal* 53 (1), pp. 43-46.

Øgård, Beathe, and Torjer Andreas Olsen. 08.10.2018. "Lesing og forståelse avhenger av leseren." *Klassekampen*. Accessed 08.10.2018.

Østby, Jon Birger. 2000. *Utlån og avhending av materiale fra museenes samlinger*. Edited by universitetsmuseene Nasjonalt utvalg for. Vol. 5:2000, *Norsk museumsutvikling (trykt utg.)*. Oslo: Norsk museumsutvikling.

Øverli, Ingvil Thallaug, Solveig Bergman and Ann-Kristin Finstad. 2017. "*Om du tør å spørre, tør folk å svare*" *: hjelpeapparatets og politiets erfaringer med vold i nære relasjoner i samiske samfunn*. Vol. nr. 2/2017, *Rapport (Nasjonalt kunnskapssenter om vold og traumatisk stress*. Oslo: Nasjonalt kunnskapssenter om vold og traumatisk stress.

References

Øyvind, Ravna. 2020. "Den tidligere umatrikulerte grunnen i Finnmark: Jordfellesskap fremfor statlig eiendom?" *Tidsskrift for rettsvitenskap* 154 (2-03), pp. 219-263.

Aagård-Dunfjeld, Maja. 1991. "Ornamentikk of dafliglivets gjøremål." In *Far etter fedrane. Årbok for Vefsn, Grane og Hattfjelldal*, 42-53. Vaapste: Vefsn Museums.

Åhrén, Mattias. 2010. "The Saami traditional dress & beauty pageants : indigenous peoples' rights of ownership and self-determination over their cultures." PhD, Tromsø: University of Tromsø.

Aarseth, Bjørn. 2006. *Norsk samepolitikk 1945 – 1990. Målsetting, virkemidler og resultater, Norsk Folkemuseums Samiske Samlinger*. Nesbru: Forlaget Vett & Viten.

APPENDIX I

THE VERDDE

Ájtte:

Ahlström, Eva. 12.11.2018. Ságastallan. edited by Liisa-Rávná Finbog.
Ahlström, Eva. 16.11.2018. Ságastallan. edited by Liisa-Ravna Finbog.

Riddo Duottar:

Olli, Anne May. 29.05.2018. Ságástallan. edited by Liisa-Ravna Finbog.

Ságastallan:

Amaut, Arely. 24.09.2020. Ságastallan. edited by Liisa-Ravna Finbog.
Black, Zoe. 28.09.2020. Ságástallan. edited by Liisa-Ravna Finbog.
Fjellheim, Unni. 27.11.2019. Ságastallan. edited by Liisa-Ravna Finbog.
Stenhammer, Trude. 12.04.2018. Ságastallan. edited by Liisa-Ravna Finbog.
Kuhmunen, Mereth. 02.12.2017. Ságastallan. edited by Liisa-Ravna Finbog.

Ságastallan:

Áile. 05.01.2018. Ságastallan. edited by Liisa-Ravna Finbog.
Áile. 11.09.2018. Ságastallan. edited by Liisa-Ravna Finbog.
Áile. 19.09.2019. Ságastallan. edited by Liisa-Ravna Finbog.

Ájsa. 23.06.2018. Ságastallan. edited by Liisa-Ravna Finbog.
Anna. 16.11.2018. Ságastallan. edited by Liisa-Ravna Finbog.
Anna. 23.04.2020. Ságastallan. edited by Liisa-Ravna Finbog.
Anne-Maja. 17.11.2018. Ságastallan. edited by Liisa-Rávná Finbog.
Anta. 01.06.2018. Ságastallan. edited by Liisa-Rávná Finbog.
Ása. 24.01.2018. Ságastallan. edited by Liisa-Ravna Finbog.
Ása. 07.01.2018. Ságastallan. edited by Liisa-Ravna Finbog.
Asta. 21.02.2019. Ságastallan. edited by Liisa-Ravna Finbog.
Ása. 24.01.2018. Ságastallan. edited by Liisa-Ravna Finbog.
Ása. 07.01.2018. Ságastallan. edited by Liisa-Ravna Finbog.
Asta. 21.02.2019. Ságastallan. edited by Liisa-Ravna Finbog.
Birthe. 23.06.2018. Ságastallan. edited by Liisa-Ravna Finbog.
Berit. 30.05.2018. Ságastallan. edited by Liisa-Rávná Finbog.
Ella. 23.06.2019. Ságastallan. edited by Liisa-Ravna Finbog.
Elle. 29.05.2018. Ságastallan. edited by Liisa-Rávná Finbog.
Elly. 17.01.2019. Sagastallan. edited by Liisa-Ravna Finbog.
Elly. 24.06.2018. Ságastallan. edited by Liisa-Ravna Finbog.
Elly. 25.06.2018. Ságastallan. edited by Liisa-Ravna Finbog.
Elsa. 13.11.2018. Ságastallan. edited by Liisa-Rávná Finbog.
Emily. 08.09.2019. Ságastallan. edited by Liisa-Ravna Finbog.
Emmy. 05.12.2017. Ságastallan. edited by Liisa-Ravna Finbog.
Eva. 24.03.2018. Ságastallan. edited by Liisa-Rávná Finbog.
Gunn. 15.05.2020. "Ságastallan. edited by Liisa-Ravna Finbog.
Hanna. 12.02.2019. Ságastallan. edited by Liisa-Ravna Finbog.
Ilse. 09.07.2018. Ságastallan. edited by Liisa-Ravna Finbog.
Inga. 15.01.2018. Ságastallan. edited by Liisa-Ravna Finbog.
Jane. 30.03.2019. Ságastallan. edited by Liisa-Rávná Finbog.
Jovnna. 14.11.2018. Ságastallan. edited by Liisa-Ravna Finbog.
Kajsa. 05.12.2018. Ságastallan. edited by Liisa-Ravna Finbog.
Karen. 08.03.2019. Ságastallan. edited by Liisa-Ravna Finbog.
Karen. 12.06.2018. Ságastallan. edited by Liisa-Ravna Finbog.
Karen. 15.05.2018. Ságastallan. edited by Liisa-Ravna Finbog.
Karl. 13.05.2020. Ságastallan. edited by Liisa-Ravna Finbog.
Lukas. 02.07.2018. Ságastallan. edited by Liisa-Ravna Finbog.
Laara. 05.04.2018. Ságastallan. edited by Liisa-Ravna Finbog.
Mari. 03.04.2018. Ságastallan. edited by Liisa-Ravna Finbog.
Marte. 13.01.2019. Ságastallan. edited by Liisa-Rávná Finbog.
Marte. 26.6.2018. Ságastallan. edited by Liisa-Rávná Finbog

Mia. 08.11.2017. Ságastallan. edited by Liisa-Ravna Finbog.
Mona. 17.08.2019. Ságastallan. edited by Liisa-Ravna Finbog.
Naja. 22.06.2018. Ságastallan. edited by Liisa-Ravna Finbog.
Naja. 23.06.2018. Ságastallan. edited by Liisa-Ravna Finbog.
Naja. 24.06.2018. Ságastallan. edited by Liisa-Ravna Finbog.
Násti. 13.08.2019. Ságastallan. edited by Liisa-Rávná Finbog.
Niila. 13.02.2018. Ságastallan. edited by Liisa-Ravna Finbog.
Ovlla. 24.04.2019. Ságastallan. edited by Liisa-Ravna Finbog.
Petra. 08.06.2020. Ságastallan. edited by Liisa-Ravna Finbog.
Pia. 17.11.2018. Ságastallan. edited by Liisa-Ravna Finbog.
Sáje. 23.11.2019. Ságastallan. edited by Liisa-Ravna Finbog.
Sanna. 02.07.2018. Ságastallan. edited by Liisa-Ravna Finbog.
Sanna. 11.09.2018. Ságastallan. edited by Liisa-Ravna Finbog.
Sara. 16.11.2018. Ságastallan. edited by Liisa-Ravna Finbog
Sara. 21.01.2018. Ságastallan. edited by Liisa-Ravna Finbog.
Sara. 29.05.2018. Ságastallan. edited by Liisa-Rávná Finbog.
Sávve. 06.05.2018. Ságastallan. edited by Liisa-Rávná Finbog.
Silje. 15.03.2018. Ságastallan. edited by Liisa-Rávná Finbog.
Solfrid. 03.05.2018. Ságastallan. edited by Liisa-Rávná Finbog.
Sunna. 05.01.2018. Ságastallan. edited by Liisa-Rávná Finbog.
Sunna. 26.01.2018. Ságastallan. edited by Liisa-Rávná Finbog.

Printed in the USA
CPSIA information can be obtained
at www.ICGtesting.com
LVHW020854310823
756660LV00030B/66